DATE DUE

OC 14 '94	DE 13 '92		
NO 4 '94	MY 11 '06		
RENEW			
DE 9 '94			
DE 19 '95			
MR 22 '96			
JY 10 '97			
DE 11 '97			
DE 19 '97			
MR 20 '98			
OC 8 '98			
NO 4 '99			
NO 4 '99			
NO 22 '99			
DE 14 '99			
AP 7 '00			

An Activities Handbook for Teachers of Young Children

Fifth Edition

An Activities Handbook for Teachers of Young Children

Doreen J. Croft

De Anza College

HOUGHTON MIFFLIN COMPANY   **BOSTON**

Dallas   Geneva, Illinois   Palo Alto   Princeton, New Jersey

Cover illustration by Jim Baldwin.
Line illustrations of people by Susan Avishai.
Other line drawings by Marcia R. Smith and Timothy Jones.

Part 1 Opener	Elizabeth Crews
Part 2 Opener	Elizabeth Crews/Stock, Boston
Part 3 Opener	Carol Palmer
Part 4 Opener	David Grossman/Photo Researchers, Inc.
Part 5 Opener	Mary Thacher/Photo Researchers, Inc.
Part 6 Opener	Carol Palmer
Part 7 Opener	Carol Palmer
Part 8 Opener	Elaine Rebman/Photo Researchers, Inc.
Part 9 Opener	Jean-Claude Lejeune
p. 4	Robert Overstreet
p. 87	Elizabeth Crews
p. 148	James Scherer
p. 172	Bruce Roberts/Photo Researchers, Inc.
p. 235	James Scherer
p. 238	Lynn McLaren/Photo Researchers, Inc.
p. 288	James Scherer
p. 291	Used by permission of the Massachusetts Poison Control Center
p. 318	Robert Overstreet
p. 372	Jean-Claude Lejeune
p. 387	Used by permission of Koala Technologies
p. 404	Richard Frieman/Photo Researchers, Inc.
p. 416	Roberta Hershenson/Photo Researchers, Inc.
p. 435	Elizabeth Crews

Printed in the U.S.A.
Library of Congress Catalog Card Number: 89-85106
ISBN: 0-395-43207-3

DEFGHIJ-S-96543

To my daughters, Karen and Colleen—
For all the love and good times they have brought into
my life

Contents

Part Three   Math Experiences   127

Part Four   Language Arts   159

Preface

AUDIENCE AND PURPOSE

My first experience as a teacher of young children took place more than forty years ago. I remember well my eagerness to work that first day in the lab school. I was nervous, anxious, and uncertain about what I might be expected to do. I watched the master teachers closely as I worked alongside them, wondering where they got all their great ideas for recipes and activities. I was impressed with how they always seemed to know just the right things to do and say with the children. In those days there were no activities handbooks to turn to, so I took copious notes and collected every handout and recipe I could find.

Through the years, I continued to collect useful materials, sharing them with others. One year I compiled some of the recipes and ideas for our co-op nursery school fund raiser. The children helped design the cover, and the parents typed and produced fifty copies of *Recipes for Busy Little Hands*. Since that time, we have sold more than fifty thousand copies of the little booklet, which was, of course, the forerunner of the much expanded *Activities Handbook for Teachers of Young Children*.

Teachers are always seeking new and better ideas for the classroom. Although some activities hold up well, we still welcome a fresh approach to them. Others reflect new perspectives in the ways we work with children. In this fifth edition, I have rewritten and revised a great many activities to reflect our understanding of how children learn. Every section has an expanded introduction that provides theoretical as well as practical information about the activities in that part.

As a student, I looked to my teachers for ideas. I observed them, modeled their behavior and language, and relied on their expertise. Although this handbook will not take the place of a master teacher, my hope is that it will be a companion of sorts for those times when teachers need some ideas for activities to enhance the joys of being a teacher of young children.

An Activities Handbook for Teachers of Young Children is suitable for preservice and inservice teachers. With its expanded introductions on theory and practice, it can be used as the primary text or as a supplement in methods and curriculum courses. This handbook is an invaluable tool both in preservice lab settings and in inservice programs. Day care professionals as well as parents find the many ideas of great help in everyday learning situations.

This fifth edition—like its predecessors—is a resource. Its activities are intended to be suggestions and examples to help the teacher be aware of the great range of possibilities for enhancing the curriculum. They should be tried, revised, and adapted to suit individual needs. As such, they should help to stimulate the imagination and to create "teachable moments" in the classroom.

SPECIAL FEATURES OF THE REVISION

Part Introductions and General Introduction   This new edition, divided into nine parts, offers activities for every major area of the curriculum. Completely revised and expanded introductions for each part present rationale and background information for each subject area to help the reader understand *why* he or she is offering a particular activity in the classroom. A new introduction to the handbook provides a theoretical background of how children learn, based on Piagetian principles.

Activity Format   Activities retain the pedagogical format of lists of necessary materials and step-by-step procedures. Many activities have been expanded to cover a broader age range, including toddlers and school-age children. Helpful suggestions and comments accompany a number of the activities.

Helpful Hints, Tips, and Related Ideas   The popular boxed feature containing helpful hints has been retained. Additional tips and related ideas are now also highlighted in box format.

Bibliographies   Each part is followed by an extensive, annotated reference list that includes books for teachers as well as children. Every list has been revised and updated to incorporate the most recent books.

Art Program   New illustrations provide ideas for setting up learning centers for *Art, Woodworking, Math, Language Arts, The Physical World*, and *Computers*. In addition, new photographs and redrawn illustrations highlight and clarify many activities.

COVERAGE IN THIS EDITION

Part One: Art and Woodworking   The *Art* section retains many time-tested recipes for preparation of art materials. Suggestions for their use with a broader age range of children are included, along with a discussion of the developmental stages of art. Comments preceding and Notes following many activities help the teacher focus on goals of the curriculum.

Woodworking is often overlooked as a valuable part of early education. The *Woodworking* section is designed for teachers who have little or no experience with tools and materials in that area. The activities have many practical applications and are highly rewarding for young children. Working with wood and related materials also can serve some special needs that other activities may not satisfy. Thus, the information is offered with the hope that teachers will make full use of its possibilities.

Illustrations identify various materials and clarify how they are used. New additions include a section on planning the curriculum and sketches showing how the special centers might be set up.

Part Two: Music, Drama, and Movement   Favorite activities remain, and new material stresses the value of teaching each area. There are suggestions for effective ways to prepare and introduce various activities as well as how the teacher can adapt them for children with special needs. Included are instructions for making simple puppets and activities that promote expression of feelings.

Part Three: Math Experiences   New material includes activities stressing the importance of developing physical knowledge. Premath skills are acquired through concrete experiences. Since numbers are symbols, they are best understood when the teacher attaches them to concrete objects familiar to the children. Piagetian principles are incorporated, along with suggested comments and observations the teacher might make to encourage further exploration.

Part Four: Language Arts   The useful section of annotated books has been updated and expanded to include many recent titles, including books about children with special needs. The introduction provides information about how language is learned and a listing of milestones in speech and language development. New information includes a section on planning the curriculum along with an illustration of how a teacher might set up a language arts area. Some popular and easy-to-learn finger plays are included.

Part Five: The Physical World   New activities reflect ways that children can construct knowledge through active learning. Useful phrases for questioning and commenting emphasize ways that teachers can enhance children's curiosity. Illustrations and suggestions help the teacher plan and design a science area in the classroom. Both physical and natural science activities facilitate reasoning and questioning through active learning. Ecology experiences, which include solar and conservation activities, introduce children to the importance of conserving our shrinking resources and taking responsibility for maintaining a healthy environment.

Part Six: Health and Safety   Maintaining health and safety is one of the biggest concerns of parents. Because youngsters are placed in the care of teachers for increasingly longer hours, health and self-care are important issues in planning the curriculum. Information about children with AIDS and what teachers can do is new to this edition.

Personal safety activities have also been updated and enhanced. The bibliography includes many new health and safety books for teachers and children.

Part Seven: Cooking and Nutrition   Attitudes and knowledge about food are developed at an early age. Teachers of young children have wonderful opportunities during these impressionable years to help youngsters become better informed and wiser consumers. An expanded introduction includes sections on nutrition, consumer awareness, and maintaining good health that can be beneficial for the teacher as well as children. Cooking projects include planning guidelines as well as a listing of skills appropriate for different age groups. Many recipes are adaptable to individual portions. Most of them incorporate whole grains, fresh fruits, vegetables, and unprocessed foods and avoid sugar, salt, and fats as much as possible. Some of the ingredients in ethnic recipes may be unfamiliar, but many are available in supermarkets.

Part Eight: Computers for Preschoolers   A summary of research in the introduction addresses some concerns that parents and teachers may have about using computers in early education. Since the last edition, however, many teachers appear to have overcome any initial reservations about introducing computers to young children. Activities are designed for the beginning teacher and student, with detailed examples to help them plan and set up a computer center. The annotated list of programs has been field-tested and can be useful to the teacher in selecting appropriate software.

Part Nine: Themes   In this final section, themes have been reorganized according to the four seasons. Many new suggestions have been added to provide ideas for unifying activities around a central topic. A theme chart is included for teachers to reproduce and use in curriculum planning. Dates of holidays and celebrations as well as a list of additional themes supplement the thematic approach.

ACKNOWLEDGMENTS

One of the pleasures of writing a book is the opportunity to thank publicly those whose time and effort helped in its production.

My friend and sometime exercise partner Barbara Irvin provided materials collected from her years of teaching young children. We combined our walks with extensive discussions about food and recipes, some of which are reflected in the cooking and nutrition section.

Janet McCarthy worked diligently on parts of the bibliography. Her cheerful manner and sincere offers to help are deeply appreciated. Thanks to Linda Hagen for her theme suggestions and to Ellie Muhlstein for her valuable contributions to the computer section, both in this edition and in the previous one.

Nancy Wilde and Susan Kempe contributed ideas for health and safety activities. They are the kind of students teachers love to have in the classroom. Kevin Carnes, of Lakeshore Equipment Company, generously shared his fun-with-science activities. I appreciate his friendly manner and enthusiasm for his work.

I am indebted to Dennis and Linda Ronberg, owners of Linden Tree (children's records and books), and to Lynn Ratliff, manager of the store. Even during their busiest hours, they managed to find time to help me locate books and records. They tolerated with good humor my many hours of research throughout their store, never knowing when they might trip over me or the many books and notes I had spread out on the floor. I am indeed grateful for their generous assistance.

Bob Hess, my former co-author, offered incisive (but always tactfully phrased) comments that improved the introduction to computers. I appreciate his continued interest in the handbook. Most of all, I value his friendship and emotional support in all that I do.

Finally, thanks to the staff at Houghton Mifflin, especially my editor, for timely assistance and gentle suggestions; also my reviewers for their patience in suffering through early drafts of the manuscript: Millie Berg, Community College of Philadelphia; Candice Bowers, Kilgore College (Texas); Mary Jane Fields, Missouri Western State College; Lois Klezmer, Miami-Dade Community College; Sim Lesser, Miami-Dade Community College; Antoinette Phillips, El Camino College (California); Leah M. Serck, Concordia College (Nebraska); Carol Woodard, State University College at Buffalo (New York); and Roberta Wong Bouvcrat, Western Washington University. Their comments were thoughtful and thorough. I hope they approve of the ways I incorporated many of their suggestions.

All of these people helped to make this handbook better than it would otherwise have been. They have my unlimited gratitude.

DJC
Palo Alto, CA

Introduction

As a teacher of young children, you will use activities to help you fashion the curriculum and organize the day at school. Activities are specific processes or procedures that can be selected and planned in advance to meet objectives for a particular child or for a group of children. They promote learning through experience—the aim of all the resources that schools offer to young children.

What children learn depends on what they already know, and how well they learn depends on what the teacher knows about how children learn. Thus, the effectiveness of your program is largely determined not by the activities themselves, but by your understanding of how children learn.

PIAGET'S INFLUENCE ON EARLY LEARNING

The most influential scholar in the field of early learning is Jean Piaget (1896–1980). His impressive theories on the development of human intelligence have altered the way we teach young children. Piaget was so fascinated by the mental processes of children that he devoted his life to the study of cognitive development. (The term *cognitive* is derived from *cognition*, meaning the act of knowing, perceiving, understanding.) His theories are based on observations and experiments, many of which he carried out initially with his own children.

He developed ways of thinking about thinking—*terms*, *concepts*, and *categories* that have greatly influenced research and have been the basis for developing curricula for teaching young children. In order to understand Piaget's theories about the way children learn, you need to be familiar with some of the terms he used:

Schema (plural: **schemata**)   Mental structure of conceptualizations. When youngsters call a rabbit "kitty" or refer to an

Adaptation or accommodation

Assimilation

Equilibrium

airplane as "bird," they are trying to make new information fit into an existing schema.

The process of blending new information with old to organize new behavior. If a child who has been nursing at the mother's breast is given a bottle, he or she will approach it applying the pattern of behavior already known from previous experience with the mother. Upon discovering that the bottle is different from the mother's breast, the child will adapt to or accommodate this new information.

The process by which new ways of dealing with the environment are incorporated into existing mental structures, or schemata. When the child discovers that the airplane is not a bird, the child revises his or her schema, assimilating this new information.

A mental state that exists when there is no conflict between existing schemata and new experiences and information. Although children strive to achieve this sense of balance, most early learning involves disequilibrium, or a sense of imbalance. It is this disequilibrium that motivates children to further accommodate and assimilate in order to restore balance.

In Piaget's view, knowledge is not absorbed from the environment; it is *actively constructed* through the interactions between children's mental structures (schemata) and their actions on the environment.

The child's environment is continually creating potential conflict and disequilibrium, which in turn leads the child to strive for equilibrium through accommodation and assimilation. Following is an example of the process of adapting behavior, also known as **equilibration.** Assimilation and accommodation occur simultaneously in equilibration. Thus, it is not useful to attempt to isolate a particular behavior in a child and label it as assimilation or accommodation.

Existing schema	The child believes that all red, round objects are apples.
Conflict	The child sees a red ball, calls it "apple," and tries unsuccessfully to eat it.
Disequilibrium	The child's usual way of thinking has been disturbed.
Accommodation	The child acts on the ball —touching it, smelling it, examining it, throwing it, and generally becoming acquainted with the properties of a ball (which the adult labels for him).
Assimilation	The child incorporates the new experiences into an existing mental structure (schema).
Equilibrium	The child now no longer confuses a ball with an apple.

Three Types of Knowledge

When an adult tells a child that a particular object is a ball and not an apple, the child is gaining *social knowledge*—that is, knowledge learned from someone else. Names of objects, numbers, and letters fall into this category. When the child throws the ball, squeezes it, and experiments with it to discover its properties, he or she is gaining *physical knowledge*. Later, when the child learns to sort and categorize balls and apples, he or she is gaining *logical-mathematical knowledge*. (See the Introduction to Math Experiences for further discussion.)

Piaget maintained that all three types of knowledge are interrelated. Physical and logical-mathematical knowledge, however, cannot be taught verbally. Children need to *construct* such knowledge through the processes of equilibration.

Piaget's theory clearly underscores the importance of children's learning through play. The challenge to teachers of young children is how best to implement the theory through appropriately designed activities.

Piaget's Stages of Cognitive Development

In Piaget's view, cognitive development is continuous and progresses through several stages. Although everyone passes through these stages in the same order, not everyone progresses at the same rate. Each stage provides a foundation for the next one. Progress, which is continuous and overlapping, is determined by the interaction of four factors: maturation (the child's physical and mental growth determined by heredity), social knowledge, physical knowledge, and equilibration.

Stages	Age Range	Operations
Sensorimotor stage	Birth to 1½–2 years	The child makes contact with the external world through the senses: sucking, crying, touching, putting things in the mouth. He or she also develops coordination, progressing from random movements to more deliberate motions (seeing, reaching for, and grabbing objects).
Preoperational stage	2 to 6–7 years	This stage is sometimes divided into two periods. In the early preoperational stage (2–4 years), the child begins to represent ideas through symbols—language, art, dramatic play, movement. The child is too egocentric to be aware of another's point of view. Judgment is based on how things look rather than on logic. In the later preoperational stage (4–7 years), the child makes better perceptual comparisons, but still deals with immediate and observable events. Conservation develops slowly; the child still has difficulty determining that an object remains the same even when its physical appearance is changed. He or she is unable to reverse operations (for example, the child cannot visualize that when water is poured from a tall glass into a short glass and back into the tall one there is still the same amount) and cannot hold abstract ideas in mind to compare with unseen objects.
Stage of concrete operations	6–7 to 11–12 years	The child can conserve and hold information in mind, can articulate consequences, and can handle two dimensions of an object more easily.
Stage of formal operations	11 years to adult	The child can use abstract symbols to solve problems in his or her mind, can consider alternatives by using symbols, is less dependent on visual or tactile information, and can see logical possibilities.

Implications for Teachers

For teachers, one of the most important implications of Piaget's findings is that children think differently than adults. Thus, they must be provided with materials and activities appropriate to their mental processes and developmental levels. The two stages of development most significant for teachers of young children are the sensorimotor and preoperational stages.

Sensorimotor Stage. During the sensorimotor period, infants and toddlers begin to accumulate ideas about the world and represent these ideas with simple words, such as *go bye-bye, bottle, kitty, no night night!* They also begin to plan and to think in advance about what they are about to do. When faced with a problem, the 2-year-old will try a new strategy if the first one fails. Teachers of toddlers are familiar with watching a youngster try one cabinet door after another until one responds to his or her tugging.

Thought is now beginning to be independent of action, separated into an activity of its own. An important clue for the teacher is the fact that children become more receptive to suggestions such as "Someone else is playing with that puzzle; can you find another one?" "Let's look for a tricycle no one is using," or "Can you try doing that a different way?"

At this stage, thinking is still tied to things that are immediately before the child in space and time. In other words, the planned acts of most toddlers are still centered on the here and now, not on a toy or person in another room or out of sight. A 2-year-old does not plan something to be carried out in half an hour or sometime in the future. That is why distraction is an effective strategy with children in the sensorimotor stage of development. A child intent on having a certain toy can usually be distracted with a different one. Similarly, a child can usually be persuaded to stop crying as soon as departing parents leave the room.

Toddlers love to play hide and seek, but have you noticed how some continue to look in the same place, even after you have moved? Sometime during the sensorimotor stage, a fascinating process takes place—the development of **object permanence**. This term refers to the knowledge that objects, including people, continue to exist even when they are not visible: "Mommy is at work now, but she'll be back after naptime." "Your friend does not come to school on Tuesdays. He will be here the next time you come." "Where is your blanket? Help me find your blanket." Studies indicate that memory plays a crucial role in object permanence. If mommy continues as an image in memory, it is easier for a child to accept the notion that she still exists even though she can't be seen.

Preoperational Stage. The preoperational stage of development is an exciting time when symbols, concepts, imagery, and other internal representations become a familiar part of the child's mental systems. The early preoperational stage (roughly ages 2–4) is when children begin to develop concepts about the patterns they have begun to identify. They become aware that things are *alike* or *different*, that water is *wet* and a block is *hard*. These and many other concepts are formed from the child's firsthand experiences.

In this stage, children begin to become aware of consistent patterns in their environment, but they are still easily misled by their perceptions. For example, several small pieces of playdough may look like more than one large piece, even though the amount is actually the same. A child whose cookie is broken into several pieces may think that he or she has more than a child with an entire cookie. At this age, children struggle with the ideas of change and sameness in objects. They begin to realize that some properties remain constant despite the fact that objects change in other ways—a concept known as **conservation**.

Conservation applies to quantity (a broken cookie versus a whole cookie), length (beads in a long line versus the same number of beads in a shorter line), and volume (liquid in a tall, slender cylinder versus the same amount of liquid in a short, wide cylinder). Typically, *number conservation* is acquired about age 5 or 6; *substance, area,* and *liquid-volume conservation* appear around age 7 or 8. Conservation of *weight* and *solid volume* appear much later, usually at about 9–12 years.

When preoperational children are given objects to sort, they are able to focus on only one characteristic (color, for example) at a time. This process is called **centering**. At this stage, children are not yet able to classify according to two features simultaneously (for example, color *and* size).

As many teachers recognize, children at this stage are **egocentric**. They view situations from only one perspective—their own. They have difficulty understanding that another person might see things differently. That is why teachers repeat over and over again phrases such as "She feels angry when you knock over the blocks," "He's crying because he feels sad," "It hurts when you hit," and "How do you think she feels? Let's ask her." The teacher's guidance and interpretations help young children gain the experience and social skills needed to move out of the egocentric phase.

Also typical of children in the preoperational stage is **animism**—the belief that nonliving things are alive. Children have difficulty understanding, for example, that puppet or cartoon characters are not alive. Magical thinking, or **artificialism**, is another feature of children's mental development at this time. They still confuse fantasy with reality, at times acting as if (and believing) they had magical powers over their environment. It is important, especially in traumatic situations such as death and divorce, to help a child understand that what has happened is not his or her fault.

ROLE OF THE TEACHER

Your role as a teacher of young children is a crucial one. The success of your program will depend heavily on your ability to match teaching strategies to how children learn.

When using the activities in this handbook, keep in mind the following principles:

1. *Children learn by doing.* Remember that preschoolers construct their knowledge through their actions on objects. They learn not by being told, but through firsthand experiences.
2. *Provide challenging activities.* Create a comfortable amount of disequilibrium by challenging children to try to make sense of their world. When confronted with unfamiliar materials or things they do not understand, they will be motivated to act on the materials to regain a sense of equilibrium.
3. *Offer developmentally appropriate materials.* During the early stages of constructing new knowledge, it is important to help children avoid failure and defeat. Materials and experiences should be appropriate to each child's level of ability—not too easy, not too difficult. A series of small successes gives children the confidence to seek more challenges.
4. *Provide materials with many variables that children can manipulate.* The most effective teaching materials are those that provide immediate feedback to children. For example, throwing a ball, building with blocks, and pouring liquids all provide direct experience with the properties of an object or material. Children also benefit from playing with materials that can be manipulated in many different ways. Clay, fingerpaint, sand, water, and other unstructured materials enable children to explore properties in a variety of ways.
5. *Allow plenty of time to explore, examine, and experiment.* Children need time to ruminate, to tinker, to try things in many different ways. By interacting with materials over and over again in many different situations, children learn that blocks are *hard*, playdough is *soft*, a feather is *light*, and wood can be *smooth* or *rough*. It takes time for such concepts to become integrated into their mental operations.
6. *Provide information at appropriate times.* Your role is not so much to tell children but to guide them to find answers for themselves. This requires careful observation and listening so that you can provide information at appropriate times (for example, "That's called a magnet," "When that goes to the bottom of the water, we say it *sinks*; when it stays on top, we say it *floats*"). The teacher is an important resource in children's development of social knowledge.
7. *Extend children's learning.* Your questions, comments, and suggestions are crucial in guiding children's learning. Questions such as "What will happen if . . .?" "Can you think of another way?" or "What's different about this?" help to focus children's attention on problems and alternative solutions. The child is encouraged when you acknowledge his or her efforts: "I notice you tried different ways to make that work. That's good thinking. I wonder what made that happen." Accept hypotheses and explanations even if they are inaccurate. They reflect the child's thought processes and current level of cognitive development.
8. *Be a good model.* Children love their teachers; they want to please them and be like them. They learn a great deal by imitation. You can show them how you try to solve a problem, explaining what you are doing and why: "That didn't work. I wonder what will hap-

pen if I try it this way. I'm going to put this larger block on top of the wide one to see if it will balance. Do you think that will work?" When they see how you deal with problems and challenges, they will have a model to emulate.

As you select activities from this handbook, read the introductions to the sections. They will help you think about ways you might want to use or adapt the tasks to best serve the way in which children learn.

Specifying Behavioral Objectives

Teachers of young children are very busy people. It is not uncommon for a school day to include such unplanned events as illnesses, minor accidents, unhappy children, and a shortage of help and time. Just attending to immediate needs can consume most of a teacher's day. Given such a schedule, how will you have time to determine whether your goals for the children are being met? What are those goals? Would you be able to state them to your supervisor or to the children's parents? And how can you be sure when you have achieved them?

One of the best ways to determine if you are achieving your goals is to develop objectives, specified in writing. List exactly what it is you want your children to learn and the behavioral changes you seek. Then select activities and appropriate teaching methods to implement your goals. Finally, assess the extent to which the desired changes have occurred (usually in terms of performance).

Some cognitive behaviors, such as counting to 10, recognizing and naming six colors, or knowing how to print one's name, are fairly simple to specify and measure in terms of behavioral objectives. But you may find it a bit more difficult to explicitly define and measure objectives in the affective domain, such as developing an awareness of others' feelings or learning to share. Such goals are too abstract and distant to be easily evaluated, and thus teachers often do not know how close they are to achieving them.

Long- and Short-Term Goals

Long-term goals are an important part of a teacher's plan, but there are many intermediate goals that lie between a specific incident and a final objective. Suppose, for example, that you want Maggie to learn to share. This goal may become attainable only after many weeks or months. In order not to lose sight of your goal, you need to state it in terms of behavioral objectives. The objective is not only that Maggie will share, but that she will do so in ways that you can actually see—that is, in terms of *observable behavior*. Thus, your objective for Maggie might be stated as follows:

By the end of June, Maggie will demonstrate the ability to share by: (1) taking turns on the swings, (2) taking only two crackers at juice time, (3) helping to pass out art materials to other children, and (4) waiting willingly to take her place in line.

Short-term goals expressed in behavioral objectives provide the teacher with guideposts toward progress. Unless you have a clear idea of the behavior you want a child to display, you aren't likely to know if your efforts have been successful.

Meaningful Objectives

There is a saying "If you're not sure where you're going, you're liable to end up someplace else." Well-stated objectives let you know where you're going. Basically, a meaningful objective is one that succeeds in communicating your intent. You may want to specify objectives so that parents, your team-teaching members, and your supervisor can understand what you intend to achieve. Or you may simply want to refer to your objectives as reminders of the behavioral changes you seek in your children.

Objectives are not rigid goals that must be met; they can be modified as you assess performance. If you provide other teachers with objectives, it is important to be clear and specific about your goals. For example, "Jonathan will know how to use a puzzle" is not a clearly stated objective. Do you mean that Jonathan should be able to take the puzzle out and return it to the appropriate box, to try different ways to complete a puzzle, to ask for help, or to take turns?

Some words that often lead to misinterpretation include *know, understand, appreciate, enjoy,* and *believe.* Instead of these words, use action words that describe what the child should *do* to demonstrate that he or she knows or understands, such as *choose* two partners, *sort* four colors, *sit quietly* for two minutes, *demonstrate* three different ways to move.

The ability to specify objectives in meaningful terms provides you with a tool for self-evaluation and increased confidence in what you are doing. When your objectives are not being met, you can systematically evaluate your process, materials, or techniques, rather than blaming the lack of progress on something outside of your control.

Your methods for organizing the children's activities and your techniques for dealing with specific events thus form a kind of unseen structure that can be used to achieve your goals. Whether you want a child to participate actively in music, learn to write his or her own name, or simply stop whining, specifying objectives will orient both you and the child toward the behavior you have in mind. The activity planning sheet on the next page may help you to formalize your objectives and proposed techniques for meeting them.

Activity Planning Sheet

Name of teacher _____ Date _____

Name of activity _____

Objectives (What do I want the children to learn? Are these goals developmentally appropriate?):

1.

2.

3.

Materials and preparation needed:

Presentation (How will I introduce the activity? What questions will I ask? What comments will I make?):

Observation (What happened? How did the children respond? What do I think they learned?):

Evaluation (What was effective? What would I change?):

An Activities Handbook
for Teachers
of Young Children

PART ONE

Art and Woodworking

Introduction to Art Activities

Imagine a scene in the art area of a busy preschool. Several children are busily engaged in painting at easels; two others are carrying a wet painting to hang up on a drying rack. One youngster is smearing finger paint all over a tabletop, exclaiming "More! More! I want more goop!" Another child is happily scooping more paint out of a large container and dumping it on the table. At the next table, a boy is working by himself, concentrating on squeezing out an elaborate design of glue on construction paper.

Children work independently and cooperatively at various projects, taking materials out, putting them away, and washing up when they have finished. The teacher is nearby, listening, observing, offering suggestions.

The apparent ease with which the children participate belies the amount of planning needed to create this kind of environment. Such scenes reflect the expertise of teachers who know how children learn and grow.

STAGES OF DEVELOPMENT

In order to make effective use of art materials in the curriculum, you need to be familiar with the way children develop in their skills. Just as they move through stages of cognitive development (see page xix), they also develop artistic skills in the following sequence. (Ages are approximate.)

Disordered scribbling
  18 mo.–2½ yr.

When toddlers (at about age 18 months) are introduced to crayons, they go through a period of exploration—making random movements, banging, and even tasting the crayons. The marks they make are purely random and reflect muscle control that is not fully developed.

In plastic art, beating and pounding randomly on playdough or

Controlled scribbling
2–4 yr.

Naming unplanned creations
(Preschematic)
3½–4½ yr.

Representational art
4½–6 yr.

clay is the stage that parallels disordered scribbling.

With repetition and greater muscle control, children begin to repeat patterns, such as by making a series of vertical or horizontal movements with a paintbrush or crayon. The patterns are not well controlled and are still somewhat random.

The parallel with plastic art materials is when the child forms balls or ropes with playdough.

At about age 3, children begin to label their scribbles. Generally, they do not plan their creation ahead, but their scribbles remind them of something familiar, to which they attach a label.

At this stage, while manipulating playdough, the child will pick up a coil and call it a snake, or will refer to a lump as a car or an airplane. The child develops from being involved in a purely kinesthetic activity to making a connection with the environment. Giving a name to unplanned creations is an important step in *symbol development*.

With practice and maturation, children begin to think ahead and plan what it is they are going to paint, draw, or make. They are now able to combine formerly random patterns into circles and lines and connect them to represent something they have decided in advance to create.

With plastic materials, they will announce that they are going to make cakes or cookies and will proceed to mold the material into objects that represent their intended creations.

The developmental stages roughly cover ages 18 months to 6 years. Children progress through these stages in the same order, but not at the same rate.

USING ART TO ENHANCE THE CURRICULUM

Because of their versatility, art materials can serve many purposes in the curriculum. For example, you might at one time encourage a youngster to relieve frustration by pounding on playdough; another time, you might use the same material to provide practice in naming colors and shapes. Both are constructive ways to use art materials and activities.

Knowing how children develop in artistic skills will help you to plan activities that are appropriate for each child. A two-year-old in the early scribbling stage will benefit more from experimenting and exploring the physical properties of fingerpaint on a tabletop than making a picture to mount. Pounding on clay, scribbling with a crayon, or making random brushstrokes at the easel may not result in something understandable to adults, but your choice of activities enhances essential skills that contribute to the physical, social, emotional, and cognitive development of children.

ART AND DEVELOPING SKILLS

Some of the many skills that art and art materials enhance include those involved in physical, social, emotional, and cognitive development.

Illustration 1.1 **Among the skills developed through art activities are fine motor coordination, cooperation, and aesthetic judgment.**

Physical Development

Muscle Coordination. Gross-motor movements include painting with broad strokes, manipulating large pieces of clay, and making foot-print murals. Fine-motor coordination is enhanced by cutting with scissors, using pens and pencils, and making collages.

Sensory perception and sensory discrimination. Awareness of how things look, sound, feel, taste, and smell is heightened through the use of art materials. Noticing and selecting different colors and being able to tell the difference between things one sees are functions of *visual perception* and *visual discrimination.* Activities such as fingerpainting, pasting, and making collages with objects from nature offer opportunities to enhance sensory perceptions and discrimination.

Perceptual motor skills. Using art materials can help a child to develop the ability to coordinate movements with perception. For example, eye-hand coordination can be improved through painting, making collages, and cutting.

Social Development

Sharing and cooperation. Children learn to work together on art projects such as mixing playdough or creating a mural, to share materials with one another, and to help each other with clean-up or hanging up art to dry.

Planning and verbalizing. Working together to plan a project for the classroom, students will talk to each other about plans, and while creating they will socialize with one another.

Appreciation of other people. Watching and hearing the teacher show appreciation for individual creations, children learn to observe and notice the work of other children.

Emotional Development

Awareness and expression of feelings. Children become more aware of their feelings by talking about how various materials or colors make them feel and by expressing feelings through artistic creations, such as paintings. They can also pound on playdough or clay to express and relieve feelings of anger, frustration, or aggression.

Development of self-esteem. By receiving appreciation from others for efforts, children can learn to feel good about making choices based on their own opinions.

Development of pride and confidence. There is a certain satisfaction in creating something unique. Children can come to feel confident in their ability to successfully carry out a project and to manipulate and control materials.

Development of aesthetic judgment. Students learn to make judgments based on their experiences with different kinds of materials. They experience the joy and satisfaction of being more aware of things in the environment, thereby developing their aesthetic judgment.

Cognitive Development

Math skills. Children develop concepts of size, shape, sorting, conservation, counting, and measuring through such activities as painting, participating in plastic arts, mixing paints, and measuring flour for playdough. They can compare different attributes, such as large and small, long and short, same and different.

Science skills. Students gain physical knowledge through manipulation of materials. They experience cause and effect in mixing different colors of paints or in gluing paper together. They learn that properties change when clay dries or when ingredients are mixed to make paste or playdough. Children gain practice in decision making, planning and carrying out a project, and predicting the outcome. They test ideas and find different solutions, noting similarities and differences among materials and objects.

Language skills. Through art activities, children learn to communicate ideas, follow directions, and express feelings.

THE ROLE OF THE TEACHER

A teacher aware of how young children develop will not be surprised or disappointed if a 2-year-old paints his hands instead of the easel paper, or if a 3-year-old decides to taste the colorful playdough instead of fashioning it into something familiar.

Art in the preschool is not a series of isolated activities consisting of painting at specific times or making something to take home. An educator with a broader view sees that there are opportunities for artistic development throughout the child's day. It may be in talking about the colors and sparkling design of frost on a window, noticing the translucent silkiness of a spider web, or reproducing the patterns of footprints in the sand. To teachers with an open perspective, no part of the curriculum is excluded from art and artistic expression.

It is helpful to have a clear idea of your goals and how you plan to use art and art materials to achieve them. The fact that you have a plan in mind does not detract from the pleasure or spontaneity of children's play. For example, you may use an activity such as making a mural of children's footprints to help youngsters become aware of body parts. Or sand painting could be an outdoor activity to engage children in exploring textures.

For all their curiosity, many children have not thought about the sensations they experience. Experience alone is not enough. Teachers can help children focus attention on such sensory experiences as how it feels when you put your feet in smooth paint, cool mud, or warm sand. Some have smelled their mother's perfume or their father's shaving lotion, but may not know the individual odors of paper, paste, leather, wood, fruit, or flowers. Children hear noise, but most have never consciously listened to silence.

A simple word or phrase at the appropriate time can help focus a child's attention on one aspect of an experience he or she may not have noticed before:

The sandpaper feels rough, doesn't it?
Your hands are gliding so smoothly over the fingerpaint!
Listen to the sounds you hear when you step on the dry leaves.
What did you do with the paints to make that new color?
Tell me about your painting.
What happened when you squeezed the playdough?

The images children create may not mean much to us, but their actions on objects—whether it is random scribbling or creating a sculpture—function as *symbols*. These symbols are used as vehicles for creative expression. Children's art and the work of famous artists have in common the notion that ideas and emotions can be symbolized and expressed through visual forms. Thus, the whole of our environment can be regarded as a source of aesthetic experience and a resource for artistic expression.

The teacher should not make judgments about children's art. Instead, he or she should guide and encourage children to grow in the creative process by making their experiences meaningful and acceptable. When a child says, "I can't paint" or "I don't know how to make a picture," you may feel uncertain about your response. What the child has not grasped is that what he or she wants to do is truly all right, and your reassurance and encouragement are needed. When children accept your permission as real, they dare to be themselves. The selves we all try to hide at some time or another in fear of rejection are our true selves, and *any expressions of our true selves are original and therefore creative.*

When you translate a child's "I don't know how to paint" into "I'm afraid you won't like what I paint," you will find responses come much more easily. Indeed, even the most inadequate "representations" are important indicators of the child's level of development and experiences of rejection. It is important that such a picture be talked about with interest and given the same recognition as pictures that may appear more impressive to an adult.

As in all aspects of the curriculum, your effectiveness in creating meaningful art experiences is very much a matter of communication. When you convey confidence, acceptance, and enthusiasm for your children's artistic expressions, you will be nurturing the creative spirit in your classroom.

THE ART AREA

A well-planned art area, such as the one shown in Illustration 1.2, invites exploration and encourages creative expression. It is set up in such a way that children can be self-reliant: they can help themselves to materials, hang their paintings up to dry, make clay sculptures, create collages, and clean up, all with minimal assistance from the teacher.

The art area should be located in a spacious, well-lit place near a source of water. Since it is a busy (and sometimes messy) place, be sure it is protected from through-traffic. Children need plenty of space where they can have elbow room to create clay and playdough sculp-

Illustration 1.2   **The art area**

tures, or work on a mural spread out on the floor without interruption. This is equally true if you decide to set up art activities outdoors.

The floor should be of material that can be washed easily. The areas under paint easels and drying racks can be further protected with sheets of plastic or drip pans, such as those designed for use under automobiles.

If space allows, place two-sided standing easels side by side so children can socialize while they paint. If you are short on space, you can still offer painting activities by protecting a wall with plastic and attaching easel paper at the proper height. There are also wall easels that can be purchased. Drying racks can be purchased or made of wooden dowels or clothesline. Leave plenty of wall space to display art work at children's eye level. Burlap-covered wallboard makes a nice background for paintings.

A pegboard with hooks for smocks can be mounted to the wall adjacent to the water supply. Wash basins, soap, and paper towel dispensers should be within easy reach.

Plastic art materials, such as clay, playdough, and plasticene, stored in unbreakable containers, should be readily available to the children. Open shelves and cabinets make it easy for children to help themselves to more paper, paste, crayons, scissors, and collage materials. Ice cream cartons with picture labels simplify returning materials to proper places.

Higher shelves and cabinets can be used by the teacher to store extra supplies such as powdered tempera, soap, starch, brushes, and sponges. Post an inventory/supply list on one of the cabinet doors to expedite reordering.

Child-height tables with smooth-surfaced tops are useful for fingerpainting, making collages, and sculpting. Provide rubber spatulas for scraping fingerpaints and plastic materials off tables. A good supply of sponges makes clean-up an interesting part of the art activity. Plastic trays (such as those used in cafeterias) are excellent for use with clay because they help to define the space and simplify clean-up. Remember to strategically place several wastebaskets.

BASIC ART SUPPLIES

Painting
Powdered tempera
Liquid tempera
Easels (two-sided, adjustable in height)
Easel paper (newsprint works well)
Fingerpaint paper (butcher paper)
Brushes (long-handled, flat- and round-bristle)
Recipe ingredients for easel and fingerpaints (soap, detergent, starch, cornstarch, flour, salt, etc.)
Aprons and smocks

Plastic art
Clay
Plasticene
Playdough (ingredients for recipes)
Tools for children to use (such as spatulas, rolling pins, biscuit cutters)

Collage
Safety scissors (right- and left-handed)
Paste
Glue
Paper (a variety of different kinds, including construction, drawing, and computer paper)
Tape (masking and cellophane)

Markers
Water-based felt markers
Crayons (good quality, large and small)
Pencils (regular-size and fat ones)
Chalk

Post a list of materials that families and volunteers can donate to enhance your art program, such as

Computer paper
Safety scissors (right- and left-handed)
Paintbrushes
Large and small crayons
Colored chalk
Water-based felt markers

Pencils
Construction paper
Magazines
Wallpaper books
Greeting cards
Fabrics
Decorative stamps and stickers

Envelopes
Stationery
Interesting materials for gluing and
    plastic art
Rubber spatulas
Styrofoam trays
Plastic lunch trays
Egg cartons
Cardboard
Masking and cellophane tape
Potato ricers
Cookie and biscuit cutters
Garlic presses
Plastic serrated knives
Tongue depresssors

Hair rollers
Empty juice cans
Rolling pins
Small baking tins
Large plastic sheets
Heavy plastic pans and buckets
Child-size mops and brooms
Blender (to mix paints)
Clean plastic spray bottles
Sponges
Clean rags
Shoe boxes
Clear plastic storage containers
Styrofoam packing materials

Guidelines for the Safe Use of Art and Craft Materials[1]

There are unique factors associated with children's use of art and craft materials that may increase health risks. Because of their smaller size, higher metabolic rates, and immature organ and immune systems, children are less able than adults to tolerate exposure to hazardous substances.

There are three ways by which children are most likely to be exposed to unsafe materials in the school:

1. **Inhalation.** Dusts, powders, vapors, gases, and aerosols are potential health hazards. Silica or asbestos present in dry earth clays can cause damage to the lungs; organ damage may occur from inhalation of solvent vapors.
2. **Ingestion.** Young children often put things in their mouths. They can accidentally ingest poisonous substances by handling tools used for mixing art materials and then putting the tools or their hands in their mouths. Another danger is using glitter, which adheres to hands and can be transported to mouths or eyes.
3. **Skin contact.** Caustic substances such as cleaning solvents or paint thinners may cause local skin damage; some solvents can pass through the skin into the bloodstream, resulting in damage to internal organs.

Exposure to toxic substances can result in either acute or chronic illness. Although the symptoms of an acute illness are immediately apparent, chronic illnesses may arise at a later time because of a build-up of substances such as asbestos or lead in the body from repeated exposure.

[1]Adapted from California State Department of Health Services, *Guidelines for the Safe Use of Art and Craft Materials,* June 1988.

WHAT THE TEACHER CAN DO

- Label and store art and craft supplies in a place that is safe from the children.
- Keep dust to a minimum by damp mopping rather than sweeping.
- Promote good hygiene habits by having the children wash their hands after working with art and craft materials.
- Prohibit the children from eating or drinking while engaged in art projects.
- Ensure proper ventilation in the art area.
- Dispose of art and craft materials according to local health department guidelines.
- Substitute liquid or nonaerosol products for those in dry form. If dry products, such as powdered tempera, are used, premix them before involving the children.
- Use water-based glues, paints, and markers instead of solvent-based rubber cement, turpentine, paint thinners, and markers.
- Avoid lead- or metal-based materials such as glazes, enamels, and paints.
- Substitute vegetable and natural dyes for commercial dyes.
- Use only black-and-white newspaper for papier-mache and other such projects; commercial papier-mache and colored printing inks may contain asbestos fibers or metal-based pigments.
- Avoid projects that use photo developing supplies and blueprint papers.
- Contact your state department of health services, department of education, or the Food and Drug Administration for further assistance.

Art: Recipes and Activities

EASEL PAINT RECIPES

A teacher who knows how to prepare paints and understands when and why to use them is like a master chef who has an intimate knowledge of the foods he or she uses to create a tasty and nutritious meal. Your expertise will greatly enhance your program.

First learn how to prepare the basic recipes; then familiarize yourself with the variations and the purposes they serve. The recipes you select will depend on the children involved and the objectives of your project. Keep notes, evaluate your projects, and revise the recipes as you work with them. You will soon develop competence and skill in preparing art materials for your students.

The easel paint recipes call for powdered tempera, which is the most commonly used ingredient. It is water soluble, dries quickly, and mixes easily with other materials. Although some schools prefer to buy their paints commercially mixed in order to save preparation time, the cost is usually higher and the teacher does not have the opportunity to control the variables of hue and density.

An important caution is to avoid letting children help mix powdered tempera, which produces potentially toxic dust. Teachers themselves need to be cautious about inhaling the powder, but children are especially vulnerable because they have a larger surface area relative to their body mass than do adults. Also, their detoxification and immune systems are not yet mature. Thus, smaller amounts of inhaled toxins can produce more injurious effects in children than in adults. (See Guidelines for the Safe Use of Art and Craft Materials, page 10.)

Mixing and Storing Paints

- Use large, clear plastic containers to mix and store paints.
- Follow the correct sequence of mixing as specified in each recipe.
- An *extender* like bentonite reduces paint cost and gives the desired consistency. It also can be added to tempera to make fingerpaint. Other extenders can be made by mixing flour or cornstarch and water; cornmeal will produce a different texture. Extra soap or detergent powder will also thicken paint.
- Soap makes paint easier to wash out and helps it adhere to slick surfaces like glass and cellophane. It's a good idea to add ⅓ cup liquid soap to each quart of commercial paint, as these paints are difficult to wash out of clothing.
- Detergent keeps paint from cracking when it dries.
- A few drops of oil of cloves or oil of wintergreen will keep paints fresh longer.
- Condensed milk or liquid starch makes the paint creamy and provides a glossy finish. (Too much liquid starch causes flakiness when the paint dries.)
- Keep a tight lid on the containers, and store paints in a cool place; refrigerate if milk is used in the recipe.
- Start beginners with clear primary colors of red, blue, and yellow. (See the color chart in Illustration 1.3.)

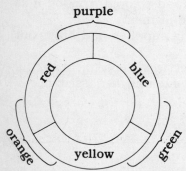

Illustration 1.3   Color chart

Basic Bentonite Extender

2 cups bentonite (Powdered bentonite can be purchased at pottery or ceramic supply outlets, also at some wallpaper and scientific supply stores.)

2 quarts water
½ cup soap powder

- Place the water in a large plastic or glass container. *Do not use a metal container.*
- Add the bentonite and soap powder. Do not mix.
- Let the mixture stand several hours or overnight. After the powder has been absorbed, stir or mix with a beater until thick and creamy. Add more water or bentonite as needed.
- If an electric blender is available, prepare the extender by filling the blender container half full of water.
- Add bentonite and soap gradually, turning the blender on and off after a few seconds to check the consistency.

• Pour the mixture into a plastic container with a tight lid. Stir well each day. The mixture tends to thicken; add more water as needed.

Easel Paint Recipe #1

6–8 tablespoons extender (If bentonite is not available, make a smooth mixture of 3 parts flour to 4 parts water; see page 12 for more suggestions on extenders.)
1 one-pound can of powdered tempera

3 cups liquid starch
2 tablespoons soap powder
water
alcohol (optional)

• Put the extender in a half-gallon container.
• Gradually stir in the tempera and liquid starch, mixing well.
• Add soap powder.
• Stir in a few drops of alcohol if desired to help ingredients mix more readily.
• Add water gradually until the mixture reaches the desired consistency. Paints that are thick will be more intense in color.

Store tightly covered. Pour into small juice cans each day as needed for easel painting.

Easel Paint Recipe #2

2 parts powdered tempera   **1 part water**

• Pour water slowly into powdered tempera, stirring to eliminate lumps.

This basic recipe can be used to mix either small or large amounts of paint, as long as you keep the proper proportions. One-half part powdered detergent can be added; preservatives and fresheners such as alum, oil of cloves, or alcohol also can be added as desired.

Easel Paint Recipe #3

⅓ cup water
¼ cup liquid starch (If none is available, mix 3 tablespoons flour with 4 tablespoons water.)

1 one-pound can powdered tempera
1 tablespoon soap powder

• Pour liquids into a blender.
• Gradually blend in the powdered tempera, using a rubber spatula to scrape the paint down from the sides of the blender jar.
• Add soap powder; blend until smooth and thick, adding more liquid as needed.

Note: A blender should be designated exclusively for use as a paint and extender mixer. Do not use the same blender for food.

Easel Paint Recipe #4

2 cups powdered tempera   **1 cup starch**
1 cup liquid soap

* Place the liquid soap and starch in a container.
* Pour the powdered tempera over the liquids, and stir the mixture just enough to cover the powder with liquid.
* Let stand for one hour or more; then stir again, breaking up any lumps.
* Pour into a glass or plastic jar, cover tightly, and shake well.

The mixture should be smooth. Consistency improves overnight. Shake gently again before using.

Note: This is a good recipe for those days when you don't have the time to stir the paints.

FINGERPAINTING

Sometimes children approach fingerpainting with reluctance—perhaps because they have been warned by adults about "messiness." Yet the values and satisfaction derived from the activity make offering fingerpainting well worth the trouble.

Fingerpainting does, indeed, require more supervision and clean-up. Teachers themselves may object to the added work and mess. Unless they are convinced of the values of fingerpainting, they probably will not offer it in their curriculum. To be successful, fingerpainting projects require careful planning and a positive attitude.

Fingerpaints offer one of the best media for tactile experiences in the curriculum. Other art projects usually require the use of tools (brushes, pens, scissors, crayons) that interfere with direct contact. Fingerpaints, on the other hand, provide opportunities (and give children "permission") to touch, smear, spread, squish, and generally explore directly. For young children, it provides an exciting medium for hands too young to control crayon and brush well enough to achieve satisfying aesthetic effects.

A good way to introduce such a project is simply to allow the children to fingerpaint on a Formica tabletop or a large piece of oilcloth. Set out several containers of fingerpaint in different colors and large spoons for scooping out the paints.

Encourage them to explore freely by making comments such as
I see you're making streaks by pulling your fingers through the paint.
That's an interesting design you made with your arm.
The paint looks interesting when you squeeze it through your fingers, doesn't it?

Children are influenced by your attitude of acceptance of what they are doing. With your comments you want to create an atmosphere that encourages spontaneity and independence rather than producing products that are results of adult ideas.

Developmental Stages

There are four stages of development in fingerpainting:

1. **Initial stage.** Children get acquainted with the medium. For some children, this may mean watching, poking with a finger, dabbling tentatively without smearing paint or moving the hands freely.
2. **Smearing stage.** Children move the paint around by smearing, not using fingers or hands in a purposeful way.
3. **Purposeful stage.** Children produce line drawings of an abstract character which result in designs that are not pictorial.
4. **Pictorial stage.** Children produce recognizable pictures.

All children go through the four stages, no matter what their ages. A 5-year-old who has not fingerpainted before could go through all four stages in the first session, but the beginning painter of any age is likely to loiter in the smearing stage. This is a valuable experience, and children should not be rushed to move on.

One of the more rewarding aspects of fingerpainting is that children can create and destroy their designs over and over again without concern about saving a picture to take home. Later on, you can refer to some of the activities in this section to let the children make pictures with fingerpaint and paper.

Children who are reluctant to participate may want to observe several times before making a commitment. Others may respond more readily to warm paints, to pastel shades, or to music being played while the activity is going on. Providing many opportunities to fingerpaint, both indoors and out, leads to successful and satisfying experiences.

(Although these media do not provide a true fingerpainting experience, some teachers find it useful to let children fingerpaint with pudding, gelatin, toothpaste, shaving cream, hand cream, or mud.)

Materials

Fingerpainting is generally done while children *stand* at a table low enough for them to move their hands and arms comfortably. Position children far enough apart to allow plenty of space for freedom of movement.

The best economical paper for fingerpainting is meat-wrapping, or butcher paper, which is available from a butcher supply or paper dealer in rolls or flat bundles cut to the desired size. Size 10" x 15" is good for 2-year-olds, and 12" x 18" is good for 3- to 5-year-olds. Larger sheets encourage larger movements; fingerpainting involves the use of back muscles as well as muscles in the arms, hands, and legs. When paper is too small, children will end up smearing rather than painting with their hands. Paper that is thin and absorbent will tear easily and discourage proper fingerpainting techniques.

Freezer wrap paper is more expensive than regular butcher paper but is excellent for fingerpainting. Commercially packaged glossy paper is quite expensive and usually too small in size to encourage large muscle movements. Paper should always be used with the *glossy side up* and kept moist.

Other things to paint on include Formica, wax paper, aluminum foil, corrugated paper, old window shades, tile, vinyl, shelf paper, cardboard, wall paper, Plexiglas, cookie sheets, and plastic trays.

Tables of hardwood, Formica, or other smooth materials are the best surfaces to work on. Dampen the surface with a wet sponge, then place the paper, glossy side up, on the damp area. You may need to add a few drops or a squirt of water occasionally to prevent the paper from slipping.

To keep old paint from contaminating the new painting and to moisten the surface again, wipe the table clean before placing each new sheet of paper.

Oilcloth or old shower curtains can be used to cover table surfaces that are not suitable for paints. After use, oil cloth should be cleaned and *rolled up* rather than folded for storage, to prevent cracking.

Suggested Procedures

* Locate the fingerpainting tables near wash basins.
* Show children where they are to wash up before they start painting.
* Place protective coverings such as newspaper or plastic on the floor under and around the tables.
* Have aprons for the children and adults.
* Place a wastebasket and a pail of slightly soapy water and paper towels nearby so that children can rinse and wipe their hands before going to the wash basins to do a more thorough job.
* Place a pan of water, several sponges, and rubber spatulas nearby for cleaning tables and moistening paper.
* Large unbreakable bowls, lower halves of milk cartons, and coffee cans make good containers for fingerpaints. At first, you may want to control the amount of paint by dishing out a tablespoonful at a time; or you can provide individual cartons with plastic spoons so that children can help themselves. Adding more as needed is easier when smaller spoons are used.
* Separate disruptive children and limit the number who can fingerpaint at any one time.
* Allow plenty of time for individual children to explore the paints.

Fingerpaint Recipe #1

1 cup dry laundry starch or corn-starch

1 cup cold water

4 cups boiling water

1 cup soap powder (Ivory Snow works well.)

¼ cup talcum powder (optional)

* Put the starch in a large saucepan.
* Add the cold water gradually, stirring until there are no lumps.
* Continue to stir while adding the boiling water; cook over medium heat until clear, stirring constantly.
* When the mixture thickens, remove from heat.
* With an egg beater or wire whisk, beat in soap powder and talcum until smooth and thick.

Store in a plastic container in the refrigerator or use while still warm.

Note: Children can help select food coloring or liquid tempera paint to be added to each batch just before using. Avoid sprinkling powdered tempera because of the danger of inhalation. Fingerpainting can also be done with easel paints, liquid starch, or liquid tempera that has been thickened with bentonite extender, buttermilk, or liquid starch.

Fingerpaint Recipe #2

1 cup cornstarch
2 cups cold water
½ cup soap powder
2 quarts boiling water

glycerin or oil of wintergreen
  (optional)
liquid food coloring

• Put 1 cup cornstarch into a pitcher or bowl.
• Gradually add 2 cups cold water, stirring until smooth.
• Pour this mixture slowly into 2 quarts boiling water, stirring constantly.
• Cook over low to medium heat until the mixture is clear and thick.
• Add the soap power, stirring until smooth
• Remove from heat, and add a few drops of glycerin or oil of wintergreen and some food coloring.

Fingerpaint Recipe #3

1 cup flour
1 cup cold water
3 cups boiling water

powdered tempera or liquid
  food coloring

• Mix the flour and water, stirring until smooth. This can be done by gradually stirring the water into the flour, or by placing the water in a jar, adding the flour a little at a time, and shaking the tightly covered mixture after each addition.
• When the mixture is smooth, pour it gradually into the boiling water and bring to a boil, stirring constantly.
• Add the coloring.

Paintings made from this recipe will dry flat and will not need to be ironed.

The following fingerpaint recipes need no cooking.

Fingerpaint Recipe #4

1 cup dry laundry starch
½ cup cold water

1½ cups boiling water
¾ cup powdered detergent

• Put the dry starch in a saucepan.
• Gradually add the cold water, stirring until smooth.
• Add the boiling water, stirring rapidly and continually.
• Add the detergent, and stir again until smooth.

Fingerpaint Recipe #5

1 cup dry laundry starch   **3 cups soap powder**
1 cup cold water

• Mix all the ingredients together for a quick, no-cook paint.

The texture will not be as smooth or thick as the cooked variety.

Fingerpaint Recipe #6

1 part liquid soap (Do not use   **powdered tempera**
   detergent.)
4 parts liquid starch

• Add the soap to the liquid starch, and let children use this mixture
  on a smooth washable surface.
• Sprinkle powdered tempera (or food coloring) as desired for color.

Fingerpaint Recipe #7

1 tablespoon soap powder   **1 one-pound can powdered tem-**
¼ cup liquid starch   **pera**
⅓ cup water

• Pour soap powder, starch, and water into blender.
• Gradually add powdered paint while machine is running and blend
  until smooth.
• Add a bit more water as needed.

This recipe calls for a large amount of pigment and is useful when
teachers want a brilliant paint to teach color concepts or to create
especially colorful fingerpaintings.

Note: Use a warm iron to flatten edges of dried paintings before
mounting and framing them.

PLASTIC ART

Modeling clay, playdough, plasticene, Silly Putty, and paste are all plastic art materials. Working with these materials offers some of the most
rewarding experiences for young children. Manipulating clay provides
excellent exercise of the small muscles of the hands and fingers.
Because of the unstructured plasticity of the materials, children are
challenged to create three-dimensional objects which they can destroy
and reshape. Children can take pride in creating something that is
uniquely individual.

     Plastic art materials also offer nonthreatening and socially accept-
able outlets for children to express feelings and release tensions. The
playdough table provides an emotionally comfortable place to observe
others, carry on a conversation, and learn to share; moreover, children

can pound, punch, rip, and poke at the dough without fear of reprimand. Here, too, the teacher can incorporate opportunities for cognitive experiences by relating such concepts as size, shape, color, weight, quantity, and conservation of various attributes to the children's physical interaction with the materials.

Playdough

Children love **playdough**. The enduring popularity of its commercial counterpart, Play-Do, attests to the universal appeal of this manipulative medium. The basic mixture of flour, salt, and water provides a wonderful material to engage a child's developmental interests at many levels. A warm, softly colored playdough is at once appealing and soothing to the touch. The pliability and unstructured qualities of the dough give children the chance to create something or simply to enjoy the way it feels.

Every teacher seems to have a favorite recipe. Try the ones in this book, and modify them to suit your needs and preferences. Be sure to make a large amount so that each child will have plenty to work with.

Let beginners start with just the playdough, in order to have direct tactile experiences with the properties of the dough. Later on, you can add such tools as rolling pins, pie and cookie cutters, blunt scissors, small baking dishes, plastic knives, and other accessories. (Potato ricers make great playdough spaghetti!) Children enjoy preparing make-believe foods, and using different kinds of tools enhances their sociodramatic play and language development.

Plasticene

One of the most popular kinds of commercial claylike products is **plasticene**, which can be purchased in different colors from art supply stores. It is a good material with which to introduce children to the plastic arts because it is not as sticky or difficult to manipulate as potter's clay. Usually sold in 2-pound blocks, plasticene comes in different degrees of softness. Experiment with different consistencies and qualities to find the one most suitable for your class. Purchasing good quality plasticene is economical because it can be used over and over again. Unlike clay or playdough, it won't dry out when left on an open shelf.

Plasticene, like playdough, can be manipulated on a smooth surface, such as a Formica tabletop. Some teachers like to provide trays or masonite boards alongside the plasticene to help children define their work space more clearly. In this way, the children can take responsibility for clean-up, returning the materials to the shelf for the next child.

Clay

Potter's or modeling clay is the familiar gray- or buff-colored material that is shaped, fired, and glazed to make pottery bowls and such. This type of clay can be purchased already prepared, or it can be obtained in powdered form and mixed according to accompanying directions. If mixing the clay yourself (not a simple task!), exercise caution to avoid inhaling the powder. Children should not participate in the preparation.

Molding potter's clay is a totally different experience from molding plasticene or playdough, and one material should not be substituted for the other. Clay needs to be kept moist at all times to be workable. It is easily shaped but sticky, so clothing should be protected; children may find clay less appealing until they become accustomed to the feel of it on their hands.

An excellent way to present potter's clay to children is simply to provide a large chunk that children can cut pieces from with wire or pie cutters; thus they can exercise their autonomy by helping themselves to as much or as little as they need for their projects. On nice days, let children work outdoors. Since clay dries quickly, the objects they create can be painted with bright tempera colors soon after they are molded.

Clay can be stored in dampened plastic bags and kept in a cool place. Other good storage containers are small plastic garbage cans or ceramic crocks. Form the clay into balls, poke a hole in each ball, and fill it with water before storing. Another method is to place several wet sponges in the container. The moisture content must be monitored. If clay dries out, it will be difficult to soften, but if it is left in an overly moist condition, it can become rancid or moldy.

Provide large amounts of clay and plenty of elbow room for each child. Indoors or out, a large Formica tabletop or an area covered with oilcloth provides an excellent work space. A spray bottle of water will enable the children to control the amount of moisture they need and also help them develop an awareness of differences in texture and composition. There is no need to provide any other tools, since you want the children to have direct tactile experiences with the clay.

Each of the materials described serves different needs of the curriculum. But all the plastic art media provide excellent resources for teachers to offer experiences that further the physical, social, emotional, and cognitive development of young children.

Playdough

4 cups flour	**1½ cups water**
¼ cup powdered tempera paint	**1 tablespoon oil**
¼ cup salt	

- Mix together flour, powdered paint, and salt.
- In a separate container, mix water and oil.
- Gradually stir the water and oil mixture into the flour mixture.
- Knead the dough as you add the liquid. Add more water if too stiff, more flour if too sticky.

Note: If the children are helping, eliminate the powdered paint and add liquid paint to the water and oil instead. If using food coloring, add it to the cold water before mixing with the flour.

Stay-Fresh Playdough

2 cups flour   1 cup water
1 cup salt   2 tablespoons oil
2 tablespoons alum   liquid food coloring

• Pour dry ingredients into a large pan, stirring together to mix well.
• Stir oil and food coloring into the water. (Have children watch and comment on what happens when oil and water are mixed together.) Pour liquid into the dry ingredients while mixing, squeezing, and kneading the dough. If too sticky, add more flour.

Alum acts as a preservative; the dough should keep for several weeks if placed in an airtight container in the refrigerator.

Note: Mix two or three different colors of playdough and let children knead portions together to make new colors.

Cooked Playdough

1 cup flour   1 cup water
½ cup salt   1 tablespoon oil
2 teaspoons cream of tartar   1 teaspoon food coloring

• Combine flour, salt, and cream of tartar in a saucepan.
• Mix liquids, and gradually stir them into the dry ingredients.
• When mixture is smooth, cook over medium heat, stirring constantly until a ball forms.
• Remove from heat, and knead until smooth.

Note: This is a very pliable and long-lasting playdough, with a more elastic consistency than uncooked dough. Student teachers voted this their favorite playdough recipe.

Chinese Playdough

3½ cups flour   1¾ cups boiling water
1½ cups sweet rice flour[2]   4 teaspoons honey
7 teaspoons salt

• Mix both kinds of flour and the salt in a large mixing bowl.
• Add 1½ cups boiling water, and work the liquid into the flour well.
• Gradually add ¼ cup to ½ cup more hot water as needed to make a dry dough mixture. The dough should stick together without feeling sticky.
• Form the dough into a flat lump, and steam it for 30 minutes.
• Remove and break into smaller pieces and place on a rack or towel to cool.

[2]Sweet rice flour, also known as glutinous rice flour, can be purchased in one-pound boxes at most Chinese or specialty food stores.

• When cool, combine the pieces into one lump and knead in 4 tea-spoons honey, a little at a time; work in food coloring or liquid tempera as desired.

The mixture keeps well in a plastic bag.

Note: This recipe was given to me by a master artist in Beijing shortly after the Cultural Revolution, when only two artists in all of China were allowed to make playdough figures for sale. This dough was modeled into colorful and delicately shaped figures of children and mythical characters.

Baked Playdough

4 cups flour
1 cup salt
1½ to 2 cups water
condensed milk

food coloring (optional)
small decorative objects such as macaroni, buttons, pebbles, and beans

• Preheat oven to 250°F.
• Let children help mix together flour, salt, and enough water to make a stiff dough.
• Have children help themselves to a big handful and press dough flat or into any shape they like (thick shapes will take longer to dry).
• Provide macaroni, beans, and decorative materials for the children to press into their dough.
• Bake completed dough projects for up to 1 hour, depending on the thickness of the shapes.

For an antiqued, glossy effect, brush on condensed milk before baking or use a mixture of condensed milk and food coloring.

Craft Clay

1 cup cornstarch
2 cups baking soda (one-pound box)

1¼ cups water

• Combine cornstarch and baking soda in a pan.
• Add water gradually, stirring until smooth.
• Place mixture over medium heat and cook until thickened and doughlike in consistency, stirring constantly.
• Turn mixture out onto a pastry board and knead well.
• Cover with a damp cloth or keep in a plastic bag.
• When ready for use, roll flat for cutting into various shapes.

This clay works well for plaques, mobiles, and other models that will be painted when dry.

Textured Modeling Clay

3 cups sand
1½ cups cornstarch
3 teaspoons alum

2¼ cups hot water
food coloring (optional)

- Mix sand, cornstarch, and alum in a saucepan.
- Add hot water and food coloring.
- Cook over medium heat until mixture thickens.
- Remove from heat and knead until smooth.

Store in an airtight container.

Note: This recipe provides an interesting tactile contrast to the smoother playdoughs. The degree of grittiness will be determined by whether fine, medium, or coarse grain sand is used. Objects made from this clay can be dried and painted.

Modeling "Goop"

⅔ cup water
2 cups salt
½ cup water

1 cup cornstarch
**beads, colored macaroni, and
    other small objects**

- Add ⅔ cup water to the salt in a pan.
- Over medium heat, cook and stir 4–5 minutes, until salt is dissolved.
- Remove mixture from heat.
- Gradually mix ½ cup water with cornstarch in a separate container. Stir until smooth.
- Add the cornstarch mixture to the salt mixture.
- Return the combination to low heat, and stir and cook until smooth. The "goop" will thicken quickly.
- Remove from the heat and use for modeling objects.

To harden projects made from this "goop," place outdoors in the sun or indoors in a warm, dry place.

Note: This mixture will not crumble when dry, as some unfired clay products tend to do. Objects like beads and colored macaroni may be added to the "goop" models. Store unused portions in a plastic bag or airtight container.

ADHESIVES

Paste, glue, and tape are important for beginners because of the way these materials feel and what they do. First, let children explore with paste and paper, applying paste with their fingers. Talk about the properties of paste and how the children can use this material to hold things together. Gradually introduce them to other adhesives such as glue, tape, and stick-em stamps. Paste brushes may be offered after the children have had many direct tactile experiences with a variety of adhesives.

Colored Salt Paste

2 parts salt   **powdered tempera**
1 part flour   **water**

• Mix salt, flour, and powdered tempera.
• Gradually stir in enough water to make a smooth paste.

This mixture can be used like regular paste. Store in an airtight container.

Note: Colored paste is appealing to young children. You can store different colors of paste in small babyfood jars.

Liquid Paste *(can be used as a lacquer)*

½ cup regular library paste   **food coloring** (optional)
4–6 tablespoons boiling water

• Stir a small amount of boiling water at a time into library paste until it has the consistency of glue.
• Add food coloring as desired.

This mixture can be brushed over a completed collage for a lacquered effect.

Thin Paste

¼ cup sugar   **1¾ cups water**
¼ cup non-self-rising wheat flour   **¼ teaspoon oil of wintergreen**
½ teaspoon alum

• Combine sugar, flour, and alum in a saucepan.
• Gradually stir in 1 cup water.
• Bring to a boil, and stir until the mixture is clear and smooth.
• Stir in ¾ cup more water, and add oil of wintergreen.

Makes 1 pint. Store in an airtight container.

Note: Thin paste can be spread with a paintbrush or tongue depressor. This is a good adhesive for scrapbooks, collages, and papier-mache.

Paper Paste

⅓ cup non-self-rising wheat flour   **1 cup water**
2 tablespoons sugar   **¼ teaspoon oil of peppermint**

• Mix flour and sugar in a saucepan.
• Gradually stir in water and cook over low heat until mixture is clear.
• Remove from heat and mix in oil of peppermint.

Makes about 1 cup. Store in an airtight container

Note: This recipe makes a smooth, thick paste that is excellent for children to use for any project because it is easy to spread with fingers and makes a good basic adhesive.

Classroom Paste

1 cup non-self-rising wheat flour
1 cup sugar
1 cup cold water
4 cups boiling water

1 tablespoon alum
½ teaspoon oil of wintergreen
(optional)

• Mix flour and sugar in a saucepan.
• Gradually stir in cold water to make a paste.
• Slowly stir in boiling water.
• Bring to a boil and stir until mixture is thick and clear.
• Remove from heat and mix in alum and oil of wintergreen.

This recipe makes about 1½ quarts. Store in an airtight container.

Note: This is an all-purpose paste, similar to the commercially prepared kind used in most schools. If the paste becomes hardened or too thick, stir in hot water to restore to desired consistency. This paste has a softer texture than paper paste and can be stored for several weeks.

Crepe Paper Paste

½ tablespoon flour
½ tablespoon salt
water

2 tablespoons crepe paper,
finely cut

• Add dry ingredients to crepe paper. (The finer the paper is cut, the smoother the paste will be.)
• Add enough water to make a paste.
• Stir and mash the mixture until it is as smooth as possible.

Store in an airtight container.

Wallpaper Paste

1 tablespoon wallpaper paste
(available from paint and wallpaper stores)

1 cup water
1 tablespoon food coloring

• Add 1 tablespoon powdered wallpaper paste to 1 cup water.
• Mix and let stand for 30 minutes.
• Stir again and add about 1 tablespoon food coloring.
• Add more powder or water as needed for desired consistency.

This paste is best if allowed to stand overnight.

Note: This paste has a translucent quality that is especially brilliant when the paste is mixed with a generous amount of color. It can be added to fingerpaints (remember to add soap for easier washing of stains), used as glue in collages, and painted on clear cellophane for a stained-glass effect.

Squeeze Bottle Glitter

1 part flour   **1 part water**
1 part salt   **liquid food coloring** (optional)

• Mix equal parts flour, salt, and water.
• Pour into plastic squeeze bottles such as those used for mustard or ketchup.
• Add liquid food coloring for variety.

Note: Squeeze this mixture onto heavy construction paper or cardboard. When it dries, the salt in this mixture provides a glistening quality.

BUBBLES

Everyone is intrigued with the ethereal quality of bubbles. Children love to chase these magical floating objects that reflect all the colors of the rainbow. Even more fun is to actually make your own bubbles—and burst them! You can always count on blowing bubbles to be a successful activity, whether it is to involve children in music and art, to encourage cooperation and language development, or simply to engage them in a fun activity. Bubble fanciers have their own favorite recipes. Try the following to decide which ones you like.

Fancy Bubbles

1 cup water   **¼ cup granulated sugar**
½ cup Joy liquid detergent   **1 tablespoon glycerin**

• Mix all ingredients until sugar dissolves.
• Let stand for 3–4 hours.

Fill individual juice cans about half full for each child. Provide bubble pipes, straws, or wire rings for children to create their bubbles. This recipe produces bubbles that float longer than those produced from commercial products. Store the mixture in a covered jar in the refrigerator.

Note: Have inexperienced children practice blowing *through* a straw into water before introducing them to the bubble mixture.

Tough Bubbles

⅔ cup Dawn liquid detergent   **1 tablespoon glycerin**
water

• Add enough water to the detergent to make 1 gallon of liquid.
• Add glycerin.
• Let the mixture sit out for one day.
• Stir before using.

Note: This recipe for long-lasting bubbles is recommended by the San Francisco Exploratorium.

Colored Bubbles

1 cup soap powder   **liquid food coloring**
1 quart warm water

• Dissolve soap in warm water.
• Stir in food coloring.

Note: This is a basic recipe calling for granulated soap rather than liquid detergent. It does not require glycerin, unlike most other recipes.

Super Bubble Brew

2 cups liquid detergent   **¾ cup sugar**
  (Joy recommended)
6 cups water

• Mix all ingredients together.
• Let stand for 4 hours at room temperature.

Note: This is a non-glycerin recipe that keeps for up to 5 days. Use berry baskets, twisted wire coat hangers, kitchen utensils, and plastic six-pack rings for bubble-blowing.

Print-Making Bubbles

2 cups powdered tempera   **½ cup liquid starch**
1 cup water   **1 cup liquid detergent**

• Stir powdered tempera into water until smooth (or use liquid tempera made from Easel Paint Recipe #2).
• Add liquid starch and detergent, and mix.
• Blend with additional water if needed to make a solution that is the consistency of thin liquid soap.
• Pour into a wide, shallow pan.

Let each child blow through a straw until bubbles are high above the container. Lift the bubbles off with a sheet of paper placed over the top of the container. When the paper dries, let children use it for felt pen art or simply enjoy the random bubble designs.

  Cover the activity area with newspapers to soak up bubble solution that spills over the container.

Note: You can vary the color intensity of the bubbles by using more or less tempera. Do not let children mix the powdered paint or suck the solution through the straws.

Another Bubble Activity

See page 235 for an additional recipe for a bubble solution that is used with a hula hoop to make person-size bubbles!

PAINTINGS, PICTURES, AND COLLAGES

Creating paintings, pictures, and collages provides attractive opportunities to extend children's learning and development. With a basic knowledge of *how* to prepare art and craft recipes, the teacher can now consider *when* and *where* to use them. After using an activity with the children, evaluate the project to determine whether it was developmentally appropriate. Revise the recipes as needed to better serve your objectives.

Cellophane Murals

MATERIALS   Large sheets of colored cellophane
Masking tape
Different colors of Easel Paint Recipe #3
Small cans and brushes

PROCEDURE   • Tape large sheets of cellophane to a window.
• Give the children brushes and cans of different colored paints.
• Let them paint on the cellophane to make translucent murals.

Notice how different the colors look when there is light shining through them.

Printing with Objects

MATERIALS   Kitchen tools with handles (potato mashers, cookie cutters)
Vegetables and sponges cut into different shapes
Plastic table toys
Easel paints
Pie tins
Absorbent paper (easel or construction)

PROCEDURE   • Provide several pie tins, each containing a different color of paint.
• Let the children make prints by dipping various objects into the paint to make designs on paper.

Spatter Painting

MATERIALS
Fine wire screen cut into 6" squares
Colored tape 1½" wide
Toothbrushes
Leaves and other flat objects such as paper cutouts
Easel paint in flat containers

PROCEDURE
- Attach and fold colored tape over the edges of the wire screen to frame the squares.
- Put the leaves, paper cutouts, and other flat objects on trays, and let the children select materials to make a design on a piece of paper.
- Place the wire screen over the design and have the children hold the frame steady with one hand while they use a toothbrush dipped in paint to "scrub" the wire mesh.

When the leaves and wire screen are removed, outlines of the objects will appear on a background of finely spattered paint.

Note: Children can work together if one child holds the screen while another scrubs. Notice how the spatter effect is controlled by the amount of paint and the angle of the brush. To contain the spatter, have children hold the materials inside a shallow cardboard box.

Paste Painting

MATERIALS
3 tablespoons paste
2 tablespoons liquid tempera paint
Tongue depressors
Construction paper or cardboard

PROCEDURE
- Mix paste and paint. Add a few drops of hot water if necessary to make a smooth, thick consistency.
- Mix several colors, and let the children use their fingers or tongue depressors to apply paste to the cardboard.

The completed paintings will have a thick, textured appearance.

VARIATION
Add tempera or food coloring to white glue; squeeze the mixture out of bottles to form designs.

String Pictures

MATERIALS
Easel paints
White glue
String and yarn of different lengths and thicknesses
Heavy construction paper

PROCEDURE
- Mix two parts paint to one part glue.
- Stir and pour mixture into pie tins or other flat containers.

• Let children dip the yarn into the paint and glue mixture, then make string designs on paper.

When dry, the strings and yarn will adhere to the paper.

Cornstarch Painting

MATERIALS   Powdered cornstarch (allow one 16-ounce box for 2–3 children)
Water
Large table with smooth surface, or shallow trays, or large unbreakable mixing bowls

PROCEDURE   • Mix enough water with the cornstarch to eliminate the possibility of the children's inhaling the powder.
• Have the children help spread and mix the cornstarch with their hands while you slowly add more water.
• While the children are mixing it, talk about the consistency and texture and how the mixture feels.

Note: Food coloring can be added if desired. This is a good "messy" activity for toddlers as well as older children.

Blow-out Pictures

MATERIALS   Easel paints
3-ounce juice cans
Plastic straws
Paper

PROCEDURE   • Pour paints into juice cans.
• Let the children dip their straws into the paint and blow out designs onto paper.
• Fold the paper in half while the paint is still wet to make Rorschach-like designs.

Note: Have the children practice blowing with straws before introducing paints. Do not use this activity with children who are likely to suck in instead of blowing out.

VARIATION   Blow black paint on glossy white paper. To make oriental-looking scrolls, dip a finger into red paint and make little "blossoms" on the black branch-like figures.

Roller Painting

MATERIALS   Empty roll-on deodorant bottles
Easel paints
Paper

PROCEDURE   • Fill roll-on deodorant bottles with different colors of paint.
• Let children use the paint to make designs on paper.

Note: The rolling motion strengthens wrist, finger, and hand muscles different from those used with brushes and crayons.

Eyedropper Painting

MATERIALS
Small juice cans
Easel paints (thinned down)
Paper
Eyedroppers of different sizes

PROCEDURE
- Provide children with small juice cans of paints.
- Let them use an assortment of different-size eyedroppers to squeeze drops of paint onto construction paper.

Note: This is a good activity to develop the small muscles of the hands and fingers.

VARIATION
Let the children squeeze different colors of paint into plastic containers of water to make new colors. Provide the primary colors of red, yellow, and blue so that they can be mixed to make orange, green, purple, and brown. Make a color chart as in Illustration 1.3 for children to refer to while they are mixing the paints.

Colored Collage Materials

MATERIALS
Rock salt
Eggshells
Pasta of different shapes
Rubbing alcohol or vinegar
Food coloring or easel paint
Plastic bags

PROCEDURE
- Make a thin mixture of coloring and vinegar or alcohol to pour over porous collage materials such as rock salt and pasta.
- Shake well in a plastic bag.
- Pour into a flat tin and let dry.
- Let children use materials for collages.

Note: If using alcohol, do not let children handle mixture during preparation.

Magic Marker Spray Painting

MATERIALS
Felt pens in a variety of colors
Absorbent paper, such as coffee filters or paper towels
Spray bottles of water

PROCEDURE
- Let the children make designs on absorbent paper with the felt pens.
- Spray the designs with water and watch the colors spread.
- Hang the paintings up to dry.

Tissue Collage

MATERIALS
Empty juice cans
Carpet yarn spools
Small containers, such as boxes and juice cans
Cardboard
Liquid starch
White glue
Paintbrushes
Colored tissue paper
Magazines
Scissors

PROCEDURE
- Mix one part liquid starch with one part white glue.
- Let the children use brushes to paint the mixture onto juice cans, spools, small containers, and cardboard.
- Apply torn-up or cut-up pieces of colored tissue paper and magazine pictures to decorate.

Note: Give the children plenty of time and encouragement to practice cutting with scissors. Provide magazines and other paper that can be cut easily (the tissue paper is better for tearing). Although cutting may seem easy, children's small finger muscles may not be sufficiently developed to manipulate the scissors successfully. Provide the best-quality blunt-nosed scissors available (both left- and right-handed). Children enjoy practicing tearing and cutting, without any concern for making a particular project. Save the paper scraps and display them attractively in see-through containers. Children can use them later in other collage activities.

Three-Dimensional Collages

MATERIALS
Collection of items such as Styrofoam pieces from packing boxes, small scraps of wood, soft wood (balsa), foil, string, yarn, pipe cleaners, colored macaroni, corks, shells, beans, rice
Glue
Plastic tape

PROCEDURE
- Let the children glue or tape various objects to pieces of wood and Styrofoam to create three-dimensional sculptures.
- Provide plenty of space and materials and encourage them to use both the materials and their imaginations freely. Some children may want to combine their efforts to make one large sculpture.

Note: Children develop and strengthen their concepts of size, space, shape, and direction with collage and sculpting activities. As they gain competence, they will become more selective in the materials they choose or find to create their projects.

Piñata Pigs

MATERIALS   Newspaper
Balloons
Water
White glue, or classroom paste thinned with water
Paintbrushes, 1" or 1½" wide
Easel paints or watercolors
Construction paper
6" pieces of curly ribbon

PROCEDURE
- Have children tear newspapers into 2"-wide strips.
- Inflate balloons.
- Soak some of the paper in water and apply two layers of damp paper to the balloons.
- Coat the paper with glue. Attach two more damp layers of paper.
- Make the pigs' legs, snouts, and ears out of construction paper and glue them onto each balloon.
- Add curly ribbon to form tails.
- Apply three more layers of shredded paper, using glue instead of water.
- When dry, paint the pigs.

Note: This activity requires more adult direction than others do. It may be useful for a special occasion or as a group project.

Sand Painting

MATERIALS   Liquid starch (or a mixture of 3 parts flour to 4 parts water)
White glue
Plastic squeeze bottles
Fine-grain white sand
Newspapers
Construction paper

PROCEDURE
- Mix equal parts of starch and glue together and pour into squeeze-bottles.
- Spread sand on large sheets of newspaper.
- Let the children squeeze glue designs onto construction paper and then turn the paper, design side down, onto the sand.

Note: If you wish to use colored sand, mix powdered tempera with sand away from the children to avoid their inhaling the dust.

Finger Etching

MATERIALS   Masking tape
Liquid tempera paints (Select a recipe containing soap.)
Liquid starch
Easel paper or colored newsprint

PROCEDURE
- Use masking tape to delineate on the surface of a smooth table an area the same size as the easel paper or colored newsprint you plant to use, as shown in Illustration 1.4.
- Supply containers of liquid paints, and let children fingerpaint on the outlined table area, using a variety of colors.
- Supply small containers of liquid starch and spoons for children to use if they wish.
- When a child is ready, lift off the design by smoothing the newsprint over the table area. Vary the colors of paper for different effects.
- Talk about the designs and how they look on the table and when lifted off on paper.

Blotter Art Pictures

MATERIALS
Easel paints
Water
Eyedroppers
Straws (optional)
Blotter paper or absorbent paper towels
Transparent self-sticking shelf paper

PROCEDURE
- Thin easel paints with water.
- Give the children small containers of paint, and let them use eyedroppers and blow through paint-dipped straws to make designs on white or colored blotter paper or absorbent paper towels.

Note: Make certain children understand that they are to blow through the straws, not suck in. (The straws can be an optional item.)

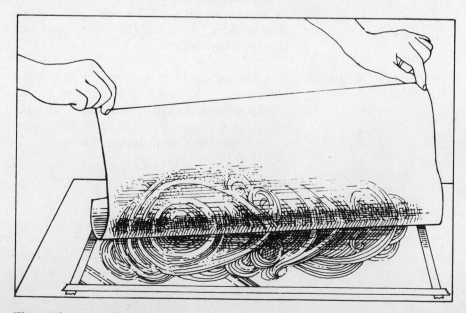

Illustration 1.4 Finger etching

Talk about the absorbency of some materials and how the liquid paint "travels," or is carried by the fibers of the blotter paper. If desired, the finished work can be mounted on contrasting colors of construction paper and covered with transparent self-sticking paper to make an effective display.

Cornmeal Painting

MATERIALS
Cornmeal
Large salt shakers with handles
Sifters
Small pie tins
White glue
Liquid starch or water
Cotton swabs
Small brushes
Plastic spoons
Paper

PROCEDURE
- Give the children small pie tins partially filled with a mixture of white glue that has been thinned with liquid starch or water.
- Let them use cotton swabs, small brushes, and plastic spoons to paint glue onto the construction paper.
- Provide an area where children can use shakers and sifters to sprinkle cornmeal over their paintings and shake off the excess.

Note: If possible, have children carry their completed paintings to an adjacent table (lined with newspapers) where the cornmeal, shakers, and sifters are located. Have a broom and dustpan nearby to sweep up spilled cornmeal. Be sure the shakers and sifters have holes large enough to accommodate the coarse cornmeal.

This activity provides opportunities for children to develop a variety of muscle skills as well as independence, cooperation, and resourcefulness.

Sandpaper Painting

MATERIALS
Old crayons of several colors
Sheets of fine-grained sandpaper
Oven

PROCEDURE
- Preheat oven to 250° F.
- Give each child a sheet of sandpaper and an assortment of crayons to make designs on the sandpaper. Have them bear down hard, making heavy strokes. Drawing with lots of color provides the best results.
- Place each drawing on a cookie sheet in the oven for 15 seconds. The oven door can be left ajar (with teacher supervision) so that children can watch the crayons melt.

• Use potholders to remove the cookie sheets from the oven; let the sandpaper paintings cool. Finished work can be mounted on contrasting colors of construction paper.

Texture Pictures

MATERIALS
Collection of items such as features, dry cereals, textured materials, scrap tiles, pine cones, seed pods, pebbles, shells, buttons, pasta, and eggshells
Glue
Brushes
Pieces of smooth scrap lumber, about 6" x 9"

PROCEDURE
• Let children make texture pictures by gluing items of different textures on wood.

Note: Extend children's experiences with texture by blindfolding them or having them close their eyes and describe or identify the objects.

Transparent Pictures

MATERIALS
Scraps of colored tissue paper
Small leaves and flower petals
Bits of crayon scrapings
Scraps of material
Waxed paper cut into 12" squares
An old iron

PROCEDURE
• Let the children make a design using the above materials on one sheet of waxed paper.
• When they have finished, cover the paper with another piece of waxed paper the same size.
• Iron the sheets together.
• Display the pictures in a window so that light can shine through.

Note: An adult should do the ironing. Be sure to have a thick pad between the iron and the tabletop or whatever surface you use. An ironing pad can be made with old mattress pads and discarded sheets or towels. For easier identification, a small slip of paper with the child's name can be inserted between the sheets of waxed paper before ironing.

Chalk Painting

MATERIALS
Pie tins or flat pans
Liquid starch
Water
Large, flat paintbrushes
Smooth paper
1" x 4" colored chalk

PROCEDURE • Provide pans of liquid starch mixed with a small amount of water for children to paint onto smooth paper (fingerpaint paper or butcher paper works well).
• When the paper has been painted with starch, have the children make designs on the wet paper with colored chalk.

Note: When the design dries, the starch acts as a fixative and the chalk will not rub off the paper.

Buttermilk Painting

MATERIALS Fingerpaint paper
Buttermilk
Colored chalk

PROCEDURE • Place about a tablespoonful of buttermilk on the paper.
• Let each child use chalk to make designs.

Note: The buttermilk acts as a carrier, and the product is similar to fingerpaint but can be more easily controlled by the child. Wash chalk or rub it on wire mesh to clean after each use.

Glass Wax Art

MATERIALS Glass Wax
Pieces of dry cloth, or sponges
A window

PROCEDURE • Let the children rub Glass Wax all over the window and allow it to dry.
• Then let them draw on the window with their fingers.
• When they are finished, they can use clean cloths to wipe the windows and erase their work.

Note: This activity gives children the opportunity to use large arm movements as well as their hands and fingers. They also gain experience in eye-hand coordination from a standing rather than a sitting position.

Footprint Painting

MATERIALS Large sheet of plastic or oilcloth
Newsprint
Two child-size chairs
Paints
Large juice cans
Paintbrushes
Dishpan of warm, soapy water
Towels

PROCEDURE
- Spread plastic or oilcloth on the floor.
- Place a long sheet of newsprint on top of the plastic.
- Place a chair at each end of the newsprint.
- At one end of the paper, place cans of paint and brushes.
- At the other end, place a pan of soapy water and some towels.
- Have children remove their socks and shoes.
- Have each child sit on a chair while you paint the bottoms of his or her feet. (You may wish to give the child a color choice.)
- Instruct the first child to walk on the paper, leaving footprints.
- At the end of the paper, have the child step into the pan of soapy water to clean his or her feet and then dry them with the towel.
- Proceed in the same manner with the other children, using the same piece of paper for all the footprints.

Note: This project works most efficiently when there are two adults supervising. You may want to label one of each child's prints. The same procedure can be used to make handprints. This project is useful for teaching *right* and *left*, size concepts, and counting fingers and toes. When the paint has dried, children enjoy retracing each other's prints.

Styrofoam Art

MATERIALS
Styrofoam meat trays
Squeeze bottles of glue
Colored pasta in different shapes
Natural materials such as leaves, pebbles, and shells

PROCEDURE
- Give each child a Styrofoam tray.
- Let each child select materials and glue them onto the tray to make a design.

Note: Children enjoy the process of squeezing and watching liquid flow from a bottle. You may need to suggest that they limit the amount of glue they use to make the materials adhere to the tray. Point out that they need only a small amount to make the objects stick and that it takes a long time for large amounts of glue to dry. You can also provide an area with squeeze bottle activities using less expensive materials, such as liquid starch and water.

Soap Snow

MATERIALS
2 cups soap powder
$\frac{1}{2}$ cup water
Egg beater
Cardboard
Cookie press or pastry tube

PROCEDURE
- Whip soap powder with water to the consistency of thick whipped cream.
- Fill a cookie press or pastry tube with the mixture, and let the children "frost" cardboard or other suitable objects.

Note: Soap snow can be molded by first dipping hands in water before shaping. The mixture will dry to a porous texture and last for weeks.

Spackle Imprints

MATERIALS
Spackling powder (available at paint or hardware stores)
Water
Tops of cottage cheese cartons
Paint (optional)

PROCEDURE
• Mix spackling powder with water to the consistency of whipped cream, making sure the mixture is free of lumps. (Children should not participate in mixing the powder.)
• Pour the mixture into cottage cheese carton tops, and let each child make an imprint of his or her hand.

Note: Spackle is superior to plaster of Paris because it dries more slowly, giving the children time to make their imprints or to make designs with other materials. Paint may also be added to the mixture. The finished product takes about 40–60 minutes to harden.

Sand Casting

MATERIALS
Imprint materials such as shells, cans, and pine cones
Wet sand
Plaster of Paris
Candle wax and wicks

PROCEDURE
• Have the children make imprints in wet sand with their hands, feet, or other objects. (See Illustration 1.5.)
• Pour plaster of Paris or melted candle wax into the imprint. Insert wicks in the wax before it hardens.
• Remove wax or plaster when cool and hard.

Note: Pouring hot candle wax is the teacher's job. Supervise children closely.

SEWING AND DYEING

As children develop more strength in their hand muscles and gain dexterity and competence in manual activities, you can offer new challenges. Sewing with needle and thread requires unique skills. Not only are the small muscles used, but also the ability to weave *in* and *out* is demanded. When embroidery loops are used, children must learn to go *down* and *up* rather than *over* and *over* around the edge of the fabric.

Dyeing materials provides opportunities for children to learn how people of different cultures dye fabrics and yarn for making clothing and rugs. You might want to combine an activity with a story such as "Pelle's New Suit" to discuss the process of making wool, dyeing it, and

Illustration 1.5   **Making sand castings**

finally sewing it into clothing. Children can save shaggy dog hair, wash and dye it, and use it for collages.

Only adults should work with the hot dye baths. Children can help select natural plant dyes, tie and wrap their materials, untie the cooled materials, and hang them out to dry.

To avoid toxic hazards, use only natural plant dyes. Some natural dyes are onion skins, outer leaves of purple cabbage, lupine, silver dollar eucalyptus, and fennel. For more information on natural dyes, see *Dye Plants and Dyeing—A Handbook*, available from the Brooklyn Botanic Garden, Brooklyn, New York 11225.

The activities in this section are suitable for children ages 4½ and up who have the manual dexterity and perceptual-motor skills to approach these as reasonable challenges, not frustratingly impossible tasks. The activities have been used successfully in schools and are quite popular. You must decide if they are appropriate for your children.

Strengthening Hand and Finger Muscles

The following activities can be built into the daily routine to help strengthen small muscles:

- Provide individual hand paper punches for children to use. Show them how to hold the paper with one hand and squeeze the punch with the other hand to make holes. It is sometimes helpful for you to hold your hand over theirs to let them get a feel of what they must do to squeeze the punch.
- Make "train tickets" for the conductor to punch when children engage in dramatic play.
- Provide kitchen tongs for children to use to pick up articles of varying weights, from cotton balls to nuts and bolts.
- Space containers at varying distances from one another and ask children to transfer items from one container to another.
- Have children use tongs to pick up and place a certain number of items in a series of muffin tins.
- Sew snaps on separate pieces of material and let children snap them together, by pushing the snaps together against a tabletop first with just the thumb, then with the first finger, and so on; do the same with the opposite hand. Then have children hold up the pieces of cloth and snap the snaps together with the thumb and first finger of the right hand, the thumb and second finger of the left hand, and so on.

Sewing Cardboard Shapes

MATERIALS   Paper punch
Pieces of cardboard cut into various shapes
Yarn or old shoelaces
Melted wax

PROCEDURE   • Punch holes about an inch apart around the edges of cardboard.
• Stiffen the yarn by dipping it in melted wax.

• Have the children use yarn or shoelaces to sew in and out of the holes in the cardboard. Talk about directional movements of *up*, *down*, *in*, *out*.

Sewing on Burlap

MATERIALS   Plastic darning needles
Yarn
Pieces of burlap or other loosely woven material
Embroidery frames or hoops

PROCEDURE   • Teach the children to thread the darning needles with yarn.
• Help them knot the yarn at one end, and show them how to place the material between the embroidery hoops to hold the material taut.
• Teach them how to insert the needle and how to sew by pulling the yarn down and then bringing the needle and yarn up through the material.

Note: Some children will tend to go around the outside of the hoop instead of up and down through the middle. Many children who have not had experience will need help and plenty of time to practice. Some will be content to simply sew around the hoop's edge, which is acceptable, except that you will need to cut the yarn to remove the hoop. Plastic berry baskets are also excellent for sewing and weaving.

Tie Dye

MATERIALS   Untreated soft cotton cloth
String and rubber bands
Liquid vegetable dye
Container of clear water
Salt
Container for dye bath, preferably stainless steel or enamel
Large strainer or mesh basket

PROCEDURE   • Fill a large container with water and bring to a boil.
• Add vegetable dye to desired strength of color. (You will need to experiment with the intensity of shade you wish to achieve.)
• Keep the dye bath simmering while you help the children prepare their cloths.
• Have the children prepare their material by taking a piece of cloth and (1) pleating it like a fan, (2) picking it up in the center, or (3) bunching it up and tying it tightly with string or rubber bands. (You may need to tighten the strings after children have tried.)
• Place tied cloths in the clear, cold water until completely soaked.
• Remove from water and place in the dye bath. Let simmer for 1–3 minutes, depending on the strength of dye and the desired color.
• Remove from the dye, place in a strainer or basket, and rinse under a faucet until the water runs clear.

• Remove the string.
• If you want to add another color, repeat the same procedure, omitting the soaking process.

Note: Children should not be involved in any of the dye preparation or simmering of the materials.

Dyeing Eggs

MATERIALS Bag of onion skins (available free at produce markets)
Squares of cloth (about 8" square)
Eggs
Bits of rice, leaves, and flower petals
String
Pot for boiling eggs

PROCEDURE • Place 6–8 layers of onion skin on each piece of cloth.
• Place bits of design material (rice, leaves, flower petals, etc.) on top of the onion skins.
• Place an egg on top of the above materials and wrap carefully.
• Tie the cloth tightly around the egg and onion skin.
• Put wrapped eggs in a pot of water and boil for 30 minutes (a teacher task).
• Remove eggs, let cool without rinsing, and then untie wrapping.

Note: This is the way Latvian children used to color their Easter eggs. Onion skin can also be used for tie dyeing by boiling the material and skins together. The color will vary from yellow to brown. Darker shades result from longer boiling in a larger quantity of onion skins.

Introduction to Woodworking

THE VALUE OF WOODWORKING

Observe the expression of pride on a youngster's face when she has finally sawed through a piece of wood, or the obvious sense of accomplishment when a child proudly displays the "airplane" he has labored so long to glue together! An ordinarily distractable child shows an unusual amount of concentration when focusing on hammering a nail; a physically aggressive child discovers he or she can work out angry feelings *and* create something original at the same time.

Teachers need not shy away from woodworking because they feel the activity is dangerous, there is inadequate supervision, or they themselves lack a sense of competence. Those who are willing to invest the time and effort to include woodworking in the curriculum soon come to appreciate the valuable experience children gain from these activities.

Through woodworking, children develop eye-hand coordination, learn to measure, and become familiar with various materials and their attributes (hard, soft, long, short, and other similar concepts). A typically quiet child will often discuss in great detail and with obvious satisfaction how he or she used tools to make something. How proud a youngster must feel to see that inventiveness and persistence result in something tangible! Such activities not only influence language development but also enhance a child's self-esteem and sense of competence.

TOOLS AND MATERIALS

Start your woodworking program with quality equipment, provide a good supply of raw materials, observe the safety suggestions accompanying the activities, and you will soon find that the enthusiastic responses of the children will make woodworking an indispensable part of your program.

Workbench

Woodworking benches can be purchased from school equipment supply houses, but you can make your own at much less cost.

You can build a woodworking table out of a hard wood, such as maple. The surface should be at least 3' x 4' with sturdy wood-block legs. The correct height is that of children's knuckles when their arms are straight down by their sides — generally about 24"–26".

A good alternative is to use a heavy table with legs cut to the desired height. Solid wood doors or heavy wood planks can be nailed to boxes or sawhorses. Individual workbenches can be made by using packing boxes, wooden benches, or old wooden chairs with the backs cut off.

Storage

Tools, wood, and woodworking materials need to be stored near the work area, designed for easy access and clean-up. Commercial tool racks or cabinets are available; depending on the location of your carpentry, you may need to have portable equipment that can be locked.

A rack can be made quite easily by using ¾" plywood held together with straps across the back so that it can be folded. Screw in hooks to hold the tools. Do not use masonite pegboard with hooks, as those come loose easily. Attach wheels for easier portability.

Use a marker to outline each tool on the rack so that children will know where each tool belongs. To encourage reading skills, you can label with the names of the tools.

A woodbox on casters is suitable for storing large pieces of wood. Smaller pieces can be stored in baskets and boxes. Sturdy see-through boxes (such as plastic food or shoe containers), tin cans, and open cardboard boxes with picture labels are useful for storing nails, screws, wires, wheels, and other woodworking accessories.

Wood and Other Materials

Use a soft wood for nailing. Pine is the best choice because it holds nails well and is lightweight, moderately strong, and relatively inexpensive. Other soft woods are fir, cedar, spruce, poplar, and balsam. Avoid redwood, which is soft but tends to be splintery.

Check for softness by scratching the wood with your thumbnail; if an indentation is left, the wood is soft enough for children to use. Hard wood can be set aside in a different bin for gluing construction.

Other board products that are suitable for carpentry projects are particle board (sometimes called chipboard), fiberboard (insulation board), and ceiling tiles.

Particle board is made by bonding wood particles into sheets to be used for shelving and floor underlayment. It is easily sawed and glues well, but tends to break apart when nailed along the edges.

Fiberboard and *ceiling tiles* are easy to nail but do not hold nails as well as soft woods. They do not saw easily, but are good for gluing.

Wood and board products that are ³/₄" to 1" thick work well for children's carpentry because pieces can be nailed together easily.

Lumber mills, cabinet shops, and high school woodworking classes are good sources for donations of scrap wood. Carpenters, contractors, grocers, and workers on construction sites are also potential donors of wood, wire, knobs, and other accessories. You are more likely to collect materials if you leave a box labeled with the name of your school, your phone number, and the date you intend to pick it up. Occasional samples of the children's work, along with a thank-you note, do wonders for public relations.

Hammers

Select some 7-ounce *claw hammers* and some weighing between 8 and 10 ounces. (See Illustration 1.6.) The ones with steel shanks are best. The weight of a hammer is important in providing the proper balance for nailing. If a hammer is too light, children will not be able to hammer nails into wood; if it is too heavy, the nails will bend.

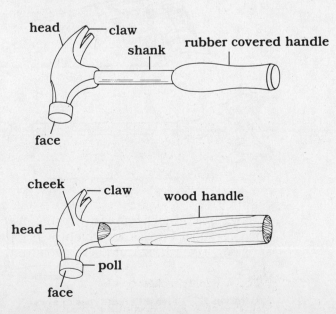

Illustration 1.6   **Two types of hammers**

Handles should be smooth and small enough for a child's hand to grip, measuring about 11½" from handle to head (the Vaughan "Little Pro" and the Estwing E3-12C are good choices). Both wooden and rubber-covered handles are suitable. Beginners tend to choke up on the handles by moving their hands up closer to the head. As they become more experienced, have them move their hands back to gain better leverage and balance.

Saws

A *crosscut saw* is the best choice for young children. (See Illustration 1.7.) It is designed to cut across the grain of the wood. Select saws with blades 16"–20" long. The more teeth or points per inch, the finer the cut. Saws with ten points are about right for children. If possible, have a child try the handle for comfort before you purchase the saw.

There are other saws that are suitable for young children.

A *keyhole*, or *compass*, *saw* is a light saw designed for sawing in tight places. It is easier to handle than a crosscut and can be less frustrating for a beginner.

A *backsaw*, like the crosscut, is used for cutting across the grain. It has a rectangular blade held rigid by a reinforcing piece of metal along the top edge that strengthens the saw and ensures a straight cut.

A *dovetail saw* resembles a backsaw. It has a screwdriver-like handle and a short blade reinforced along the top edge. The blade has fine teeth.

A *coping saw*, or *jigsaw*, consists of a slender, short blade that can be inserted in a U-shaped frame. The advantage of the coping saw is that the direction of the teeth of the blade does not matter. The

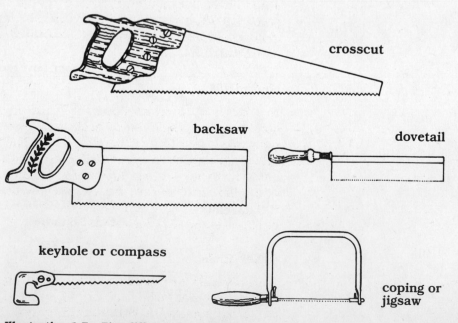

Illustration 1.7   **Five different types of saws**

blade is less likely to bind against the wood if the child uses too much pressure. A supply of replacement blades should be kept on hand. (Use medium or fine blades only; coarse blades will break too easily.)

All these saws are good choices for young children because they are shorter than the common crosscut saws and easier to handle.

Sawing with a dull blade causes binding and pinching against the wood. Except for the coping saw, all saws should be sharpened at least once a year. Store saws so that they do not come in contact with other metal that can dull blades. Wipe blades with lightweight machine oil from time to time.

Clamps

Clamps are used to hold pieces of wood together while the glue between them dries or to secure a piece of wood to the workbench so that it can be drilled, nailed, or sawed. A clamp allows the child to use both hands for working. *C-clamps* come with different size jaws or openings, ranging from 1" to 8". A good size for the preschool is 4". The *sliding bar clamp* is similar to the C-clamp except that it is more easily adjusted by the child. Be sure to select clamps that will fit the depth of the workbench or table and still leave room for the wood you will be securing.

Vise

A *vise*, like a C-clamp, is used to hold pieces of wood. It can be mounted permanently to the workbench so that children can secure their own wood.

Miter Boxes

Miter boxes are made of hardwood and have two sets of grooves in them for sawing straight lines and 45° angles. The miter box helps children saw correctly and can be secured to the workbench or table. (See Illustration 1.8.)

Hand Drill

Buy *hand drills* with handles that fit the child's grip comfortably. A good length is 10¾". Some drills have removable caps on the handles for storing drill bits of different sizes. The teacher should change the bits for the children. Hand drills are used to drill small holes such as guide holes for screws. It is easier to start the drill if a small hole is made first with a nail and hammer. Show children how to hold the drill handle with one hand and turn the crank handle forward with the other, as shown in Illustration 1.9.

Other Tools

Screwdrivers are good tools for children who have had experience with more basic tools

A *try square*, or *carpenter's square*, is useful for marking off a right angle.

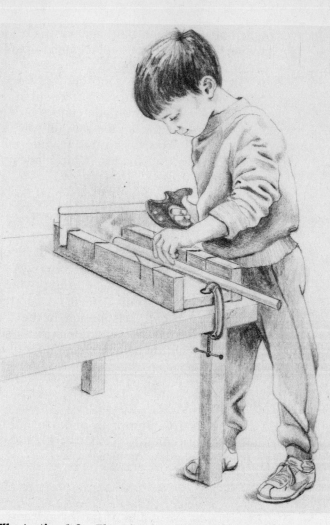

Illustration 1.8   **The miter box helps children saw correctly.**

Rulers and *tape measures* are handy for teaching children to be more exact, but do not hesitate to encourage the use of fingers, hands, and feet for measuring.

Sandpaper of varying grades is useful for calling the children's attention to wood grain. There are several grades, or "grits," of sandpaper. The fine grit is 220, medium is 120 grit, and coarse is 80 grit.

Sanding blocks with screws can be purchased to hold the paper, or you can wrap a piece of sandpaper around a small block of wood.

Nails

The proper kind of nails is important for successful woodworking experiences. Most nails are graded in size by the penny system, abbreviated with the letter d. Standard-length nails are identified as follows:

Size	Length in inches
2d	1
3d	1¼
4d	1½
5d	1¾
6d	2

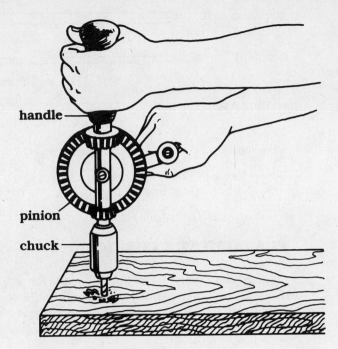

Illustration 1.9   **Hand drill**

Common nails have large, round, flat heads and come in the sizes listed above. (See Illustration 1.10.) For the preschooler, a selection of 4d and 6d nails is the most practical.

Roofing nails have large, flat heads. The galvanized ones produce toxic fumes when heated, so do not use them if there is a chance the child's woodwork might end up in the fireplace.

Box nails and *wire nails* also have large heads relative to their size.

Other Materials

Post or send home notices so that parents can contribute materials such as the following:

coffee cans (to hold nails and other materials)
cottage cheese cartons
plastic lids of all sizes
cardboard
wire (especially the colored plastic-coated kind)
babyfood jar lids (for wheels)
paraffin or bar soap (to rub across the blades of saws)
spools
rubber bands
carpenter's pencils
Styrofoam

clean rags
toilet paper and paper towel tubes
yarn
old drawer pulls
pieces of leather and plastic
used Tinker Toys
pieces of inner toys
end cuts of pegboard
ceiling tiles
plastic meat trays
egg cartons
bottle caps

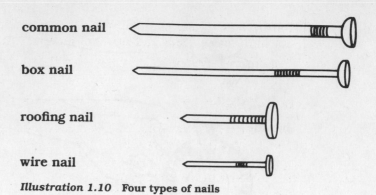

Illustration 1.10 **Four types of nails**

PLANNING THE CURRICULUM

Most preschoolers have limited experience with carpentry, and many do not yet have the coordination to handle some of the tools. Two-year-olds are not ready for complicated projects with hammers and saws. Thus, it is important to start slowly, offering simple activities that guarantee success.

Give children (especially 2- and 3-year-olds) practice in using vertical wrist movements, such as in pounding wooden pegs with mallets. Or let them use their mallets to hammer golf tees or nails with large heads into big pieces of Styrofoam. Pounding large spikes into firm soil offers another opportunity to practice. Wood stumps make excellent spots for hammering nails. Projects such as gluing and sanding give youngsters the chance to become familiar with some of the characteristics of different kinds of wood and woodworking materials.

Process versus Product

Young children enjoy opportunities to use their senses to explore the properties of woodworking materials. They will work diligently at hammering a nail or sawing a piece of wood, without any thought of what the finished product will be. Just the act of working with and controlling materials is satisfaction enough. They may give the final product a title when they have finished, but their joy is derived from the *process* of hammering and sawing.

Ages and Stages

Age is not the only factor in a child's skill level. Much depends on previous experience, physical abilities, perceptual-motor development, and the child's interests. A beginner, no matter the age, will generally spend time getting acquainted with the tools and how they work.

Prior experience and success with such related activities as those mentioned above help motivate children to try new and more challenging tasks.

After *exploring*, the next stage is one in which children attempt to *combine* two or more pieces of wood or other materials. The stages closely parallel those of artistic development. At about age 3½ or 4, children begin to name the pieces of wood they have combined. This is comparable to the *preschematic stage* in art, discussed earlier. It is not until later (age 5 and up) that children enter the *representational stage*, when they are able to plan ahead about what they are going to make.

Introducing Tools

Offer one tool at a time. The younger and less experienced the child, the simpler the task should be. Just pounding with a mallet to explore the properties of Styrofoam or wood is a worthwhile activity.

When you do introduce a tool, start with the hammer. Show it to the children, name it, and demonstrate what it is designed to do, how to hold it, and where to store it. Show them how to select the right size nail by measuring it against the wood to be sure it is not longer than the wood is thick. For beginners, hammering will be an end in itself.

To start a nail, hold it steady with one hand and tap the head of the nail lightly with the hammer, making sure to get the nail straight. When the nail is standing firmly on the wood, move your hand away and hammer harder. Getting the nail started straight is more important than hitting it hard.

A good way to protect your fingers is to first push the nail through a piece of cardboard or heavy paper. Hold the paper by the edge, and hit the nail squarely to get it straight. (See Illustration 1.11.)

To remove a nail, hold the wood or clamp it down, slide the claws of a hammer under the nail head, and pull the handle of the hammer back toward you. With long nails, it is sometimes helpful to place a block of wood under the hammer head to get more leverage, as shown in Illustration 1.12.

As children become more experienced, introduce the saw, again describing it and demonstrating how it is to be used. Younger and

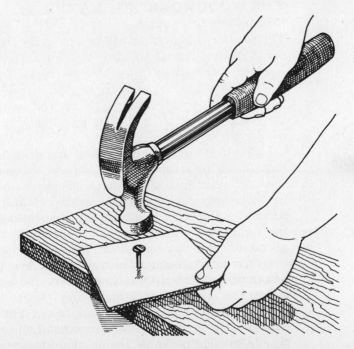

Illustration 1.11   Protecting fingers while nailing

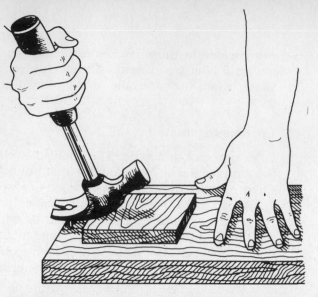

Illustration 1.12 **Removing a nail**

smaller children will have more success with a short-handled tool such as the dovetail saw. They can start by sawing on Styrofoam or balsam wood.

To begin, select a piece of soft wood and mark the place to be sawed with a pencil line. Clamp the wood down or secure it in a vise so the part of the wood to be sawed extends beyond the edge of the table. Hold the wood down with one hand, and, with the saw in the other hand, start a groove in the wood by gently pulling the saw toward you. After the groove is started, saw the wood using more forceful motions on the cutting (forward) strokes.

THE WOODWORKING CENTER

The woodworking center will be one of the most popular—and *noisy*—areas in the school. An ideal location for carpentry is in a sheltered outdoor space adjacent to the classroom. If you need to stay indoors, find a location that is away from regular traffic but not too isolated.

You want to encourage girls as well as boys to participate, and if the center is out of sight, it is less likely to entice curious onlookers who might be tempted to tease.

Children enjoy painting their handiwork, so it is a good idea to locate near the art area, where youngsters can conveniently avail themselves of paint and collage materials to enhance their creations.

A permanent location where tools and other materials can be secured is best. If you have a table earmarked exclusively for carpentry, mount a permanent vise to one corner of it. If you need to be portable, refer to page 44 for ideas on making tool racks. Keep the woodbox near the woodworking tables, keeping in mind that wood is flammable and needs to be sorted out and kept neat. It is important to sweep the area for nails and other sharp objects. Keep one or two large magnets on the shelf or tool board; children love to use them to help pick up stray nails and other metal objects.

Cover the floor with plastic or newspapers, and let children paint their creations. Have a felt pen and masking tape nearby to label their

Illustration 1.13   Woodworking area

work. Collect a few wooden crates from the local produce market in which to display woodworking products until children take them home. (See Illustration 1.13.)

THE TEACHER'S ROLE

Your confidence in knowing how to use tools properly sets the stage for children to gain worthwhile experiences with woodworking. This means that you need to spend time getting acquainted with the materials yourself. Take some time alone or with other adults to try some of the simple techniques outlined above. You will be surprised how much confidence you can gain with just a short practice session.

When working with children at carpentry:

1. *Limit the ratio* of children to adults. Depending on the children's ages and ability levels, one adult to two or three children makes supervision comfortable. Maintain a waiting list for additional children who want to participate.

2. *Limit the number of tools* available, in order to avoid clutter and confusion. Children should use one tool at a time and use it only for its intended purpose.

3. *Allow children to use tools only when an adult is present.* Maintain constant supervision by monitoring all children, even when you are helping one child.

4. *Keep work areas free of clutter* by maintaining proper storage of equipment and materials. Remind children to return things to their proper places. Work spaces should be free from extra wood pieces, bottles of glue, bent nails, and so on.

5. *Examine finished products* for potential hazards. Hammer down protruding nails, and sand or file splintered edges.

6. *Enforce safety rules.* Children who are disruptive or who are using the tools inappropriately should not be allowed to remain in the work area.

Your attitude and teaching style will help children to develop their woodworking talents and other skills as well. For example, a question like **"How far do you think this nail will go into the wood when you hammer it?"** can get a child started on thinking about a problem. Having to select a nail long enough to attach two pieces of wood provides children with practice in estimation, measurement, and prediction. They see cause and effect when they observe how a large nail can split a thin piece of wood. Their efforts teach them to persist at a task, overcome frustration, and experience pride in accomplishment.

Woodworking also offers the chance for social and language development when children discuss, plan, and carry out projects. The problem-solving skills acquired from such activities not only establish a foundation for future learning, but also provide a unique opportunity for young children to experience the joys of working with wood.

Woodworking: Processes and Projects

Gluing Wood and Other Materials

MATERIALS
Variety of small wood scraps
Pieces of Styrofoam
Pieces of corrugated cardboard
Twigs, sticks, natural materials
Styrofoam trays
Masking tape
Felt pens
White glue

PROCEDURE
• Protect a large, low tabletop with newspapers or a plastic cover.
• Give each child a Styrofoam tray and a small bottle of glue.
• Place containers with a variety of objects within easy reach of each child.
• Let children glue their choice of objects to the Styrofoam trays.
• Demonstrate how a small amount of glue is enough to hold things together and explain that a large amount of glue will take much longer to dry.
• Label completed work with a felt pen and masking tape.
• The finished products may be painted when dry.

Note: This activity provides a good opportunity to talk about differences in size, shape, and texture.

Making a Holiday Candle

MATERIALS   Slices of round wood about 6" in diameter (Enlist the help of tree-service workers and someone with a power saw to cut the slices from tree branches.)
Candles
Holly berries, nuts, small pine cones, seeds, leaves, and ornaments
Glue

PROCEDURE   • Have the children glue a candle in the center of each wood round.
• Let the children arrange decorations around the candle and glue them onto the wood.

Nailing Different Materials

MATERIALS   Variety of types of wood
Large, thick pieces of Styrofoam
Corrugated cardboard
Hammers
Nails

PROCEDURE   • Place materials on the carpentry table so that they can be reached easily by the children.
• Have the children nail different kinds of materials and talk about qualities of hard and soft.
• Talk about the materials that are easy to nail; use a felt pen to label these materials *soft*. Identify the hard-to-nail materials, and label them *hard*, accordingly.
• Talk about the texture, weight, shape, and thickness of materials as the children work with them.

Nailing Wood Together

MATERIALS   Variety of pieces of soft wood of different sizes and thicknesses
Variety of nails of different sizes and lengths

PROCEDURE   • Show children how to start a nail in a piece of wood (page 51).
• Suggest that those who are interested might nail two or more pieces of wood together. (Do not make available any material for nailing except wood.)
• Observe how children approach the task. Ask questions and make comments and suggestions as appropriate—for example,
Why did you decide to choose that nail?
How far do you think the nail will go into the wood?
What do you think you have to do to make these two pieces of wood stay together?
What do you think you can do to stop the wood from moving?
What happened to the wood when you put a nail through it?
Why do you think this fell apart?

• Help children discover that nails must be selected based on the size of the wood. Large nails will split thin wood. Two pieces of wood cannot be nailed together if the nails are not long enough. Show the children that it is easier to start a nail in one piece of wood first, without hammering it all the way down, and then place the first piece on top of the second piece and attach them. Warn the children to avoid nailing wood into the workbench. And remember that nails bend if they are too thin or too long or if they are hit at an angle (the workbench may be too high). See page 51 for instructions on removing nails.

Note: After carpentry time, have children show and talk about their constructions. Talk about some of their initial problems and how they overcame them. Praise them for thinking about the problem, persisting at the task, and adapting their techniques to solve their problems. Tie in the concepts of size, length, width, measurement, hardness, softness, and so on.

Nailing and Removing Nails

MATERIALS   Corrugated cardboard
Pegboard
Large pieces of Styrofoam
Soft wood such as pine and balsam
Ceiling tiles
Nails
Hammers with claws

PROCEDURE   • Let children practice hammering nails into pieces of Styrofoam and cardboard.
• Then let them nail pieces of pegboard into Styrofoam.
• As they become more adept, let the children nail ceiling tiles and soft wood.
• Have the children practice removing nails by slipping the claw of the hammer or nail puller under the nail head, with the handle pointing away from them, and then pulling until the handle is in a vertical position.
• For longer nails, have the children slip a block of wood under the hammerhead. (See Illustration 1.12.)

Note: You might want to try *furring nails*, which have washers around the shanks, as they can be held more easily.
Refer to page 51 for information about teaching children how to get a nail started.

Sanding Wood

MATERIALS   Variety of wood scraps (Cabinet shops are good sources of woods with different grains.)
Sand blocks
Sandpaper of varying grades

Linseed oil
Small plastic squirt bottles
Old rags
White glue
Tagboard

PROCEDURE
- Precut wood into small pieces about 4" or 5" square.
- Have children examine, feel, and use different grades of sandpaper and notice the results.
- Let children smooth the rough edges and surfaces of the wood with medium-grit sandpaper, then with fine-grit sandpaper.
- Call their attention to the grain of the wood. Discuss the concepts of *rough* and *smooth*.
- Have the children wipe the wood clean and squirt a small amount of linseed oil on the surface.
- Let them work the oil into the wood by rubbing with a soft rag. As they work, call their attention to how the oil brings out the grain of the wood.
- Glue samples of different kinds of wood onto tagboard, and label each kind for a display in the carpentry area.

Sawing Wood and Other Materials

MATERIALS
Variety of saws (see page 46)
Wood clamps
Vise
Pencils
Variety of soft woods, including balsam
Particle board
Large pieces of Styrofoam

PROCEDURE
- Before putting saws out, talk with the children about using tools to help hold pieces of wood steady while they saw. Demonstrate and let them try using clamps and vises to secure wood.
- Encourage children to show and help each other.
- Help each child learn the techniques of sawing (see page 52).
- Use a pencil to mark a sawing line on the wood. When they are sawing, have children keep their eyes on the cutting line, not the saw.
- Observe, ask questions, and make comments:
  What happens when the wood moves while you are sawing?
  What do you think you can do to steady the wood? (Tighten the clamp and move the saw—or cutting line—as close to the clamp or vise as possible.)
  Let's see what happens if you hold your saw so that it points down. (Saws operate most efficiently when held at about a 45-degree angle.)
  What happens when you use the tip of the saw?
  What happens when you use the blade?
- Let children practice on Styrofoam, particle board, and balsam if they are having difficulty with regular wood. Emphasize using more

force on the downward, or forward, motion. Wood should be secured to a work surface that is low enough for children to make a strong downward thrust.

- Encourage children to talk about their experiences, what problems they encountered and how they solved them. Make notes of your observations.
- Reinforce that saws must be maintained properly.

Creating Original Wood Projects

MATERIALS   Assorted wood scraps
Spools
Lids from babyfood jars and juice bottles
¼" Dowels cut into 3" or 4" lengths
Pencils
Rulers
Paper triangles
Hand drills with ¼" bits
Nails
Hammers
Glue
Yarn
Hole punches
Saws
Clamps

PROCEDURE • As children demonstrate competence with individual tools, introduce other tools one at a time to provide plenty of experience. A toolbox containing various tools such as those listed above can be made available for carpentry, provided the children know how to use them. You may need to limit the number and kind of tools you put out, depending on the children's level of ability and experience.
- A variety of wood scraps and accessories such as spools and bottle tops spark a child's imagination. For example, a piece of wood with a spool glued on it can become a boat with a smoke stack. An airplane can be made by nailing two long, flat pieces of wood together.
- To make a sailboat, clamp a piece of wood for a child to drill. The child can then insert a piece of dowel, punch two holes in a paper triangle, and attach it to the wood.
- Nailing lids on a block of wood makes a car with wheels.

Note: As children become more sophisticated with tools and materials, they will want to plan a woodworking project before they start. Be careful not to throw away pieces of wood, thinking children did not make anything. Often a piece of wood sawed in two or a nail hammered into a block represents a lot of effort and is a treasured project.

When children are done nailing, turn their work over to check for protruding nails. Talk about safety and how they can flatten the nails or select shorter nails by measuring them against the depth of the wood.

Making Rollers and Floaters

MATERIALS   Wood scraps, including balsam
Styrofoam
Popsicle sticks
Circular objects suitable for wheels, such as milk bottle caps and plastic caps for food jars
Small nails
Accessories for floating objects, such as toothpicks, lightweight material, corks, and such

PROCEDURE   • Talk about things that float and sink.
• Have the children examine the different materials and guess which ones will float and which will sink.
• Talk about cars, trucks, trains, and other vehicles that travel on wheels. Also talk about ships, boats, rafts, and other vehicles that provide transportation on water. Suggest that children build their own vehicles that roll on the ground or float in the water.
• Have them plan what they want to build, and talk about why they think their creation will roll or float.
• Help the children construct their vehicles using the wood scraps, Styrofoam, caps, nails, and toothpicks.
• Let them test their completed projects in a tub of water and on a smooth surface.
• Have a show-and-tell time when the children can discuss how they planned and carried out their work.

Note: A "wheel" will rotate if the nail that attaches it to a vehicle is not hammered in all the way.

The activities that follow are more structured and are suitable for older or more experienced children.

Making Sanding Blocks

MATERIALS   Blocks of wood to fit a child's hand
Large pieces of sandpaper
Scissors
Pencils
Tape measures
Tacks or glue
Hammers
Clamps or vises

PROCEDURE   • Let each child select a block of wood.
• Show the children a sanding block and explain that to make one they need to cut a piece of sandpaper large enough to wrap around their block of wood.
• Help them figure out how to measure the sandpaper, making appropriate suggestions as to how they might use a pencil to mark the width of the block on the back of the sandpaper.

• If children cut the paper too large or too small, encourage them to think about what they did wrong and try again.
• Sandpaper can be glued or tacked onto the blocks. If hammer and tacks are used, have the children secure their wood blocks with a C-clamp or vise.

Note: This activity is appropriate for children who demonstrate a readiness for figuring out something independently. It provides experience in measurement and in comparing size, length, and width. The child must also make judgments based on past experience and apply accumulated knowledge to a new challenge.

Making Musical Sand Blocks

MATERIALS

Scrap wood ¼" or ½" thick, cut into pieces about 4" square (enough for each child to have a matching pair)
Two wooden spools for each child
Sandpaper
Pencils
Rulers
Scissors
Glue
Paint

PROCEDURE

• Have each child pick two squares of wood.
• After they place each piece of wood on the smooth side of a large piece of sandpaper, have the children hold the wood down firmly and trace around the edges with a pencil.
• They can then cut the sandpaper along the lines.
• Have them glue the sandpaper, rough side out, to each piece of wood.
• Tell the children to mark the centers of the other smooth side of the blocks by drawing diagonal lines from corner to corner.
• Children can then glue a spool in the center of each of the wooden blocks, where the lines intersect.
• When their blocks are dry, children can paint them and use them as rhythm instruments.

Note: When the goal of an activity is to create a final product, it is helpful to show the children a sample of what it is you want them to make. Children should be allowed freedom to create the musical blocks in their own ways, however, because it is the process, not the product, that matters.

Making a Nailboard

MATERIALS

Precut boards 1" thick and 12" square
1¾" Nails with heads
Pencils
Rulers
Colored rubber bands

PROCEDURE
- After they select their boards, help the children use a ruler to mark dots an inch apart near the edges of each board.
- Have them hammer nails into the wood where marked, but not all the way through. Tell them to start hammering the nails from the center and work out.
- Let children stretch rubber bands from nail to nail to make designs.

Note: This is a challenging activity for children with a great deal of experience at hammering.

Nails need to be hammered in about $3/4$", leaving 1" above the surface of the wood to attach the rubber bands. If nails are not pounded in deep enough, they will pull out when rubber bands are stretched across them. This is a good exercise in estimating and comparing. In order to keep nails level, children need to vary the force with which they strike the nails, stopping to compare the heights and tapping gently to make them level.

Making a Hanging Scroll

MATERIALS
$1/4$" Dowels about 2' or 3' long
Saws
Pencils
Miter boxes
Vises or C-clamps
Heavy string or cord
Stapler
Art scrolls (see Blow-out Pictures, page 30)

PROCEDURE
- Have children make scrolls as described on page 30.
- Help each child to mark with a pencil where to cut a dowel so that it will extend beyond the width of the scroll.
- Have the children place the dowels in a miter box and saw them to the desired length. (Remind children to start sawing by pulling the saw toward themselves several times to make a groove.) They can use a vise or C-clamp to secure both wood and miter box to the workbench.
- Instruct the children to measure, fold, and staple the top and the bottom of the scrolls, leaving enough space for the dowels to be inserted.
- A cord can be tied at the top of each scroll for hanging.

Making a Nature Hanging

MATERIALS
Pieces of plywood $1/4$" or $1/2$" thick, about 12" x 14"
Drill
Clamps
Rulers
Pencils
Cord or heavy string
Glue

Collection of leaves, twigs, shells, pebbles, and other natural objects suitable for collages

PROCEDURE
- Have the children measure and mark two spots, each about 2" from the top of the piece of wood and about 2 inches in from the sides.
- Instruct them to use clamps to secure the wood to the table.
- Have the children drill into the wood at the marks.
- Tell the children to turn the wood over and drill through the holes from the other side.
- Let the children glue objects to the wood to make collages.
- A cord can be inserted through the holes for hanging.

Making a Picture Frame

MATERIALS
One 12" square of colored tagboard per child
Lengths of lath or thin, soft woods, about 1" or 2" wide
Saws
Try square
Rulers
Pencils
Picture hangers

PROCEDURE
- Help each child measure four lengths of lath to fit around the edges of a piece of tagboard.
- Have the children mark each piece of lath with a pencil, making sure the lath doesn't overlap at the corners.
- If the tagboard needs cutting, let the children learn how to measure with a try square. (Have them press the handle of the try square firmly against the tagboard while marking with a pencil.)
- Use a miter box or clamp to hold the wood while children saw the lath.
- Let the children paint the lath pieces.
- When the pieces are dry, have the children glue them around the edges of the tagboard.
- Then the children can tape inside the frame a painting or other piece of art that has been measured to fit.
- Finally, have the children attach a picture hanger to the back of the frame.

Bibliography of Resources

BOOKS ABOUT ART AND OTHER CURRICULUM ACTIVITIES

Adcock, Don, and Marilyn Segal. *Play Together Grow Together, A Complete Curriculum for Teachers of Young Children.* White Plains, NY: The Mailman Family Press, 1983. A book to help teachers design a curriculum focusing on early development of social skills, sharing, cooperation, playing in a group, and making friends. Includes possible scripts with opportunities for the teacher to extend social learnings into the various areas of the class such as art, sandbox, waterplay, blocks, and dramatic play.

Bond, Carol Taylor. *Marmalade Days: Winter.* Livonia, MI: Partner Press, 1987. A book of nine complete units, to be used in teaching children ages 4 through 8. Each unit includes a daily topic for each of the curriculum areas—language arts, social studies, science, math, art, cooking, music, etc. Includes patterns for stories, finger-plays, and recipes. This is one of three books in a series which includes *Spring* and *Fall*.

Bos, Bev. *don't move the muffin tins.* Roseville, CA: Turn-the-Page-Press, 1978. This is a hands-off guide to art for the young child. Each section covers a variety of activities dealing with one medium or topic. Included for each project are a list of materials, a description of the process, and an alert to possible "traps." Underlying all of the activities is the author's respect for the individuality of each child, the creative experience, and the ways to bring them together.

Brashears, Deya. *Dribble Drabble: Art Experiences for Young Children.* Fort Collins, CO: DMC Publications, 1985. A collection of hands-on, process-oriented art activities. The experiences, including painting, crayons, collage, modeling, printing, chalk, holidays, and themes, are designed for children ages 2 and up.

Cherry, Clare. *Creative Art for the Developing Child.* Belmont, CA: D. S. Lake, 1972. A handbook for teachers setting up an art program for young children. Discusses children's development in the arts and gives descriptions of various art media (including paints, pastes, and manipulatives) and basic recipes.

Claycomb, Patty. *The Learning Circle.* Mt. Rainier, MD: Gryphon House, 1988. A book of activities grouped into categories such as seasons, music and movement, games, senses, communication, and crafts.

Dodge, Diane Trister. *The Creative Curriculum for Early Childhood.* Washington, DC: Creative Associates International, 1988. This book provides a basic structure for a developmentally appropriate curriculum for children from 3 to 5 years of age. Focuses on setting the stage and preparing the environment in the following areas: blocks, house corner, table toys, art, sand and water, library, and outdoors.

Faggella, Kathy. *Crayons, Crafts, and Concepts.* Bellingham, WA: Bright Ring Publishing, 1985. Art projects designed to be integrated into all aspects of the curriculum. Gives suggestions for setting up the art area, making smocks, safety rules, and basic recipes for paints and doughs.

Flemming, Bonnie Mack, and Darlene Softley Hamilton. *Resources for Creative Teaching in Early Childhood Education.* New York, NY: Harcourt Brace Jovanovich, 1977. A curriculum book with resources on self-concept, the senses, families, celebrations, seasons, animals, transportation, and more.

Froschi, Merle, et al. *Including All of Us: An Early Childhood Curriculum About Disability.* New York, NY: Educational Equity Concepts, 1984. An activities book incorporating disability awareness into the curriculum—how to do it, answering children's questions, and using activities to teach the concepts of same/different, body parts, and transportation. Includes information about hearing and visual and mobility impairment, plus other helpful resources for the teacher.

Hibner, Dixie, and Liz Cromwell. *Explore and Create.* Livonia, MI: Partner Press, 1979. Covers areas in art, games, cooking, science, and math, with one activity per page.

Houle, Georgia Bradley. *Learning Centers for Young Children.* West Greenwich, RI: Tot-lot Child Care Products, 1987. Ideas and suggestions for setting up areas of the preschool, including staff and parent areas. Pencil illustrations show how to set up for painting and sculpture, carpentry, collage, physical science, math, blocks, and the computer.

Kingore, Bertie W., and Glenda M. Higbee. *We Care, A Preschool Curriculum for Children Ages 2–5.* Glenview, IL: Scott Foresman, 1988. Activities in art, blocks, cooking, language arts, math, music, movement, role playing, and science.

Kohl, Mary Ann. *Scribble Cookies and Other Independent Creative Art Experiences for Children.* Bellingham, WA: Bright Ring Publishing, 1985. Activities include using toothpicks, straws, Styrofoam, craft sticks, and other common objects. Each experience is set up in an independent art center and enjoyed without adult models to copy. Includes wood prints, weaving, playdough, chalk art, and other crafts.

Mitchell, Grace, and Harriet Chmela. *I Am—I Can! A Preschool Curriculum.* Marshfield, MA: Telshare Publishing, 1987. The book consists of three parts. The first is designed to be a resource to directors about the ages and stages of child development, working with parents, and health and daily routines. The second part is designed for teachers and deals with whys and hows of various areas of the curriculum, such as language development, art, math, and science. The third part contains lists of suggested activities, with diagrams and illustrations for a developmental curriculum.

Sanford, Anne R., et al. *A Planning Guide to the Preschool Curriculum.* Winston-Salem, NC: Kaplan Press, 1983. Introduces the preschool teacher to the curriculum, what it is, and how to develop it. Offers 44 curriculum units, including holidays, body parts, seasons, foods, and pets.

Stavros, Sally, and Lois Peters. *Big Learning for Little Learners.* Livonia, MI: Partner Press, 1987. Suggested daily learning plans on a month-by-month basis from September through June. Includes art, music, math, science, social studies, physical education, cooking, and books.

Wilmes, Liz and Dick. *Exploring Art.* Elgin, IL: Building Blocks, 1986. By-the-month activities, with suggestions for preparation, gathering materials, how to talk with the children, what to do, displaying the products, and extending the learnings.

BOOKS ABOUT WOODWORKING ACTIVITIES

D'Amato, Janet and Alex. *Cardboard Carpentry*. New York, NY: Sayre Publishing, 1966. Activities for making simple and fun creations from milk cartons, cereal boxes, shoe boxes, and cardboard. Includes instructions for making a shoe-box diorama, puppet stage, and Martian mask. Good for an introduction to handling wood and other three-dimensional objects.

Dawson, Sheila. *Woodshop for Children Ages 3 Through 8.* San Diego, CA: Children's Woodshop Publications, 1984. A practical book designed for adults who teach woodworking to young children. Includes description, selection, and proper use of tools and instructions for projects such as making floating, flying, and rolling objects.

Jackson, Albert, and David Day. *Tools and How to Use Them.* New York, NY: Alfred A. Knopf, 1978. An illustrated encyclopedia of hand and power tools, their history and uses, and how to operate and maintain them.

Skeen, Patsy, et al. *Woodworking for Young Children.* Washington, DC: NAEYC, 1984. Provides information about tools and woodworking with young children. Offers teaching suggestions and ways in which woodworking can be integrated with the development of the whole child.

Thompson, David. *Easy Woodstuff for Kids*. Mt. Rainier, MD: Gryphon House, 1981. Simple wood projects for children ages 4 to 10, with accompanying drawings of tools and each project. Sticks, twigs, nuts, and berries are used in beginning projects; older preschoolers use scrap lumber and plywood to make things with hammers and hand drills.

Walker, Lester. *Carpentry for Children.* Mt. Vernon, NY: Consumers Union, 1982. Description of tools appropriate for woodworking with children. Detailed sketches accompany photos of each project, such as making a tugboat, block set, and lemonade stand. Suitable for older children, but a few activities are adaptable for preschoolers.

Note: Teachers can write to Campus Films, Overhill Road, Scarsdale, NY 10583 for purchase or rental of a filmstrip entitled *Woodworking* (Early Childhood Curriculum No. 802). This filmstrip includes a cassette and guide for developing skills and concepts that young children need in woodworking, such as patterning, matching, measuring, eye-hand coordination, and motor skills.

PART TWO

Music, Drama, and Movement

Introduction to Music, Movement, and Drama

Teachers who have worked with young children for any length of time know that they can often rely on the use of a song, a movement activity, or a game of pretend to involve children who otherwise would not participate. A bilingual child, too shy to speak, will often respond to "Where is Thumbkin?"; a hyperactive youngster will calm down to the strains of Vivaldi; and long after the last morsel of popcorn has been consumed, you will hear some child repeating in a sing-song manner the "Popcorn Song" sung much earlier in the day.

Why do some of these activities work with young children? When and how should a teacher use music, movement, and drama?

THE ROLE OF MUSIC IN EARLY CHILDHOOD

Research studies show that even before birth, a fetus responds to calming or stimulating music. It appears that music with rhythms corresponding to the heartbeat has a calming effect on the unborn, whereas loud rock music seems to be upsetting. Researchers report that after babies are born, they tend to respond most favorably to the same calming music that was played during their gestation period.

At as early as three weeks of age, infants are able to discriminate among small differences in rhythm, speech, and musical sounds. Although the centers controlling music and visual skills are located in different parts of the brain, singing appears to further speech development, and children naturally weave music into their lives.

During the preschool years, music continues to play an important role in development. Teachers routinely rely on musical finger plays and children's name songs to hold the youngsters' attention. Gentle background music helps relax children during rest or nap time, and moving to a fast-stepping rhythm enables a restless group to work off extra energy. Music not only provides pleasure and comfort; it also helps improve a child's ability to concentrate and discriminate. Music helps mentally disturbed children communicate more easily, and it has even been shown to have a calming effect on hyperactive youngsters.

MOVEMENT IS NATURAL

Have you ever noticed how rhythms such as gentle rocking or shaking a rattle engage an infant's attention? It is during the early months that babies first use their mouths for touching and feeling, and then gradually begin using their hands as a major source of information about the environment. That is when, to the dismay of many parents, children seem compelled to move about and touch everything within reach.

Our bodies were meant to move, not only for growth and exercise, but also to enable us to make sense of our world. Through movement, touch, and exposure to sensory-perceptual stimuli, children learn about themselves and the environment.

According to Patty Zeitlin in *A Song Is a Rainbow,* ". . .the difference in how young children and adults learn is that adults learn from the neck up, and children, from the neck down. Children learn less through being told about things, and more through direct experience, using the senses of touch, taste, smell, sight, and sound. That's why the language of childhood is sense-oriented rather than abstract."

Learning requires many experiences that stimulate the senses, and young children learn best when they are actively engaged in an environment that provides many opportunities to use their natural tendencies to move and explore. The young child's spontaneous movements to music also help develop body strength, sensorimotor control, and a better understanding of spatial relationships.

THE IMPORTANCE OF DRAMATIC PLAY

Music and movement activities are naturally entwined with drama and the child's sense of pretend. Observe and listen to young children at play and it will soon become apparent that their fantasy lives are rich, indeed.

There is much to be learned and integrated into a preschooler's psyche; curiosity is at a peak, and things need to be investigated and understood. Yet children at this stage have a very limited background of experiences, so it is no wonder they sometimes become confused or misinterpret what they see or hear. In order to integrate new information, they have to find acceptable ways to make sense out of their perceptions. One of the socially acceptable avenues is through dramatic play.

Teachers will find some children reluctant to express feelings or talk about themselves, especially when attention is focused on them exclusively. Yet these same children will engage readily in an extended conversation while holding a puppet or wearing a costume. By assuming different roles, children are able to hide behind a protective facade that shields them from criticism.

It is during the preschool years that children develop their consciences and a sense of morality. They need to be able to play out their fantasies and to express forbidden thoughts without fear of chastisement. Dramatic play provides that outlet, as well as opportunities for language enrichment and healthy emotional development.

Given a nonthreatening environment, young children are naturally open to creative expression and dramatic play. A child's inner life is most dramatically displayed when he or she is playing house, talking on the telephone, or assuming any number of creative roles.

EDUCATIONAL VALUES OF MUSIC, MOVEMENT, AND DRAMA

Many adults feel that children are simply having fun when they recite little finger plays, move around to music, or play pretend. It is difficult for grownups to understand how these activities can be related to more serious school-related skills such as reading and math. Yet pre-reading skills require that a child understand the basic design of a story. Finger plays provide a simple introduction to just such design. For example, children experience the *beginning* of a story when the "eensy weensy spider climbed up the water spout," a suspenseful *climax* when "down came the rain and washed the spider out," and a happy *ending* when "out came the sun and dried up all the rain; so the eensy weensy spider climbed up the spout again."

Children are intrigued with finger plays, which are, in reality, little stories that help them experience the use of language to communicate ideas and feelings. These plays also give children practice in eye-hand coordination, listening skills, cooperation, and creativity.

Dancing a story or acting it out offers a further opportunity for children to internalize language concepts. Not only do they hear and learn new words, they use these words in different contexts. Dramatizing a word that has been recited helps a child to relate that word to a physical experience. For example, dancing through a tunnel, climbing up the stairs, and turning round and round are physical experiences that help children internalize concepts. Such experiences are nonthreatening, appealing to children, and fun, and they serve to further strengthen cognition.

Research shows that poor readers generally suffer from low self-esteem. They are afraid to make mistakes or to risk appearing foolish or stupid, and they lack the confidence to face the challenge of trying something new. When children can create their own stories, express them in a nonjudgmental environment, and experience satisfaction and success, they are more likely to gain the confidence needed to succeed in more highly structured school-related tasks.

Some children enjoy singing their stories or songs into a tape recorder and then listening to a play-back. Others delight in performing for a video camera and then sharing the tape with the class. Such experiences give children a sense of accomplishment and pride as well as opportunities to practice articulation, enunciation, voice quality, pitch and volume control, and physical expression. Youngsters learn that they can use their voices and bodies as instruments of communication. Confidence in these areas carries over to the use of language as an important means of expression.

THE PLACE OF MUSIC, MOVEMENT, AND DRAMA IN THE CURRICULUM

Music and movement need not, and perhaps should not, be set aside as a formal activity in the classroom. It is easy to include music, rhythm, and spontaneous movement in other aspects of the curriculum. Music can enhance the informal, unplanned experiences that result spontaneously in children's play. Teachers can play the guitar or autoharp while children are busy at other activities in the classroom. A tape of soothing background music can accompany snack or lunch time. Chants and simple jingles help to keep a group together during field trips. Preschoolers enjoy the challenge of learning how to whistle a tune; and few children can resist an invitation to be held and rocked while an adult hums the restful notes of a lullaby.

There will be times when the teacher will want to use music and creative expression to achieve specific goals–that is, to calm a group of active children, to make a transition from one activity to another, to engage children with special needs, or to establish a foundation for further skill building.

TEACHERS' ATTITUDES SET THE STAGE

Teachers need not possess any special skills in voice or dance to be successful in offering music, movement, or dramatic play. Perhaps the most important attribute an educator can have is a positive attitude of acceptance and appreciation for children's expressions. A child needs an environment that says "It's safe here; what you do is okay; your creations are wonderful because they are you!" The teacher can impart an atmosphere of trust through actions and words reflecting a philosophy of belief in the importance of creative movement and drama. The children will come to know that the teacher respects and appreciates their individual expressions as extensions of themselves, and that therefore there is nothing wrong with their movements, songs, or dramatic play. When positively reinforced, the child has a natural urge to try new movements and to seek broader avenues of expression. As confidence builds, children feel good about themselves and develop healthy attitudes of "I can do it!"

PREPARATION

Before beginning any music activity with a group of children, it is a good idea for the teacher to plan a variety of activities that will provide a good balance between quiet and noisy, active and restful. An experienced teacher will soon learn to sense the mood of the group and will have enough resources on hand to select an appropriate activity. It's best to have more in your repertoire than you will use and stop before the children get bored.

Doing stories, dramatic play, or music with a group of children calls for serious planning and rehearsal, just as though you were performing for an adult audience. If you have to refer to a book while leading the children in a finger play, you will not be able to make eye contact or look for feedback from the audience. If you lack confidence in your ability to recall the words of a song, you will have less energy to devote to engaging the children. Effective teaching requires that you do some homework. Just as the children gain confidence from practice, so will you.

INTRODUCING ACTIVITIES

Start simply by selecting finger plays, chants, tunes, and songs that are easy to memorize. You can enhance these activities with a good selection of recorded music.

A common procedure is to use a finger play or chant to get the group's attention, then move quickly into a longer story. Depending on the ages and size of group, teachers usually follow up with an activity that enables the children to move about. Finally, they cool the youngsters down with a relaxing tune or exercise. Have enough resources on hand to revise your plans if the children are not responding. It seems that teachers get best results when they make smooth transitions from one activity to another. You are likely to lose the children's attention if you have to pause to prepare for the next activity.

When planning group music and creative expression, keep in mind that infants and toddlers have short attention spans. They are likely to wander and should not be expected to sit quietly. Activities that work well with very young children and with children who have had little group experience are short activity chants such as "Clap, Clap, Clap Your Hands," "Put Your Finger in the Air," and "The Bear Hunt." Another simple but popular activity is for the teacher to have a puppet or stuffed animal greet each child by name as the group sings "Good morning [name of child], we're glad to have you here." (See the Bibliography of Resources at the end of this section for books of action songs and chants.)

These simple activities lay a foundation for more complex behaviors as the children gain experience and confidence. They are easy to learn and repetitive and provide a nonthreatening way to engage youngsters in new activities. For many children, being a member of a group can be frightening. It requires compliance and surrendering some of one's identity to the group. Gradually, children learn that there are advantages to group play and that it is fun to share an experience with others.

As children become more familiar with music experiences, the teacher may wish to add props such as hats or simple costumes and ask the children to create a dance to go with the costumes. Comments reinforcing the child's creativity help to establish an environment of acceptance: "I like the way Joni makes heavy and then light movements with her feet." "Tommy really opens his arms out wide." "You seem to be flying!" Avoid making judgmental comments containing the words good, bad, right, and wrong. (See Creative Movement Activities later in this part.)

Simple stories such as "Caps for Sale" can be danced or acted out. Children can pretend to reach way up high to put caps on top of their heads and then show how they would walk wearing dozens of caps piled on top of each other. "Jack and the Beanstalk" can evoke giant steps and climbing motions.

Children become aware of body parts and learn how to control their muscles when they do a "rag doll" activity; with repetition, they learn to relax more fully. One of the best ways to prepare them for rest time is to engage them in a calming activity accompanied by some familiar restful music, turn the lights down, and have individual mats ready for them to lie on.

CHILDREN WITH SPECIAL NEEDS

Songs and chants work well with children who have special needs. Shy children may take longer to participate; others may prefer to learn by watching. Some children for whom English is a second language may enjoy rehearsing at home with their parents. Other adults can help in the group activity by sitting with children who need special attention. For example, a physically handicapped child or one who is developmentally delayed will benefit from sitting on an adult's lap and having the adult help with the motions. Holding a child's hands to tap out a rhythm may give the child just what he or she needs to get started.

Children with language handicaps often respond well to acting out feelings. Playing a part in acting out a story can provide a satisfying outlet for expression. It is especially important for all children to realize that they cannot fail when they participate in creative movement and dramatic play.

Some of the stretching and relaxing activities are especially useful with physically handicapped children and children who are hyperactive or tense. Regardless of the degree of physical limitation, every child can be involved through music. Blind children still respond to sound and touch; deaf children can feel rhythms; physically handicapped children can "dance" with streamers and scarves. The number of ways in which children can be helped to internalize music and movement is limited only by the teacher's imagination.

The activities in this section offer young children a variety of creative experiences in music, movement, and drama. The explanations and suggestions are offered as general guides for the teacher, who should adapt them to suit the children.

Whatever the teacher's objectives in using the expressive arts, the overriding goal should be to provide a stimulating and joyful time for all.

MUSICAL TERMS

Rhythm: A regular patterned cadence or beat

Form: The design, structure, or pattern of a composition. For example, a tune might begin with theme A, change to theme B, and then return to theme A.

Mood: A state of feeling, as inspired by listening to music

Tone: A sound of distinct pitch, quality, and duration. For example, high and low, loud and soft are some characteristics of tone.

Melody: A sequence of tones organized to create a particular musical phrase; the prominent or leading part of a musical composition.

COMMENTS TO THE TEACHER

The activities in this section are intended to be used as general guides, not formal presentations. The music activities—categorized as rhythm, tone, melody, text, mood, and form—are suggested patterns for the teacher to expand and incorporate into the spontaneous and creative aspects of the program. For example, playing a tape of rhythmic sounds can reinforce related spontaneous rhythmic movements. Or it might be a lead-in to a dramatic play or story-acting experience.

The same caution holds for questions and comments suggested for use with children in the creative movement and dramatic play activities. The sentences in boldface type are merely models for teachers to adapt to their own styles and personalities.

If you have not done so, please read the introduction to this part before beginning the activities.

Music Activities

RHYTHM

Hearing Rhythm in Words

MATERIALS   None

PROCEDURE
- Sit with the children in a circle.
- Say,
  Let's clap our hands.
  After children have had time to clap in their own ways, say:
  There are lots of ways to clap. Do you know that we can clap our names? Listen, I'm going to clap some of your names.
- Go around the circle saying the names of the children, clapping the syllables as you call out the names. Say:
  Each of your names has a rhythm. (For example, Ja-son, clap-clap; Mel-a-nie, clap-clap-clap.)
  Listen, and help me clap your names.
- When children are familiar with the activity, go around the circle and have each child clap to "My-name-is- ____ ____ ." The teacher can accompany each syllable with a drum beat. Add middle and last names for variety.
- Use this activity as a lead-in to or part of a rhythmic experience with music and movement.
- On other days, repeat this activity using words as well as names, so that children can have practice in hearing and clapping rhythm.
- As children become more familiar with clapping in unison, divide them into groups according to the number of syllables in their names. Have each group clap the appropriate pattern, and suggest

that they experiment with the various rhythms (all clap at the same time and listen for new rhythms; one group claps and another responds; alternate rhythmic patterns).

Note: Some children may simply enjoy clapping their own way. There is no need to impose conformity. This kind of activity may take only a few moments as a transition to another experience. On other days, it may engage most of the children in a more extended exercise.

VARIATIONS   Some other ideas that may be helpful:

- Have children clap to a metronome or wood block.
- The book *Mandala* by Arnold Adoff (New York, NY: Harper & Row, 1971) is good for exploring rhythm, chanting, singing, and language development. The author develops a poem from the Sanskrit word *mandala*, meaning "magic circle," that is chanted by an African family.
- Another good book is *Waltzing Matilda* by A. B. Paterson (New York, NY: Holt, 1970). With this well-known Australian song, the children can explore the rhythm of words like "coolabah," "billabong," and "tucker-bag."
- Two record albums with clapping songs are Hap Palmer's *Folk Song Carnival* and Nancy Raven's *Singing in a Circle*.

Moving the Body in Response to Rhythm

MATERIALS   Recorded instrumental music, or an instrument the teacher can play

PROCEDURE   • Play some simple selections with the ABA form: songs that start with theme A, change to theme B, and end with theme A—for example, "Baa baa, black sheep, have you any wool? Yes sir, yes sir, three bags full" (theme A); "One for my master and one for my dame, and one for the little boy who lives in the lane" (theme B); then back to original theme A.

- Listen to the songs with the children, and sing them together. (There is no need to call their attention to the changes in themes.)
- While the music is playing, suggest that the children move to the music in any way the music makes them feel. You may want to take the hands of reluctant children and move along with them at first to get them started, but avoid modeling movements for them to imitate.
- Repeat the music and suggest that they move in ways different from the ones they used the first time.
- When you stop the music, comment on some of the different ways you noticed each child move.

Note: "Pop Goes the Weasel" is a bouncy tune that entices children to move. Also, listen to some of Ella Jenkins's albums, such as *Rhythm and Games Songs for the Little Ones*; *This a Way, That a Way*; and *You Sing a Song and I'll Sing a Song*. These albums will give you lots of ideas for conducting music time with a group of young children.

Making Rhythmic Sounds with the Body

MATERIALS   None

PROCEDURE
- Sometime when the children are especially noisy, say something like
  I wonder if any one of you here can show me how to make a sound without using your voice.
- Praise and reinforce the children who come up with ideas:
  Good thinking, Johnny, you're making a noise by clapping your hands (stamping your feet, snapping your fingers, slapping your legs).
  What are some of the sounds you can make while sitting down? standing up?
- Ask the children to mimic the sounds you make with your mouth—tongue clacking, teeth clicking, lip smacking, hissing, sighing.
- Tell the children there are many people in the world who make sounds with their bodies to accompany their songs. Sometimes we clap our hands while we sing; some people clap parts of their bodies, move their feet, or cluck their tongues to make rhythms.

Note: Long before instruments were devised, humans used their bodies to produce rhythmic sounds. The cultures of West Africa and Samoa are noted for their body-slapping rhythms.

Playing Rhythm Instruments

MATERIALS   Rhythm instruments of top quality, including drums, wood blocks, tambourines, and rhythm sticks (If no instruments are available, substitute wrapping paper tubes or plastic golf ball tubes that have been cut to 16" lengths. These can be purchased very inexpensively at any sporting goods store.)
A recording such as Ella Jenkins's *Play Your Instruments and Make a Pretty Sound* or Melody Midget's *Music for Rhythm Band* or Henry "Buzz" Glass's *Rhythm Stick Activities*

PROCEDURE
- Keep the instruments out of the children's reach until you have demonstrated how each is to be used.
- If you are using tubes, have children hold them, one per child, under their arms until the music starts.
- Let children make their own rhythms. Suggest that they listen to the music for loud and soft sounds, stops and starts, fast and slow rhythms.
- Do not expect children to follow a prescribed beat in the beginning.
- If children are using tubes, suggest that they tap them on their hands, heads, shoulders, legs, and floor (but not each other).
- Repeat this activity frequently during the year, giving children the opportunity to use a variety of instruments. As they become more

***Illustration 2.1* Making rhythmic sounds with the body**

familiar with the instruments, the children will be more interested in producing different kinds of sounds, rhythms, tempo, etc.

Making Kazoos

MATERIALS Toilet tissue tubes
Assorted fabrics, cut into different shapes
Glue made up of 1 part white glue mixed with 2 parts liquid starch
Paintbrushes
Wax paper or aluminum foil
Rubber bands

PROCEDURE
- Have children paint the toilet tissue tubes with the glue mixture
- Let them decorate the tubes with fabric pieces.
- They can then apply another light coat of glue and let the tubes dry.
- Have them punch a hole about 1½" from the top of the tube.
- Let each child cut a circle of wax paper or foil large enough to cover the bottom of the tube; attach with a rubber band.

Note: Children can hold the kazoos up to their mouths and make humming sounds.

Reproducing Rhythmic Sounds

MATERIALS   Empty cardboard containers, such as those used for oatmeal

PROCEDURE
- Make up a story based on the children's everyday experiences at home and in school.
- Tell the story, using the empty container to produce appropriate sound effects. For example:
  Early in the morning, before it was time to get up for school, Johnny heard shuffle, shuffle. (Rub your hand across the top of the container, to make a rhythmic shuffling sound.)
  What was that? It was mother shuffling to the kitchen in her slippers. Johnny closed his eyes and listened again. Then he heard . . .
- Use simple rhythmic sounds at first, such as click, click, click (scrambling eggs with a fork); clump, clump (Dad's footsteps); tap, tap, tap (the dog). Then increase the difficulty with combinations of sounds—bump, bump, bumpety, bump (brother going down the stairs, dog dragging a slipper or playing with a ball, and so on).
- After the children have had several opportunities to listen and watch how you do it, select two or three children to help tell a story.
- Give each of the selected children a container. Vary the story so that they have to listen and watch.
- Over a period of time, gradually increase the size of the group of storytellers and vary the rhythmic sounds as the children become more skilled. Have them guess occasionally about what the sound represents.
- Start simply and proceed slowly. The purpose of the activity is to give children practice in listening and reproducing sounds. Keep the stories short at first. Handing out too many containers can cause distraction and confusion. Limit the number until children understand the purpose for which the containers are intended.

Identifying Rhythmic Sounds

MATERIAL   Tape recorder

PROCEDURE
- Identify and tape rhythmic sounds familiar to the children, such as walking, dancing, hammering, sawing, snoring, bouncing a

ball, hopping, typing, clapping hands, chewing, clicking the tongue, breathing, using an eggbeater, and brushing teeth.

• Play each sound and have the children guess what it is. Allow plenty of time for guessing, questioning, and discussing. Give clues to help, and encourage the children to try to reproduce the human sounds.

• Have the children help decide what kinds of rhythmic sounds the class should tape for other guessing games.

• Let the children who can identify the sounds be the "teacher." Let them ask questions and give clues to the others.

Note: Use *Adventures in Sound* (MH-55) from Melody House, which gives sounds and a three-second pause so that children can identify them.

TONE

Recognizing High and Low Sounds

MATERIALS   Piano or other musical instrument

PROCEDURE   • Have the children sit on the floor and listen while you play a middle C and then follow it with a C an octave higher. Repeat this sequence twice.
• Ask:
Did both of these notes sound the same?
What can you do to show me when you hear the high note?
What can you do for the low note?
• Play the notes again, and let the children respond in the agreed-upon manner.
• Use another instrument, such as resonator bells, resonator blocks, a harmonica, or any bells or whistle.
• Play a melody that has obvious high and low changes in it. Have the children respond by stretching high for the high notes and crouching low for the low notes.

Recognizing Loud and Soft Sounds

MATERIALS   Recordings by Ella Jenkins: *Call and Response—Rhythmic Group Singing* and *Jambo and Other Call and Response Songs and Chants*

PROCEDURE   • Have the children make their voices loud when yours is loud, and soft when yours is soft.
• Sing or play a simple call-response song.
• Have the children listen to the song the first time, then participate in the call-response.
• Have the children follow your pattern of call-response using a pattern of loud-soft.
• When they are familiar with alternating the loud-soft pattern, vary it by building up to three or four soft sounds before you make a

loud sound. (This will create a sense of anticipation in the children.)
- Talk about how the children felt while waiting for the loud sound. Explain that composers do the same thing to create that feeling in their listeners.[3]
- Play examples from a variety of recordings such as *Shout and Whisper* (Tickly Toddle 597) to demonstrate the difference between loud and soft.

Note: This activity is suitable for children 4 years and older. Familiarize yourself with the music, and identify the sections before using them with the children.

Learning That Different Instruments Have Different Sounds

MATERIALS   Records with a variety of instrumental solos
Pictures of people playing those instruments

PROCEDURE
- Show a picture of someone playing a violin.
- Play a record with a violin solo, then play another with a solo in a different style (first a classical piece, then "Hot Canary" or "Pop Goes the Weasel," for example).
- Play a trumpet solo for contrast. Show a picture of a person playing a trumpet.
- Show the children how to pretend they are playing a violin.
- If possible, find a violinist to come and play for the children.
- Use the same procedure to introduce a woodwind, a brass instrument, and a percussion instrument.

HELPFUL HINTS

- Call your local music store and inquire about guitar rentals and lessons. If you learn just two simple chords on the guitar (A and E7), you will be able to play all these songs and more: "This Old Man," "My Dreydl," "Hush Little Baby," "Old MacDonald Had a Farm," "Row, Row, Row Your Boat," "Polly Wolly Doodle," "Clementine," "Go Tell Aunt Rhody," "Billy Boy," "On Top of Old Smokey," and "Oh Susanna."

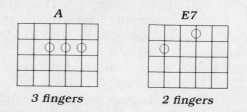

- Refer to the bibliography at the end of this section for books on learning the autoharp.

---

[3]Suggestions: *Concert in the Park* (RCA Victor LM-2677); *The Light Music of Shostakovich* (Columbia LM-6267); *Gaiete Parisienne* (Offenbach, Columbia ML 5348).

MELODY

Singing a Song from Memory

MATERIALS | Tape recorder
A musical instrument for the teacher to play
Ella Jenkins's recording *Early, Early Childhood Songs*

PROCEDURE
- Have children make a list of their favorite songs.
- Tell them you are going to make a tape of them singing their favorites, to play back for the class (or for a special occasion, such as an open house or family day).
- If appropriate, have individual children announce the title of each song.
- Replay the tape during other times of the day.
- For beginners and very young children who may not have an extensive repertoire of songs they can sing from memory, use Ella Jenkins's recording of simple classics such as "Mary Had a Little Lamb," "Farmer in the Dell," "London Bridge." One side of the recording has Ella singing with children; the other side is instrumental accompaniment only, for your children to sing along with.

Recognizing Identical Melodies

MATERIAL | Musical instrument or recordings

PROCEDURE
- Select some familiar melodies, such as "Muffin Man," "Mulberry Bush," and "Skip to My Lou."
- Play one melody several times, play a second melody, then return to the first melody.
- Ask the children to raise their hands each time they hear the first melody.
- Continue to alternate between several melodies, having the children identify the first one each time.
- This game can be made increasingly more challenging by using songs with similar melodic phrases and rhythmic patterns.

VARIATIONS | Refer to *Piggyback Songs*, by Jean Warren (Everett, WA: Warren Publishing, 1983), for new words sung to familiar tunes. Discuss how the words of a song can change even though the melody remains the same.

Have children help make up new words to some of their favorite melodies.

Creating Original Melodies

MATERIALS | Tape recorder, piano, or xylophone

PROCEDURE
- Have individual children experiment with making sound sequences using either an instrument or their voices.
- Ask the children if they can play or sing the same melody twice.

• Tape each child's original melody. Then play it back for the child and add words.

Note: This activity is for children who are sufficiently motivated and self-directed to stay with the task.

TEXT

Listening and Responding to Words in a Song

MATERIALS   Musical instrument or recordings such as the Dance-a-Story Series, by Anne Lief Barlin, or *Berman/Barlin Dance a Story, Sing a Song*

PROCEDURE   • Have children listen carefully and respond to the words in the songs.
• Play simple finger-play songs, singing the words for the children to act out. If you use recordings, preview them to determine which are appropriate for dramatization.

Note: For children under age 4, refer to some of Tom Glazer's records, such as *Activity and Game Songs for Children* and *Music for 1's and 2's/Songs and Games for Young Children.*

Learning How Music Complements Text *(for ages 5 and up)*

MATERIALS   Recording of *Peter and the Wolf* by Leonard Bernstein and the New York Philharmonic Orchestra

PROCEDURE   • Play the record in one session simply as a listening experience to familiarize the children with the story.
• Talk about the story, and listen for children's responses to determine their interest and ability levels.
• During a second session at another time, have them listen to only the first part of the story, which associates themes with animals. Discuss how the sounds of instruments describe the animals.
• Ask if the children would like to take turns acting out the story. If so, assign each child a theme to act out with the music.

MOOD

Responding to the Mood of a Song

MATERIALS   Recordings such as Hap Palmer's *Movin'*[4]

---

[4]Suggestions: *Suites from Gayne* (Khatchaturian, Capitol P8503); *The Courtly Dances from Gloriana* (Britten, Victor LM 2730); *Zorba, the Greek* (20th Century Fox TFM3167); *Going Places* (Herb Alpert's Tijuana Brass, A&M Records LP112); *Souvenirs from Sweden* (Epic LF18010); *Toshiba Singing Angels* (Capitol T10252); The Beatles' *Yellow Submarine* (Capitol Records SW153).

PROCEDURE
- Ask the children to listen carefully to the songs you select, and tell them the title of each one before you play it.
- Invite them to move to the music if they wish.
- Play a series of songs, each with a different tempo and mood. For example, three songs from Hap Palmer's *Movin'* that work well are "Gentle Sea," "Haunted House," and "Funky Penguin."
- After each song, talk about the name of the song and how the music made the children feel (peaceful, quiet, scared, spooky, funny, happy).
- Ask what each of these songs made the children think about. Follow their lead in building on ideas about feelings and how they are expressed.
- Some children may wish to express their feelings with movement, others with words.

FORM

Learning That Music Has a Form—A Beginning, a Middle, and an End

MATERIALS   Piano, guitar, autoharp, or record and record player

PROCEDURE
- Ask the children to stand, with space between them.
- Tell them that you are going to play parts of a song and they are to move to the music, stopping as soon as the music stops.
- Play short phrases of a lively tune.[5] Gradually play several phrases together. Then play the whole piece.
- In contrast to the lively piece, play a slow, flowing song.[6] Have the children lie on the floor and move their arms to the music.

VARIATIONS   Set up chairs in a circle, one per child. Ask the children to begin moving around the chairs when the music starts and sit down on the chairs as soon as it stops.
Give the children rhythm instruments to play with the music.

Learning That Music Has Patterned Forms

MATERIALS   Piano, guitar, autoharp, or record and record player
Triangles for half of the children; drums for the other half of the children

PROCEDURE
- Play a selection that has the ABA form (starts with theme A, changes to theme B, and ends with theme A).

---

[5]Bouncy, lively records: *The Tartan Ball* (EMI SZLP2118); *Pop Goes the Weasel* (RCA Victor 45–6180).

[6]Slow, flowing records: *Duets with Spanish Guitar* (Capitol 8406): *Songs in Spanish for Children* (Columbia 91A02029).

- Give half the children triangles (or substitutes). Play the first theme again. Tell the children with triangles that this A theme is their part. When they hear that theme, they can play along on their triangles.
- Give the drums to the other half of the class. Play the B theme, identify it as such, and tell the children with drums that this is their theme. Ask what they will do when they hear their theme.
- Ask the children to listen while you play the whole ABA pattern again.
- Ask them to play their instruments when they hear their themes this time.
- After the children have done this exercise several times, encourage them to find new combinations as they play without music (for example, AABB and ABBA).

Note: Use this activity with children who are sufficiently experienced to understand the ABA form.

Creative Movement

Some types of dancing involve following a pattern of movements the dancer has been taught. The dancer's movements are judged "right" or "wrong" by the teacher, with the goal being performance for others of a practiced and perfected skill. Creative movement, however, is not a performing art; rather, it is a nonintellectual activity in which the dancer's body is an interpretive tool for inner expression. Under this philosophy, dancing becomes a successful experience filled with music, freedom, and joy. Because the feeling of success is engendered by the teacher's positive and approving attitude, the role of the teacher in guiding creative movement is of primary importance. In addition to the comments made in the introduction to this section, the following basic concepts should be reviewed before working with young children in creative movement.

GUIDELINES

- Movement activities are most effective when presented in a noncompetitive way. The goal is for every child to feel successful; no one should be seen as better or more correct than anyone else.
- Whatever the child does is all right, so long as it is safe for himself or herself and others. There is no standard of performance for the class.
- The child need not do anything that anyone else is doing; children should be encouraged to follow what the music "tells" them. You can explain that it is okay for children to copy each other, but that we are all different and so we each move in a different way. If children have difficulty initiating their own movements, you can begin by giving them some suggestions, such as

This sounds like a good tune for jumping.
Then as children begin to follow your suggestion, branch out by making comments such as
Can someone show me a new way to jump?
Who can move their arms in a different way?
Reinforce children with statements such as
I see Noah is making his arms go in big circles.
Rachel looks like she's flying with her arms.
These comments give children a point of reference from which to begin thinking creatively.
- Challenge children to progress individually with questions that are specific, yet allow for different interpretations, such as
Can you show me another way to move from here to there?
What are some other ways to use your feet?
When the teacher makes nonjudgmental comments about new movements observed, individual children will feel free to expand their own ideas about movement.
- Removing shoes, socks, and other restrictive clothing allows for greater freedom of movement.
- You might move with the children to get them started or to illustrate a suggestion, but draw back when they get involved.
- Do not pressure children to participate if they prefer to watch. Invite them occasionally, or look for "safe" opportunities for them to join in.
- Disruptive children who cannot be redirected should be asked to leave the group until they are able to participate without spoiling the experience for others.

DESIRED OUTCOMES

- Creative movement should be an integrating experience that strengthens and unifies the whole child.
- Creative movement should be seen by the children as a fun and healthy experience requiring no particular talent or skill.
- Children should experience the feeling of freedom in movement and should explore the relationship of their movement to space and to the movements of others.
- A greater sense of confidence and an enhanced awareness of self should be the results of participating in creative movement experiences.

PACING

- Practice timing your comments and questions to reinforce and support the children. Watch to see their reactions to your words.
- Children are often distracted by too many questions or statements from the teacher. Err on the side of observing rather than talking too much.

- Suggesting and redirecting are very important aspects of a successful movement experience. On the teacher's part, this requires careful observation and sensitivity to individual children.
- With very young or inexperienced children, short explorations are most effective. Introduce and practice movement skills in spurts of a few minutes at a time.
- Pacing allows a smooth transition between vigorous and less active movements so that no one becomes overstimulated, provides a shift from moving actively through space to sitting with a group in a more confined (and sometimes safer-feeling) area, and allows a smooth transition between loud and quiet activities.

BODY PARTS

Learning to Relax

MATERIALS   One limp rag doll
Recording of slow, quiet music[7]

PROCEDURE
- Have the children sit on the floor around you.
- Hold the rag doll with both hands and show the children how limp it is. Shake it gently, calling their attention to the way its head, legs, and arms hang loosely.
- Have the children shake their hands and arms and let them hang limp. Then have the children do the same with their heads and bodies.
- Play the record, and let the children move around the room as if they were rag dolls.
- Ask the children to lie down. In turn, lift each one's arms and legs and let them drop gently, saying
Feel like a rag doll. Make your arms and legs heavy and floppy.
- Other images that stimulate relaxation are melting ice and Jello. Let the children watch and touch melting ice cubes or gelatin and verbalize the process.

Note: In addition to enriching children's lives creatively, imagery of all kinds—in literature, music, dance, and singing—can also help them develop visual memory skills.

Learning to Stretch

MATERIALS   Chinese jump ropes (stretchy ropes)
Records appropriate for stretching movements[8]

[7]Hap Palmer's *Sea Gulls* has slow, restful melodies and includes a guide for the teacher in the use of relaxation techniques. It is good for toddlers and older children. Other suggestions are *Songs in Spanish for Children* (Columbia 91A02029) and *Duets with Spanish Guitar* (Capitol 8406). Try the different songs to find the most suitable mood.

[8]Suggestions: *Natay, Navajo Singer* (Arizona 6160); *Balalaika* (Elektra EKS7194); *A Child's Gift of Lullabyes* (JTG, arranged by David Huntsinger).

Illustration 2.2 **Learning to stretch**

PROCEDURE
- Demonstrate how the Chinese jump rope stretches.
- Give each child a jump rope.
- Say:
  Show me how you can stretch this rope with your hands and arms.
  Show me another way you can do it (holding rope with foot and stretching with the arm; holding rope with both feet; holding rope around various parts of the body).
- Play the record and ask children to stretch to the music.
- Suggest long, slow movements.
- Collect the ropes and continue to play the music.

- Say:

Now stretch to the music. Stretch all parts of yourself. Stretch your arms, stretch your legs, stretch your body as you move to the music.

You should stretch along with the children. Say:

Remember how it felt when you were pulling the rope?
Stretch as if you were still pulling on the rope.
Stretch your hands up; feel the top of your head reaching up toward the ceiling. Lie on the floor and stretch your fingers and arms and legs. Stretch your fingers as far as you can from your toes.

Practicing Moving Individually

MATERIAL   Recordings of bouncy tunes

PROCEDURE
- Have children stand in a circle, with adequate space between children to avoid crowding.
- Ask the children to locate and place their hands over their stomachs.
- Suggest that they pretend there is a bouncy ball inside their stomachs, and the ball loves to bounce to music.
- Start the music softly and begin by "bouncing" your upper body gently without picking up your feet. Remind the children to "feel" the ball getting started.
- Explain that the stomach area is the center of the whole body and after bouncing it, the children can start letting the ball bounce other parts of their bodies—hands, head, legs, and even ears and nose.
- Gradually increase the loudness of the music and tell the children that they can bounce around the room and let the music tell them what to do.
- Gradually soften the music and slow the children down.
- Follow up with a bit of quiet music, and talk about the way each person bounced different parts of the body in different ways.

Note: Many excellent musical selections for use in creative movement are still on 45 and 33⅓ rpm records. Premarking record bands will help you to find the songs you want quickly. You can also tape record the sequence of tunes to match your planned activities.

Learning to Move Every Part of the Body

MATERIALS   Records of both fast and slow music[9]
Small finger puppet

PROCEDURE
- Have children sit in a circle.
- Say:

[9]Suggestions: *Music of Golden Africa* (Universal DC 6485); and *Walter the Waltzing Worm* by Hap Palmer.

> **HELPFUL HINT**
>
> Use the book *Dancing Is*, by George Ancona (New York, NY: E. P. Dutton, 1981), to introduce children to a creative movement activity. This colorful book is illustrated with photographs of people moving and dancing. The simple text corresponding to a photo of a child skipping says "dancing is a skip [a jump, wiggle, hop, etc., with appropriate photos]; dancing is just feeling good. . . ; dancing is moving to music—just listen to the music; the rhythm will tell you how to move."

We can dance with many parts of our body. We don't have to use just our feet. Our fingers can dance too.
- Demonstrate with the finger puppets.
- Let each child play with a finger puppet.
- Play the recording, and suggest that the children let their fingers dance to the music. Say:
  Pretend your fingers are candles with flames moving.
  Pretend your fingers are sparklers with sparks flying from them.
- Suggest that children sit still and dance with other parts of their body. Say:
  Dance with your whole arm.
  Move your head to the music.
  Dance with one arm and your shoulder.
  Move just your arms and head.

> **HELPFUL HINTS**
>
> - Provide ample space for children to observe.
> - Not everyone has to participate.
> - Invite children with comments like
>   **We have a place here, Mary.**
>   **We need another dancer.**
>   **You can hold my hand, Jimmy.**
>   **There's room if you decide you'd like to join us later.**

Learning to Isolate Body Parts in Movement

MATERIALS   Any record with a bouncy, spirited beat, such as "Funky Penguin" from Hap Palmer's *Movin'*

PROCEDURE   • Have the children stand in a circle.
              • Say:
              Let's pretend there is popcorn popping inside of us. Here it goes inside of our hands—pop, pop, pop. See our hands go popping.

- Show the children how to bounce and shake just their hands. If a child is using total body movement, you can hold the child gently by the wrists to isolate that body part.
- Then let the popcorn move inside different body parts—head, shoulders, elbows, knees, hips, fingers, toes.
- Name each of the body parts so the children learn to identify them. Encourage their suggestions. This type of practice will help young children develop total body coordination and increase body awareness.
- Have children bounce their whole bodies up and down as if popping. This will lead into jumping, hopping, galloping, and other movements that children enjoy.

Note: You may want to precede the activity with an actual corn-popping session. Place a large sheet on the floor, with a corn popper in the middle. Have the children sit around the outside edges of the sheet. Play the bouncy tune, and when the corn pops, remove the cover and let the corn pop out onto the sheet. Have children listen for the popping sounds and watch how the corn pops up and out.

MOVEMENT IN SPACE

Learning to Relate Movement to Space

MATERIALS   Large and small cardboard containers
Records of medium to slow music[10]

PROCEDURE
- Play a record, and suggest that children dance in and around the cartons.
- Say:
**We all need space to move. Move into a small space.
Now use big spaces.**
- Suggest climbing, crawling, hiding in and under various spaces in the room. Tell the children to fit into different spaces.
- Say:
**When you are in a small space, you make small movements.
Show me how you moved when you were inside the box.
When you are in a large open space, you can make big movements. Show me how you moved when you had lots of space.**

Note: Use books by Helen Borten (such as *Do You Move as I Move? Do You See What I See?*) to start a discussion of different kinds of movement. Have children create their own movements based on themes from the books. Take color slides of children painting to music; project these slides while playing the same music, and have each child create dance movements in front of the projector so that his or her shadow is superimposed on the painting.

---

[10] Suggestion: Hadjidakis, *Lilacs out of the Dead Land* (Odeon).

Learning to Make Heavy and Light Movements

MATERIALS   Balloons, scarves, heavy blocks
Records of slow "heavy" music and "light" music[11]

PROCEDURE
- Ask children to watch how the balloon moves when you toss it in the air. Reach up with stretching movements to grasp the balloon as it comes down.
- Say:
A balloon is very light. Move like the balloon.
- Give each child a balloon, and comment on the way each one moves, stretches, lifts up on his or her toes, and so on.
- Praise the movements that convey the feeling of lightness:
I like the way you bounce so lightly on your feet, Mei-ling.
Max, that's a lovely way to move your arms. Your whole body is moving in such a light way.
- If balloons are too distracting, use scarves.
- Demonstrate with heavy blocks by having each child move with a block in his or her hands.
- Play heavy-sounding music and say:
Move as though you are as heavy as a block. Move your feet and arms and body in a heavy way.
- Contrast heavy and light music, and comment as children move to each kind of music.
I see you're putting your whole foot down at once.
You're dragging your shoulders, and your arms and hands are so heavy.
Listen to what the music tells you to do.

MOVEMENT WITH OTHERS

Learning to Move with a Partner (for ages 5 and up)

MATERIALS   Scarves
Chinese jump ropes
Records appropriate for dancing and skipping[12]

PROCEDURE
- Ask the children to hold hands with partners and skip.
- If some children can't skip, let those who know how hold hands with those who don't. Skipping-like movements are all right. Practice the activity in pairs.
- Let pairs of children hold hands and skip around the room, trying not to bump.

[11] Suggestions: "Shalom" from *Orcha Bamidbar* for heavy mood (Elektra ELK146); *Newest Hits in Israel* by Geula Gill (Epic LF18045); *Iron Butterfly*—drum part in middle of record (Altco SD33-250); *Bantu Folk Songs* (Folkways FW6912); *Sea Gulls—Music for Rest and Relaxation* by Hap Palmer.
[12] Suggestions: *Original Score of Butch Cassidy and the Sundance Kid* (A&M Records SP4227); "Raindrops" or "Seven Jumps" from *Perceptual Motor Rhythm Games* by Jack Capon (Educational Activities).

- Give a Chinese jump rope or a scarf to each pair of children to share.
- Play music and say:
  It feels different to move with someone else. Show me how you move with your partner using the rope or scarf.
- Keep each pair together, and comment on movements that indicate that a child is aware of the other child's presence.
  I like the way you both move so close to each other without touching.
  That's nice the way your back and arms touch while you move and turn to the music.

Note: Remember that preschoolers are more concerned about themselves than others and need to be encouraged to work with partners.

Learning to Relate Movements to Others

MATERIALS
A scarf or ribbon streamer for each child
Recorded music of a soft, swaying melody and a bouncy, spirited tune

PROCEDURE
- While the children are seated, hand each of them a scarf or streamer. Ask the children to feel the prop and touch it to their bodies.
- Then have the children stand and begin to move their scarves to the soft music.
- Say:
  Listen to the gentle music. Let's see how we can move our scarves with that sound.
- Encourage new ideas and incorporate movements that you see the children using.
- You may wish to let the children move about the room, swaying their scarves as they go.
- After a period of free movement, have the children sit together in pairs. Say:
  We are going to move our scarves again with the music. When the music stops, you and your partner will put your scarves together on the floor.
- Look for interesting designs the two scarves make on the floor, and comment on the patterns you see.
- Keep the music segments short. Change from gentle to more spirited music. Encourage the children to listen and move appropriately to the different sounds.
- Once the children are interrelating well with their partners, let them hold hands as they move their scarves and walk around the room.
- You may wish to continue using the pauses in the music as a stop signal while the children move around on their feet.

VARIATION
If you have a parachute, use it for movement activities along with the recording *Playtime Parachute Fun* (Kimbo). Also see the parachute activity on p. 108.

Where to Write for Additional Materials

Children's Book and Music Center, 2500 Santa Monica Blvd., Santa Monica, CA 90404.

Educational Activities, Inc., P. O. Box 392, Freeport, NY 11520.

Folkways Records, 632 Broadway, New York, NY 10012.

Kids on the Block, 1712 I St. NW, Suite 1008, Washington, DC 20006. An educational group dedicated to developing programs to build awareness about the handicapped among the nonhandicapped. The organization has kits with puppets, manuals, and activities on the six disabling categories plus other areas such as drug abuse.

Kimbo Educational, P. O. Box 477, Long Branch, NJ 07740.

Learning Through Movement, P. O. Box 22, Claremont, CA 91711.

Linden Tree, 170 State St., Los Altos, CA 94022. Specializes in children's books and records. This company will locate and mail-order most of the records and music/movement books listed in this section.

Nancy Renfro Studios, 1117 W. 9th St., Austin, TX 78703. Offers an extensive collection of puppetry materials and resources for use with young children. The company also has many materials and activities for children with special needs.

Puppeteers of America, 15 Cricklewood Path, Pasadena, CA 91107. A national organization with members in many parts of the world. This group sponsors an annual puppet festival and has a puppetry store that sells books and puppet items.

Touch Toys, 3519 Porter St. NW, Washington, DC 20016. Sells handcrafted stuffed toys designed to provide tactile joy to blind students. Many of the toys may be adapted as puppets.

Sensorimotor Explorations

BODY AWARENESS

Learning Parts of the Body

MATERIALS   None[13]

PROCEDURE
- Say:
  Do you know what your body is? It's you from head to toe. It's all of you.
- Tell the children that you and they are going to play a game. They will touch the body part that you name.

[13] See the Bibliography of Resources at the end of this section for records and books useful in enhancing motor explorations.

- Work from top to bottom—head, eyes, nose, ears, mouth, chin, neck, shoulders, chest, back, arms, and so on.
- Repeat. Then name parts of the body in random order.
- Ask if anyone would like to be the leader. As the children learn the names for their body parts, they can name the part as they touch it.

Practicing Tensing and Relaxing Body Parts

MATERIALS   Mats or pads for comfort

PROCEDURE
- Ask the children to show how they can make a fist.
- Ask them to make their fists very, very tight, then very loose.
- Watch and check each child to be sure they all know how to tense and relax.
- Have the children sit on a comfortable mat and tighten and relax upper body parts—face, arms, fingers, hands.
- Have them lie down and make other body parts loose and tight, gradually substituting the terms *tense* and *relax*.
- Go from head to toe, monitoring how well each child is doing.
- After many repetitions of this activity, you will notice how individual children improve in their abilities to control various muscle groups and attain deeper relaxation.

Note: Some children will tense up when you come around to check their degree of relaxation. Just hold their hand or foot and wiggle it loosely, suggesting they be like a rag doll. When they loosen up, tell them, "Now you're relaxed."

Learning to Relax

MATERIALS   One balloon
             Quiet music (optional)

PROCEDURE
- Blow up the balloon, and talk about how the air makes the balloon get larger (expand).
- Tell the children that when they breathe in, their lungs fill with air just like the balloon.
- They can help get a lot of air into their lungs by pushing out on their stomachs when they take a big breath. Practice with them, having them put their hands on their stomachs.
- Have them stand and breathe in deeply through their nostrils, expanding their stomachs as they inhale.
- Tell them to exhale through their noses, pulling their stomachs in.
- When children are able to do this, have them lift both arms to the side and high over their heads with each inhale, and lower their arms with each exhale. Deflate the balloon to show how you want them to exhale completely.
- After the breathing exercise, tell the children to sit down on mats or comfortable carpeting.

- Have them sit with straight backs and bent knees and then lean forward and hold their legs under their knees with both hands.
- Still holding their legs, the children should begin to rock back and forth gently (to slow rocking music). As they continue rocking, allow the children to experiment with movements. Remind them at first to continue to hold their legs.
- Have the children lie flat on the mats and continue with the breathing exercise and total body relaxation.

Note: Suzy Prudden's *Creative Fitness for Children* is a useful record for exercises. She also has a recording for children with special needs: *Special Exercises for Exceptional Children* (Kimbo).

Practicing the Movement of Body Parts

MATERIALS   None

PROCEDURE
- Have the children stand with enough space around them that they can move freely.
- Ask them to show how they can move different parts of their bodies.
- Ask them how they can move their heads in different ways. Note the different kinds of responses, and repeat them with the children.
- Ask them how they can move their eyes, necks, mouths, shoulders, elbows, chests, arms, fingers, waists, hips, legs, ankles, toes.
- Play a game in which they move the body part you name.
- As the children develop their body awareness, have them concentrate on two or more body parts. Give directions such as
Put your arms between your knees.
Stand with your shoulder touching someone else's shoulder.
Show me how you can walk with your leg stuck to your partner's leg.
These variations are appropriate for children ages 5 and up who have had many experiences with simpler activities.

SPACE AWARENESS

Space awareness activities need not be presented in a formal fashion. The following suggestions are intended merely to provide ideas, which the teacher can use in conjunction with story concepts or spontaneously either on the playground or in the classroom.

Experiencing Space in Relation to the Body

MATERIALS   None

PROCEDURE
- Ask the children to sit on the floor and curl up, trying to make themselves round as a ball. You might show them a party noise-

maker—the kind that unrolls when you blow it. Ask them to roll up as the noisemaker. Go around looking for spaces. Show them where the empty spaces are by patting—for example, behind their calves.

• Ask children to use more space by stretching their arms, then their legs.
• Ask them how they can use more space behind themselves, to the side.
• Have them repeat the entire sequence with their eyes closed.

Experiencing Limitations of Space

MATERIALS   Several large cardboard boxes

PROCEDURE
• Set the boxes on their sides in a circular pattern, like a corral. Leave enough room so that when the children are standing in the middle, they will have to take at least three steps to reach the boxes.
• Ask children to walk slowly, stopping when they touch the boxes. Ask them to walk back to the middle of the circle.
• Move the boxes farther out. Have the children walk out and back again. Then ask them if they had more space to move in or less.
• Ask them to repeat steps 2 and 3 with their eyes closed.
• Remove the boxes. Ask the children to walk out as far as they can until something stops them and then return.
• Have the children sit down. Talk about how sometimes we can change the size of the space around us, and sometimes we can't. For example, ask if there is any way to change the space when we are riding in a car (rolling windows down, folding the seat of a station wagon down). Ask whether they have more space in their bathroom or their living room, their living room or their front yard or the street. Talk about how sometimes it feels good to be in a small space—when tucked into bed, for example.

Note: *Over, Under & Through,* by Tana Hoban (New York, NY: Macmillan, 1973), provides picture presentations of 12 spatial concepts that you can use to reinforce movement exploration activities. Photographs show children crawling through a pipe, leapfrogging over a hydrant, and so on.

Experiencing Spatial Relationships

MATERIALS   One chair per child
Table
Group of objects to place on or under chair: dolls, books, cars, blocks

PROCEDURE
• Direct each child to take a chair and put it somewhere so that he or she can walk around it without touching someone else.
• Tell the children to walk around their chairs. Ask if they can move around their chairs in another direction.

- Ask whether they can move around their chairs without walking.
- Ask:

  Who can get on top of his or her chair? In front of it? Behind it? To the side of it?
- Ask whether they can get under their chairs. (If not, why not?)
- Ask if they see anything they can get under (the table). Let them get under the table in suitable groups.
- Ask:

  Do you see anything on top of the table?

  Pick one of those objects and put it on top of a chair.

  Put your objects under the chair.

  Who can think of another place to put his or her object?

FORM AWARENESS

Experiencing Form Through Touch

MATERIALS Enough boxes to form the outline of a square with a 3' x 3' base and 3' sides

Enough boxes to outline a triangle with a 4' base and 3' walls

Corrugated cardboard 3' x 12' to make a circle

One or two aides

PROCEDURE
- Allow one child at a time to get inside the circle and walk around it, running his or her hand on the side to feel the curve.
- Let the same child get inside the boxes that form the square and walk or skip around, running his or her hand on the side to feel the straight plane and sharp angles. While the first child is doing this, another child can start in the circle.
- Introduce the triangle in the same manner.
- After everyone has had a chance to experience the shapes until they are satisfied, sit down and talk about how each space felt different. Ask what was different about each one—curves, straight lines, number of angles (corners).
- Arrange the boxes so that each child can be directed to go in the circle and come out of the square, and so on.

LOCOMOTOR SKILLS

Locomotor movement is defined as movement that carries one through space on a moving base. This base can be either "footed" or "non-footed." Typically children first move on a non-footed base, propelling themselves by rocking, rolling, scooting on their bottoms, crawling (with tummy in contact with the floor), and later creeping on hands and knees. When children are able to stand, they learn the eight locomotor skills that are basic to all movement activities. The first five locomotor movements are done to a single, steady rhythmic beat: walking, running, jumping (with both feet leaving the floor together), hopping (on one foot only), and leaping (pushing off from one foot and landing on the other). The next three movements are done to an uneven, short-long rhythmic beat: galloping (a step sequence in which the same foot consistently leads the other); sliding (a step sequence in which one foot consistently slides behind the other on the floor, often done moving sideways); and skipping (a step-hop sequence with a leg swing). One rarely sees preschoolers use leaping movements because of the strength required to perform more than one leap. Skipping is a complex locomotor skill that requires the child to use both sides of the body in a cross pattern. The left arm swings forward as the right leg swings up. Because the awareness of left and right body sides does not occur until sometime between 4½ and 7 years of age, skipping is generally the last locomotor skill a child acquires. Most children use the galloping pattern until they are ready to internalize the skipping process.

Experiencing the Changing Forms of Shadows

MATERIALS   None

PROCEDURE
- Have children stand in the sun to cast a shadow.
- Say:
  What is a shadow?
  Is your shadow bigger or smaller than you?
  Can you make your shadow move?
  How can you make your shadow bigger? Smaller?
  Make your shadow bounce up and down.
  Make the arms of your shadow move like the wings of a bird.
  How can you make your shadow say "yes"?
- Encourage the children to show one another how they create different shadow patterns.

VARIATION   Have the children work in pairs. Encourage the pair to move together, with their bodies touching in some way. They might hold hands and stretch, bend, jump, or walk to make a shadow design together.

   This version helps develop a child's ability to interrelate in movement with others and improves balance skills.

Learning the Feeling of Direction (up, down, forward, and so on) and Developing Strength and Coordination

MATERIALS   Drum or whistle

PROCEDURE
- Have the children stand far enough apart that they can put their arms out without touching anyone else. Explain that when you hit the drum (or blow the whistle), you want them to stop and listen.
- Ask:
  Who can jump?
  As children jump around, watch and comment on each child.
  Can you jump another way? I see you are jumping forward (back-

ward, sideways, crouched, and so on). **Can you take a big jump toward me? A little jump?**
Can you move a part of your body while you are up in the air?
Find someone to jump with.
How would you jump if you were mad?
How would you jump if you were sad?
How would you jump into a swimming pool? ·

* Use the drum to call children's attention to the objectives you have in mind—different ways of moving in different directions, for example.

Note: There is no right or wrong way to move; the goal here is to have each child explore a variety of ways.

VARIATION　Do the same with hopping, walking, tip-toeing, and so on:
Who can hop?
Can you hop and change feet?
How tall can you make yourself while you hop?
Who can walk without touching anyone?

Learning the Feeling of the Directions Across and Over (*for toddlers through primary-level children*)

MATERIAL　Large mattress (king-size, if possible) with sturdy box springs covered with canvas

PROCEDURE　**Note**: Allow only one child at a time on the mattress when doing these directed exercises.

* Have the child jump from one corner of the mattress to the other.
* Suggest that the child land on all fours and jump up again.
* Have the child turn while jumping so that she or he changes direction.
* Have the child land on his or her seat and bounce up again.
* Ask the child to close his or her eyes and jump from one end of the mattress to the other.
* Have the children roll over and over again from one end of the mattress to the other.
* Then ask the child to "log roll" over and over again across the mattress. The log roll is done with arms extended over the head and legs out straight. This movement helps the child integrate use of both sides of the body together.

VARIATIONS　Use a waterbed mattress to provide a more flexible surface and increase tactile input as the child rolls or jumps across the mattress. This activity stimulates the inner-ear balance center as well.

　　This activity can be varied even further by changing the surface material. Cover the mattress with a rough canvas tarp, a nylon parachute, or a carpet remnant. New tactile experiences are provided as the child rolls, creeps, or jumps across the surface.

HELPFUL HINTS

- Teachers sometimes assume that a child who is highly verbal and intellectually above average is also physically well coordinated. This is not necessarily true.
- Children who need more practice in physical coordination may be resistant, requiring firm but gentle guidance.
- Be supportive of children who need help. Hold the child's hand while he or she jumps on the balance board, praise the child, let the child have more turns, and protect the child from those who are faster and likely to push him or her aside. Provide many positive experiences and lots of praise.
- Observe individual children, and keep a record of the activities each favors and those each avoids.

Learning the Feeling of Direction While Walking

MATERIAL   Drum or whistle

PROCEDURE
- Tell the children:
  When I hit the drum (or blow the whistle), **it means I want you to stop. I'm going to watch how you walk. Show me how you walk.**
- Give directions:
  Show me how slowly you can walk.
  Now show me how fast you can walk.
  See how close to someone else you can walk without touching.
  Walk taking giant steps. Walk taking small steps.
  Walk using a lot of space. Walk using a little bit of space.
- Ask the following questions:
  How can you walk and make noise with your feet? (shuffle, stamp)
  Can you walk and then turn and walk in a different direction when I beat the drum twice?
  How would you feel if you were walking to the store to buy ice cream?
  How would you walk if you were going someplace you didn't want to go?

Note: Children often need help moving to a specific tempo. Be prepared to clap or drum the speed you want them to adopt. For further variation, select instrumental music with a moderate tempo. Have the children walk with the beat, which you accent further by clapping. When the music stops, the children are to stop also.

This activity helps build listening skills as well as coordination and sense of direction.

Learning the Feeling of Direction While Running

MATERIALS   Four barrels, large storage cylinders, or boxes
Drum or whistle

PROCEDURE
- Find an area (preferably grassy) at least 20' long and wide enough that the children can stand side by side in a row, about an arm's length apart.
- Before setting up the barrels, ask the children to line up on one side of the grass. Stand at the other side.
- Ask them to show you how they can run to your side of the grass as you play the drum and stop quickly when the drum stops.
- Ask:
  Can you run quickly and reach to the sky, be as tall as you can?
- Set up barrels in a line with about 3' of space between them. If children need more space, use only 3 barrels spaced farther apart.
- Have them run in and out around the barrels quickly, then slowly, then moving another part of the body along with their feet.
- Ask:
  How would an airplane fly around those barrels?
  Can you show me how a train would move around the barrels?
  What else could you be?

Experiencing the Feeling of Direction (*for children who are adept at bouncing a ball*)

MATERIAL   Large ball for each child

PROCEDURE
- This activity is best done with one child at a time—certainly no more than three children, all of whom are able to follow directions.
- Have the children bounce a ball exactly the same way you do, stopping when you stop.
- Vary the action by bouncing the ball to the right, the left, and in ways that are not too difficult for the children to follow.
- Verbalize actions with statements such as:
  Now the ball is bouncing fast.
  Now it is moving backwards.
  This time we'll bounce the ball to the right.
- This activity helps children build their vocabulary of directional words, as well as coordinate their physical movements with visual and auditory cues.
- It is difficult for a child to have a ball in hand without simply bouncing it for fun in his or her own way, so allow time for the child to play with the ball. Then you might redirect the child's attention by saying:
  Can you bounce the ball and keep it in this circle?
  Can you throw it to me and make it bounce once (twice) **before I catch it?**

Note: When outdoors, use a whistle to signal *stop*. Practice with the children so that they respond to the whistle before you introduce difficult tasks. Indoors, use a drum beat, a hand clap, or tone blocks as a signal to stop. Remember that young children often are quite sensitive to loud sounds.

Keep activities simple for very young children. Do not expect them to respond to a large number of variations.

Learning to Skip

MATERIALS   Drum or sand blocks
Barrels (optional)

PROCEDURE
• Ask the children to show if they know how to skip. If some children can and some cannot, ask them all to join hands and skip toward you. Those who are learning to skip will receive movement and rhythm cues from those who can already skip. Children also can do a slow step-hop pattern together.
• Play an uneven rhythm pattern with the sand blocks to accompany the skipping movement (two beats in an uneven, short-long combination).
• If the children have mastered the skipping pattern, they can go on to explore other movement possibilities, such as jumping, hopping, walking, and running.

Note: Skipping is a difficult motor skill for children to master, requiring an internal integration of both sides of the body. Children master the skill between the ages of 4½ and 7.

Learning Directional Placement of the Feet

MATERIALS   Vinyl tiles
Water-base paint

PROCEDURE
• Paint the bottoms of a child's bare feet, and make a dozen or more prints of each foot on separate tiles.
• Arrange the printed tiles in a path the children can walk. Vary the footprints so that children must criss-cross, go sideways, and move their feet in different directions.
• Ask each child to place his or foot to match the pattern.
• When all are familiar with the pattern, ask them to move more quickly along the path.
• Move the tiles to form different patterns.

BALANCE

Experiencing Directional Changes in Space (*for preschoolers and primary-level children*)

MATERIALS   A walking board (1' wide x 8' long x 2" thick) supported by small saw horses 8" off the ground

PROCEDURE   **Note**: Use a grassy area. Work with one child at a time.

• Say:
Show me how you can walk across the board.
Can you walk across touching your heel to your toes?
Try walking backward.
Can you walk sideways on the board? Can you go the other way?

Show me how you can walk to the middle, turn around, and walk back toward me.
How else can you get to the middle and change?

- Ask what other ways the child can get across the board. (Possibilities include jumping, hopping sideways and backward, and using different body positions, such as squatting and stooping.)

VARIATIONS   These variations require children to shift their center of gravity even further and stimulate the inner-ear balance system as well:

- Place the walking board at a slight slant by putting a 6-inch block under one end.
- Place the walking board on a mat or mattress to further emphasize the uneven surface.
- Place a bean bag on the walking board. First have the children step over it as they walk across the board. Next have them stop, pick up the bean bag, and carry it to the end.

HELPFUL HINTS

- Provide an object at eye level for the children to focus on (such as another adult or a streamer tied to a branch). The children should be encouraged to watch the target rather than their feet.
- For preschoolers, start with the walking board placed on the ground. Raise it later.

Learning to Coordinate Weight Shift and Experiencing Right and Left Sides of the Body

MATERIALS   A wooden balance board (16" x 16" x 1")
A wooden base (5½" x 5½" x 2") placed under the center of the board

PROCEDURE   **Note:** Use a grassy area. Work with one child at a time.

- Show the children the equipment. Say:
See what happens when you push with your foot on this side of the board?
What happens when you push the other side with your foot?
- Ask a child to get up on the balance board. He or she may need to hold your hands at first in order to maintain balance. Try to keep most of the child's weight on the board rather than on your hands.
- Ask the child to push down on one foot, then the other. The goal is a smooth shifting of weight, and the child will probably need a good deal of practice before the goal is reached. Singing "See-Saw, Margery Daw" might help the child to develop a smooth, rhythmic pattern of movement.
- Ask:
What happens if you lean on your toes?
What else could you lean on? (heels)
Ask the child to combine the movements.

• As the child becomes skilled, you can talk about pushing forward, backward, and side to side.

Practicing Balance and Experiencing Directional Changes

MATERIALS   One hula hoop for each child
One red cardboard circle and one red cardboard square (8" x 8") for each child

PROCEDURE   • Give each child a hula hoop. Ask children to put the hoops on the ground in a place where there is room to move around them. Ask children to stand behind their hoops, facing you. Call that their "home" position.
• Say:
Can you jump into your hoop with both feet?
Can you jump out the other side?
Turn around and jump back through.
• Ask:
Who can hop on one foot into the hoop and hop out the other side?
Can you hop back through?
Hop through using your other foot?
• Say:
Hop into the hoop using both feet and stop.
Can you see a place to jump where you haven't been yet? (to the side)

Have them practice jumping to the side on both feet, then on one foot.

• Tell them they are going to play a game. Put the red circle on the side of the hoop that is to their right; put the red square to their left.
• Play the game by asking them to jump into the hoop and out onto the circle. Ask them to jump into the hoop and out onto the square, then back again. Once the children are aware of the possible bases, encourage them to explore different combinations (for example, jump in and out toward you and go back and land on the circle). Ask what different way they could go back besides straight to "home."

Practicing Balance on an Uneven Surface

MATERIALS   Small circular trampoline or rebounder. (These are sold in most sporting-goods stores. Be sure the edges are padded, the legs are secure, and the trampoline is no more than a foot off the floor.)
Recorded music and record player
Hula hoop

PROCEDURE   **Note:** Let children use the trampoline only when an adult is in attendance or when it is surrounded by tumbling mats. Children may go on the trampoline in stocking feet indoors or may keep their shoes on if outdoors. This activity is appropriate for 2-year-olds and up, as long as the trampoline will bear the child's weight.

- Have children jump on the trampoline one at a time. (With very young children, two may go at a time.)
- Stand next to the trampoline as a spotter while each child is jumping.
- Play some recorded music with a steady, moderate beat to set the pace.
- To help inexperienced children maintain balance while jumping, hold one side of a hula hoop as you stand on the floor, while the child faces you and grasps the other side of the hoop with both hands.

Note: As a child nears kindergarten age, he or she should be able to answer questions, recite simple rhymes, count, or say his or her phone number while continuing to jump. This demonstrates the ability to perform a cognitive or learned skill while performing a basic motor skill and maintaining balance.

Jumping on an uneven surface is an excellent activity for developing the child's inner-ear balance system.

COMBINING MOVEMENTS

Combining Movements Using Tires

MATERIAL   One automobile tire for each child (get used ones free from a service station), placed flat on the ground with space between them.

PROCEDURE
- Assign each child a tire.
- Ask how the child can get from one side of the tire to the other side without touching the tire (walk around it, hop into the middle and out).
- Ask how the child can get from one side of the tire to the other by touching the tire (walk around the edge, hop on one edge, jump into the center, jump over the edge and out, jump around the edge). Encourage the children to explore all the possibilities by offering indirect clues (to use one foot, to touch twice, and so on).

Using Various Body Postures

MATERIALS   Walking board
Saw horses
Mattress

PROCEDURE
- In a grassy area, set up the walking board so that it is at the edge of the mattress.
- Let the children take turns moving across the board in any manner they choose and end by jumping on the mattress. Encourage them to try new movement combinations by saying you like what

HELPFUL HINTS

- Begin with simple activities, and do not end on a failure.
- Demonstrate what you want before distributing materials.
- If the group is large, use a whistle to signal the beginning and ending of an activitiy.
- Don't expect children to stand still and pay attention after you have handed them a ball, a tire, or a hula hoop. Let the children experiment with free movements.
- Play recorded music as a background. Use a moderate tempo appropriate for jumping and hopping. Tell the children that when the music stops they are to "freeze." This helps maintain control of the group and also reinforces the tempo at which you wish to maintain the activity. The "freeze" will allow the children to rest.
- Remember that hopping is difficult for young children. By age 4½ a child may be hopping on one leg, usually the dominant one. By age 5, the child will be able to hop on one leg and then the other.

they are doing. Help them think of new things to do by asking if they can move their hands, if they can use one foot, and so on. Other possible questions include

Can you look somewhere different when you land?
Can you go higher as you move across?

- Once they land on the mattress, the children can explore the space available, the movement combinations, and the various body postures.

Moving Through a Maze

MATERIALS   Any or all of the following to make a maze:

big wooden blocks (for walking around, jumping over, hopping onto and off of)
four chairs
two or more yardsticks (use with chairs or blocks for going over or under)
walking board
mattress
big boxes or barrels
auto or bicycle tires (for hopping into, running through, walking on)
chalk for drawing guidelines through the maze
rope at least 9' in length
footprint patterns (See the following activity.)

PROCEDURE   • Set up a maze.
- Allow the children to go through the maze any way they want the first time, as long as they follow the guidelines. Keep the children spaced 15' apart.

- The second time they go through, ask them to do something specific at one point (hop off the blocks, for example).
- Each time, change the point at which they are to do something specific.

Making Footprints on Butcher Paper

MATERIALS
One 10' long sheet of butcher paper per child
A plastic dishpan holding ½" of easel paint (See "Easel Paint Recipes," pp. 13–14.)
Two child-size chairs
A basin of soapy water
A towel

PROCEDURE
Note: Have an aide help the children wash their feet.

- Seat the barefooted child on the chair, which has been placed at one end of the butcher paper.
- Have the child put his or her feet in the dishpan of paint. Help the child to step onto the paper.
- Say:
Show me how you can move on your feet across the paper to the other end. (He or she may simply walk straight across the paper.)
- Have the aide stand at the other end of the paper with the other chair placed beside the pan of soapy water and a towel. The aide can help the child be seated, place his or her feet in the soapy water, and clean and dry the feet.
- Note on the paper who walked across it and when.
- Within the next day or so, show the child his or her footprints from the first experience and have the child walk on the prints. Set up a blank sheet of paper, and ask the child to go across the paper differently than he or she did before. Should the child balk while on the paper, the teacher can guide him or her by asking
Can you hop?
Other movement possibilities include jumping on both feet, stepping sideways with either foot, and crossing one foot in front of the other.

Walking and Crawling Through Inner Tubes

MATERIAL
Ten or more inner tubes

PROCEDURE
- Arrange the inner tubes in a variety of patterns.
- Ask the children to put one foot in each inner tube and walk through the pattern.
- Ask them to put two feet in each tube as they move through the pattern.
- Ask them to show you how quickly they can go through the pattern.
- Ask them to show you other ways they can go along the tubes

(using hands and feet, on their knees, touching only the tops of the tubes).

Combining Clapping with Body Movements

MATERIALS   Record player and square-dance record

PROCEDURE
- Listen to the regular beat of the square dance.
- Have the children follow you in clapping in unison.
- When the children are familiar with clapping to the beat, ask them to slap their thighs.
- Call out other parts of the body:
  Touch your toes; squeeze your waist; nod your head; touch your elbows; rub your tummies.
- Combine clapping with hopping, jumping, walking, skipping, and so on.

Combining Movements Using a Parachute

MATERIALS   One small cargo parachute (available from surplus stores)[14]
Two or three lightweight balls about 8–10" in diameter

PROCEDURE
- Have the children grip the edge of the parachute and pull back tightly.
- Ask if they can shake the chute.
- Ask them to shake the chute up and down in unison to fill it with air.
- Have them hold the parachute up as high as they can.
- Ask for a volunteer to run under the chute from one side to the other without letting it touch him or her. (You may want to demonstrate and to tell each child when it is time to start running.)
- Have everyone let go and run under the chute at the same time.
- Place one or more balls on top of the parachute, and ask the children to bounce the balls up and down.
- Ask if they can shake the chute to make the balls bounce off it.
- For variation and to provide further sensory stimulation, have a few children lie in the center of the parachute while it is on the ground. Have the others shake the chute up and down so that it ripples around those in the center. They can pretend to be noodles cooking in a pan of bubbling water.

Note: It may be helpful to use a whistle to signal when to start and stop.

    If you wish to combine the activity with music, try the recording *Playtime Parachute Fun* (Kimbo).

---

[14]Parachutes of varying sizes are available from Mosier Materials, Inc., 61328 Yakwahtin Court, Bend, Oregon 97702.

Exercising to Music

MATERIAL

Record player and records suitable for exercise movements (The theme from *Rocky* works well.)

PROCEDURE

- Have the children sit on the floor or a mat, facing you. Allow 3' to 4' on either side of each child for movement.
- Have the children start with slow movements to the music—nodding the head and moving the head from side to side.
- Ask them to reach high with their arms, stretching at the waist and sitting very tall.
- Have the children bring their arms down and extend them behind the body, leaning forward and letting the head touch the knees.
- Tell the children to stand up, put hands on hips, and bounce on the balls of their feet.
- Have children hop to the left and then to the right.
- Let them climb an imaginary ladder with arms and legs.
- Show them how to do jumping jacks.
- Have children lie on their stomachs, face down. Tell them to reach back with their hands and hold their feet and then rock back and forth.
- Have the children lie on their backs with legs extended over their heads; have them pedal an imaginary bicycle.

Drama and Creative Expression

Dramatic play is one of the most powerful avenues through which children come to discover and understand their worlds. During the early years of life, children are basically self-centered. They learn about their worlds by imitating the adults around them. In doing so, they "try on" the roles of those who are more powerful; thus, they get a sense of what it must be like to be big and strong.

Preschoolers lack the maturity and experience to have a clear perspective of the world. Their senses are bombarded daily with new and confusing stimuli. They are expected to learn new things and behave in ways that seem unnatural to them, all within what appear to be very limiting constraints. Dramatic play offers them a satisfying and socially acceptable avenue to express some of their confusion, fears, and needs, as well as to release usually unacceptable impulses. It's not okay to hit mommy or daddy, but when you're playing pretend it's okay to spank your doll.

THE VALUE OF DRAMATIC PLAY IN THE CLASSROOM

The early education classroom can be a place where young children work out their feelings, act out their fears, and expand their knowledge of themselves and others in ways that are both healthy and creative.

The teacher who appreciates the value of dramatic play can do many things to nurture the activity within the classroom. A positive attitude and acceptance of children's natural urge to fantasize are fundamental to establishing a safe environment for dramatic play. Although playing pretend is usually a favorite pastime, there are ways a teacher can help to enhance such an activity.

Among the most common enticements for make-believe are the dress-up and housekeeping areas in a classroom. When children are given a few props—some "grown-up" clothes, a few child-size housekeeping items—their imaginations take wing. Add a telephone and some plastic food, and watch their dramatic play extend even further. The amount of equipment does not determine the quality or degree of make-believe, however. It is probably safer to start with a limited number of props; too many can become distracting and confusing, stifling the children's imaginations. Add a few at a time as needed to maintain interest. Most young children need only the simplest props to support their fantasy lives.

PLANNING DRAMATIC PLAY ACTIVITIES

The ways in which a teacher plans and introduces dramatic play activities into the classroom depend on the children's ages, ability levels, needs, and interests. It is simple enough to purchase and set up equipment; but to be most effective, a teacher must monitor what the children are doing with it.

Some children will play-act situations to rehearse roles they admire or fear; others may need to work out some particularly difficult problem facing them at home, such as a power struggle or sibling rivalry. Still others may be practicing the skills necessary to get along with their peers.

Listen to the talk. Are they re-enacting roles of adults? Is the quality of the conversation such that you sense a degree of satisfaction and release for the children?

The introduction of a new prop can change the direction of the play dramatically. For example, a few baby dolls and a crib will engage children who need to act out baby-related roles. The teacher can have boxes of different kinds of props available, to be brought out as needed. The quality of play will dictate the kind, quantity, and appropriate time for the introduction of props.

When collecting items for dramatic play, don't overlook parents, who can be a valuable resource for both ideas and contributions. Keep in mind, also, that opportunities for such activities exist throughout the school and need not be confined to a particular area. For example, children can pretend to be mail carriers with a hat and pouch; a delivery person can make rounds on a trike; ice cream, popcorn, or flower vendors can hawk their wares from a wagon. Other community workers such as grocery clerks, doctors, dentists, nurses, teachers, veterinarians, bankers, and cobblers can ply their trades in most any area of the classroom.

Sometimes it is a good idea to introduce simple props in a variety of places throughout the school, to attract children who may tend to avoid the traditional dress-up or housekeeping corner.

Field trips and visits to the school by community workers provide additional background knowledge to facilitate and extend children's sociodramatic play. (*Sociodramatic play* is the term used to refer to dramatic play in which children assume roles and interact along the lines of a theme; see Dramatic Play Kits, p. 118.) Stories, puppet shows, and film strips are also useful in enhancing children's fantasies.

From time to time, the teacher may need to redirect children if their fantasy play appears potentially harmful to themselves or others. You understand that monsters are supposed to act ferocious, but you can't let them hurt the other children. You remain sympathetic to the child's need to assume such a role, but you set limits and suggest other equally satisfying ways a child may play-act aggressive feelings.

Music activities, such as those presented earlier in this section, offer excellent outlets for fantasy play. Learning to recognize and express feelings by talking about pictures of people or using art materials may open up new avenues of creative expression. Some of the organized dramatic play activities, such as acting out a story, can offer children the chance to assume formerly avoided roles. Sometimes children who are either passive or aggressive need help and "permission" from the teacher to assume a role in which they may feel self-conscious at first. But when, through an accepting and supportive attitude, the teacher assures children that it is safe to experiment, they are more likely to work out possible solutions to their needs.

EXPRESSING FEELINGS

Learning to Imagine and Project Feelings

MATERIAL   Pictures from magazines and other sources, mounted on heavy tag board, showing such situations as

a mother scolding or spanking a child
two children fighting
a serious accident
joyous interactions among people

PROCEDURE   • Hold pictures up one at a time for children to see.
   • Let the children volunteer their observations. (Most will be descriptive. Give children plenty of time to talk about the pictures.)
   • Then ask:
   What is happening in this picture?
   What do you think happened just before this picture was taken?
   • Later in the discussion, ask:
   What do you think will happen next?
   How do you think the story will end?
   • Repeat some of the stories from beginning to end, to help children realize that a picture can stimulate imaginings of the past, present, and future, as well as project their own wishes.

Recognizing and Expressing Feelings

MATERIALS   Pictures from magazines or other sources, mounted on heavy tag board, showing individuals (all ages) in emotional states, such as

a man laughing
a person looking sad
a child smiling
a woman looking exasperated

PROCEDURE   • Hold the pictures up one at a time for the children to see. If working with an individual child, let the child hold and examine each picture closely.
• Say:
Tell me about this picture. (Many first responses will be simple identification. Let all children have plenty of opportunity to comment.)
Look at this woman's face. How do you think she feels? (Usually the responses will be simple descriptions.)
• Continue to encourage all the children to look at details of expression. Say:
Look at her eyes. Do your eyes get that way?
Look at her mouth. Can we try to make our mouths look like that? When do you look like that? (Children will volunteer personal and sometimes seemingly unrelated experiences.)
• Notice, respond to, and encourage the children's individual expressions of feeling.
• Use a mirror during this activity. As the children volunteer facial expressions to illustrate a feeling, let them check themselves in the mirror. Encourage them to make any adjustments they want. Say:
Can you make your eyes look angry too?
Now that you are making a sad face, how can you make it happy again?

VARIATIONS   Re-create experiences and have children act them out. For example, pantomime the following:

• Get out of bed, get dressed, tie your shoes, and brush your teeth.
• Spread mustard, ketchup, and relish on a hot dog and eat it.
• Pour sugar and cream into coffee or tea; stir it, cool it and taste it.

Re-create feelings and have children express them. For example, pantomime the following:

• Pour a glass of milk and spill it.
• Scoop some ice cream into a cone and drop it.
• Pick beautiful flowers and smell them.

Encourage expression of feelings rather than superficial acting.

Expressing Inner Feelings Through Color, Line, Movement, Shape, and Form

MATERIAL   Color pictures and photographs showing scenes not emphasizing people, such as

a colorful day in fall or spring
a wintry landscape
a dismal, dreary scene
a bright, cheerful scene

PROCEDURE
- Hold pictures up one at a time for the children to see. Let them comment on what they see.
- Say:
  Look at the colors! (Children will usually begin to name them.)
  How does this color make you feel?
  How do all the colors in the whole picture make you feel? I wonder why. (Young children will have difficulty expressing their inner responses to color. Try to call their attention to the effects colors can have.)
- Repeat the same procedure with lines. Say:
  Look at how the artist made his brush strokes go (up/down).
  Are these lines straight or crooked?
  Notice the thick paint and the big hard lines. Do you think these lines help to make you feel happy? Sad?
- Comment on the movement in the pictures. Ask:
  What is happening to the leaves in this picture?
  What is moving?
  Why is the girl's hair back like that? What makes your hair do that?
- Comment on the other shapes in the pictures. Ask:
  How do you think this feels—round or flat?
  Let's try to think about how the artist made this look round instead of flat.
- Comment on the textures within the pictures. Ask:
  Do you think this is rough or smooth?
  I wonder why it looks that way.
  Do not expect young children to contribute sophisticated comments at first. They should be given many, many opportunities to learn to look at pictures, people, and nature from the standpoint of the characteristics of color, line, form, and so forth.

Learning That Art Is a Medium of Expression[15]

MATERIAL
Reproductions of paintings, all on the same subject, such as children; for example,

"A Girl with a Broom"—Rembrandt (Dutch)
"Portrait of a Boy"—Soutine (Russian)
"A Girl with a Watering Can"—Renoir (French)
"Don Emanuel Osorio De Zuniga—Goya (Spanish)
"Girl with Braids"—Modigliani (Italian)

(Other subjects include birds and animals, flowers, work, or places.)

[15]Adapted from "Elementary Level Pilot Program, Art Appreciation: A Step Toward Aesthetic Awareness," pp. 1–7, prepared by the Palo Alto Unified School District.

PROCEDURE   • Begin the discussion by saying
When we look at children, we see that they do not always look the same. If you are sad, your face will look a certain way. (Let one child demonstrate.)
If you are feeling very happy, your face might look quite different. Many things make us see the same children in different ways.
• Darken the room and have the children look at one another.
• Introduce a light and say:
Light can come into a room and change the way a child looks.
• Introduce the paintings by placing them on low tables or on the floor.
• Have each child look at the paintings and tell you which one he or she likes best and why. (You may want to keep a list of the number of children who choose each painting.)
• Encourage the children to use easel paints to "tell" about the way they feel.
• Discuss how artists also tell the way they feel through their paintings.
• Discuss how color and light affect the way a person feels.

Learning About Three-Dimensional Objects

MATERIALS   Paper large enough for a mural
Three-dimensional objects such as driftwood, sculptures, fruits, vegetables, rocks, flowers, seashells, and nuts

PROCEDURE   • Select several items that have different textures.
• Talk to the children about how the objects feel.
• Have the children close their eyes. Give them an object to pass along, and ask if they can tell what it is by touching and feeling it.
• Have them turn each object over and look at it another way.
• Take the children on a nature walk to collect three-dimensional objects.
• Have the children cooperate in making a large wall mural with the objects they collect.
• Hang the mural low enough that children can touch it.

Learning the Meaning of Pretend

MATERIAL   The book *What You Can Do*, by Bill Gillham (New York, NY: Putnam, 1986)

PROCEDURE   • This is a good book for a beginning exercise in talking about the meaning of pretend.
• Show the pictures, allowing plenty of time for children to discuss personal experiences that they can relate to the book. For example, say:
What can you do with pillows?

In addition to the book's suggestion of building a den under the table, have the children talk about other things they can do to pretend with pillows. The colorful photos of real children are easy to relate to, and the topics are familiar to all young children.

- Use the opportunity to let children know that other people also play pretend, and that it is fun and okay to do so.

Note: You can follow the story with Hap Palmer's recording of *Pretend*.

VARIATION   If the book is not readily available, you can improvise, using bath bubbles to make a beard or empty eggshells to make boats.

Acting Out Different Characters

MATERIAL   Hap Palmer's recording *Pretend*

PROCEDURE
- Preview the recording, and select the bands that are appropriate for the children with whom you will be working.
- Play the side that has verbal instructions for the children to pretend to be such things as rag dolls, friendly giants, and clowns.
- Talk about the meaning of "pretend" and let the children assume the different roles.
- Afterwards, encourage the children to talk about how they felt when they pretended to be something or someone else.
- If appropriate, play the side that is instrumental music only and let the children create their own pretend characters.

Note: Suzy Prudden's *Creative Fitness for Children* has some play-acting songs, such as "Snuggles the Snail" in which the children engage in directed exercise movements.

Acting Out a Story with Puppets

MATERIALS   A familiar story such as "Peter Rabbit," or "The Three Bears."
Hand puppets of the main characters in the story (Refer to the bibliography at the end of this section for some excellent resources on the use of puppets with young children; see Illustration 2.3 for some ideas for puppets.)

PROCEDURE
- Tell the story with the puppets, emphasizing the dialogue of the characters. Tell the story dramatically as you assume each role.
- Watch the children's facial expressions while you are talking.
- When you have finished the story, ask if the children would like to hear the story again. Tell them that you will need their help this time.
- You may want to be the narrator and invite each character to show the others what he or she sounds like.
- If you do not have time to accommodate all the volunteers, assure them that you will write their names on a list for future acting roles.

Illustration 2.3   **Various kinds of puppets**

Note: It is a good idea to imagine in your own mind the strategies you will use to keep the activity running smoothly.

Practicing Creative Dramatics Using Props

MATERIAL   Props to denote characters familiar to the children, such as a police officer's hat or badge, a firefighter's hat, a nurse's hat, an Indian headband, a fairy princess's wand

PROCEDURE   • Ask the children to help you act out a story.
    • Keep the props hidden from their view.
    • Start the story with "Once upon a time, there was a police officer . . . " (or whatever you choose).
    • Have children volunteer to be the characters, and ask them to tell the group what they are doing in the story.
    • You may need to help by suggesting some possibilities for the plot, but have in mind a suspenseful climax and an ending with plenty of flexibility and room for creative license.
    • Some children may want to be invited to join in after the first round.

Note: This is the kind of activity that bears repeating, because many children are not accustomed to making up a story as a group. Keep the activity simple in the beginning, increasing the length and complexity as children become more familiar with the technique.

Acting Out a Story

MATERIAL   Storybooks such as *The Turnip, The Three Billy Goats Gruff, Elephant in a Well, Too Much Noise, The Greedy Old Fat Man, Where the Wild Things Are* (See Part Four for annotations.)

PROCEDURE   • Read a story with feeling and drama.
• After you have read the story, talk about how each of the characters might feel and act.
• Ask the children how they would feel and act if they were the characters.
• Offer to help them act out the story by getting some simple props and reminding them of the general format.
• Act as the director, narrator, and prompter while each child takes his or her part.

Note: This activity requires that the children have a bit of prior acting experience. It is best to use this form of creative drama after the children have had many opportunities to participate in less extended play-acting.

After they become more confident in their roles, you might want to videotape the play and invite parents to attend the premiere.

PUPPETS

The following are some suggestions for making simple puppets from simple materials. The books listed in the annotated bibliography at the end of this section provide many more ideas, as well as directions for making more elaborate puppets.

Practice telling stories with puppets in front of a mirror. Remember to tip the face of the puppet toward the children to maintain eye contact. Shy children will often respond more easily to a puppet than to the teacher.

Paper Bag Puppets   Use a felt marker to draw a face on a small paper bag. Make a hole for the mouth so that the child can poke fingers through for a tongue.

Mitten or Sock Puppets   Use an old mitten or sock with buttons for eyes and nose. Attach a small piece of colored material for the mouth, and yarn for the hair.

Hand Puppets

A hand can be a puppet. Using a washable, water-base felt marker, draw eyes, nose, and mouth in the creases of a child's palm. By moving the fingers and stretching them, the child can create many amusing expressions.

Potato or Apple Puppets

In a small apple or potato, cut a hole large enough for a child's finger. With toothpicks, attach slices of olives, cloves, or pieces of the potato and apple to make the eyes, nose, and mouth. A handkerchief wrapped around the hand will become the body.

Shadow Puppets

Trace figures on construction paper, and glue them onto poster board. Cut out the shapes, and attach them to handles made of flat sticks or heavy plastic straws.

DRAMATIC PLAY KITS

The young child re-creates and integrates many personal experiences through dramatic play. In this way, the child tries to make sense out of his or her world. You can facilitate dramatic play by supplying props to help children use their imaginations. Chairs become trains, cars, or boats. A table covered with a blanket or bedspread becomes a cave or a secret hiding place. Empty cardboard cartons convert into airplanes, houses, forts, and fire stations. Providing kits containing the materials suggested below can add to the reality of the experience and help children expand their imaginative play.

Bakery

Pots, pans, rolling pins, sifter, playdough, cupcake molds, cookie press, cake decorator, bread wrappers, plastic plates to display baked goods, aprons, bakers' hats, cash register, play money, paper bags.

Unisex Hair Style Shop

Plastic brushes, combs, hair dryer, makeup, cotton balls, hair rollers, curling irons, colored water in nail polish bottles, empty shampoo bottles, wigs.

Garage Mechanic/Gas Station Attendant	Tire pump, tubing for gas pump, wrench, clean empty oil cans with spouts, spray bottles of water, rags for wiping engine parts and cleaning windshields, shirt, hat.
Druggist	Empty plastic pill and medicine containers, typewriter, stick-em labels, telephone, delivery wagon.
Doctor/Nurse	Tongue depressors, stethoscope, satchel, adhesive bandages, cotton balls, uniforms.
Dentist	Chair, large doll to be the patient, small mirror, dental floss, toothbrush.
Postal Worker	Hat, badges, envelopes, mail satchel, postage stamps (save stamps from promotional mailings), index card file, rubber stamps, stamp pads, crayons, pencils.
Plumber	Wrench, pieces of plastic pipe, tool box, plunger.
Firefighter	Hard hat, raincoat, boots, short length of garden hose.
Shoe Repair Shop	Shoes, small cans of clear (natural) shoe polish, sponges, buffs, soft cloths, mallet, shoe strings.
Veterinarian	Stethoscope, toy animals, empty plastic hypodermic syringes (without needles), bandages, splints.
Travel Agent or Escort	Badges or pins (such as flight attendant's wings), hat, tickets, play money, clipboard, plastic trays, paper cups, plastic food, small pillows, blankets.
Bank Teller	Deposit slips, play money, rubber stamps, stamp pads, pens, pencils.
Restaurant	Cash register, play money, menus, paper and pencils, plastic food, empty plastic condiment bottles, napkins, empty drink containers, straws, uniforms, pots and pans, egg beater, spoons, pitchers, salt and flour shakers, tablecloth, napkins, aprons, chef's hat.

Police Officer   Hat, badge, book of tickets, whistle.

Supermarket   Cash register, play money, pad of paper, empty and clean food cartons, pencils, paper punch, paper sacks, plastic food, grocery boxes, cans with smooth edges.

Bibliography of Resources

ACTIVITY SONG BOOKS

Beall, Pamela Conn, and Susan Hagen Nipp. *Wee Sing Series.* Los Angeles, CA: Price/Stern/Sloan. This series of small paperback books offers titles such as *Children's Songs and Fingerplays* (1986); *Musical Games and Rhymes for Children* (1988); and *Nursery Rhymes and Lullabies* (1985).

Burton, Leon, and William Hughes. *Music Play.* Menlo Park, CA: Addison-Wesley, 1979. A book of activities designed to help children learn about the characteristics of sound and how sounds may be combined to produce sound patterns. Records included.

Chroman, Eleanor. *Songs That Children Sing.* New York: NY: Oak Publications, 1970. Seventy-one international folk songs for children, some with English translations. Charming photographs of the world's children accompany the guitar chords and piano arrangements.

Jenkins, Ella. *The Ella Jenkins Song Book for Children.* New York, NY: Oak Publications, 1966. Twenty-six of Ella Jenkin's most popular songs used in her rhythm workshops.

Nye, Robert, Vernice Nye, Neva Aubin, and George Kyme. *Singing with Children.* 2nd ed. Belmont, CA: Wadsworth, 1970. A collection of songs for the elementary grades, but the teacher of young children will find the sections on action songs and singing games useful. The book also includes a section of songs to be accompanied by the autoharp, ukele, and percussion instruments. Teaching objectives are listed at the beginning of each section, and suggestions for other uses for songs are given.

Nye, Robert, and Meg Peterson. *Teaching Music with the Autoharp.* Northbrook, IL: Music Education Group, 1982. A useful book teaching simple chords and songs for the autoharp. Rhythm, melody, and harmony are some of the concepts that can be taught with the autoharp. Includes 37 songs with strums.

Peterson, Meg. *Autoharp Parade.* Northbrook, IL: Oscar Schmidt International, 1967. One hundred favorite songs for young people, with autoharp chords and strums.

Raffi. *The Raffi Singable Songbook.* New York: Crown, 1987. Piano arrangements and guitar and ukelele chords to 51 songs for young children. Includes "Five Little Pumpkins," "My Dreydel," "Brush Your Teeth," "Mr. Sun," and "Peanut Butter Sandwich."

Reynolds, Malvina. *Tweedles & Foodles for Young Noodles.* Berkeley, CA: Schroder Music, 1961. This classic and *Malvina Reynolds' Songbook* (1984) contain charming originals written by a delightful protestor who says, "You can't be meaningfully angry unless you burn because you care truly about people and small children and birds, fishes, ladybugs and wilderness places, and there are songs here about all that."

Seeger, Ruth Crawford. *American Folk Songs for Children in Home, School, and Nursery School.* New York, NY: Doubleday, 1980. The author originally compiled these folk songs for use at a cooperative nursery school. The preface contains an excellent discussion on the rationale for introducing young children to American folk music, with suggestions for parent and teacher improvising, accompanying, and using the songs at home and school. The classified index includes such topics as name play, finger play, small dramas, buttons, babies, and days of the week.

Zeitlin, Patty. *A Song Is a Rainbow.* Glenview, IL: Scott, Foresman, 1982. A book of more than 50 tunes for the teacher who can't carry a tune or play an instrument. Lots of good advice and ideas for using instruments, creative movement, and other musical activities.

BOOKS ABOUT CREATIVE MOVEMENT

Barlin, Anne Lief. *Teaching Your Wings to Fly.* Santa Monica, CA: Goodyear Publishing Co., 1979. An excellent collection of movement activities, including relaxation, emotional expression, and body techniques. The book is generously illustrated with photographs. Two 33⅓ records are included with the book.

Burton, Leon, and Kathy Kuroda. *Arts Play.* Menlo Park, CA: Addison-Wesley, 1981. A collection of creative activities in art, music, dance, and drama for young children. Dance activities include *Balloon Persons, Popcorn, Falling Leaves, Spider's Dance.* Record included.

Cherry, Clare. *Creative Movement for the Developing Child.* Belmont, CA: Pitman, 1971. A nursery school teacher's collection of ideas on involving the young child in such activities as creeping, crawling, walking, and balancing games.

Hendricks, Gay, and Kathlyn Hendricks. *The Moving Center.* Englewood Cliffs, NJ: Prentice-Hall, 1983. Simple movement activities for the teacher to incorporate into the daily curriculum. Appropriate for K–6, but can be adapted for younger children.

Sheehy, Emma D. *Children Discover Music and Dance.* New York, NY: Teachers College Press, 1968. A useful text for the teacher of children of all ages. It includes discussions of the use of singing, instruments, dance, movement, and recordings in the classroom.

Sullivan, Molly. *Feeling Strong, Feeling Free: Movement Exploration for Young Children.* Washington, DC: National Association for the Education of Young Children, 1982. Considers movement exploration as a teaching method for the total development of the child. The techniques encourage children to apply problem-solving techniques to activities and to explore fantasies and relationships with others.

Wax, Edith, and Sydell Roth. *Mostly Movement.* New York, NY: Mostly Movement, Ltd., 1982. Book I (*First Steps*) and Book II (*Accent on Autumn*) contain many original movement activities for preschoolers.

Weimer, Tonja Evetts. *Creative Dance and Movement for Handicapped Children.* Pittsburgh, PA: The Easter Seal Society, 1984. Lesson plans include finger plays, action songs, and creative movement for children, with all levels of physical involvement.

BOOKS ABOUT SENSORIMOTOR EXPLORATIONS

Allen, Marsha. *Sensory-Motor Integration.* Bend, OR: Mosier Materials, 1983. A practical book with a simple explanation of sensory integration, diagnostic tests, and 30 lesson plans for grades K–8. A wide range of activities and equipment are included. Many suggestions can be applied to the preschool child as well.

Ayres, A. Jean. *Sensory Integration and the Child.* Los Angeles, CA: Western Psychological Services, 1982. A basic text for any teacher interested in the theory of sensory integration.

Capon, Jack. *Perceptual-Motor Lesson Plans.* Byron, CA: Front Row Experiences, 1975. A book and cards presenting activities for preschool through first grade. Included are plans for 25 weeks of activities with evaluation scales, objectives, introductory information, and illustrations. Many of the lessons can be simplified further as needed. The book contains a detailed technical presentation of the tactile and inner-ear balance systems.

Cratty, Bryant J. *Active Learning, Games to Enhance Academic Abilities.* Englewood Cliffs, NJ: Prentice-Hall, 1985. A book of activities designed to incorporate action into the curriculum, based on the premise that children learn through action. An approach to changing hyperactive behavior is included.

Curtis, Sandra R. *The Joy of Movement in Early Childhood.* New York, NY: Teachers College Press, 1982. Uses photographs to illustrate various stages of fundamental motor patterns—walking, running, jumping, kicking, throwing, and catching. The author offers games and activities for preschoolers based on these patterns and suggestions for setting up creative play spaces.

Furth, Hans, and Harry Wachs. *Thinking Goes to School: Piaget's Theory in Practice.* New York, NY Oxford University Press, 1981. Offers games that develop movement thinking (eye-movement thinking games, auditory thinking, logical thinking, social thinking, etc.). The emphasis is on the development of visual skills. Designed for use in the classroom from kindergarten on up, many of the activities are appropriate for preschoolers as well.

Graselli, Rose N., and Priscilla A. Hegner. *Playful Parenting.* New York, NY: 1983. Games and exercises for infants and children up to age 3, designed to encourage physical and mental skills according to developmental stages.

Hackett, Layne C. *Movement Exploration and Games for the Mentally Retarded.* Mt. View, CA: Peek Publications, 1970. Noncompetitive, child-centered activities that provide successful experiences. For example, children are asked to show "how far you can reach with your hands" or "how you can put your heels together." Most of the activities are designed for older children, but the teacher can adapt the ideas to suit younger children.

Hackett, Layne C., and Robert G. Jenson. *A Guide to Movement Exploration.* Mt. View, CA: Peek Publications, 1973. The movement exploration activities are designed for the elementary school child but can be adapted for the preschooler. These tasks allow the child to develop and progress at his or her own rate. Helpful teaching techniques are given.

Hendricks, Gay, and Kathlyn Hendricks. *The Moving Center.* Englewood Cliffs, NJ: Prentice-Hall, 1983. Simple movement activities for the teacher to incorporate into the daily curriculum. Appropriate for K–6, but can be adapted for younger children.

Kamii, Constance, and Rheta DeVries. *Group Games in Early Education: Implications of Piaget's Theory.* Washington, D.C.: National Association for the Education of Young Children, 1980. A book based on the premise that play is a powerful factor in fostering the social life and constructive activity of the child. It outlines the criteria for meaningful group games and then presents examples of aiming, chasing, hiding, and guessing games; races; and games involving verbal commands. Appropriate for preschool and the elementary grades.

Levy, Janine. *The Baby Exercise Book.* New York, NY: Pantheon, 1975. Simple exercises by a kinesiotherapist based on natural movements. For newborns through 15 months.

Lovinger, Sophie L. *Learning Disabilities and Games.* Chicago, IL: Nelson-Hall, 1979. Describes the procedure and intrinsic developmental tasks of the standard and beloved games of childhood. The text emphasizes the usefulness of these games in contributing to the self-esteem and skill development of the learning-disabled child. Appropriate for elementary level, but some games can be easily adapted for preschool.

BOOKS ABOUT CREATIVE DRAMATICS

Carlson, Bernice Wells. *Picture That!* New York, NY: Abingdon Press, 1977. A collection of folk tales with a related dramatic activity. Another book of dramatic play activities by the same author is *Let's Pretend It Happened to You.*

Champlin, Connie. *Puppetry and Creative Dramatics in Storytelling.* Austin, TX: Nancy Renfro Studios, 1980. Ideas for teachers who wish to use puppets and creative dramatics to stimulate interest in children's literature.

Cottrell, June. *Teaching with Creative Dramatics.* Lincolnwood, IL: National Textbook Co., 1975. A good introductory book for anyone interested in using creative dramatics with children. It includes a bibliography of stories to dramatize with various age groups, plus ideas for involving children through sensory and pantomime experiences.

Gowan, John Curtis, et al. (eds.). *Creativity: Its Educational Implications*. Dubuque, IA: Kendall-Hunt, 1981. A collection of readings that gives the teacher some insights into the creative potential of children and provides ideas for practical application of research in the curriculum.

Hartley, Ruth E., et al. *Understanding Children's Play*. New York, NY: Columbia University Press, 1952. A classic text in which many observations of young children are used to discuss the way children integrate reality into their lives through dramatic play.

Renfro, Nancy. *Puppetry, Language, and the Special Child*. Austin, TX: Nancy Renfro Studios, 1984. This unique book presents ways in which puppetry can be used to discover alternative languages with children who have special needs in six major disability areas. It includes activities for creative movement using bodi-puppets.

Renfro, Nancy, and Nancy Frazier. *Imagination: At Play with Puppetry & Creative Drama*. Austin, TX: Nancy Renfro Studios, 1987. Imaginative uses of puppetry to engage young children in creative drama.

Torrance, E. Paul. *Guiding Creative Talent.* Melbourne, FL: Krieger Publishing, 1976. A discussion of creative talent at all ages and educational levels. The author presents research findings and gives examples of specific tasks used to assess creativity. He examines some of the difficulties that educators face in understanding and maintaining creativity.

PART THREE

Math
Experiences

Introduction to Math Experiences

A FOUNDATION FOR MATHEMATICAL CONCEPTS

How often a teacher hears from a proud parent, "My 4-year-old knows the whole alphabet and can count to 100!" Most young children do learn letters and numbers from their parents—their first teachers. What the parents teach is rote memory; that is, they teach their children to memorize and recite the names of letters and numbers. The youngster's ability to recite these names is called *social knowledge.* (See the Introduction at the beginning of Part One for a more detailed explanation of Piaget's stages of learning.)

Social knowledge results from listening over and over to such things as "A, B, C" or "1, 2, 3." Children repeat letter and number names until they have committed them to memory. They do not yet understand, however, that numbers are *symbols*, representing a certain number of things. They do not realize that the number 3 stands for three of something—three years, three cookies, three days.

Although social knowledge is an important aspect of learning, we must not confuse the ability to recite with true understanding.

HOW CHILDREN DEVELOP PREMATH SKILLS

Many young children start school with an impressive amount of social knowledge. In addition to being able to recite letters and numbers, they know the names of many common objects and familiar phrases.

Their natural urge to explore and touch things leads them to develop *physical knowledge*, which is derived from their action on things. For example, a child learns what "ball" means by handling a ball, throwing it, watching it bounce, and generally playing with it. Through direct action, he or she learns about properties of balls: shape, size, color, texture, smell. Children do not gain physical knowledge by being told; they learn through direct hands-on experience.

Premath skills are also developed through concrete experiences. Since numbers are symbols, they are best understood if the teacher attaches them to concrete objects that are familiar to children.

The classroom provides many opportunities to acquire physical knowledge about numbers: "I drank three cups of juice and ate six crackers at snack time." "Measure two cups of flour for the play-dough." "I need five more blocks to build my house."

Children continue to reinforce social knowledge when they recite their numbers in finger plays or sing the letters of the alphabet. In addition to these activities, the teacher can provide other opportunities for children to acquire prenumber skills—matching coats to hangers, cups to saucers, small blocks to larger ones. Children practice one-to-one correspondence when they help the teacher distribute a basket of crackers: "One cracker for you, one for Mary, and one for me."

Use of ordinal numbers is apparent when children say things like "I get to go first," "You're next," and "He's last." They compare numbers and quantities: "I have more than you do," or "We both have the same."

Numbers are all around children in the classroom: "It is 10 o'clock, time for juice;" "Four children can go for a walk today;" "We need two cups of fruit for the salad;" "There's room for six children at this table."

In cooking activities, children learn sequence and how different measures correspond: "Put the flour in first, the sugar second, and the baking power last." "*Three* of these teaspoons equal one tablespoon."

Children also become familiar with shapes that are around them: the circular clock face, the edge and angle of a unit block, the round ball they bounce, the square or triangular shape of a sandwich.

Numbers, sizes, shapes, sequences, correspondence, and other pre-math concepts are so much a part of a child's daily experiences that teaching opportunities arise naturally. The teacher needs to be aware of the kind of knowledge children are acquiring—social or physical. Both have their place in the curriculum; however, it is during the preschool years that children establish a basic foundation for later learning, and thus the early childhood classroom is the ideal place to provide opportunities to acquire physical knowledge.

HOW CHILDREN CONSTRUCT LOGICAL MATHEMATICAL KNOWLEDGE

The social knowledge that children acquire, such as the names of numbers, is meaningless unless they have direct experiences with numbers of objects. A number is not just a name; it is a symbol that represents a relationship, such as how many objects or what place in order.

One other important characteristic of numbers is that they are constant despite spatial rearrangements. This concept, known as *conservation*, is one of the fundamental principles most important for success in math.

How do children learn about conservation, and how can teachers teach it? One thing is certain: children do not learn by being told, or even by being shown.

In a classic study of the way young children reason, Swiss psychologist Jean Piaget made a ball of clay and asked a child to make another one of the same size. When the child was satisfied that both balls were exactly the same, Piaget rolled his out into a long sausage shape and asked the child if there was still the same amount of clay in each shape. Piaget found that children in the preoperational stage (about 2 to 7 years of age) usually said there was more clay in the rolled out shape because the sausage was longer than the ball.

Another way to determine how a child reasons is to have two glasses with the same amount of liquid in each. After the child has ascertained that the amounts are equal, pour the liquid from one glass into an empty, taller glass and ask if there is now more, the same amount, or less liquid than there was in the shorter glass. A preoperational child will say there is more because the glass is taller. Although you may pour the water back and forth, the child will have difficulty understanding that the amount can remain the same even though the appearance is altered.

Young children think this way because they have not yet developed the concept of conservation of quantity. Their judgments are based on how things look, rather than on logic.

Unlike social knowledge, *logical mathematical knowledge* cannot be taught verbally. Number relationships, to be truly understood, must become internally consistent systems that are constructed in the child's mind. Children develop logical mathematical knowledge by acting on objects and internally structuring their actions. They learn not from the objects themselves, but from their actions on the objects.

PLANNING THE CURRICULUM

By the time children enter preschool, they have already had many premath experiences. Helping to set the table by counting out enough silverware and napkins, choosing one or two boxes of cereal at the grocery store, helping mom and dad count the number of apples and bananas needed—these and many other family-related activities provide a sound basis for learning math.

The classroom offers many other opportunities for purposeful activities that help young children construct their knowledge of math. For example, while playing with blocks, children learn that they need a certain size or number in order to build a structure. When there are not enough of one kind of block, they discover that a combination of smaller ones equals the larger size. In addition to *equivalence* among sizes, they learn, through unit blocks and pattern blocks, that there are a variety of shapes within a set. When children copy patterns, build different structures, and explore with concrete objects, they are integrating their experiences with a true understanding of mathematical concepts.

Whenever possible, relate activities to children's natural interests. For example, you might want to display a height and weight chart, talk about how children can be measured, and let them practice different ways of recording their own statistics. Shelling peas for snack time can be turned into a game of counting the number of peas in each pod. Guessing the number of marbles in a jar is an excellent experience in estimation, an important mental tool in mathematics.

Concentrate on concrete experiences rather than on abstract labels. This is true not only for numbers, but for all learning experiences for young children. For example, let's say you want the children to learn about apples. You could show them the word *apple*, read stories about apples, and have them color pictures of apples. All these techniques are abstract ways to teach the concept of apple. A concrete way would be to have the children pick apples from a tree or select them at a produce market; talk about the color, weight, shape, size, and smell of the apples; cut the apples up; taste them; cook with them; and describe what they know about apples from their active learning experiences. A child's understanding of abstract labels, whether apples or numbers, takes on more meaning when it is based on concrete experiences with the real objects.

The ability to develop mental images is also important to conceptual growth. You can suggest that the children imagine and describe how the apple tasted. What did it look like when it was whole? When it was cut up into pieces? Extend their problem-solving skills by having them close their eyes and identify different kinds of fruit. (Or blindfold them, if they do not object.) Before they arrive at a decision, they will gather more information by touching, pinching, smelling and tasting the fruit.

Through such experiences, children learn how to think about a problem, use past knowledge in new situations, work from different perspectives, eliminate possibilities, and apply familiar strategies to new challenges.

As a teacher, you will find that there are times when providing social knowledge is appropriate, since symbols serve as useful labels for children in constructing their relationships with objects. At other times it will be more effective to let children act on materials in order to find things out for themselves. In most instances, children's questions are best handled by responding with another question that encourages them to develop their own reasoning. Your questions, personal interest, and enthusiasm will help to stress that what is important is the process of arriving at an answer, not the answer itself.

The activities offered in this section are not intended to be carried out as formal tests. They can be adapted for use in spontaneous situations. One-to-one correspondence, for example, can be practiced on the playground, with equipment such as trikes and balls; during music and movement, with scarves and rhythm instruments; or at meal time, with eating utensils, crackers, cups, napkins, and chairs.

Whenever practical, plan activities that involve children as *active learners,* encouraging them to act on objects and observe the results of their actions. Your role is to help children to structure their knowledge by asking questions such as

What happened?

Why do you think that happened?

What do you think will happen if you try it another way?

Use the activities to help you determine each child's level of functioning. One child may be a conserver of length but not of number. Another may be able to count but not understand equivalence. By presenting variations of the activities, you can determine where there is conflict between a child's perceptions and logical understanding. The activities are merely a beginning for you to adapt and expand to meet the unique needs of each child in your class.

THE MATH CENTER

Use of teacher-directed activities is not the only way to impart math skills. Many children learn more effectively when they are free to construct their own knowledge through experimentation. A math center enables them to explore and discover at their own pace.

Locate the math center near the block play, cooking, or science area. The concepts taught in each of these areas are closely related, and one can build on or expand from the other.

Set up a child-height table with intriguing equipment such as weighing and balance scales and measuring cups and spoons. Provide clear plastic containers of things that can be weighed and measured, such as beans, rice, small blocks, balls of yarn, and materials of different lengths and widths. Attach a clearly marked tape measure or yardstick to the tabletop.

Display different sizes and shapes of unit blocks, pattern blocks, playing cards, geoboards, dominoes, sequence boxes, cuisinaire rods, and rulers on open shelves.

Provide a changing display of books about math concepts on a nearby table or shelf. Exhibit posters of things that children can measure and count.

Attach a flannelboard to one wall, or provide an easel-type flannelboard near some shelves where children can help themselves to containers of felt numbers, shapes, and figures such as those suggested in the activities on the following pages.

HOW TO MAKE A FLANNELBOARD

- Select a piece of ³⁄₈" plywood, and cut it to measure 24" x 32". You can also use heavy cardboard, such as the cover from a wallpaper sample book or part of a packing carton.
- Cut one piece of heavy flannel or coat lining 28" x 36". A light color provides a good contrast for most flannel figures.
- Staple flannel over the edges of the plywood, pulling the material taut. Miter the corners.
- Use 1" tape to cover the staples and the raw edges of the flannel.
- Figures can be cut out of felt or made with heavy construction paper backed with flannel, coarse sandpaper, or commercial flocking paper. Use rubber cement rather than glue to attach backings.
- Pellon, a lightweight lining material, works well for figures or background scenery, because you can use crayons, felt pens, or paint on it.

Post a colorful measurement chart on the wall, with a graph on which to record the children's heights on various dates. Post a weight graph next to a bathroom scale.

Place a large clock with clearly designated numbers on the wall low enough for children to see. Beneath the real clock, post tagboard clock faces that show the times when familiar events occur during class. Accompany them with sketches or photos of the children at snack, lunch, nap, rest, story, and clean-up times. (See Illustration 3.1.)

Depending on the ages and abilities of the children, you will want to simplify or add to the collection of materials. Do not overwhelm them with too many choices. Watch and listen to the children for cues to introduce different materials. Children's toy and school equipment catalogs are a good source of ideas as to materials you may want to make, collect, and use.

Call on parents and volunteers to help make some of the activity materials described in this section for your math center. Be sure to encourage girls to participate. Since our culture tends to reinforce the notion that boys excel at math, science, woodworking, and computers, it is important for preschool girls to develop competence in these areas at an early age. The same holds true for encouraging boys to participate in music, movement, art, and cooking.

Vary the displays by removing some items and introducing new ones as you notice an interest or need. Coordinate the materials with the themes currently being carried out in other parts of the curriculum. Change tends to stimulate children (as well as teachers) to try new ways to test their skills. Make your math center an enticing and fun place, and math will soon be one of the most popular parts of your curriculum.

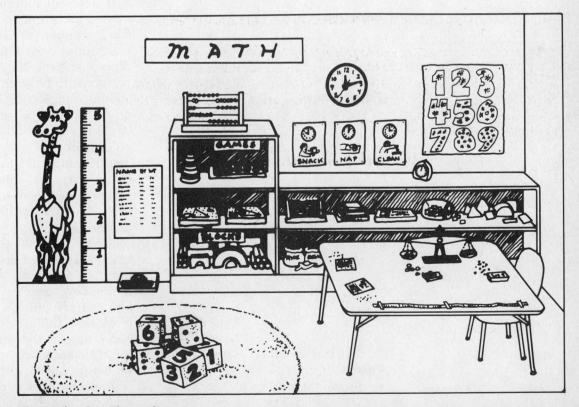

Illustration 3.1 **The math area**

Defined below are some important mathematical terms. Familiarity with these terms will help you to recognize chances to incorporate the concepts in the daily activities and learning experiences of the children.

Classification

Grouping objects according to similarities in such characteristics as color or shape. Preoperational children (ages 2–7) will often lack consistency in classifying objects; they may start grouping by color but be distracted by some other attribute, such as shape. Activities in sorting and comparing objects provide the basis for understanding classification and, ultimately, mathematics.

Conservation

The principle that the quantity of matter remains the same regardless of the shape the matter assumes. Conservation applies to number, length, liquid amount, solid amount, area or space, weight, and displacement volume.

Seriation

Ordering according to increasing size, number, or length. The child must be able to compare objects and mentally retain the relationship between them.

Equivalence

Matching and pairing one object or set of objects with another to determine if they are equivalent.

One-to-one correspondence

A relationship that exists when one element is equal to another—when one set has the same number of members as another set.

Set

A collection of things. Things belonging to a set are its members, or elements. A set may have many, few, or no members. (A set with no members is called a *null* or *empty set*.) For example, the members of the class are a set.

Subset

A set within a given set. If the set is the members of the class, then one subset is all the boys in the class.

Comparison of sets

Relating two or more sets in terms of *more than* and *fewer than*. This concept is taught more easily after pairing has been introduced. Note that *more than* is learned more easily than *fewer than*.

Counting

Naming the numbers. Cardinal numbers tell us how many — for example; he has two hands and ten toes. Ordinal numbers tell us which one and express succession in a series—for example; the fifth child in the first row.

Rote/verbal counting

Reciting number names with little or no understanding of their meaning. This is one of the first number activities learned by children.

Rational counting

Matching and comparing in order to determine one-to-one correspondence; matching number names with objects.

Logical/cognitive counting

Placing numbers in a logical mental relationship; understanding that numbers represent quantity. The child arrives at logical counting by manipulating objects and internally structuring his or her knowledge.

SUGGESTIONS FOR MAKING COMPARISONS

Use opportunities during spontaneous play to give children practice in making comparisons.

Greater than/less than

This set of blocks is greater than that set. There is less water in my glass than in yours.

More/fewer

I have fewer crackers than you; you have more than Janey. Does Janey have more or fewer crackers than I?

Taller/shorter

Let's measure to see who is taller than 36". How can we tell if this string is shorter than that one?

Heavier/lighter	Jon is 1 pound heavier than he was the last time we weighed him. The baby guinea pig is lighter than this big brother.
Higher/lower	The red balloon is higher than the green one. What color balloon is lower than the green one?
Wider/narrower	You will need to make your road wider for the truck to fit on it. Can you find a truck that is narrower than the one you are holding?
Larger/smaller	My feet are larger than yours. Can you find someone whose feet are smaller than yours?

MATH ACTIVITIES

CLASSIFICATION: SORTING AND COMPARING

The following activities give children the opportunity to sort a variety of objects into groups according to such characteristics as color, size, shape, and design. They can then compare the groups to determine which one has more than or fewer than the other.

Sorting Beans

MATERIALS   An assortment of beans of different colors and shapes, such as red and white kidney beans, pinto beans, black beans, lima beans
Cloth on which to display the beans
An individual cloth placemat for each child

PROCEDURE
- Work with individual children or small groups of two to four children.
- Spread the beans out on a cloth.
- Give each child a placemat and ask:
  Do you want to sort beans?
- See if the children understand what it means to sort something. Some may simply pick up a handful of beans and begin to play with them. Watch and listen to see what the children do.
- Take a mat yourself and put a handful of beans on it. If the children need some subtle suggestions, sort the beans on your mat by color, saying:
  I think I'll put all the red beans in this pile. Let's see, what else can I do?
- Wait for suggestions from the children, or, if they are busy sorting, watch to see what characteristics they use to sort their beans.

- Encourage the children to think of different ways they can sort, and comment on what they are doing:

    I see Jamie is sorting his beans by shape. He's picking out kidney-shaped beans. Some are red and some are white, but they're all the same shape. Good thinking, Jamie.

    Margie, I see you sorted all your black beans into one pile. How else can you sort the rest of your beans?

Note: As children become familiar with sorting by size, shape, and color, you can introduce the concept of class inclusion—that is, all the members of one group can be part of another group at the same time. For example, a group of red kidney beans and a group of black beans are all beans. They are subsets of the set of beans.

Sorting Objects by a Common Characteristic

MATERIALS   A variety of objects in sets of three or more that are suitable for sorting, such as buttons or beads of different colors, sizes, numbers of holes, or shapes; marbles; table toys; or attribute blocks (small blocks of various colors and shapes)
Empty containers

PROCEDURE   • Ask the children to help sort the given objects by a common characteristic—for example, putting all the buttons in one container, all the beads in another, and so on.
- Watch to see how children decide to group the objects. Ask questions to determine why children made certain selections—for example, did they choose their favorite colors?
- When children are using beads or buttons, have them sort the objects into separate containers according to a common property they choose. Ask why they put a bead or button with a particular group.
- When children have had many opportunities to sort objects, suggest some simple characteristics they might sort by, such as color, shape, size, or number of holes.

Note: Clean-up time offers an excellent opportunity for sorting and classifying different kinds of objects (blocks, cooking equipment, dress-up items, wheel toys) and generally returning things to their proper places. Sorting and classifying provide the basis for all logical thought. In order to solve a problem, children need to learn how to sort available information and use that information to make decisions.

Matching Geometric Shapes

MATERIALS   Geometric shapes cut from construction paper or felt, including a circle, square, triangle, and rectangle
Paper clips
Pole (suitable for "fishing")
Magnets
String

PROCEDURE
- Cut 20 or more geometric shapes.
- Attach one paper clip to each form.
- Attach a magnet to a string about 25" long; attach the string to a pole.
- Spread forms on the floor.
- Hold up a shape, and let the children take turns fishing for the shape that matches yours. Ask the children to name to the shapes as they catch them.
- Hold up another shape, and repeat the process. Be sure every child has an opportunity to catch, match, and name a shape.
- Vary the activity by letting the children fish for any shape at random, naming each one as they catch it.

Sorting and Matching Geometric Shapes

MATERIALS
A large assortment of circles, triangles, squares, and rectangles cut from construction paper
A box divided into four equal compartments, with one of the shapes pasted in each of the compartments

PROCEDURE
- Mix all the shapes together.
- Have each child sort shapes into the appropriate compartments, naming the shapes as he or she matches them.
- Vary the activity by using different size shapes, using shapes of different colors, or having children sort shapes in any way they choose. (Many will sort by color first, then by shape, and finally by size.)

VARIATIONS
Cut sandwiches, cookies, and snacks into geometric shapes, and talk about the shapes as children eat. Or cut sponges into different shapes and have the children use them to paint designs on construction paper, posters, or wrapping paper.

Note: Have children help make a large poster of different shapes to display in the math center, along with materials for the above activity.

Matching Geometric Shapes

MATERIALS
Flannelboard
Felt or construction paper with sandpaper backing

PROCEDURE
- For each child, make two of each of these four shapes: circle, square, triangle, and rectangle. Keep one set for yourself.
- Put the shapes into a box and mix them up.
- Let each child take one shape.
- Place one of your shapes (for example, a triangle) on the flannelboard and ask:
  What is this shape called? Who has a triangle?
- Let each child holding a matching shape put his or hers on the flannelboard and pick out another shape.
- Continue playing the game until all the shapes have been used, or continue replacing the shapes from the flannelboard.

VARIATION   Have children take turns holding up their shapes, naming them, and finding someone in the group who has a matching shape.

Naming and Matching Geometric Forms

MATERIALS   Cards of heavy tagboard, each divided into a grid, with a shape in each square (see figure)
Cutout cardboard shapes to match those in the grids

PROCEDURE   • Give one grid card to each child playing the game.
• Place all the cardboard shapes in a pile in the middle of the table.
• Let each child take a turn picking a card from the pile, naming its shape, and placing the card on the appropriate square. If the child has no square to cover, he or she may put the shape back into the pile or give it to another child who needs it.
• As children learn the shapes, give each one a selection of cutout shapes. Then draw (or have one of the children draw) shapes from the box one at a time, calling them out as in Bingo. When you call a shape, the children cover that shape on their grids with the appropriate cutout.

VARIATION   Let children play with the game on their own in the math center, or have cardboard or tagboard shapes for children to trace or copy with crayons.

Making Geometric Shapes Using a Nailboard

MATERIALS   12" square of wood, $3/4$" thick
25 nails, 1– 1 $1/4$" long
Box of rubber bands

PROCEDURE   • After marking the wooden square, hammer the nails into but not through it in a 5 x 5 array.
• Use a rubber band to make a square shape, and ask each child to make a shape just like yours. (See Illustration 3.2.)
• Do the same with triangular and rectangular shapes, naming each shape as you make it.
• Place the nailboard and rubber bands in the math center, and let children experiment with making shapes.

Note: The nailboard can also be made with golf tees glued into a pegboard.

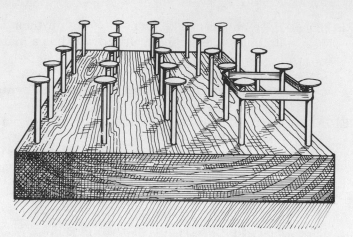

Illustration 3.2 **Using a nailboard to learn geometric shapes**

VARIATIONS   Some other things you can do:

- Have the children squeeze out white glue shapes on construction paper and cover the glue with yarn.
- Have the children look around the classroom and describe the shapes they find in the windows, doors, chairs, bookcases, blocks, balls, musical instruments, clocks, and so on.
- Distribute shapes at transition time, saying, for example:
  The children with triangles may go to the juice table.
  The children holding circles may get ready to go home.

Comparing Amounts and Weights

MATERIALS   Bathroom scale
Food scale (if available)
Homemade scale constructed from a wire coat hanger, string, and two large paper cups
Items suitable for weighing (beads, buttons, small blocks, marbles)

PROCEDURE   • Cut away the bottom of the wire coat hanger, leaving about 2" at either end to twist up; or pull the center section up and bend the ends of the hanger up. (See Illustration 3.3.)
- Cut two lengths of string each 10" long.
- Make two equidistant holes under the rim of each cup; attach the strings so as to suspend a cup from each end of the hanger.
- Hang the scale from a door knob or heavy nail.
- Have the children count out two sets of suitable items, weigh the sets, and compare them. Tell the children to add or subtract some of the items and then weigh and compare the sets again. Ask:
  How can we make them balance (equal)?
  Which group has more (fewer)?
  What do you need to make them weigh the same?
- Have them guess (estimate) how many items they might need to add or subtract to make the sets equal.

Illustration 3.3 **A coat hanger scale**

- Use the food scale to weigh fruits, vegetables, and nuts. Have the children place enough items on the scale to weigh one pound. As they become familiar with weighing, have the children estimate how many items will equal one pound before they weigh them.
- Let the children weigh themselves on a bathroom scale and then compare their weights. Make a chart or graph for them to keep a record of how much they weigh.

Note: Lead children to discover ways to compare amounts and weights of things that they cannot count, such as rice, sand, and liquids.

Provide cans and containers of varying sizes and shapes in the sandbox and housekeeping areas for children to use to compare amounts of sand and water.

CONSERVATION

The law of conservation states that the quantity of matter remains constant regardless of the shape the matter assumes. Preschool-age children need many opportunities to build their knowledge and understanding of conservation through hands-on play experiences. The ability to conserve develops gradually with many experiences over a period of years.

Conservation of Number

MATERIALS   Plastic chips or markers, all the same color
Egg cartons

PROCEDURE   • Work with individual children or small groups.
- Give each person an empty egg carton.
- Place a pile of plastic chips on the table.
  Have everyone put one chip in each cup of his or her carton. (With very young children, you may want to start with half a carton, or 6 cups.)
- Ask:
  Do we each have the same number?
  Do you have as many as I do?
  How can we tell if we each have the same number?

- Combine several of your chips into one cup while the children are watching.
- Ask:
  Do I still have the same number as you?
  How do you know?
- Have the children count their own and your chips.
- Let the children play with the chips in their own ways. Watch and listen as they count their chips.
- Ask:
  How can you make equal rows of chips?
- Rearrange the chips, keeping the numbers constant. Have the children count to see if the numbers are the same, even after the chips have been rearranged.

Conservation of Quantity—Volume and Number

MATERIALS   Playdough

PROCEDURE
- Work with a small group of children informally at a table.
- Make pretend cupcakes, loaves of bread, and cookies for a pretend bakery.
- As children begin to make their own items, copy their shapes and ask:
  Do we have the same number of cupcakes?
  Do I have the same amount of dough as you do?
- Re-form your pieces of playdough into a rope shape and ask:
  Now do I have the same as you?
- Continue comparing, shaping, and reshaping the playdough, and talk about how the amount of dough remains constant.

Note: The value of conservation activities lies in providing opportunities for children to *act on* objects rather than arrive at a correct answer. It is through their errors that young children learn. Make the activities fun and challenging by extending concept learning to other areas of the school.

Conservation of Quantity—Volume

MATERIALS   Clear plastic measuring cups
Clear plastic containers of different sizes and shapes
Water or other materials that can be poured, such as beans, rice, flour or sand
Food coloring (optional)

PROCEDURE
- Work with a small group of children at a table or some other area where they can pour water, beans, rice, flour, or sand. (A few drops of food coloring added to the water helps children see the level more easily.)

- Provide cups and other containers so that the children can pour the water or other materials back and forth. (See Illustration 3.4.)
- Place your measuring cup of water next to each child's glass and ask: **Do I have the same amount of water as you?**
- Let the children practice pouring liquids into a measuring cup to a certain level. Compare amounts by looking at the measurements indicated by the lines on the cups.
- When they have poured equal amounts into separate measuring cups, have the children pour the liquid from one of the cups into a different shaped container that you have selected. Ask: **Do you think I have as much water in here as you have in there? How can we find out? Let's pour this back into another measuring cup and see.**
- Let the children practice pouring all kinds of materials into different size containers. When they are participating in such activities as cooking, carpentry, and sand or water play, help them to observe how weight, number, length, quantity, and volume remain the same when the shape changes.

Illustration 3.4 **Practice pouring liquid**

SERIATION AND MEASUREMENT

Seriation is the ordering or sequencing of objects in relation to each other—for example, from largest to smallest. Seriation requires the ability to measure and compare. Although 4- and 5-year-olds are able to compare two objects at a time, they may have difficulty ordering a series of objects.

Ordering by Size

MATERIALS   Flannelboard
10 felt figures of people in a graduated series of sizes
10 felt hats of graduated sizes to fit the figures

PROCEDURE   • Line up 4 to 6 of the figures on the flannelboard, in order by size. Place the corresponding hats beneath the figures.
• Place the flannelboard where children can play with the figures and move them around on the board.
• Watch to see if they place the hats on the figures and order them according to size.
• Ask if the figures look alike:
  How are they different? (bigger/smaller)
  How are the hats different? (taller/shorter)
• Depending on the ages and experience of the children, you may want to start by using only a few figures, then add the hats and more figures as the children progress.

VARIATION   Use witches with hats or Christmas trees with stars.

Note: Children may want to simply manipulate the figures and tell stories with them, which is fine. Each time you set the flannelboard up, let the children help and watch while you place the figures and hats in proper order. Alternate ordering so that the children can see the series graduating from small on the left to large on the right and then from large on the left to small on the right. As you place the figures, ask the children to help you find the next larger or smaller figure.

Let them help you discover how they might simplify the task by locating the largest and the smallest figures and placing them at either end, to use for comparing and locating the remaining figures.

Children who are unable to grasp the concept of sequencing may have success with a set of graduated nesting barrels.

Ordering by Number

MATERIALS   String
Colored macaroni or beads

PROCEDURE   • Have the children help one another measure appropriate lengths of string to make necklaces.

Illustration 3.5 Using beads to make comparisons

- Have a model string of colored macaroni or beads in graduated numbers for children to copy (for example, one red macaroni, two blue, three green, four orange, etc.). Tape the model string horizontally to a piece of cardboard.
- Talk about the pattern of the sample necklace:
  What are the colors of the beads? (Name them.)
  How many red beads are there? (Count the beads of each color in graduated sequence, noticing that the string has one red, two blue, three green, and so on.)
- To help children who want to copy the sample string of beads, compare the sequential numbers by counting the beads of each color and naming the numbers that follow. They can also place their beads next to the sample string to compare.
- Some children will want to string the beads without regard for following a pattern, and that's okay, too.

Ordering by Size and Height

MATERIALS   Flannelboard
Two colors of felt or construction paper with sandpaper backing

PROCEDURE   • Cut 8–12 figures of cakes in graduated sizes, all of the same color.
- Cut 8–12 candles in graduated heights, all of the same color, but a color different from that of the cakes.

- Place 4 to 6 cakes in random order on the flannelboard.
- Working with one or two children, ask how the cakes are different. When the youngsters recognize that the cakes differ in size, ask if they can line the cakes up according to size. (You might want to pretend to be having a party for a large number of children, a smaller number of children, etc.)
- Place a corresponding number of candles in random order on the flannelboard. Ask how the candles are different. When the children recognize that the candles differ in height, have them place the candles on the appropriate cakes.
- Add more figures as children expand their abilities to order by size and height. Use the terms *bigger, smaller, taller,* and *shorter,* and encourge children to verbalize why and how they ordered the figures.

Ordering by Size and Number

MATERIALS   Construction paper
Shredded green plastic grass (the kind used for Easter baskets)
White egg-shaped beans (Great Northerns)
Glue

PROCEDURE
- Cut 6 to 10 construction paper circles in graduated sizes.
- Have the children help glue grass onto each circle to make nests.
- Begin by having the children place 3 to 5 nests in order by size.
- Provide egg-shaped beans for the children to place into the nests.
- As they play with the nests and eggs, suggest that they count out one egg for the smallest nest, two eggs for the next larger nest, working up to whatever number you feel is appropriate.
- Stress the concepts of *larger/smaller, more/less,* and *greater/fewer.*

Note: Allow plenty of time for the children to simply play with the materials. This activity works well with children who prefer three-dimensional materials over flannelboard figures.

Ordering by Height, Width, and Number

MATERIALS   Flannelboard
Brown felt material
Red felt material

PROCEDURE
- Cut 6 to 10 tree shapes out of brown felt. The trees should be graduated in terms of *width, height,* and *number of branches.*
- Cut enough apples out of the red felt to place one on each branch of each tree.
- Place 3 to 6 trees on the flannel board in random order, along with a number of apples.
- Working with one or two children, watch to see how they order the trees.
- Ask them to tell you how one tree is different from another (bigger/smaller; wider/narrower; taller/shorter; more or fewer branches).

- Suggest that they place one apple on each branch and arrange the trees in order according to height, width, and number of branches with apples.

Note: This is a complex activity requiring the ability to order by three different criteria. Do not expect most preschoolers to be able to do it quickly. It may be enough just to expose the children to materials that provide opportunities for them to construct their own knowledge from experience. Let them play with the trees and apples in their own ways. You can add other figures from previous activities to enable the children to make up stories.

Ordering by Length and Width

MATERIALS
Cloth tape measures
Rulers
Varying lengths of dowels
Strings
Straws
Blocks

PROCEDURE
- Give each child a tape measure.
- Talk about the numbers on the tape; identify and count the numbers if appropriate.
- Talk about ways measurement is used (to see how tall you are, how long the block is, how wide the door is, etc.).
- Provide easily measured objects so that the children can practice measuring and identifying the number of inches.
- Suggest that they find things that are of equal length and width.
- When talking about their measurements, use the terms *longer/shorter* and *wider/narrower*.

VARIATION
Instead of a tape measure, give each child a ball of string. Have the children measure different objects by cutting a string segment to the same length or width. Label each string with the name of the corresponding object.

Note: Include experience with measuring in other areas of the curriculum that provide opportunities for seriation and measurement, such as block, playdough, sand, and water play; cooking; and carpentry. Look for other ways to introduce children to sequencing by size, length, width, height, weight, and volume.

EQUIVALENCE: MATCHING AND PAIRING

Matching is one of the most direct ways of comparing objects to see if they are equivalent. Because children can make a one-to-one correspondence without understanding number concepts, comparing without counting is a prenumber activity. Such activities provide a foundation for understanding number.

Matching Objects *(one-to-one correspondence)*

MATERIALS Black buttons and white buttons, red beans and white beans, or similar contrasting objects

PROCEDURE
- Start by placing one black button on the table; ask a child to place one white button under yours.
- Continue to place one button at a time on the table, making sure the child is matching the buttons on a one-to-one basis. (See Illustration 3.6.)
- Count each row of buttons to reinforce equivalency. Say:
  You have five white buttons and I have the same number of black buttons, so your row of buttons is equal to my row.
- The next time you do this activity with the child, place several buttons in a row before you ask the child to make an equivalent row with his or her buttons. When the child has matched your row, count both rows simultaneously to determine if they are equal.
- Continue in this manner, changing the number of buttons and placing them closer or farther apart.
- Simplify or increase the complexity of the activity, depending on the ability of each child.

Note: Make the activity fun without stressing right or wrong. Take turns making the rows to be copied. Adapt one-to-one correspondence activities to other areas of the curriculum, such as block or playdough play, cooking, and carpentry.

Illustration 3.6 **Using buttons to practice one-to-one correspondence**

Matching and Pairing Pictures

MATERIALS   Blank 3" x 5" index cards
Assorted pairs of stickers

PROCEDURE   • Attach one sticker to each card
• Place all the cards face down on a table.
• Play a game with a small group of children, in which the children take turns picking up two cards.
• Say to the first child:
  Are your pictures the same?
  You have a pair because the pictures match; they're the same.
  Have the child place the cards next to him or her and take another turn.
• If the child selects two cards that are not the same, state that they are not a pair because they do not match. Replace those cards face down on the table.
• Let another child take a turn.

VARIATION   To increase the complexity of the game, use cards from a deck of playing cards.

Note: This game is popular among 5-year-olds and is a good activity for stimulating memory and recall.

Matching and Pairing Playing Cards

MATERIALS   One deck of playing cards, with jokers and face cards removed

PROCEDURE   • Work with small groups of older preschoolers. To begin with, you may want to use only cards with low numbers.
• Depending on the experience and abilities of the children, deal one or two cards, face up, to each child.
• Talk about the cards, the colors, the designs, and the number of spots on each card. Identify red hearts, red diamonds, black spades, and black clubs.
• After dealing the cards, turn the top card of the rest of the deck face up. Ask the first child to your left if he or she can match the card in suit or number. (For example, a 3 of hearts would match a 3 of spades, diamonds, or clubs; a card of one suit would match any other card of the same suit, regardless of the number.)
• If the child can match the card, he or she keeps the card, face down.
• Turn up another card for the next child, unless the first child did not make a match with the top card. Continue in this manner until the children have collected all the cards. (You can vary the procedure by letting children turn up two new cards of their choice from among the pack they have accumulated.)
• Let them count and match the cards they are holding.
• Encourage them to talk about how they matched and paired the cards.

Matching and Pairing Geometric Forms

MATERIALS   Felt or construction paper cut into squares, rectangles, circles, and triangles

PROCEDURE   • Place a sample of various shapes on a table or flannelboard.
• Hold up a shape, and ask the children to find another one just like it.
• Name the shapes as the children match them. Encourage the children to say the names, too.
• Let them practice pairing and matching shapes themselves, or have them take turns being the teacher.
• Suggest that they put a triangle on top of a circle (a circle on top of a rectangle, etc.) and pair that shape.

Note: Extend matching and pairing activities throughout the curriculum by having children match a set (2 pencils, 2 spoons, etc.), a group (3 bears with 3 beds), or two sets (3 hearts with 3 triangles).

Matching and Pairing Groups of Objects

MATERIALS   Flannelboard
Felt or construction paper cutouts of the characters from "The Three Little Pigs" (three different-colored pigs and the three kinds of houses—straw, twig, and brick) and "The Three Bears" (three different size chairs, bowls, and beds)

PROCEDURE   • Using the flannelboard and felt figures, tell the story of "The Three Little Pigs," emphasizing which pig goes with which house.
• When the children are familiar with this pairing, mix the houses and the pigs and let the children indicate which pig goes with which house.
• Repeat the same procedure using "The Three Bears."
• Leave the felt cutouts and flannelboard out for the children to play with.

VARIATION   Cut out matching felt shapes in the same and different colors. Let children match and pair shapes in similar or dissimilar sets.

NUMBER CONCEPTS

Young children first learn to recite numbers; later they learn to match the names of numbers with objects. The final stage is to learn logical counting—that is, to understand that numbers represent quantity.

Practicing Counting: Matching Objects to Dots

MATERIALS   Sheets of paper
Felt pens
Objects to count, such as chips, beans, buttons, or pennies

PROCEDURE
- Use a felt pen to mark 20 or more sheets of paper, each with 2 to 6 large dots. Run the dots in a straight line horizontally on some sheets, vertically on others, and in a random design on still others.
- Work with individual children or with small groups of children who are about equal in ability.
- Start simply, using a sheet that has no more than 4 dots.
- Ask the children to count out enough objects to cover each dot on the sheet; count out loud with them as they place each object on a dot.
- Have them practice with other sheets that have the same number of dots but placed in different designs.
- When the children are able to count and match objects to the dots accurately, have them count a given number of objects onto a blank sheet of paper.
- Increase the difficulty of the sheets by adding more dots and varying the designs. Give children plenty of time to practice before adding new sheets.

Note: When children are familiar with this activity, you can place it in the math center for them to use on their own.

Practicing Counting Objects

MATERIALS
Empty dozen-size egg cartons, one per child
20 or more small objects, such as pebbles or beans

PROCEDURE
- Have each child take a handful of pebbles or beans and sprinkle them randomly into an egg carton.
- Have the children close the cartons and shake them to distribute the objects.
- After opening the cartons, the children can count the number of objects in each cup by taking one object out at a time.

VARIATION
If peas in the pod are available, have the children shell the peas, counting each pea as they take it out of the pod. Then have them place the peas in the egg cartons, shake the cartons, and count the contents of each cup.

Note: If children are skipping objects or counting them more than once, use fewer objects.

Counting in Sequence

MATERIAL
7–10 small objects that are alike in shape and size, such as small blocks or beans

PROCEDURE
- Place the blocks in a container, and have a child count and remove one block at a time, counting out loud as he or she places the block on the table.
- If the child counts each block correctly, change the number by removing or adding blocks. Then ask the child to count them again.

- Have the child count blocks that have been arranged horizontally, then blocks that have been arranged vertically.
- After moving the blocks around on the table so that they are in a random pattern, ask the child to count the blocks again. Remove and add extra blocks each time to determine if the child knows how to attribute one number to each block or is simply counting randomly.
- Instruct the child to count and remove 6 blocks from a group of 10 or more.

Note: Four-and five-year-olds who know how to count verbally in the correct order may not recognize the need to order the objects (count them in sequence) in order to avoid missing some or counting some twice.

Give the children many opportunities to count objects by adapting the above procedure to other curriculum activities.

Sequencing Numbers

MATERIALS   2 wire coat hangers
15 clothes pins
5 pieces of tagboard
Felt pens
Cellophane tape

PROCEDURE
- Cut two pieces of tagboard 2½" square, two pieces 3" square, and one piece 4" square.
- Beginning with the smaller squares, mark each piece of tagboard in sequence. (See Illustration 3.7.) Use the largest square of tagboard for the numeral 5.
- Tape the tagboard numbers in sequence from left to right on one of the coat hangers
- Clip 15 clothes pins to the other hanger.
- Hang the hangers side by side on a pegboard or in some other convenient spot in the math center.
- Let the children work alone or together to clip the corresponding number of clothes pins to the numbered tags. (Stress the left-to-right progression.)

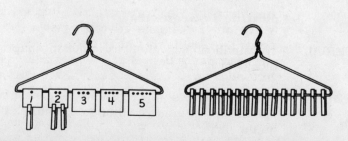

Illustration 3.7 **Using hangers to sequence numbers**

Practicing One-to-One Correspondence

MATERIALS   Egg carton
                 12 plastic eggs (the hollow kind that twist open), all the same size and color
                 Objects suitable for counting, such as buttons, Styrofoam packing beads, Cheerios, or beans

PROCEDURE   • With a felt pen, number the eggs from 1 to 12 and draw the corresponding number of dots on each egg.
                 • Place some eggs in the carton, the number depending on the child's ability. Put the counting materials in a separate container.
                 • Have the child place in each egg the number of buttons corresponding to the number indicated on the outside of the shell.
                 • Check for correct counting after each series. As children become more capable, add larger numbers and mix up the eggs.

Note: When the container is empty, ask the children how many buttons are left (none). Print 0 on a card, and tell the children that *zero* means the same as *none*. Place this activity in the math center once children are familiar with its use.

Counting with Dice

MATERIALS   3 clean half-pint milk cartons
                 Construction paper
                 Glue
                 Felt pen
                 Dice
                 Buttons, play coins, or other uniform small objects in a container

PROCEDURE   • Cut the tops off the milk cartons to make them into the shape of dice.
                 • Glue construction paper onto the cartons, to cover all sides of each die.
                 • Mark one die with dots only, one with dots and numerals, and one with numerals only.
                 • Have the children take turns throwing the die that has the dots only.
                 • Let each child count the number showing on the die and take an equal number of objects from the container.
                 • Introduce the dice according to children's developmental levels.
                 • When all the objects have been selected, have children sort and count the objects they have collected, and compare the objects using the terms *more than, less than*, and *same as.*
                 • Introduce regular dice after children have had success with the large ones.

VARIATION   Make a board game by marking spaces on a large piece of tagboard. Have the children throw the dice and move their markers (while counting out loud) the equivalent number of spaces. Notice whether they are counting correctly and moving one space for each number. When children are familiar with this game, place it in the math center.

Counting with Dots and Numerals

MATERIALS   Sandpaper or felt
Glue
Construction paper
A large piece of cardboard
Felt pen
Dot stickers all of the same size, shape, and color

PROCEDURE   • Cut the numerals 1 to 12 out of sandpaper or felt. Mount each number on a separate piece of construction paper.
• Have the children name the numerals as they trace each one with their fingers.
• Use a felt pen to mark 12 squares on the piece of cardboard.
• Moving from left to right, place the appropriate number of dots in each square. (See Illustration 3.8.)
• Have the children count the number of dots in each square and place the corresponding numeral in the square.

Note: You may find it helpful to make a simple number line showing the numerals and dots in correct sequence, which the children can refer to as they work.

ORDINAL NUMBERS

Ordinal numbers tell us *which one* and express succession in a series—for example, the *fifth* child in the *first* row.

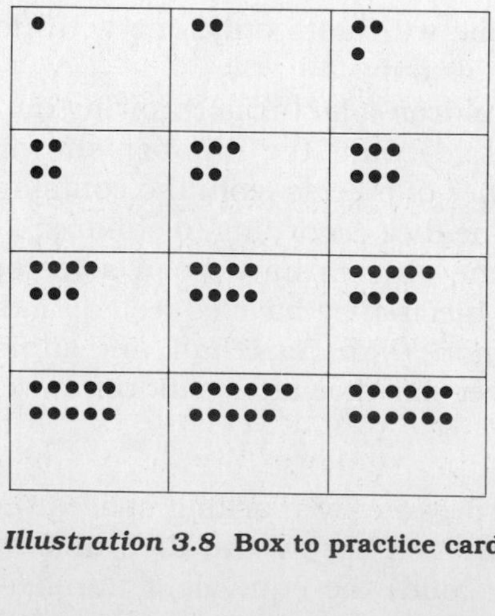

Illustration 3.8 **Box to practice cardinal numbers**

Practicing with Ordinal Numbers

MATERIALS   Bean bags
Tagboard
Paint and paintbrush

PROCEDURE
- Paint a target on the tagboard.
- Give each of four or five children a bean bag and say:
  How many bean bags are there?
  Let's count them: 1, 2, 3, 4, 5.
  Let's take turns throwing the bean bags at the target.
  Do you think you can hit this spot (point to the center mark) **on the target?**
- Assign each child a number by pointing to them one by one and saying
  You are first, you are second, you are third, you are fourth, and you are fifth.
  Let's say the numbers together: first, second, third, fourth, fifth.
- Have the children throw the bean bags in the proper order, repeating their respective ordinal numbers.

Practicing with Ordinal Numbers

MATERIALS   5 paper cups
Felt pen
Button or coin

PROCEDURE
- Label the bottoms of paper cups as follows: 1st, 2nd, 3rd, 4th, 5th.
- Place the cups upside down on a table.
- Have the children close their eyes while you hide a button under one of the cups.
- Have the children open their eyes and take turns (identify who goes first, second, etc.) guessing which cup the button is under. The child must say, "The button is under the first (second, third, fourth, fifth) cup."
- Children who are unable to identify the labels may point to a cup, but they must verbalize the ordinal number.

VARIATION   Collect paper plates and container tops, both round and square, in graduated sizes. Label them 1st, 2nd, 3rd, 4th, 5th, etc. Put them in the math center for children to use to practice sequencing.

Note: Reinforce the use of ordinal numbers when children are taking turns ("Jimmy goes first, Nancy is second, and who wants to be third?"). Use ordinal numbers when children sign up for turns at the computer or the woodworking table. Instead of calling on children, identify the order in which they can participate during group time. Ask children to recall whether they were first, second, third, etc.

Using Ordinal Numbers with Matching and Nonmatching Items

MATERIALS   A box filled with matching pairs of items such as bottle caps, spools, buttons, marbles, small toys
Two place mats

PROCEDURE
- Place seven nonmatching items in a row on a place mat. This row will serve as a model.
- Give a child another place mat, making certain that it is at least 10" away from the model.
- Ask the child to copy the model by placing matching items in the order shown.
- Provide help as needed, encouraging each child to verbalize the ordinal sequence (for example, "The first item is a marble, the second is a button, the third is a bottle cap," and so on).

VARIATION   Collect simple drawings or pictures that show a sequence of experiences familiar to children (for example, getting up in the morning, washing, eating breakfast, going to school). Place each set of pictures in a separate envelope. Let the children sort the pictures into the proper sequence, telling what happens first, second, third, etc.

Sequence pictures can also be made for the flannelboard and stored in the math center for children to use.

Bibliography of Resources

Baratta-Lorton, Mary. *Workjobs II: Number Activities for Early Childhood.* Menlo Park, CA: Addison-Wesley, 1979. A popular resource book of manipulative tasks in math readiness, using common materials. Appropriate for prekindergarten and early elementary. Many ideas can be adapted for younger children.

Brown, Sam (ed.). *One, Two, Buckle My Shoe.* Mt. Rainier, MD: Gryphon House, 1982. Activities of varying degrees of difficulty, designed for parents and teachers to use with young children. For each activity, the text describes the common materials needed, the concept to teach, and the vocabulary to use.

Debelak, Marianne, et al. *Creating Innovative Classroom Materials for Teaching Young Children.* New York, NY: Harcourt Brace, 1981. Provides teachers with ideas for developing games that are suitable for teaching young children basic math concepts.

Ginsburg, Herbert. *Children's Arithmetic: How They Learn It & How You Teach It.* Austin, TX: PRO-ED, 1982. Discusses children's strategies with arithmetic, the sources of their mistakes, and appropriate ways to teach young children.

Golick, Margie. *Deal Me In! The Use of Playing Cards in Teaching and Learning.* Austin, TX: Monarch, 1985. More than 100 games for children ages 4 and older, classified by age level.

Holt, Michael. *Math, Puzzles, and Games.* New York, NY: Walker, 1983. Puzzles and games of logic for children ages 4 and older.

Kamii, Constance. *Number in Preschool and Kindergarten.* Washington, DC: NAEYC, 1982. A Piagetian-based resource encouraging teachers to build on number relationships derived from children's personal experiences, rather than use workbooks.

Nuffield Foundation. *Nuffield Maths: Three & Four.* White Plains, NY: Longman, 1981. A series of booklets and worksheets designed to help young children perceive the patterns and relationships of mathematics. It includes many useful projects and activities that give preschool children experience with space, shape, size, matching, and measuring.

Sharp, Evelyn. *Thinking Is Child's Play.* New York, NY: Avon, 1982. Forty games based on Piaget's work, stressing learning concepts through manipulation of objects. Each activity is presented in a simple format, with purpose, materials, comments, and illustrations. The simply written text makes it possible for parents and teachers of young children to appreciate and put into practice some of Piaget's impressive research findings.

Zaslavsky, Claudia. *Preparing Young Children for Math, A Book of Games.* New York, NY: Schocken Books, 1986. A simply and clearly written book that tells how parents and teachers can make mathematics a part of the everyday life of the child 2–8 years old. Activities are designed to help children acquire math concepts while doing daily chores and playing.

PART FOUR

Language Arts

Introduction to Language Arts

LANGUAGE AND COMMUNICATION

One of the most exciting and complex achievements of a preschooler is learning to talk. A teacher is privileged to be part of the most dramatic period of language development in a child's life.

Teachers share in the daily discovery of words and phrases as a child's language skills mature and new avenues of communication are explored. Observing the change from the compressed style of a toddler's message ("all gone" or "more milk") to the complex forms of a 3-year-old's "I don't want to do that anymore," the teacher encounters one of the most impressive feats of a young child's development.

HOW LANGUAGE IS ACQUIRED

Children seem not to be taught a language so much as to acquire it on their own. Preschoolers are not passive learners. They absorb words during play, imitate adults' conversational phrases, and repeat stories read to them. By the age of 6, a child has learned most of the adult patterns of speech.

Although imitation and modeling are important factors in speech development, researchers are not clear about the exact way in which children learn to speak. One principle of significance to early education, however, is that *children learn to speak by speaking*. Thus, opportunities for children to practice speaking are very important.

Studies show that imitation and instruction do not adequately account for language acquisition. They do, however, play a role. Expanding vocabulary, labeling, and clarifying the exact meanings of words are among the skills that probably respond to reinforcement and imitation.

Interestingly, however, findings point to the fact that these familiar learning processes do not account for much of children's speech or for the phases through which it develops. Most children will use double negatives (for example, "I don't want no juice") for a short time during their language learning, despite the fact that they may never hear their parents or other adults use this form of speech.

Teachers will recognize how children, in making up words, seem to be applying principles they learned to use in solving problems of phrasing or tense. The familiar errors in past participle ("He goed to school," "I holded the rabbit") are not imitations. They are words that seem to be applications of the rule that actions which took place in the past are indicated by adding *ed* to the end of a verb. No one teaches children this rule and they certainly could not describe it, but somehow they come to sense and apply it. Usually it works, but occasionally results in an error. Children make up and form their own language by applying such rules. It is in this sense that language grows through the interaction between the child's capabilities and the language of his or her surroundings. This is a dramatic example of the role of the child's own inner curriculum in the preschool classroom.

SEQUENCES IN SPEECH AND LANGUAGE DEVELOPMENT

There are great differences among children in the age at which they begin to acquire language and the rapidity with which they reach adult levels of competence. The sequence in which language is acquired, however, appears to be similar for most children.

Age	Ability
1 year	Responds to own name; recognizes names of family members and familiar objects. Is interested in new sounds. Can vocalize a variety of sounds to indicate desire for attention, pleasure, and displeasure. Babbles and may have several words such as *mama, dada,* and *ball* in his or her vocabulary.
2 years	Is able to follow simple commands without visual cues: *David, get your hat and give it to Daddy; Debbie, bring me your ball.* Uses a variety of everyday words heard at home: *Mommy, milk, ball, hat, bottle.* Can put several words together (*more juice, go bye-bye car, milk all gone*), and begin to ask routine questions such as *Where Daddy?*
3 years	Understands and uses words other than for naming—for example, descriptive words such as *big, little, hot, cold*; spatial words such as *in, under, on top of*; pronouns such as *he, she, mine, yours.* The child is able to fit simple pronouns, verbs, adjectives, prepositions, and nouns together to make complete sentences: *I pushed the big ball down the hill.* The 3-year-old has a vocabulary of between 300 and 600 words and is now asking questions like *Why? Who is it? What is that?*
4 years	Speaks in more complete sentences. Can follow multistep directions: *Bobby, go find the guinea pig and put it*

back in its cage. The 4-year-old is able to give a connected account of a recent experience (with some gram-
matical errors), asks lots of questions, and can carry on
a simple conversation. The child is beginning to understand size and shape concepts.

5 years   Speaks intelligibly, although some sounds may still be
mispronounced. Can listen to a story and answer questions about it. Is interested in meanings of words and
can define common words. The 5-year-old is able to
communicate ideas, acquire information, and generally
carry on more complex social interaction by listening
and speaking.

6 years   Has learned most of the adult patterns of speech and is
using language to learn new skills, such as reading and
writing.

PLANNING THE CURRICULUM

In planning the language arts curriculum, keep in mind that children
learn to speak by speaking. Opportunities to practice conversation
with adults are especially important during the preschool years.

Children will talk more about things that are important to them
than they will about other subjects. Monitor teacher-child talk for a
period of time, and certain patterns will become clear. Some adults
tend to lean toward the interview technique: "What is your name?"
"How old are you?" "Where do you live?" "Do you have brothers and
sisters?" and so forth. These questions usually prompt simple one- or
two-word replies. The teacher who consciously picks up on topics and
activities that are of interest to children will get more elaborate verbal
responses.

Teachers are in danger of carrying on monologues if they do not
listen to themselves. Directions ("Put the brush in the paint can"),
comments ("I like what you're doing"), and warnings ("Be careful not
to spill") constitute much of a teacher's verbalization during a work-
day. Such utterances do not encourage extended conversations. Equal
interaction between adult and child does not happen accidentally;
teachers need to monitor themselves and plan an environment where
such interaction can take place naturally.

Provide activities that lend themselves easily to verbal interaction,
and relate verbal exchange to the real world whenever possible. Set up
snacks and meals for small groups so that individuals can speak and
listen to one another. Allow plenty of time and space during stories or
sharing for children to express themselves. Plan an environment in
which conversation is natural and enjoyable.

When teachers make informative comments ("I notice that you
helped Janie put the toys away today"), ask open-ended questions
("What do you suppose Seth wanted to do?"), and encourage thinking
responses ("I wonder why that happened"), children are more likely to
respond and be motivated to carry on extended conversations.

The teacher who is most likely to succeed in motivating children
to talk is the one who listens carefully and watches for clues about the

child's interest and concerns. Attending totally to children means not finishing their sentences for them or assuming that you already know what they want to say. Ask children to elaborate and explain what it is they mean when they make comments. For example, if a child complains that another child "won't share," ask the youngster to tell you what he or she means and to verbalize in greater detail how such a conclusion was reached. When children expand on their ideas, they gain practice in verbalizing and also clarify their thought processes for themselves and the listener.

Sometimes teachers are guilty of using comfortable phrases ("That's nice, honey," "I like that," "You're doing a good job," "How are we doing here?) without really expecting any response from children. Such phrases do not encourage the child to think; they become hollow, and soon the children learn to tune them out.

Teachers can help stretch a child's verbal abilities by using a wide variety of expressions that are a bit more complex than those the child is using. Instead of saying "Marty, think of another way to do that," the teacher might say, "Marty, have you considered other possibilities?" Marty might not be able to define all the teacher's words, but he will be challenged in a nonthreatening way to think about the meanings of words in a given context. The teacher must be careful, however, to see that the child does not have to stretch too much to comprehend.

Use language to help children focus on their activities: "Joshua uses both hands to hold on"; Claudia is hopping on her right foot"; "Peter knows how to go down the slide slowly. Now he's going very, very slowly."

Make comments that encourage responses: "I wonder how you made this design"; "That's an interesting way to do it"; "I'd like to have you tell me more."

Phrase comments and questions so that they require more than a yes or no answer. Instead of "Do you want to read a story?" you might say, "I wonder if you remember the funny story we read yesterday about the silly bear."

Teachers tend to address their remarks to the children who respond. Unless the adult is sensitive to this tendency, he or she is likely to overlook the shy or quiet child who is reluctant to talk. Sometimes there may be a language or hearing deficiency or handicap of some sort. It is important that the teacher initiate conversations with reluctant youngsters and persist in talking and encouraging discussion. Quiet children appear to respond favorably to the friendly, warm, and chatty teacher who makes no demands for verbal response. The interview technique would be least successful with these children.

Young children for whom English is a second language may have difficulty in making the transition to verbalizing, even when they understand what they hear. Some cultures discourage children from questioning an adult or making eye contact. A sensitive and loving teacher—one who does not treat these children as though they were less intelligent than the rest of the class—can do much to help them risk speaking in a less familiar tongue.

Although many of the activities that follow are presented in a structured format, they are intended to be adapted and extended for use in a friendly, safe environment. Teaching language does not require a formal teacher-directed setting, where the child sits and listens passively and then responds to questions. Young children learn to speak best when they are actively engaged in doing something of real interest to them and relating their physical activities to appropriate speech. Language competencies are enhanced by activities that encourage cooperation and interaction: select cooking recipes that enhance cooperation, establish guidelines for the computer that require children to work together, suggest a large group building project with blocks and woodworking, introduce enticing dramatic play materials, assign quiet children to be partners of more verbal youngsters. The teacher who is sensitive to opportunities for language enhancement will create an atmosphere where talking and listening are fun, where adults and children enjoy themselves and each other, and where language competence can grow and flourish.

The activities in this section cover the following areas:

Speaking	Developing fluency, acquiring new words and concepts
Listening	Learning to attend to speech and stories, discriminating sounds
Prereading	Recognizing letters and numbers, discriminating visual patterns, developing vocabulary, becoming familiar with printed materials, following the sequence of a story, developing perceptual skills
Prewriting	Developing motor skills, becoming familiar with writing

PLANNING THE LANGUAGE ARTS AREA

Locate the language arts activities in a part of the classroom that is well lit, quiet, and somewhat secluded. The area should be a place where children can relax and be free from distractions.

Provide some cozy and comfortable places to curl up with a book, such as a bean-bag chair, large pillows and cushions, a rocking chair, and other soft furniture. Include a child-size table and chairs. (See Illustration 4.1.)

There should be as much natural light as possible, supplemented by floor lamps with three-way incandescent bulbs. Avoid direct fluorescent lighting, which is too harsh. Hanging plants and other greenery will add a warm touch.

Decorate the walls with book jackets, posters depicting storybooks, and appropriate photos. Display some books in an upright position so that children can see the covers. Have a theme table, where selected topics can be highlighted with books and related objects (for example. seashells, dinosaurs, or rocks).

Ideally, the book area should lead into an adjacent listening and writing center, where children can select and listen to audio tapes of music or stories. Word/picture instructions along with color-coded pushbuttons on tape recorders can help children become more independent. Tapes of stories can be attached to the appropriate books with Velcro. Provide open shelf space for easy storage of listening materials.

A writing area might consist of a chalkboard at child's height, a simple typewriter, a table, and a shelf with tracing materials, felt pens,

Illustration 4.1 The library area

crayons, pencils, and lined paper. Colorful eye-level displays of rebus stories (see page 185) and the children's own dictated stories are attractive and help the youngsters build a sense of pride in their work.

For selections of storybooks and related language arts materials, see the annotated bibliography and resource lists at the end of this section.

Language Arts Activities

SPEAKING

The activities in this section are designed to give children the opportunity to practice speech. The emphasis is on active participation in verbalization.

Using Sentences to Describe Pictures

MATERIALS   Magazine pictures of subjects familiar to the children
Candid photos of the children engaging in activities at the school

Tagboard
Glue
Felt pen

PROCEDURE
- Mount the pictures and photos on tagboard, leaving enough space below each picture to attach paper for writing.
- Hold up a picture and ask the children to tell what is happening in it.
- Invite each child to help dictate what you should print under the picture. Encourage, but do not insist on, the use of complete sentences.
- Help children associate speaking with writing by asking them to help you repeat the sentence after it is written.
- Show the pictures another time and, with the children's help, read and add to the existing descriptions.

Note: Add new pictures from time to time. Large ones are most effective for group use.

Work on an individual basis with youngsters who are reluctant to speak in a group.

Combining Actions with Words

MATERIAL   None

PROCEDURE
- Do one or more of the following finger plays slowly, enunciating clearly.

Open, Shut Them (Use appropriate hand and finger movements.)

Open, shut them, open, shut them;
Make a little clap.
Open, shut them, open, shut them;
Put them in your lap.

Open, shut them, open, shut them;
Clasp them very tight.
Open, shut them, open, shut them;
Shake them out so light.

Creep them, creep them,
Creep them, creep them,
Right up to your chin,
Open up your little mouth,
But do not let them in.

Creep them, creep them, slowly upward
To your rosy cheeks;
Open wide your shining eyes,
Through your fingers peek.

Open, shut them, open, shut them;
To your shoulders fly.
Let them like the little birdies
Flutter to the sky.

Falling, falling, downward falling,
Nearly touch the ground,
Quickly raising all your fingers,
Twirl them round and round.
Slower, slower, slower, slower,
STOP!

Where Is Thumbkin?

Where is Thumbkin? Where is Thumbkin?
Here I am. [Hold up one thumb.]
Here I am. [Hold up other thumb.]
How are you today, sir? [Wiggle one thumb.]
Very fine, I thank you. [Wiggle other thumb.]
Run away, run away. [Hide hands behind back.]

[Do the same movements with your other fingers, calling them
   Pointer, Tall Man, Ring Man, and Pinky.]

Eensy Weensy Spider

The eensy, weensy spider climbed up the water spout. [Place left
   thumb on right forefinger, and repeat the climbing motion with
   fingers.]
Down came the rain [starting above head, drop both hands, wrig-
   gling fingers.]
And washed the spider out.
Out came the sun
[Make "sun" with both hands over head.]
And dried up all the rain.
And the eensy, weensy spider climbed up the spout again. [Repeat
   climbing motion.]

Mr. Brown and Mr. Black

Note: This one requires a bit more eye-hand coordination, but is
very popular. Children like to add to the story by having Mr.
Brown and Mr. Black ride motorcycles (making appropriate
sounds when they start up the engines), meet for tea (going
through the motions of adding a number of sugar cubes, pouring
the cream, stirring, sipping, and blowing on the tea to cool it
down), go home to take a nap, and so on.

[Make two fists, with thumb in each fist.] This is Mr. Brown's
house [show one fist], and this is Mr. Black's house [show other
fist]. One day Mr. Brown decided to visit Mr. Black, so he opened
the door [open fingers], went out the door [thumb up], and shut
the door [close fingers]. He got into his car [or bike, or motorcycle]
and went up the hill and down the hill [make up and down movements with fist and thumb] until he got to Mr. Black's house. He
knocked on the door [make knocking sounds with tongue on roof
of mouth], but there was no answer, so he rang the bell [make
ringing or buzzing sounds]. Still there was no answer, so he got
back into his car and went up the hill and down the hill [etc.] until
he got home, opened the door, went inside the house, and shut the
door. [Use appropriate motions, ending with thumb in fist.]

The next day, Mr. Black decided he would visit Mr. Brown. [Repeat the story and actions above, exchanging the names.]

Finally, both Mr. Brown and Mr. Black decide to go visiting, and both open their doors [etc.] until they meet each other at the top of a hill. "Why, how do you do, Mr. Brown?" "How do you do, Mr. Black?" [Wiggle thumbs at each other.] "Good to see you [etc.]" Both go up and down the hill to get home, open the doors, close the doors and go to bed.

- Repeat each play several times, watching individual children to determine the degree to which each is able to recite and follow the actions. Sometimes children respond well if they can sit on an adult's lap and have the adult help them with the actions and recitation.
- Reinforce the finger plays at other times throughout the day—for example, at the lunch table and during transition times.
- Make copies of the finger plays, with descriptions of appropriate movements. Tell the children the finger play you just did is written on the piece of paper. Ask if they would like to take a copy home to teach their parents and other family members. You may wish to print each child's name on a paper, but make the papers available to all parents.

A statement such as the following should accompany the copies sent home to parents:

For many young children, finger plays are an excellent introduction to the language arts. These simple activities are really short stories, with a beginning, a climax, and an end. They require the child to listen, to follow a sequence, to verbalize, and to coordinate movements with words. They do not require a long attention span. Their rhythmic repetitiveness and simplicity are engaging and fun!

Note: See the bibliography at the end of this section for books of finger plays.

Telling Stories Using Wordless Books

MATERIAL   Picture books without words, such as *Moonlight* and *Sunshine*, both by Jan Ormerod (Lothrop, 1982) (See the section of the bibliography "Picture Books Without Words" for other selections.)

PROCEDURE   • Look at the books with one child at a time. Let the child take the lead in turning the pages and making comments about the pictures.
- Encourage the child to use descriptive words and phrases rather than simply name objects.
- Use comments such as "Sometimes we don't want to go to bed . . ." and "I wonder what is happening here. . . ." Wait for the child to talk, and then build on his or her comments.
- Accept the child's story, noting the complexity of speech and the ability to accurately describe and develop a story by interpreting the sequence of pictures.

• At a later time, offer to write the child's story to accompany the pictures.

Note: Add other wordless books as children become more adept at telling stories. Since the vignettes in both books offer familiar family scenes, allow time for the child to talk about his or her family and whatever other thoughts the pictures may elicit.

Telling a Story in Correct Sequence

MATERIALS   Flannelboard
Flannel or Pellon pictures based on simple books such as *The Carrot Seed*, by Ruth Krauss (New York, NY: Scholastic, 1971); *The Adventures of Paddy Pork*, by John S. Goodall (New York, NY: Harcourt, 1968); *Pig Pig Grows Up*, by David McPhail (New York, NY: Dutton, 1980)
Construction paper
Strip magnets (available at craft stores)
Magnetic board
Envelopes or ziplock bags

PROCEDURE   • Copy the pictures of the stories onto flannel or Pellon. (Enlarge the small pictures, such as those in Paddy Pork.)
• Package the pictures for each story in separate envelopes or ziplock bags.
• After you and the children have told a story using the book, put the book away and let them retell the story using flannel pictures.
• Make magnetic board stories by copying the illustrations onto construction paper. Back the cutout characters with strip magnets. The pictures will adhere to a magnetic board, a cookie sheet, or a refrigerator.

Note: Practice in sequencing is important for the development of reading and writing skills.

Select books that have a simple repetitive theme.

Leave the flannel figures out for children to use in telling their own stories.

Recognizing and Describing Objects

MATERIALS   Pictures of familiar objects, such as animals, furniture, vehicles, food, play equipment
Cardboard
Adhesive

PROCEDURE   • Mount each picture on a piece of cardboard.
• Display one picture at a time, and invite the children to help you describe each one. Call attention to details of color, size, shape, how the subject of the picture is used, where it is found, and the group to which it belongs (animal, food, wheel toys, etc.).

USING A FLANNELBOARD

- When using a flannelboard, place it on an easel or a stand so that all the children can see it easily. To avoid neck strain, children need to be seated farther away from the teacher than when a book is being read.
- Arrange the figures in correct sequence, and keep them in a folder out of sight of the children. Staple the story to the outside of the folder for easy reference.
- Maintain eye contact with the audience. Beginners have a tendency to concentrate so much on placing the figures that they direct their voices and attention to the board rather than to the children.
- Make an extra set of figures for the children to play with at other times of the day.

- After the children are familiar with the pictures, play a game in which you keep the pictures hidden from their view. You describe a picture, giving additional clues as needed, until they can guess which picture you are describing.
- Hand pictures out to the children, and let each child take a turn describing the picture he or she is holding while the others guess what it is. Encourage them to use complete sentences and descriptive phrases.

Note: When working with very young children or those with limited vocabularies, use pictures of one class of objects, such as food; display pictures to provide visual clues. For older and more verbal children, you can add "secret pictures" that they have not seen.

Naming and Describing Single and Plural Objects

MATERIALS   Pictures of animals, people, familiar objects—some showing a single object, others showing more than one object (for example, one car/several cars, one child/several children)
Construction paper or cardboard
Adhesive
Paper clips
Small poles
String
Small magnets

PROCEDURE
- Mount pictures on cardboard or construction paper.
- Attach a paper clip to each picture.
- Make fishing poles by attaching string and a magnet to each pole.
- Place the pictures with paper clips in a container.
- Let the children fish for pictures.
- Have each child identify and describe the object(s) he or she has caught, using the correct singular or plural words. Make it clear that

the statement "This is a ___ " refers to one thing, and the statement "These are ___ " means more than one.

• When children become adept at describing singular and plural objects, vary the game by having them use more than one sentence and compound sentences to describe the object(s). For example, "This is a car. It is red and has four wheels."

Sorting and Describing Objects by Size and Color

MATERIALS   Red buttons and white buttons (Include large and small buttons of each color, as well as buttons with different numbers of holes.)
Cigar box, shoe box, or similar container
Two smaller boxes or two paper mats for each child to use for sorting buttons

PROCEDURE   • Working with one or two children at a time, hold up a large red button and ask:
Can you tell me what this is called?
• Have the children describe the shape of the button, the color, and the number of holes. Allow plenty of time to talk about buttons and related subjects.
• Compare a red button with a white one. Talk about the differences in size, shape, color, and number of holes.
• Have them pretend to buy a button from you to replace one that is missing from their coat. Have them use words and sentences to describe what the button looks like. If their descriptions are not detailed enough, make a game of the process by bringing out buttons that do not match.
• Giving two mats or boxes to each child, let them sort the buttons in any way they choose.
• Have them describe why they sorted them the way they did.
• Ask if they can sort them in other ways (small, large, two holes, four holes, etc.).

Learning to Say Names, Addresses, and Telephone Numbers

MATERIALS   List of children's names, addresses, and telephone numbers
Police officer's hat and badge, if available
Fairy wand (wooden dowel with star attached)

PROCEDURE   • To introduce a game about being lost, talk about how it might feel to be lost. Ask the children who might help them find their way home.
• Ask:
Do you think a police officer could help you?
How would you tell the officer where you live?
• Put on a police officer's hat, badge, or some other identifying symbol. Let children take turns telling you their names, addresses, and phone numbers.

• Play another game of pretend in which you are a fairy granting one wish to each child. The children must leave their names, addresses, and phone numbers for you so that you can deliver their wishes.
• Print a separate card for each child as he or she dictates the information.
• When the game is over, give each child his or her card to keep.

LISTENING

There are different levels of listening:

Appreciative   Listening to music, poetry, or stories without necessarily understanding the meanings of all the words

Purposeful   Following and responding to directions

Discriminative   Being aware of changes in sounds, pitch, loudness

Creative   Responding imaginatively and emotionally to words, stories, and other listening experiences

Critical   Evaluating and formulating opinions based on what one hears

Listening to a Puppet

MATERIALS   Styrofoam ball
Colorful material
Velcro
6" length of wooden dowel
2 rubber bands
Felt pen

Illustration 4.2   **Children using puppets**

Selection of poems and nursery rhymes (See the Note below or refer to the bibliography at the end of this section.)

PROCEDURE
- Cut a triangular bandanna to fit the Styrofoam head of the puppet.
- Attach Velcro to hold the bandanna together under the puppet's chin.
- Invite the children to watch while you make a puppet.
- Describe what you are doing as you build the puppet. It is all right to use words that the children might not understand if they can infer meanings from what you are doing. Enunciate clearly and speak slowly:
  This is the way I make a puppet. First, I take a Styrofoam ball. Next, I insert this length of wooden dowel into the Styrofoam ball . . . .
- After making a hole, remove the dowel, center a piece of cloth over the tip of the dowel, and reinsert the dowel into the Styrofoam.
- Insert your hand under the cloth. Gather some of the cloth around your middle finger, and secure it with a rubber band; repeat the procedure with your thumb. You will now have a puppet figure with two wiggly arms. Your first finger should be behind the dowel, the thumb and other fingers pressing against the dowel.
- Make eyes, nose, and mouth with the felt pen.
- Give the puppet a name.
- Tell the children that the puppet wants to recite some poems or nursery rhymes. (You can dramatize the incident by having the puppet whisper in your ear because it is shy.) Ask the children to listen carefully while you recite a selection of poems and rhymes, using the puppet with animation.

Note: You may wish to have materials ready for the children to make their own puppets after they are finished listening. Send copies of the poems home for family members to read to the children. *Poems to Read to the Very Young*, by Josette Frank (Random House), has many time-tested, easy-to-memorize poems. The popular rhymes of Mother Goose are presented in rebus form (picture words) in *Mother Goose Picture Riddles*, illustrated by Lisl Weil (Holiday House).

HELPFUL HINTS

When working with children for whom English is a second language, take slides of their experiences at school—even their unhappy moments. Include pictures of the child's parents to show what they are doing while the child is in school.

Write a story about the child's adjustment to school over a period of time. Have the story translated into the child's native language. Tape-record the story, synchronizing the tape with the slides. The audio portion accompanying each slide should present the child's native language first, followed by the English translation.

There are fairly inexpensive tape recorders and slide projectors that a child can operate.

Listening to and Following Directions

MATERIALS
Noise-making objects, such as bell, rattle, tambourine, egg beater, two wooden blocks
Other objects such as a chair, cap, book, ball

PROCEDURE
- Invite the children to play a game that requires careful listening.
- Have the children help you name the objects as you place each one in front of them.
- Explain the game:
  Listen carefully while I tell you what to do. Then I will ask who wants to do it.
  First shake the rattle; then put on the baseball cap. Who wants to do this?
- Continue giving directions two at a time until the group finds following them easy.
- Increase the number of tasks, adjusting the degree of difficulty for each child.

Note: Following directions in sequence is a complex task requiring the ability to hold one or more ideas in mind while acting on another one.

During spontaneous play situations, look for opportunities to give children additional experiences in following directions, such as
Take two big steps, hop, and turn around.
Hop-hop-hop, jump, hop.

Discriminating Sounds

MATERIALS
Bag or box containing sound-making objects, such as bells, whistles, rattles, paper to tear, rhythm instruments
Tape recorder
Tape of familiar sounds such as an alarm clock ringing, telephone ringing, train whistle blowing, automobile horn blowing, dog barking, cat meowing, clock ticking

PROCEDURE
- To play a game of guessing sounds, have the children turn their backs toward you or cover their eyes while you make a sound with one of the objects from your box.
- When the children are able to identify the sounds easily, make two different sounds for them to identify.
- Add new sound-making objects to further test their ability to discriminate sounds.
- Play the tape and have the children identify the sounds, gradually increasing the number of sounds in the sequence.
- Have children take turns making sounds with their bodies while others cover their eyes and guess how the sounds were made. Some children may need suggestions for sounds they might want to make, such as clicking the tongue, clapping hands, stomping feet, patting the body, coughing, whistling.

Hearing Rhyming Sounds; Matching Rhyming Objects

MATERIALS   Shoe box or similar container

Collection of small objects with rhyming names, such as tire/wire, hook/book, shell/bell, fork/cork, cane/plane, mouse/house

Construction-paper mat, marked off into six equal squares (See Illustration 4.3.)

Tagboard cards

PROCEDURE

- Give a child the box of objects to explore.
- Ask the child to name each object, providing the names if the child does not know them.
- Call the child's attention to the names of two objects that sound the same, such as tire and wire. Explain that the two names rhyme because they have the same sound.
- Ask if he or she can find other objects with names that sound the same. If the child needs help, line up three objects—two that rhyme and one that doesn't. Have the child name the three objects, and ask him or her which ones rhyme.
- When the child hears the rhyming sounds and can find matching items, have him or her select rhyming pairs and place each pair in a square on the construction-paper mat.
- Have the child name the rhyming objects in each square.
- Add new items as children become more proficient.
- Encourage children to think of rhyming words that you can print on tagboard cards for them to keep.

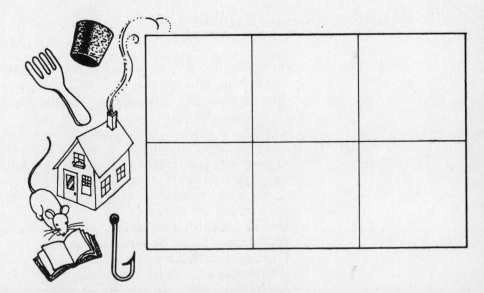

Illustration 4.3 Materials for rhyming activity

Clarifying Different Aspects of a Story

MATERIAL   A book that includes action, conflict, and expresses feelings, such as *Where the Wild Things Are*, by Maurice Sendak; *I'll Fix Anthony*, by Judith Viorst; or *Harry the Dirty Dog*, by Gene Zion

PROCEDURE
- Read the story with dramatic emphasis.
- After reading the story, go over it again, stopping to ask children about words, abstract concepts, character motivations, and processes.

  Ask if children know what certain words mean—for example, *lost, curious, friendly, sad*. Re-read segments of the story, using the unfamiliar words to help the children discover how the story explains the words.

  If a book includes abstract concepts such as fast, round, soft, secret, or mystery, ask if children can tell what the words mean. Read segments of the story that will help the children discover what the words mean. Encourage children to give their own examples and to expand on the meanings of words that relate to their personal experiences.

  Talk about character motivations by asking why a character in the story is feeling sad or frightened. Why does the character feel this way? How can the children tell? Pictures and words in the book can be used as clues.

  Ask the children why they think some process happened, what will happen next, and what the main character of the story could do to solve the problem in another way.

- Encourage children to participate by accepting their answers and expanding on them. If necessary, clarify meanings. Show that their thoughts are important and interesting to you.

Creative and Critical Listening

MATERIAL   Storybooks that include a conflict and express negative as well as positive feelings and actions, such as *The Runaway Bunny*, by Margaret Wise Brown; *The Tale of Peter Rabbit*, by Beatrix Potter; and *The Gunniwolf*, by Wilhelmina Harper

PROCEDURE
- Read the story aloud with dramatic expression. Read intimate passages softly and exciting passages forcefully. Read slowly to build suspense and faster during the action parts.
- As the story progresses, engage the children in discussion through open-ended questions:
  How do you think he feels?
  Why do you think he feels that way?
  What do you think will happen?
  What do you think he can do about it?
- Accept the children's responses and expand on them. Show them that their thoughts are important and interesting.
- Ask what-if questions to encourage critical thinking.

Note: Psychologist Grover Whitehurst at State University of New York measured the language skills of 29 children between the ages of 21 and 35 months. All the children had similar language skills. The researcher then gave the parents of half the children a brief training session in which they were told to ask evocative questions of their children while reading—to avoid yes/no questions and to ask open-ended questions that offered children a chance to elaborate. Members of the control group were asked to continue with their usual read-aloud style. After only one month, the children whose parents had received training scored six months ahead of the others on a test of vocabulary, and more than eight months ahead in expressiveness in describing objects. Nine months later they were still maintaining their lead.

HELPFUL HINTS

- Squat or kneel down to the child's eye level when you talk with him or her.
- Get into the habit of putting your arm around a child or making some kind of physical contact when you communicate verbally.
- Be conscious of the way you stand and sit. Your posture invites or discourages physical contact from others.

READING READINESS

Children who are ready to read will show a strong desire to do so. For example, they will ask to be read to, or they may memorize some of their favorite stories and "read" them aloud to others. Their speaking and listening skills will be well developed, and they will be interested in connecting printed words to pictures in a book.

Some of the skills that lead to reading include recognition of letters and numbers, recognition of the sounds of letters, and familiarity with printed materials. Most of the activities in this section are suitable for older preschoolers (4- and 5-year-olds) who indicate a readiness and desire to learn to read.

Do not push children to learn. If they are easily distracted, seem frustrated, or show little interest in the activities, offer something less difficult. There is no rush.

Learning Directional Words

MATERIAL   Play equipment such as climbing boards, boxes, chairs, and other objects suitable for making an obstacle course with which to experience different directions

PROCEDURE   • Play Follow the Leader with the children, asking them to follow you while you climb up and down, crawl in and out, walk across, through, and into various areas.
- Label your actions as you do them, stressing the directional words.

• Let the children take turns being the leader while you help them verbalize the directions they are taking.

Learning Relational Concepts

MATERIALS   Cardboard box for the teacher
Shoe box for each child
Clown puppet
Doll or stuffed toy for each child

PROCEDURE   • Introduce the clown puppet to the children.
• Tell the puppet about your school, the names of the children, and how they sit in front of you when you tell a story.
• Have the puppet confuse *in front of* with a different position.
• Involve the children by having the puppet continue to make silly mistakes.
• Bring the cardboard box out, and use it to demonstrate to the puppet (and the children) what you mean by *front, back, beside, top, inside, outside, behind.*
• Ask the children to help teach the puppet by giving each child a shoe box and stuffed toy with which to demonstrate the various locations as you call them out.
• Have the puppet thank each child by name for helping it to learn about relational concepts.

Note: Adapt this technique with the clown puppet to teach other concepts, including large/small, hard/soft, round/square, fast/slow, hot/cold, light/dark, right/left.

Have the clown wear a necklace of colored beads of macaroni, and ask the children to identify and count the various colors.

Reinforce relational concepts throughout all areas of the curriculum. Review and repeat these concepts frequently, having children demonstrate what they have learned.

Matching and Naming Letters of the Alphabet

MATERIALS   Large magnetized board
1 set each of uppercase and lowercase letters, all of one color
1 set each of uppercase and lowercase letters, all of another color
Tagboard cards (also adaptable for use with a flannelboard)

PROCEDURE   • Place three or four lowercase letters of the first color in a column on the left side of the magnetic board.
• Place matching letters of the other color in a different order on the right side of the board.
• Point to the first letter in the left-hand column, and ask if anyone knows what the letter is called.
• When the letter has been identified, ask the child to find a matching letter from the right side of the board. Place the matching letter next to its mate.

- Have children match the remaining letters in the same way.
- Increase the number of letters as children progress. Add some letters that do not correspond.
- Repeat the same activity with uppercase letters.
- Help children print their names on tagboard cards using upper- and lowercase letters. Let them use the magnetic letters to copy their names on the board.
- Ask the children to think of a word they would like to have you print for them on a card. Let them keep the card to use with the magnetic letters. Add to their card collection each time they succeed in matching the letters.

Note: Use the same activity to provide children with practice in learning numbers.

Matching Letters and Words with Objects; Recognizing Beginning Sounds of Words

MATERIALS   Shoe boxes or other such containers
A variety of toys and objects familiar to children
Tagboard cards

PROCEDURE   • Print one letter of the alphabet in uppercase and in lowercase on the top of each shoe box.
- Next to the letter, draw or paste a picture of a common object whose name begins with that letter.
- Place several objects whose names begin with that letter inside each shoe box.
- Begin by passing one box around to a small group of children; let each child select and name one object.
- Repeat the name of the object, stressing the beginning sound. Associate the sound of the word with the letter on top of the box: **This is a ball. It begins with the letter b. Make the sound of b.**
- Bring out a second shoe box, with a different letter on it. Repeat the above procedure.
- When the children have successfully named and identified the beginning sound of each object, mix two boxes of objects and let the youngsters select and name each object and replace it in the appropriate box. Continue to mix boxes, varying the degrees of difficulty according to individual abilities.
- Print the name of each object on a tagboard card. Place the appropriate cards in each shoe box, along with the matching objects.
- Let the children match cards with objects.

Recognizing Addresses

MATERIALS   Simple map of your city, showing streets where the children live
Colored squares of construction paper
5" x 7" cards, one for each child
Felt pen

PROCEDURE
- Talk about the numbers on the outside of houses and other buildings and about the names of streets.
- Ask if the children understand the word *address*. Explain its meaning, and talk about why addresses are important.
- Tell the children that you are going to read an address to see if anyone can tell you who lives there.
- When a child recognizes his or her own address, give him or her the card. If children do not know their addresses, give clues, such as hair color, and clothing, to help the children identify the owner of the address.
- Help the children print their names on squares of construction paper and pin them onto the map, to show where they live.
- The same procedure can be used to teach children to recognize their telephone numbers.

Recognizing Right and Left Hands

MATERIALS
7 pages of 8½" x 11" paper
Felt pen
7 plastic inserts, 8½" x 11", or clear contact paper
3-hole punch and binder (optional)

PROCEDURE
- Make a hand book by tracing your own hands or those of a child, as follows.
- First put the left hand on the paper, palm down, with fingers and thumb spread. (Draw in fingernails on all tracings made with the palm down.) Print the word LEFT beneath it.
- Then trace the right hand, palm down, with fingers and thumb spread. Print the word RIGHT beneath it.
- Now do the left hand palm up. Print LEFT beneath it.
- Next do the right hand palm up. Print RIGHT beneath it.
- Trace the left and the right hand on the same page, palms down. Print LEFT and RIGHT beneath the tracings.
- Trace the left and the right hand on the same page, left palm up and right palm down. Print LEFT and RIGHT beneath the appropriate tracings.
- Do the left and the right hand again, this time with the left palm down and the right palm up. Label appropriately.
- Use a plastic insert or contact paper to protect each page.
- Make a cover, or place the pages in a binder. Print the title HANDS on the cover.
- Introduce the book to individual children as follows:
  This is a book about hands. This word on the cover says HANDS. There are pictures in the book showing hands. See if you can make your hands look like the hands in the pictures.
  Here is a picture of a left hand. Can you make one of your hands look like this left hand?
  Put your left hand on the table, below the picture in the book. Are your fingernails showing?
  Do your thumb and the finger next to it make a shape that looks like an L?

Which way is your thumb pointing?
- Repeat these instructions, this time using the top of the right hand.
- For tracings with the palm up, ask:
Are your fingernails showing?
Which way is your thumb pointing?
- When using the pictures of two hands, help the child to get one hand positioned first, then the other.
- If a child is able to copy hand positions quickly, ask how he or she did it.
- Help children make their own hand books, and let them help you label right and left hands.

Matching Identical Symbols

MATERIALS Flannelboard
Pairs of familiar matching objects (for example, candy canes, toys) and of letters (both upper- and lowercase), either made from flannel or cut from construction paper or magazines and backed with sandpaper

PROCEDURE
- Divide the pairs of objects into two groups.
- Divide the children into two groups.
- Give each child a flannel picture from the corresponding group.
- Have one child from the first group place his or her picture on the flannelboard.
- Have the child from the second group who has the matching picture place it alongside the first picture. Have the children name the object or letter as they place it on the board.
- When everyone has had a turn, reverse the roles of the two groups.

Recognizing Patterns

MATERIALS Triangles cut from pieces of cardboard or construction paper 2" square
Sample cards with different triangular designs drawn or colored in (Use 3 to 6 triangles to a card; see Illustration 4.4.)

PROCEDURE
- Show the children the sample cards with different triangular designs on them.
- Talk about the designs, and help the children identify the shapes as triangles.
- Display the cut triangles, and ask the children to place them on the sample cards, duplicating the design. Help the children decide which corner a triangle should go in and which way it should point, but do not place the triangle for them.
- Increase the difficulty of the activity by introducing more designs or by using parquetry blocks with colorful patterns made up of a variety of shapes.

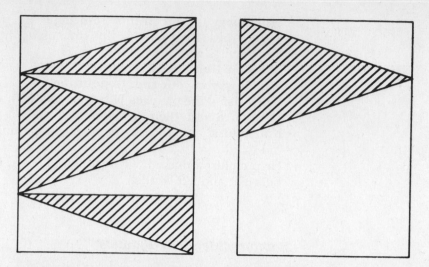

Illustration 4.4 Sample cards for recognizing patterns

Matching Identical Letters

MATERIALS   Cardboard squares (one per child), each divided into nine squares, with a different letter of the alphabet printed in each square
Plastic or cardboard letters of the alphabet
A box or can to hold the letters

PROCEDURE   • Give each child a card.
• Talk about the letters on each of their cards. Notice that each person has different letters.
• Explain that you are going to play a game. Say:
In the can are letters of the alphabet. Some of these letters will match the ones on your card.
• Have the children take turns drawing one letter at a time from the container.
• As each letter is drawn, have the child call out the name of the letter. If that letter appears on the child's card, he or she places it on the matching square.
• If there is no match, the child puts the letter back into the container and the next child takes a turn.
• Continue until someone fills in one row across, down, or diagonally from corner to corner.

Recognizing Differences in Objects

MATERIALS   Strips of cardboard about 4" x 20" on which you have drawn or attached four objects that are identical and one that is different (for example, four squares and one circle, four F's and a fifth one facing backward, four cups with spoons and one cup without a spoon)

Note: Use a copying machine to make multiple copies of objects to attach to the cardboard. Vary the placement of the nonmatching object, to keep children from using placement as a clue.

PROCEDURE
- Start with simple patterns that have obvious differences. Say:
I have some cards with pictures on them. On each card all the shapes are the same except one. Can you find the one that is different?
- Help children notice and talk about the differences in shape. Note, for example, that squares have four sides and pointed corners and that the circle has no corners.
- Suggest that children trace the shapes with their fingers.
- Praise them for recognizing differences and encourage them to tell how they were able to identify the nonmatching object.

Illustration 4.5 **Materials to use for sequence activity**

Arranging Story Pictures in Sequence

MATERIALS   Manila folder or large envelope on the outside of which 4 to 6 squares have been drawn and consecutively numbered

A set of 4 to 6 pictures showing the sequence of an activity, mounted on cardboard cut to fit the squares (See Illustration 4.5.)

PROCEDURE
- Glue the first picture in the sequence onto the first square on the folder cover.
- Place the remaining pictures inside the folder.
- Let individual children place the pictures in the appropriate squares to show the story in a logical sequence.
- Talk about each picture with the child, encouraging discussion about what is happening and why a picture should be placed in that particular position.
- Put the pictures in an illogical sequence, and talk about that sequence with the child.

Note: To find pictures for sequential stories, cut up old storybooks.

VARIATIONS   Cut out simple flannel pictures for children to use to tell stories on a flannelboard; or take pictures of the children carrying out an activity, such as cooking, and place them in proper sequence along with the recipe.

PREWRITING ACTIVITIES

Children scribble and try to draw long before they are taught to write. Many recognize their names in written form and are aware of the importance of writing from their own experience. They may pretend to write with crayons and pencils. Many 4- and 5-year-olds can make simple letters and can distinguish between printed letters on the basis of their structural configurations.

The activities in this section are designed to be introduced by teachers, but can be adapted for children to use on their own.

Developing Eye-Hand Coordination with Tracers

MATERIALS   Clear plastic folders, one for each child
Paper
Felt pens or crayons, one for each child
Sponges or paper towels

PROCEDURE
- On separate sheets of paper, print each child's name using uppercase and lowercase printscript letters. (Request a printscript chart from your local school district or library.) Put each paper inside a clear plastic folder.
- Hand each child the folder with his or her name on it, reading the name and then tracing over each letter with your finger as you spell the name out loud.

MAKING A REBUS STORY

A rebus story is one in which pictures replace some of the words. Two- and three-year-olds enjoy "reading" the pictures, and it helps them learn that words stand for things.

Select a story with a simple plot, or make up a story based on a child's experiences. Write the story down, identifying the words that can be depicted with pictures. Draw simple, clear pictures to illustrate the words you are replacing. For example:

Once there was a little [picture of a cat]. One day a big [dog] chased the little [cat] up a [tree].

You don't need to be an artist to make a rebus story—just use simple line drawings and print the words clearly. Or use pictures from discarded storybooks and magazines.

Protect the rebus stories with clear contact paper. After reading them with the children, put them in the library corner for children to look at by themselves.

Note: See *Mother Goose Picture Riddles*, illustrated by Lisl Weil (Holiday House), for rebus rhymes.

MORE SUGGESTIONS

When working with very young or inattentive children, try involving them first by drawing or painting large pictures of the characters in a story such as "The Gingerbread Man" or "The Three Bears." Encourage the children to help color or paint the characters. (They need not paint within the lines.) Talk about the story while the children are helping with the art work.

Mount the pictures on tagboard or flannel backing.

Finally, tell the story using the characters.

On another day, read the story and show the book.

• Show the children how to trace their names on the outside of the folder, using a felt pen or crayon, and then wipe the plastic clean with a damp sponge or paper towel. They should start by tracing the initial capital letter, then do the following letters one at a time, always printing from left to right.

Note: Children who skip around and trace portions of a letter can benefit from tracing the following dot pattern. Have them draw a line from one dot to another, starting at the left, without lifting their pen.

• •   •   •   •   •   • • •

Make other dot-to-dot patterns for them to trace.

Provide a chalk board that children can use to practice writing skills.

Make other patterns of shapes, letters, and numbers for children to insert into their folders and trace.

Collecting Words to Create Sentences

MATERIALS   Heavy construction paper cut into 3" x 6" cards
Felt pen
Sandpaper letters
Clear plastic folder

PROCEDURE
- Ask the children to choose words that they would like you to print for them to keep.
- Carefully print the word each child chooses on one of the 3" x 6" cards. Give it to the child to keep.
- Suggest that he or she place the card inside a plastic folder and trace it, copy the word onto a blackboard or a piece of paper, or replicate the word with sandpaper letters and trace them with the forefinger.
- When children have collected several words and become familiar with them, help them create a sentence using some or all of the words. Let them print their names after their sentences.
- Invite them to read their sentences to the class, post the sentences on a bulletin board, or add the sentences to a collection in an album for the library corner.

Note: Suggest that children create a parent-child diary (for example, "Karen's and Daddy's Diary"). Each evening the child dictates events of the day for the parent to enter in the diary. Both can work together on an illustration to highlight something that was written. The child can bring the diary to school to share with the class.

MORE SUGGESTIONS

- To celebrate special holidays, invite parents to share stories and food.
- Send notes home to let parents know what books their children enjoy in school.
- Let children check out books over weekends and holidays.
- Suggest books that parents might buy for gifts to the school. Libraries often have sales of used books.
- Make annotated lists of children's books available at the local library, and suggest that parents take their children to the library to check them out.
- Contact local libraries, storytellers' guilds, and book clubs to invite storytellers to your school.

Writing and Sending a Letter

MATERIALS   Paper
Felt pens or pencils

Copying machine
Mailing envelopes
Stamps, either postal or decorative

PROCEDURE
- Talk about the mail carrier's job, or invite a mail carrier to visit the class.
- Invite the children to talk about their experiences with the postal service.
- Determine how much they know about writing letters as a form of communication.
- Suggest that the class write a letter either to another class in the school or to family members, to invite them to an open house or to visit the class.
- Let the children dictate a letter while you print it on a piece of paper. Leave space for a child to print his or her name at the bottom. (You may prefer to use a chalkboard or chart-size paper to take dictation so that children can watch their ideas develop. Read the letter, make revisions, then transfer it to letter-size paper.)
- Make enough copies for each child to have one to sign. Some children who are able to copy simple sentences might wish to add a sentence of their own to the letter.
- If the invitation is going to another class, assign each of your children a child from the other class to invite. Provide a model of the address for children to copy on their envelopes. (Collect decorative stamps for children to use in mailing their letters within the school.) A decorated mailbox and a postal carrier's outfit will add to the appeal of the activity.
- If the invitation is being sent home, help those children who want to add something personal to the letter. They may need help addressing the letter, or they may need you to print or type the address for them. If possible, take a field trip to the post office to mail the letters.

MORE SUGGESTIONS

- Print parts of a favorite story on a large chart. Let children run their hands along the lines of the story and "read" along with the teacher.
- Tell children the title, author, and illustrator of each story you read. Show them several books by one illustrator. Help them become familiar with and identify the style of an illustrator.
- Print portions of stories on 3" x 5" cards. Read familiar passages, and have children guess what story the passages are from.
- Make some large, colorfully illustrated book envelopes that children can use to check out favorite books to take home. As the children learn to write, let them copy the titles and authors of the books on the envelopes.

Writing a Story

MATERIALS   Paper
              Felt pen
              Typewriter or word processor
              Art materials

PROCEDURE   • After an interesting experience such as a field trip, special celebra-
                tion, visit by a community worker, or party, invite the children to
                help tell the story of what happened.
              • Invite children to take turns dictating the experience while you print
                their sentences on separate pieces of paper. For example:
                Today we went to the park. —Marc
                We walked a long time. —Sally
                I stepped on a snail. —Robert
              • Help maintain some sequential order by rereading the sentences and
                asking
                Then what happened?
              • Give each child his or her sentence to illustrate. Save the papers to
                read on another day.
              • Have the children recall the proper sequence of the story, and let
                each one read his or her sentence to the class.
              • Fasten the pages together, and place them in a decorated folder. Give
                the storybook a title.

VARIATION   Use a typewriter or word processor so that the children can see their
              words produced by means other than hand printing. The finished
              story can be printed out and posted in the library area for children
              to read again.

Forming Associations Among Talking, Writing, and Reading

MATERIALS   Materials conducive to children's language involvement, such as pho-
              tographs of children engaged in school activities, magazine pictures
              depicting interesting actions familiar to the children, familiar story-
              book pictures, or some of the children's art work
              Paper and pen
              Construction paper
              Stapler

PROCEDURE   • Initiate storytelling by using a book suggested in the bibliography at
                the end of this section, or take advantage of a child's spontaneous in-
                terest.
              • Print the story as the child tells it, repeating the words as you print
                them.
              • Staple together the dictation pages and the pictures, if any.
              • Suggest that the child give the story a title and design a cover for the
                book.
              • Let the child print his or her name on the cover.

• Paste an envelope with a library card inside the front cover.
• Place the children's storybooks in the reading area; let the children check out the books to read at home.

CHOOSING BOOKS

• Does the theme reflect the children's interests?
• Is it attractively illustrated with pictures that go with the text?
• Is it a good size for a child to hold?
• If you plan to read it to a group of children, are the illustrations large enough to be seen by everyone?
• Are the binding and pages sturdy?

READING BOOKS

• Select a book that is suitable for your audience. If the children are very young and have short attention spans, select a story with a simple, short theme.
• Read the book to yourself first.
• Hold the book so that everyone can see the pictures comfortably. You should not be so far above the children that those close to you have to strain their necks backward to look up.
• Know your story well enough that you can retain eye contact with the children most of the time. Watch their facial expressions to see if they need a word explained or if they are losing interest.
• Read slowly, enunciate clearly, and project your voice. Read with feeling and a sense of drama.

TELLING A STORY

• Choose a story you like that is easy to memorize (for example, "Caps for Sale").
• Read the story over several times.
• Repeat it to yourself during the day while driving, doing the dishes, and the like. There is no need to memorize it word for word, but stick to the plot.
• Visualize the incidents in the story.
• When you tell the story, watch the children and speak directly to them, making eye contact with each one.
• Speak slowly, enunciate clearly, and use pauses for effect.
• Identify with the characters in the story; show enthusiasm.
• After you have told the story, show the book and mention the author's and illustrator's names.
• Vary the story with props. At times, let the children participate by acting out some of the scenes or reciting some of the repetitive phrases.

Bibliography of Books for Children

A very useful resource available in most libraries is *The Bookfinder*, a two-volume listing of thousands of children's books categorized under 450 developmental, behavioral, and psychological headings. Headings include adoption, courage, death, divorce, fighting, friendship, imaginary friends, jealousy, siblings, and teachers.

The books marked with an asterisk (*) are no longer in print, but are worth looking for in the library. If your library does not have the book you want, it can get it for you through the American free public library system by making a computer search throughout the United States.

ALL-TIME FAVORITES

Anglund, Joan Walsh. *A Friend Is Someone Who Likes You.* New York, NY: Harcourt, Brace, 1983.

_____. *Love Is a Special Way of Feeling.* New York, NY: Harcourt, Brace, 1960. Both of these books are excellent to look at, read, and talk about with one child. They are small, easy to hold, and delightfully illustrated. Topics are geared to the young child's experiences.

Bemelmans, Ludwig. *Madeline.* New York, NY: Viking, 1939. "In an old house in Paris that was covered with vines, lived twelve little girls in two straight lines." So begins the charming tale of Madeline. This amusing rhyming story is set against a background of illustrations showing the Eiffel Tower, Notre Dame, and other famous scenes of Paris.

Brett, Jim (illus.). *Goldilocks and the Three Bears.* New York, NY: Dodd, Mead, 1987. Everyone loves the story of little Goldilocks, who made herself quite at home in the house of the three bears. Exquisite illustrations transport children to the enchanting world of this favorite of all nursery tales.

Brown, Margaret Wise. *Goodnight Moon.* New York, NY: Live Oak Media, 1984. An old standby about a bunny in bed who says goodnight to the moon, stars, and noises until he falls asleep.

_____. *The Indoor Noisy Book.* New York, NY: Harper & Row, 1942. A book about the noises a little dog named Muffin hears. The text encourages children to participate and guess about noises indoors. The teacher can use this story for telling without a book. Other books in this series include *The Quiet Noisy Book, The Summer Noisy Book,* and *The Winter Noisy Book*.

_____. *The Runaway Bunny.* New York, NY: Live Oak Media, 1977. A bunny tells his mother he is going to run away, but his mother tells him she will find him because he is her little bunny. This pretend story is told and illustrated in a gentle, tender way.

Burton, Virginia Lee. *The Little House.* Boston, MA: Houghton Mifflin, 1978. A Caldecott Medal winner about a little house in the country that eventually becomes surrounded by urban development, and the happy ending when it is jacked up and moved back to the country again.

————. *Mike Mulligan and His Steam Shovel.* Boston, MA: Houghton Mifflin, 1977. A classic story about how one steam shovel found a permanent home. See also *Katy and the Big Snow,* by the same author.

Carle, Eric. *The Very Hungry Caterpillar.* New York, NY: Puffin, 1984. A book of beautiful bright pictures, with holes in the pages made by the hungry caterpillar. As the days of the week pass, the number of holes grows, and so does the caterpillar. Good for flannelboard.

Carlestrom, Nancy White. *Jesse Bear, What Will You Wear?* New York, NY: Macmillan, 1986. Lilting verse and exuberant paintings combine to make Jesse Bear's day of playing in the sandbox, chasing butterflies, and swinging in the swing a special one. A favorite among teachers.

Charlip, Remy. *Mother, Mother, I Feel Sick. Send for the Doctor, Quick, Quick, Quick.* New York, NY: Macmillan, 1980. A child has a stomachache, and the doctor finds all kinds of hilarious things in the child's stomach, from a plateful of spaghetti to a two-wheeled bike. This funny story can be adapted for the flannelboard or presented as a shadow play.

Cook, Scott (illus.). *The Gingerbread Boy.* New York, NY: Knopf, 1987. A classic tale, illustrated in subdued tones, about the gingerbread boy who ran away from a series of people, repeating "Run, run, as fast as you can. You can't catch me, I'm the Gingerbread Man!" . . . until he met up with a crafty fox.

Daugherty, James. *Andy and the Lion.* New York, NY: Viking, 1938. After Andy removes a thorn from a lion's paw, the grateful lion helps to make Andy a hero.

de Regniers, Beatrice Schenk. *May I Bring a Friend?* New York, NY: Macmillan, 1964. When the king and queen invite the hero of the story to tea, he asks to bring a friend, who turns out to be an animal. The boy is invited to lunch, dinner, breakfast, Hallowe'en, and more; each time he brings different kinds of animals, until the king and queen finally go with him to the zoo. Can be adapted for flannelboard by using crowns to depict the king and queen, and simple silhouettes of zoo animals.

Emberley, Barbara. *Drummer Hoff.* Englewood Cliffs, NJ: Prentice-Hall, 1967. A brightly illustrated adaptation of a folk tale in rhyme. The soldiers help to build a cannon, but Drummer Hoff "fires it off" in a colorful blast at the end. The repetitive rhyme is fun to recite. Trace the figures to adapt to the flannelboard.

Ets, Marie Hall. *Play with Me.* New York, NY: Penguin, 1976. A little girl goes out to the meadow to play, but the animals are frightened of her. When she sits quietly, they gradually come out to "play." Record and cassette also available.

Flack, Marjorie. *Ask Mr. Bear.* New York, NY: Macmillan, 1986. An old favorite about a little boy who doesn't know what to give his mother for her birthday, so he asks a series of animals to make suggestions, which he rejects. Finally, he asks Mr. Bear, who gives him a wonderful solution. Good for the flannelboard; also easy to tell without the book.

Forrester, Victoria. *The Magnificent Moo.* New York, NY: Macmillan, 1983. When a cow trades her moo for a cat's meow because she thinks it's too loud, the moo gets traded in turn to several other animals, until it finally returns to a more satisfied cow.

Freeman, Don. *Corduroy.* New York, NY: Viking, 1968. A little girl falls in love with a teddy bear no one else wants. Look for other books by this popular author. Also available in sound filmstrip, record, and cassette.

Gag, Wanda. *Millions of Cats.* New York, NY: Putnam, 1977. A familiar classic about an old man and an old woman who collect so many cats that they end up with "hundreds of cats, thousands of cats, millions and billions and trillions of cats." Fun to read, and an easy story to tell without the book. Show the pictures after telling the story.

Galdone, Paul. *The Teeny-Tiny Woman.* New York, NY: Clarion, 1984. "Once upon a time there was a teeny-tiny woman who lived in a teeny-tiny house in a teeny-tiny village." The artist's droll rendition of this old English ghost story will engender shivers of delight in young listeners.

————. ***The Three Billy Goats Gruff.*** New York, NY: Clarion, 1973. The three Billy Goats Gruff brave the fearsome Troll in order to reach a meadow of grass and daisies. Illustrations were developed from sketches of actual goats that live on a farm near the author's home. This is a good story for telling without a book and for acting out.

Geisel, Theodor (Dr. Seuss, pseud.). *The Cat in the Hat.* New York, NY: Random House, 1987. One of the most popular in a series of Dr. Seuss books. Children love the clever rhyming stories and amusing illustrations. This limited-vocabulary book is fun to read aloud, with lots of repetition of words. Other equally clever read-alouds include ***And to Think That I Saw It on Mulberry Street, How the Grinch Stole Christmas, Horton Hatches the Egg,*** and ***If I Ran the Zoo.***

Harper, Wilhelmina. *The Gunniwolf.* New York, NY: Dutton, 1967. A suspenseful and humorous tale about a little girl who wanders too far into the woods in search of flowers and is accosted by the Gunniwolf. This is an excellent story for telling without the book. Show pictures afterward.

Hutchins, Pat. *Happy Birthday, Sam.* New York, NY: Greenwillow Books, 1978. Sam turns a whole year older, but he still can't reach the light switch or the front doorknob. His parents give him a beautiful boat for his birthday, but he can't reach the sink to sail it. But then his grandfather's present arrives.

Krasilovsky, Phyllis. *The Man Who Didn't Wash His Dishes.* New York, NY: Doubleday, 1950. An amusing story about a man who is always too tired to do the dishes, so he lets them pile up until he has to eat out of his ashtrays, soap dish, and flower pots. He finally piles all his dirty dishes into his truck, sprinkles soap on them, and drives around on a rainy day.

_____. *The Very Little Girl.* New York, NY: Doubleday, 1953. A story about a little girl and how small she is compared to a big chair, a kitchen stool, a rose bush, and other things, until one day she realizes that she is bigger than all those objects. Adapt to flannelboard to show relative size.

Krauss, Ruth. *The Bundle Book.** New York, NY: Harper & Row, 1951. Children identify easily with the strange bundle under the blankets, which moves and puzzles mother, who tries to guess what it is.

_____. *The Carrot Seed.* New York, NY: Harper & Row, 1945. Simple illustrations show a child's faith that a carrot seed he plants will grow into a carrot, even when everyone tells him it won't. See also, by the same author, *A Hole Is to Dig* and *The Happy Day.*

_____. *The Growing Story.* New York, NY: Harper & Row, 1947. A little boy watches the animals and plants around him grow, but his arms and legs look the same to him until he tries on some of his old clothes and discovers he has grown too.

Lionni, Leo. *Inch by Inch.* New York, NY: Astor-Honor, 1962. An inchworm uses his ingenuity to stay alive by measuring different birds, but a nightingale decides to eat him.

Lord, John Vernon (illus.). *The Giant Jam Sandwich.* Boston, MA: Houghton Mifflin, 1973. "One hot summer in Itching Down, four million wasps flew into town." Imaginatively detailed illustrations and verses tell a delightful story of how a town cooperates to rid itself of wasps with a giant jam sandwich. Encourage children to look at and talk about the details.

Martin, Bill, Jr. *Brown Bear, Brown Bear, What Do You See?* New York, NY: Holt, 1967. One of the most popular books in early reading classes. Colors and animals are shown in large double-page spreads with rhyming text. Adaptable for flannelboard.

McCloskey, Robert. *Blueberries for Sal.* New York, NY: Viking, 1948. A standard book for preschoolers about a little girl who goes out with her mother to pick blueberries and a little bear who goes out with his mother at the same time to eat blueberries. The youngsters get mixed up, to the surprise of both mothers. Other titles by this popular author and illustrator include *One Morning in Maine* and *Make Way for Ducklings.*

McPhail, David. *Pig Pig Grows Up.* New York, NY: Dutton, 1980. A charmingly illustrated book about a pig who doesn't want to grow up, until his mother collapses pushing him up a hill in his stroller. Then the adventure begins, and Pig Pig grows up in a hurry. Excellent for telling with a flannelboard.

_____. *The Bear's Toothache.* Boston, MA: Little, Brown, 1972. What do you do when a huge bear with a big toothache sits under your window at night and cries so loudly you can't sleep? Do you tell him to go away, send him to a dentist, or try to help? This imaginative, humorous story is simple to read. A good attention-getter when the reader starts the story by howling like the bear.

Nash, Ogden. *Custard the Dragon and the Wicked Knight.* Boston, MA: Little, Brown, 1961. Every child should be familiar with Ogden Nash's humorous tale in rhyme about a cowardly dragon named Custard.

Payne, Emmy. *Katy No-Pocket.* Boston, MA: Houghton Mifflin, 1944. Poor Katy Kangaroo doesn't have a pocket like other mother kangaroos. She needs a pocket for her boy Freddie to ride in. She asks all her animal friends, whose solutions are of no help. Finally she goes to the city and meets up with a carpenter wearing a most wonderful apron.

Piper, Watty (ed.). *Mother Goose, A Treasury of Best Loved Rhymes.* New York, NY: Platt, 1972. One of the most effective ways to engage very young children (as well as children for whom English is a second language) in literature is through the wonderful rhymes of Mother Goose. This version has 102 of the best-loved rhymes depicted in large, easy-to-see illustrations.

Potter, Beatrix. *The Complete Adventures of Peter Rabbit.* New York, NY: Warne, 1982. Four of the classic original tales—*The Tale of Peter Rabbit, The Tale of Mr. Tod, The Tale of Benjamin Bunny,* and *The Tale of the Flopsy Bunnies*—are all in this one volume, which offers the original art every child should have the opportunity to see. Children identify most easily with the first and simplest of the four tales, about Peter Rabbit, who has a naughty sense of adventure and barely escapes from the clutches of Mr. McGregor.

Rey, H. A. *Curious George.* Boston, MA: Houghton Mifflin, 1941. George is a monkey whose curiosity gets him into many adventures. Among the ten books in this classic series are such titles as *Curious George Flies a Kite . . . Goes to the Circus . . . Learns the Alphabet* and *. . . Rides a Bike.*

Sendak, Maurice. *In the Night Kitchen.* New York, NY: Harper & Row, 1970. A highly imaginative story about a child's dream of falling into cake batter and bread dough. A good story to tell with dramatic gestures. Be sure to show the wonderful illustrations.

————. *Where the Wild Things Are.* New York, NY: Harper & Row, 1963. A fantasy about a little boy named Max, who is sent to his room for misbehaving. Max imagines that he sails away to a place where the wild things are. Illustrations are highly imaginative. Some teachers like this book very much; others think the pictures are frightening. Winner of the Caldecott Medal.

Shaw, Charles G. *It Looked Like Spilt Milk.* New York, NY: Harper & Row, 1947. Some large white shapes look like all kinds of things, but turn out to be clouds in the sky. A popular book for encouraging imaginative discussion. For flannelboard use, trace the shapes onto Pellon, and let the children answer "no" as each shape is named and placed on the flannelboard.

Slobodkina, Esphyr. *Caps for Sale, A Tale of a Peddler, Some Monkeys & Their Monkey Business.* New York, NY: Scholastic,

1984. This all-time favorite of teachers and children is easy to tell without the book. Children love to hear this story about a peddler trying to sell the colored caps that he carries around on top of his head.

Ungerer, Tomi. *Crictor.* New York, NY: Harper & Row, 1983. The fantastic antics of a snake named Crictor, who is the friend of a French lady, Madame Bodot.

Viorst, Judith. *I'll Fix Anthony.* New York, NY: Harper & Row, 1969. Young children can relate to this humorously written story about little brother, who is planning all kinds of revenge on big brother. Also by the same author: *Alexander and the Terrible, Horrible, No Good, Very Bad Day.*

Wildsmith, Brian. *Brian Wildsmith's ABC.* New York, NY: Merrimack, 1982. One of the best alphabet books available. Upper- and lowercase letters form the names of familiar objects, colorfully depicted one to a page. Winner of many awards.

Zion, Gene. *Harry the Dirty Dog.* New York, NY: Harper & Row, 1956. One of a series of stories about a little white dog with black spots. Children identify with Harry, who hates to take a bath. Simple sentences and excellent illustrations.

BOOKS ABOUT ABC'S

Bishop, Gavin. *Apple Pie.* Auckland, New Zealand: Oxford University Press, 1987. *A* stands for apple pie. *B* (bee) bounced to it; *C* (cow) cried for it. The letters are illustrated with animals, all of which want some pie. Frog fiddles for it; walrus warbles for it. But who eats it in the end? Lots of animals are up to crazy antics in this clever and humorous rendition of an alphabet book. Lovely old-fashioned illustrations.

Brown, Marcia. *All Butterflies.* New York, NY: Macmillan, 1981. These brightly colored butterflies, which fly through the ABC's, will trigger the imagination of any child.

Children's Television Workshop (Harry McNaught, illus.). *The Sesame Street ABC Book of Words.* New York, NY: Random House, 1988. In busy scenes, characters from Sesame Street are involved in a variety of activities. Each page introduces objects and vocabulary words to match the letter of the alphabet.

Dragonwagon, Crescent. *Alligator Arrived with Apples. A Potluck Alphabet Feast.* New York, NY: Macmillan, 1987. It's a potluck party, and the guests are an alphabetical menagerie laden with good cheer and plenty of food. Here comes Parrot, who is providing pumpkin pie and pickled peaches. And there is Mouse with lovely mocha mousse. By the time Zebra zips in with a zaftig zucchini, the table groans under the weight of the comic, cumulative repast—a feasting full Thanksgiving fest!

Gag, Wanda. *The ABC Bunny.* New York, NY: Putnam's, 1933. An old favorite, with original lithographs and hand lettering.

Gardner, Beau. *Have you ever seen. . . ? An ABC book.* New York, NY: Dodd, Mead, 1986. "Have you ever seen an Alligator with Antlers?. . . a Banana with Buttons?" A colorfully clever approach, with a zany twist of humor.

Hawkins, Colin, and Jacqui Hawkins. *Busy abc.* New York, NY: Viking, 1987. Cartoon-like illustrations of children and animals doing things that begin with each letter of the alphabet, in lower case. For example, "b" is illustrated with a child *banging* on a drum, another child *blowing bubbles*, and a cat holding its ears, saying "I think blowing is better."

Hoban, Tana. *A, B, See!* New York, NY: Greenwillow, 1982. A collection of objects that begin with a particular letter of the alphabet. Hoban's books are well-designed selections for preschoolers.

Kitamura, Satoshi. *What's Inside? The Alphabet Book.* New York, NY: Farrar, Straus, Giroux, 1986. Whimsical paintings intrigue children who already know enough of the alphabet to participate.

Knightley, Rosalinda. *ABC.* Boston, MA: Little, Brown, 1986. One of a brightly illustrated series of concept and letter books. Each letter of the alphabet (in upper and lower case) is illustrated with one object or animal.

Owen, Annie. *Annie's abc.* New York, NY: Knopf, 1987. Each letter is accompanied by an illustration of several objects whose names begin with that letter. There are lots of tiny word pictures on each page.

Wildsmith, Brian. *Brian Wildsmith's ABC.* New York, NY: Franklin Watts, 1963. An award-winning book by a famous painter. Stunning illustrations bursting with life and color combine to make an alphabet book of rare quality. Some subjects will be familiar to young children; others will be a source of wonder and surprise.

BOOKS ABOUT BABIES

Andry, Andrew C., and Steven Schepp. *How Babies Are Made.* Boston, MA: Little, Brown, 1984. Honest answers to children's questions about sex. Illustrations of colored cut-out paper.

Arnstein, Helene S. *Billy and Our New Baby.* New York, NY: Human Sciences Press, 1973. A good book for preschoolers who must deal with jealousy over a new baby. Billy acts out his conflicts by being aggressive, crying, and regressing to bottle feeding. He learns that it is all right to have angry feelings, but that he may not hurt others. Gradually, Bill's parents help him to understand his importance in the family. Includes a helpful guide, with suggestions and information about sibling rivalry.

Hamilton-Merritt, Jane. *Our New Baby.* New York, NY: Simon & Schuster, 1982. A boy adjusts to the birth of a baby brother and looks forward to being friends with him. Beautiful photos illustrate this sensitive book.

Hoban, Russell. *A Baby Sister for Frances.* New York, NY: Harper & Row, 1964. One of several books about a badger named Frances. When a new baby comes to the house, Frances is unhappy because she does not get enough attention.

Holland, Vicki. *We Are Having a Baby.* New York, NY: Macmillan, 1972. Four-year-old Dana is just as excited as her mother and father about the birth of their baby. But when the baby arrives home, Dana is not sure if she likes the idea. Dana narrates the story, and the expressive photos capture her reactions to this new event.

Keats, Ezra Jack. *Peter's Chair.* New York, NY: Harper & Row, 1967. Peter's old cradle, high chair, and crib are painted pink for his new baby sister. He is so unhappy that he decides to take his little blue chair and run away from home.

Manushkin, Fran. *Baby, Come Out!* New York, NY: Harper & Row, 1984. Mrs. Tracy was growing a baby, and the baby didn't want to be born. A humorously illustrated tale showing the various positions and facial expressions of a baby inside the mommy, and the baby's responses to other members of the family waiting for it to be born.

Selsam, Millicent E. *How Puppies Grow.* New York, NY: Scholastic, 1977. Actual photos showing six newborn pups and how they grow until they are old enough to be adopted.

Sheffield, Margaret, and Sheila Bewley. *Where Do Babies Come From?* New York, NY: Knopf, 1973. A very explicit book designed for use by parents with their children. Simple, direct explanations cover conception, reproduction, and the life cycle. The softly colored illustrations convey feelings of tenderness and warmth. Adapted from the award-winning BBC program of the same title in England, this is one of the most honest books available on sex education for children.

Showers, Paul, and Kay Sperry Showers. *Before You Were a Baby.* New York, NY: Harper & Row, 1968. A simply written and well-illustrated book appropriate for use with preschoolers. Allow plenty of time for discussion.

Weiss, Nicki. *Chuckie.* New York, NY: Greenwillow, 1982. When Chuckie arrived, Lucy was as disagreeable to him as she knew how to be. Whatever Lucy did was fine with Chuckie, but whatever he did was wrong with her. Finally, Chuckie speaks his first word! A humorous book that touches on jealousy of a new baby.

CHANUKAH STORIES

Gellman, Ellie. *It's Chanukah!* Rockville, MD: KAR-BEN Copies, 1985. Scuffable board pages contain colorful illustrations of games, shapes, snacks, and other activities associated with the Chanukah season. Good for use with toddlers.

Hirah, Marilyn. *I Love Hanukkah.* New York, NY: Holiday House, 1984. Simple story of a child's Hanukkah celebration, with his grandpa telling him the story of the holiday.

Kimmel, Eric A. *The Chanukkah Tree.* New York, NY: Holiday House, 1987. A Chanukkah tree? The people of Chelm were Jewish and had never heard of such a thing. "That's right," said the peddler. "A Chanukkah tree. From America. Over there Chanukkah trees are the latest thing. Every Jewish home has one." In this rollicking tale, the townspeople discover a wonderful and unexpected use for their tree. A Chanukkah tree? Only in Chelm.

Shostak, Myra. *Rainbow Candles, A Chanukah Counting Book.* Rockville, MD: KAR-BEN Copies, 1986. A rhyming text and colorful illustrations of the menorah on wipeable, fingerproof board pages. "My menorah is ready, shining and bright. With my shamash I'll light the candles each night."

Zalben, Jane Breskin. *Beni's First Chanukah.* New York, NY: Henry Holt, 1988. Beni the bear eagerly prepares for the Chanukah festivities. He cooks latkes and doughnuts, lights the menorah, listens to the story of Chanukah, spins the dreidel, and opens presents. This story, with soft pastel-colored illustrations, captures the warmth of the timeless celebration.

CHRISTMAS STORIES

Bemelmans, Ludwig. *Madeline's Christmas.* New York, NY: Puffin, 1988. This is the paperback edition of the popular tale of Madeline's adventures, illustrated against a Paris background.

Brett, Jan (illus.). *The Twelve Days of Christmas.* New York, NY: Dodd, Mead, 1986. This is the most lavishly illustrated version of the traditional song, with the musical score reproduced at the beginning of the book. Every page invites the reader to look at the delightful details; look closely and you will see a love story woven into the text.

Another rendition of the same verse is illustrated by Sophie Windham (New York, NY: Putnam's, 1986). This book has lift-up flaps for the reader to discover the various objects. Good for reading with one child at a time.

de Paola, Tomie. *Baby's First Christmas.* New York, NY: Putnam's, 1988. An excellent first book for toddlers who are beginning to recognize such holiday symbols as a wreath, holly, ornaments, stockings, and Santa. Pages are of heavy wipeable board.

Ets, Marie Hall, and Aurora Lambastida. *Nine Days to Christmas.* New York, NY: Viking, 1959. This Caldecott Medal winner tells about Mexican customs at Christmas time.

Geisel, Theodor (Dr. Seuss, pseud.). *How the Grinch Stole Christmas.* New York, NY: Random House, 1957. Dr. Seuss's imaginative treatment of a grinch who tries to put a stop to Christmas. The rhythmic format will be familiar to children and teachers who enjoy Dr. Seuss books.

Hazen, Barbara Shook. *Rudolph, the Red-Nosed Reindeer.* New

York, NY: Western, 1985. The delightful song is colorfully illustrated. This book plays the music when the cover is opened.

McCully, Emily Arnold. *The Christmas Gift.* New York, NY: Harper & Row, 1988. A wordless book showing the mouse family preparing for Christmas, opening gifts, visiting the grandparents, and encountering a disaster with a new toy. Grandpa mouse provides a solution in this tenderly illustrated story about the gift of love. Excellent for language enhancement.

Moore, Clement C. (Tasha Tudor, illus.). *The Night Before Christmas.* New York, NY: Rand McNally, 1975. One of the most popular treatments of this classic tale. The lovely, large picture book has old-style illustrations.

Another edition worth having is published by Random House, (New York, NY: 1976), with paintings by Grandma Moses.

Wenning, Elizabeth. *The Christmas Mouse.* New York, NY: Holt, 1959. A true story of "Silent Night, Holy Night," written in an appealing way for young children. The story can be told without the book and then the pictures shown afterward.

OTHER HOLIDAY STORIES

Adams, Adrienne. *A Woggle of Witches.* New York, NY: Macmillan, 1971. On a certain night when the moon is high, all the witches fly on their brooms way up into the dark sky. They have fun on their night out until they run into a parade of little monsters who frighten them. Beautifully imaginative illustrations.

Balian, Lorna. *Humbug Witch.* New York, NY: Abingdon, 1965. A little girl dresses up like a witch and tries to make magic potions with such things as paprika, hair tonic, pickle juice, and peanut butter. Good for adaptation to the flannelboard.

Bright, Robert. *Georgie's Halloween.* New York, NY: Doubleday, 1971. One of a delightful series about Georgie, a friendly ghost.

Bunting, Eve. *How Many Days to America? A Thanksgiving Story.* New York, NY: Clarion, 1988. Set in the Caribbean, this large picture book tells a dramatic and touching story of present-day refugees who, like the original Pilgrims, have a very personal reason to celebrate Thanksgiving. Beautiful color illustrations by Beth Peck help tell the story through the eyes of a child who asks, "How many days to America?"

Calhoun, Mary. *Wobble, the Witch Cat.* New York, NY: William Morrow, 1958. It wasn't easy for Wobble the witch cat to ride on his mistress's broom with the slippery handle. The thought of falling off again made him cranky enough to do some mean things, including pushing the broom into the trash barrel. Wobble has the last laugh when, riding comfortably on his vacuum cleaner, he flies by all the other witch cats.

Child, Lydia Marie. *Over the River and Through the Wood.* New York, NY: Scholastic, 1974. This classic, with music included, is illustrated in an old-fashioned Christmas-card style.

Dalgliesh, Alice. *The Thanksgiving Story.* New York, NY: Macmillan, 1954. The story of one family during their first year in the Plymouth colony. Told simply enough for beginning readers.

Holl, Adelaide. *The Remarkable Egg.* New York, NY: Lothrop, 1968. A coot finds a round red egg in her nest and demands to know who laid it there. Lovely color illustrations by Roger Duvoisin.

Milhous, Katherine. *The Egg Tree.* New York, NY: Macmillan, 1950. Children will want to make their own egg tree after hearing this story. Hollow decorated eggshells can be used to demonstrate the subject of this Caldecott Medal winner.

Another good book to use in making an egg tree is *Easter Eggs for Everyone,* by Evelyn Coskey (New York, NY: Abingdon, 1973).

Miller, Edna. *Mousekin's Golden House.* New York, NY: Treehouse, 1964. Mousekin climbs into a jack-o-lantern to make a house for himself. A popular book with youngsters.

Titherington, Jeanne. *Pumpkin, Pumpkin.* New York, NY: Greenwillow, 1986. A good book for the fall season, about a little boy who plants a pumpkin seed and watches it grow.

Zolotow, Charlotte. *The Bunny Who Found Easter.* Boston, MA: Houghton Mifflin, 1959. A bunny searches for Easter through summer, autumn, and winter, until he finds its true meaning in the spring. A good lap book.

CONCEPT BOOKS: COLORS, SHAPES, NUMBERS, AND TIME

Anno, Mitsumasa. *Anno's Counting Book.* New York, NY: Crowell, 1977. Children who read this counting book will get not only a mathematical learning experience, but also an aesthetic one. The setting is a rural village. Readers must search to find what has been added to the village to make one more. Contrasting groups emerge also, such as fruit trees versus evergreens. Children will be stimulated by this beautiful and imaginative counting book.

Argent, Rod, and Trinca Argent. *One Wooly Wombat.* Brooklyn, NY, Kane/Miller, 1982. Humorous illustrations depict 14 Australian animals, introduced in rhyme, along with the numbers from 1–14.

Bradbury, Lynne. *Tell Me the Time.* Lewiston, ME: Ladybird Books, 1981. This colorful book introduces children to the idea of time in relation to things that they do, see, and experience throughout the day. For each hour, the pictures illustrate a variety of activities that could be taking place, and the simple text asks a question designed to promote discussion about the child's own experience.

Carle, Eric. *1, 2, 3 to the Zoo: A Counting Book.* New York, NY: Philomel, 1987. Each bright, full-color, double-page spread shows the number of animals in a train. After one large elephant on a flat car, the book shows ascending numbers of animals on their way to the zoo. The book ends with a fold-out picture of the populated zoo and an empty train. This is the twentieth-anniversary edition of an old favorite.

Carter, David A. *How Many Bugs in a Box?* New York, NY: Simon & Schuster, 1988. This vivid pop-up book is an entertaining introduction to counting. Children pull the tab on each brightly colored box to reveal the cheerful surprise within: two polka-dot bugs, four fast fleas, and eight noodle bugs, just to name a few.

Children's Television Workshop. *The Sesame Street Book of Shapes.* New York, NY: Preschool Press, 1972. Photos and illustrations developed from material provided by the Sesame Street series on TV are used to introduce size comparisons.

Feeney, Stephanie. *Hawaii Is a Rainbow.* Honolulu, HI: University of Hawaii Press, 1985. Each color of the rainbow is represented by photos of people, places, plants, and animals of Hawaii.

Friskey, Margaret. *Chicken Little Count-to-Ten.* Chicago, IL: Children's Press, 1946. Chicken Little's quest for water adds up to a delightful counting book.

Gardner, Beau. *Can you imagine. . .? A Counting Book.* New York, NY: Dodd, Mead, 1987. "Can you imagine . . . one whale wearing a veil? two ducks driving trucks?" Bold colors on two-page spreads appeal to children's love of nonsense.

Giganti, Paul, Jr. *How Many Snails? A Counting Book.* New York, NY: Greenwillow, 1988. A clear, colorful book that is not just a counting book. The child must look for specific details—spots on dogs, stripes on snails, icing on cupcakes.

Gillham, Bill, and Susan Hulme. *Let's Look for Shapes.* New York, NY: Coward-McCann, 1984. One of a series of four books designed to encourage children to look for basic concepts of color, shape, number, and opposites in their everyday world. By getting children to talk about the topics illustrated with photos, this book encourages them to think of other examples and so further develop their mastery of language and thought.

Gretz, Susanna. *Teddy Bears 1 to 10.* New York, NY: Four Winds, 1986. A simple book for the beginner, with warm, gentle illustrations.

Hoban, Tana. *Count and See.* New York, NY: Macmillan, 1972. This author presents creative ways to engage the young child in counting, as well as grouping by ten.

_____. *Dots, Spots, Speckles, and Stripes.* New York, NY: Greenwillow, 1987. Young children have many opportunities to sharpen their observation and classification skills when they look for dots, spots, speckles, and stripes in the full-color photos of these designs that can be found almost anywhere.

_____. *is it red? is it yellow? is it blue?* New York, NY: Mulberry, 1978. A wordless book with colorful photos showing common objects such as leaves and cars. Each page has appropriate colored dots under the photo.

————. **Look Again!** New York, NY: Macmillan, 1971. Look once, look twice, look again! A collection of photos in an amusing format, showing that there is more than one way of seeing a picture. Children enjoy guessing the surprise answers. Good for language involvement. See also, by the same author, **Push, Pull, Empty, Full.**

————. **over, under, & through.** New York, NY: Macmillan, 1973. Black-and-white photos demonstrate the spatial concepts expressed in 12 words, including *around, across, between, against, behind, below,* and *beside.*

————. **Shapes and Things.** New York, NY: Macmillan, 1970. A wordless book showing such common articles as a comb, a brush, a hammer, and letters in white on a black background.

Hutchins, Pat. One Hunter. New York, NY: Greenwillow, 1982. Walking through the forest, one hunter is observed by two elephants, then three giraffes, and so on.

Keats, Ezra Jack. Over in the Meadow. New York, NY: Scholastic, 1971. Lovely illustrations of different animals are accompanied by a rhyming text using numbers: "Over in the meadow, in the sand, in the sun, lived an old mother turtle and her little turtle one. 'Dig!' said the mother. 'I dig' said the one. So he dug all day, in the sand, in the sun." Good for adaptation to the flannelboard.

Kitamura, Satoshi. When Sheep Cannot Sleep. The Counting Book. New York, NY: Farrar, Straus, Giroux, 1986. One restless evening, Wooly the sheep goes strolling in the meadow. There are no numbers in this book, but the objects in each setting—such as apples on a tree, fireflies in a meadow, and squirrels—are highlighted in color to entice the child to count.

Knightley, Rosalinda. Shapes. Boston, MA: Little, Brown, 1986. Bold illustrations with simple text. One side of each two-page spread is used to teach concepts of shapes. The series also offers **Colors** and **Opposites.**

Krasilovsky, Phyllis. The Very Little Girl. New York, NY: Doubleday, 1953. Introduces comparison of sizes.

Lief, Philip (The Group). Big and Little. New York, NY: Random House, 1986. This is one of a series of wipeable books with board pages that are divided in half horizontally so that the child can leaf through to match big and little objects. Others in the series of Matchem books include **How Many?** and **Opposites.**

Lionni, Leo. Inch by Inch. New York, NY: Astor-Honor, 1962. A worm explores the world in this book teaching measurement.

Patty, Kate, and Lisa Kopper. what's that noise? Los Angeles, CA: Price/Stern/Sloan, 1986. Illustrations depict common objects that make familiar sounds, such as a balloon being blown up and popped, and a washing machine swooshing and humming. See also, by the same author, **what's that taste?**

Serfozo, Mary. *Who Said Red?* New York, NY: Macmillan, 1988. A beautiful introduction to colors, illustrated with large paintings by Keiko Narahashi. "Did you say red?" a little girl asks her small brother. "A Santa red. A stop sign red. A cherry, berry, very red. Did you say red?" "Yes, I said red," he replies. "You don't mean green?" she inquires. "A pickle green. A big frog green" and so on, through other illustrations of the primary colors plus purple, orange, pink, brown, black, and white.

Tudor, Tasha. *1 is one.* New York, NY: Checkerboard Press, 1956. "1 is one duckling swimming in a dish; 2 is two sisters making a wish . . ." and so on to "20 is twenty geese flying toward the dawn." Lovely pencil sketches.

Wildsmith, Brian. *Brian Wildsmith's One, Two, Three.* Auckland, New Zealand: Oxford University Press, 1984. Basic shapes are related to numbers in this beautifully illustrated book by an award-winning artist.

BOOKS ABOUT DEATH

Aliki. *The Two of Them.* New York, NY: Greenwillow, 1979. A sensitive description of the relationship of a grandfather and his granddaughter from her birth to his death. Growth and change are realistically portrayed. "She knew that one day he would die. But when he did, she was not ready, and she hurt inside and out."

Brown, Margaret Wise. *The Dead Bird.* New York, NY: Young Scott, 1958. A simple story, touchingly illustrated by Remy Charlip, about some children who find a dead bird and bury it in the woods. The description of death is factual and handles the subject in a way that a child can understand and accept.

Bunting, Eve. *The Happy Funeral.* New York, NY: Harper & Row, 1982. A Chinese-American girl deals with her feelings after her grandfather dies, and assists in the preparations for his funeral. Excellent, simple descriptions of the entire funeral. Best for ages 5 and older, though it can be adapted for younger children.

Coutant, Helen. *First Snow.* New York, NY: Knopf, 1974. A snowflake changing to water helps a Vietnamese-American girl understand the meaning of dying.

de Paola, Tomie. *Nana Upstairs & Nana Downstairs.* New York, NY: Putnam, 1973. "Nana Downstairs kept busy in the kitchen by the big black stove. Nana Upstairs rested in her bedroom. She was ninety-four years old. Tommy loved visiting them on Sunday afternoons. But one day, when Tommy ran up the steps to see Nana Upstairs, her bedroom was empty." This is the heartwarming story of that special relationship between the very young and the very old and the moment when the two must part.

Fassler, Joan. *My Grandpa Died Today.* New York, NY: Human Sciences Press, 1983. A realistic treatment of a young boy's close relationship with his grandfather and his adjustment to the grandfather's death, written by a child psychologist. Look for other books from this publisher's series dealing with sensitive topics.

Harris, Audrey. *Why Did He Die?* Minneapolis, MN: Lerner, 1965. A mother's poem explains to her child about the death of his friend's grandfather. Good for use with young children.

Mellonie, Bryan, and Robert Ingpen. *Lifetimes, The Beautiful Way to Explain Death to Children.* New York, NY: Bantam, 1983. "There is a beginning and an ending for everything that is alive. In between is living." Colorful illustrations accompany explanations of how it is natural for all living things—fish, trees, birds, animals, plants, insects, and people—to live and die. A good resource to have for the science area of the school.

Miles, Miska. *Annie and the Old One.* Boston, MA: Little, Brown, 1971. When the new rug is taken from the loom, Annie's grandmother, the Old One, will return to Mother Earth. Her family all understands the cycle of nature, but Annie can't. A poignant story of a little Navajo girl and her very special relationship with her grandmother. Peter Parnall has provided lovely illustrations of life in a hogan. Read with a small group or with one child.

Rogers, Fred. *When a Pet Dies.* New York, NY: Putnam's, 1988. Color photos show children caring for pets of all kinds. The text discusses how it feels to have a pet die. "The best place is to be near someone you love." Children are reminded to talk about their feelings and to realize that both happy and sad times are part of everyone's life.

Stiles, Norman. *"I'll Miss You, Mr. Hooper.* New York, NY: Random House, 1984. Big Bird and the rest of the Sesame Street gang try to come to terms with Mr. Hooper's death. A sensitive approach that young fans of Sesame Street will find comforting.

Varley, Susan. *Badger's Parting Gifts.* New York, NY: Lothrop, 1984. Badger was a friend, and almost everyone who knew him had warm and loving memories of when he was living with them. This story is about the death and life of someone special. It makes the point that when people recall something about the dead, it makes those who are gone part of their lives once more.

Viorst, Judith. *The Tenth Good Thing about Barney.* New York, NY: Macmillan, 1975. A young boy tenderly narrates the story of his pet's death. He must remember ten good things about his cat, Barney, to tell at the funeral. A realistic treatment of the death of a pet and how a child deals with his loss.

Wilhelm, Hans. *I'll Always Love You.* New York, NY: Crown, 1985. This warmly illustrated book sensitively portrays the close relationship between a boy and his dog. As the years go on, the boy grows taller and his dog Elfie grows rounder and slower; and then one night she dies. Grief-stricken, the boy takes comfort in having told Elfie every night of her life, "I'll always love you." A good book to encourage communication of feelings.

Zolotow, Charlotte. *My Grandson Lew.* New York, NY: Harper &

Row, 1974. A boy lovingly recalls his grandfather, who died when the boy was quite young.

BOOKS ABOUT SEPARATION

Barkin, Carol, and Elizabeth James. *I'd Rather Stay Home.* Milwaukee, WI: Raintree, 1975. Jimmy isn't sure he wants to go to school. "What if no one will play with me?" At first Jimmy is hesitant, but later he joins in to help another child build a block tunnel. By the end of the school day, Jimmy realizes he has made a friend.

Bram, E. *I Don't Want to Go to School.* New York, NY: Greenwillow, 1977. Jennifer resorts to all kinds of ploys to avoid going to kindergarten the first day—her doll is sick, her shoes are missing, etc. She finally decides to go when she sees other children happily on their way to school. She returns home after school to tell of her new friends.

Breinburg, Petronella. *Shawn Goes to School.* New York, NY: Crowell, 1973. Shawn wants to go to school, but when he finally enters nursery school, he cries. The book describes a first-day routine and how Shawn eventually adjusts enough to manage a teeny smile.

Caudill, Rebecca. *A Pocketful of Cricket.* New York, NY: Holt, 1964. A 6-year-old Appalachian boy takes his pet cricket to school with him on the first day, but is embarrassed when his pet disrupts the class. He is pleased, however, when the teacher suggests that he share his cricket at show-and-tell.

Cohen, Miriam. *Will I Have a Friend?* New York, NY: Macmillan, 1967. Everyone in preschool is busy—building with blocks, painting, working with clay. Jim wonders if he will have a friend to play with. After rest time, Paul shows him a truck he brought from home, and Jim offers to bring his gas pump the next day.

Hamilton-Merritt, Jane. *My First Days of School.* New York, NY: Julian Messner, 1982. Kate, Mommy, and Bear visit kindergarten. Bear goes with Kate on the first day; on the second day, Bear stays in her cubby while Kate makes new friends. By the third day, Bear stays at home.

Howe, James. *When You Go to Kindergarten.* New York, NY: Knopf, 1986. A series of photos show what it is like to go to kindergarten: arriving, looking around the building, having a fire drill, eating snacks, etc. An introduction for parents is included.

Hurd, Edith T. *Come with Me to Nursery School.* New York, NY: Coward-McCann, 1970. "What will I do at my school?" The photos and text, which show everyday activities in a nursery school setting, are useful in introducing children to their first school experience.

Kantrowitz, Mildred. *Willy Bear.* New York, NY: Parents' Magazine Press, 1976. A young boy's fears about going to school are projected onto his Willy Bear. He tells his bear he will go to school first to meet the bear's new teacher. Brave Willy watches from the window as the boy waves and walks to school.

Rockwell, Harlow. *My Nursery School.* New York, NY: Greenwillow, 1976. A simple text and colorful illustrations depict the daily activities in a typical nursery school setting.

Rogers, Fred. *Going to Day Care.* New York, NY: Putnam, 1985. Mr. Rogers offers a warm, supportive text to accompany the lovely color photos, which show a variety of day care settings serving children from toddlers to older preschoolers. The book includes a section for parents to discuss with their children.

Soderstrom, Mary. *Maybe Tomorrow I'll Have a Good Time.* New York, NY: Human Sciences Press, 1981. Marsha Lou does not want her mother to leave her at the child care center, so she refuses to participate. Later Marsha Lou tells her mother that she was mad and sad, but "maybe I'll have a good time tomorrow."

Viorst, Judith. *The Good-Bye Book.* New York, NY: Atheneum, 1988. A boy's mother and father are getting dressed to go out to dinner, and he doesn't want them to go. It's a familiar struggle between grown-ups and a child who is fiercely determined to make them stay—but maybe laughter helps make saying good-bye a little easier.

BOOKS ABOUT DIVORCE AND WORKING PARENTS

Blaine, Marge. *The Terrible Thing That Happened at Our House.* New York, NY: Macmillan, 1980. Things were fine until mother went back to being a science teacher. That's when everything began to be different. The young child's feelings of confusion, frustration, and lack of attention are finally resolved with cooperation from family and friends.

Brown, Laurene Krasny, and Marc Brown. *Dinosaurs Divorce.* Boston, MA: Atlantic Monthly Press, 1986. If dinosaurs got married, no doubt they, like many families today, had to cope with divorce too. This reassuring book is a good resource to help young children and their families deal with the confusion, misconceptions, and anxieties apt to arise when divorce occurs. The simple text and lively, often funny illustrations depict situations young children can relate to. Positive ways of handling new situations are suggested.

Caines, Jeannette. *Daddy.* New York, NY: Harper & Row, 1977. This book about the children of separated parents deals with one aspect of the situation that has often been overlooked: What do Daddy and his daughter do on their Saturday visiting days? Here we read not only about the places they go, but also about the things they do with Daddy's new wife. The people in this black family have warm, loving relationships, beautifully expressed by the artist.

Goff, Beth. *Where Is Daddy?* Boston, MA: Beacon, 1969. This book was written by a psychiatric social worker to help a child adjust to her or his parents' divorce. The story is good for reading aloud on a one-to-one basis, so that the child can be given plenty of opportunity to discuss the situation and identify with the child in the story. An honest, realistic treatment of a subject that is difficult for the young child to understand.

Hazen, Barbara Shook. *Two Homes to Live In.* New York, NY: Human Sciences Press, 1978. This child's-eye view of a painful divorce stresses the fact that the child did not cause the divorce and that life will stabilize again.

Lindsay, Jeanne Warren. *Do I Have a Daddy?* Buena Park, CA: Morning Glory Press, 1982. A little boy wonders why he never sees his father. Designed to help children increase their understanding of different lifestyles and their acceptance of single-parent friends, the book includes a special section for single mothers and fathers, giving suggestions for dealing with a young child's feelings and discussing the roles of never-married parents as well as divorced parents.

Perry, Patricia, and Marietta Lynch. *Mommy and Daddy Are Divorced.* New York, NY: Dial, 1978. A sensitive, realistic look at the feelings of two children when their parents are divorced. The photos and text about family relationships are honest and direct.

Sanford, Doris. *Please Come Home. A Child's Book about Divorce.* Portland, OR: Multonomah Press, 1985. Jenny holds Teddy tight and whispers, "I'm afraid, I'm lonely, I'm sad, I'm lost." Teddy speaks to her, giving many helpful suggestions.

Stein, Sara Bennet. *On Divorce. An Open Family Book for Parents and Children Together.* New York, NY: Walker & Co., 1979. Black-and-white photos, accompanied by large-type text to be read aloud to children and smaller adjoining text for adults. The Open Family Series includes books on adoption, phobias, hospital stays, new babies, making babies, handicaps, and dying.

Stinson, Kathy. *Mom and Dad Don't Live Together Anymore.* Toronto, Canada: Annick Press, 1984. Simple watercolors and sketches depict a child's narrative, with one sentence per page: "I wish I could make them happy together . . ."; "I love my mom and dad . . . and my mom and dad love me too."

MULTI-ETHNIC BOOKS

Adoff, Arnold. *Black is brown is tan.* New York, NY: Harper & Row, 1973. Brown-skinned momma, white-skinned daddy, and children who are all colors of the race growing up happy in a house full of love. A story-poem about a multiracial family delighting in one another.

Baker, Betty. *Little Runner of the Longhouse.* New York, NY: Harper & Row, 1962. Little Runner is envious of his older brothers, who are allowed to participate in the Iroquois New Year's ceremonies. Young children will be able to identify with his persistence in trying to convince his mother that he is not too young.

Behrens, June. *Fiesta! Cinco de Mayo.* Chicago, IL: Childrens Press, 1978. Color photos with simple text acquaint the reader with the national holiday of the Mexicans. The celebration includes dancing, breaking of a piñata, and other contests.

Carlstrom, Nancy White. *Wild Wild Sunflower Child Anna.* New York, NY: Macmillan, 1987. An engaging story of a little girl all children can identify with. She digs in the garden, skips through snaggle brush, and splashes in a creek. Award-winning illustrations are by Jerry Pinkney. Appropriate for ages 4–8.

Cheng, Hou-tien. *The Chinese New Year.* New York, NY: Holt, 1976. A factual, colorful account of the Chinese New Year celebration, illustrated with paper cuts.

Ets, Marie Hall. *Gilberto and the Wind.* New York, NY: Viking, 1963. A little Mexican boy finds in the wind a temperamental playmate —one who can fly kites, capture balloons, scatter leaves, and run races. The wind can be a stormy and quiet companion. Charming pencil sketches.

Ets, Marie Hall, and Aurora Labastida. *Nine Days to Christmas.* New York, NY: Viking, 1959. A story about Ceci, a 5-year-old Mexican girl, who selects her piñata for Christmas. The illustrations and text give the reader a picture of how Christmas is spent by children in modern-day Mexico. The story may be a bit long for reading to a large group of very young children, but it lends itself to sharing with a small group who can look at and talk about the pictures.

Flack, Marjorie, and Kurt Wiese. *The Story about Ping.* New York, NY: Viking, 1933. An old favorite about a little duck who lives on a boat on the Yangtze River and his adventures when he hides from his master in order to avoid getting a spank on the back. Children can identify easily with not wanting to be spanked.

Greenberg, Polly. *Oh Lord, I Wish I Was a Buzzard.* New York, NY: Macmillan, 1968. A black girl goes to work in the cottonfield "with the sun shining pretty on the land." Before the day's end, she has imagined changing places with a buzzard, a butterfly, a dog, and other creatures. Written in simple, rhythmic style, with bright, warm illustrations.

Hazen, Barbara Shook. *Why Are People Different? A Book about Prejudice.* New York, NY: Western, 1985. Terry's grandma helps him look at other children in school when he complains that no one likes him because he is different. He notices others are different in color, shape, size, and ability. He makes friends and realizes that being different doesn't have to make a difference. It's really getting to know someone that counts.

Keats, Ezra Jack. *Goggles!* Toronto, Canada: Collier-Macmillan, 1969. Two black children find a pair of motorcycle goggles, but have to outsmart a gang of "big guys" in order to keep them. The author is well known for his excellent stories and illustrations, and in this book he "tells it like it is" for a little boy in the big city.

Mao-chiu, Chang. *The Little Doctor.* Peking, China: Foreign Languages Press, 1965. Ping Ping, the little girl doctor, helps make her sister's doll well, gives her brother's teddy bear a check-up, and even repairs a broken rocking horse with hammer and nails. This story is used with young children in China to teach the importance of caring for play equipment and being responsible to others.

Chinese storybooks written in English are available from China Books and Periodicals, 125 Fifth Ave., New York, NY 10003, or 2929 24th St., San Francisco, CA 94110.

Rosenberg, Maxine B. *Living in Two Worlds.* New York, NY: William Morrow, 1986. The children who are photographed in this book are biracial: white and black, Chinese and Cherokee. About 2 percent of all children born in the United States are of mixed racial and ethnic heritage. Children tell how they feel about themselves and the special challenges and benefits of belonging to more than one culture. Appropriate for ages 5–10.

Scott, Ann Herbert. *On Mother's Lap.* New York, NY: McGraw-Hill, 1972. Michael, a young Eskimo boy, loves to rock on his mother's lap. But when the baby cries, he is sure there will not be enough room for both of them. Charming illustrations.

_____. *Sam.* New York, NY: McGraw-Hill, 1967. Everyone in the family is too busy to pay any attention to Sam until finally he begins to cry. Then they find a job that is just right for him.

Showers, Paul. *Your Skin and Mine.* New York, NY: Crowell, 1965. This book shows three boys (an Oriental, a black, and a Caucasian) examining and finding out about skin—how it protects you, its different colors, and so forth. Good for use with a group of children small enough that each child can share in the discussion. Filmstrip available with record or cassette.

Stanek, Muriel. *We Came from Vietnam.* Niles, IL: Albert Whitman, 1985. Photos of a Vietnamese family in the United States, showing their efforts to adjust to life in Chicago.

Steptoe, John. *Baby Says.* New York, NY: William Morrow, 1988. A delightful first book for a baby just beginning to talk. Nice illustrations of a black baby. Good for use with infants and toddlers.

_____. *Mufaro's Beautiful Daughter.* New York, NY: Lothrop, 1987. A memorable modern fable of pride going before a fall. Illustrations glow with the internal vision of the land and people of the author's ancestors. Winner of the 1988 Coretta Scott King award for best illustrations.

_____. *Stevie.* New York, NY: Harper & Row, 1969. Robert, a black child, is jealous when his mother takes care of a younger child, Stevie, in their home. The text is written as if Robert were telling the story. He learns about his sensitive feeling for Stevie when his mother no longer has to babysit.

Yashima, Mitsu, and Taro Yashima. *Momo's Kitten.* New York, NY: Penguin, 1977. Momo finds a kitten that becomes her "nyan-nyan." She nurses her pet back to health and takes on new responsibilities when the cat becomes a mother.

Yashima, Taro. *Umbrella.* New York, NY: Viking, 1958. Lovely illustrations complement a story about Momo, a little Japanese girl who lives in New York, and her eagerness to use her new umbrella.

BOOKS ABOUT SCIENCE AND ECOLOGY

Barton, Byron. *Machines at Work.* New York, NY: Crowell, 1987. Straightforward book with minimal text and bold illustrations depicting construction workers and the machines they use. This same author/illustrator has created a number of other books for young children: *Airplanes, Trains, Boats, Trucks, Wheels,* and *Building a Home,* as well as a series about workers, including *I Want to Be an Astronaut.*

Branley, Franklyn. *What Makes Day and Night.* New York, NY: Crowell, 1961. A simple but detailed explanation of the mechanics of the earth's rotation.

Brenner, Barbara. *Faces.* New York, NY: Dutton, 1970. Photos and script about the sense organs on the head—eyes, ears, nose, and mouth. The text is clear and concise. Photos show how one uses each of the organs and how, although every face is different, they have some things in common. Good to use in conjunction with the study of body parts and exploration of the senses.

Carle, Eric. *The Very Hungry Caterpillar.* New York, NY: Putnam, 1981. A simple and colorful book showing stages of growth in a caterpillar. There are holes in the bright illustrations of leaves and fruit, showing what the caterpillar consumes as it grows.

Coats, Laura Jane. *The Oak Tree.* New York, NY: Macmillan, 1987. A day in the life of an old oak tree, from breakfast for baby birds to visits from a variety of animals and people. Easy text and lovely full-color illustrations on each double-page spread.

Ermanno, Cristine, and Luigi Puricelli. *In My Garden; In the Pond;* and *In the Woods.* Saxonville, MA: Picture Book Studios, 1985. The child's-eye view of nature in this trio of picture books opens new worlds for discovery. Each illustration by the award-winning artists reveals the plant and animal life abounding in the setting. A good introduction to nature for ages 5 and under.

Fitzsimons, Cecelia. *My First Fishes and Other Water Life: A Pop-Up Field Guide.* New York, NY: Harper & Row, 1987. This pop-up book is a good resource to use before going on a field trip to the seashore, as different habitats and their residents are identified. It is also good for displaying on a science table. Other titles by this author include *My First Insects: Spiders and Crawlers; My First Birds;* and *My First Butterflies.*

Gans, Roma. *It's Nesting Time.* New York, NY: Crowell, 1964. An informative and highly educational book designed to teach young children to observe and respect the nests of various birds. Illustrations show how different birds build their nests with different kinds of materials and designs.

Gans, Roma, and Franklyn M. Branley (eds.). *Let's Read and Find Out Science Books.* New York, NY: Crowell. A well-planned series of books designed for children. Titles include *Air Is All Around You, How a Seed Grows, What Makes a Shadow?, Your Skin and Mine,* and many more.

One book in the series, *My Hands,* by Aliki (1962), describes the fingers and thumb, shows how hands are necessary for work and expression, and gets the child to think about his or her own hands. The concepts are geared to the young child, and the easy-to-read text is colorfully illustrated. *My Five Senses* is also by Aliki.

Find Out by Touching, by Paul Showers (1961), suggests that by feeling common objects such as the book, a window, or a carpet, the child can find out many things about the world. Through touch, the child learns about the concepts of hard/soft, smooth/rough, cold/warm, and so on.

Garelick, May. *Where Does the Butterfly Go When It Rains?* New York, NY: Young Scott, 1970. When it rains, the bee flies back to its hive and water slides off a duck's back, but where does a butterfly go? The text encourages children to look and discover the answers for themselves. Blue-hued illustrations give the impression of rain.

Heller, Ruth. *Chickens Aren't the Only Ones.* New York, NY: Grosset & Dunlop, 1985. "Chickens lay the eggs you buy, the eggs you boil or fry or . . . dye! Chickens aren't the only ones. Most snakes lay eggs and lizards, too, and crocodiles and turtles do." Beautiful large-page illustrations express the wonder of nature through poetry.

Another nature book by the same author is *The Reason for a Flower* (New York, NY: Putnam's, 1985). Heller's colorful paintings and surprising rhymes brilliantly fulfill the title's promise. For children ages 3–6.

Hirschi, Ron. *What Is a Bird?* New York, NY: Walker & Co., 1987. Full-color photos introduce children to different kinds of birds in their natural habitats. The simple text makes this a good resource for ages 4 and up.

Jonas, Ann. *Reflections.* New York, NY: Greenwillow, 1987. A cleverly designed book illustrating a day at the seashore. When you come to the end, you turn the book over and read from back to front, reinterpreting the art work from the new perspective, with the help of new captions. The book encourages children to observe and predict.

Krauss, Ruth. *The Carrot Seed.* New York, NY: Harper, 1945. There are some things little children just know, that's all. And even when everyone said it wouldn't come up, the little boy knew his very own carrot seed would grow.

Lionni, Leo. *Fish Is Fish.* New York, NY: Pantheon, 1970. "The minnow and the tadpole were inseparable friends." But the tadpole grows up and becomes a frog and goes off to explore the world. He returns to tell his friend about the extraordinary things he has seen and convinces Fish that he too should venture out of the pond. The sketches of Fish's dreams are humorous. This is a good book to use with tadpoles and fish in a science project.

Mari, Iela, and Enzo Mari. *The Apple and the Moth.** New York, NY: Dial, 1970. This lovely picture book without words shows the stages in the metamorphosis of a moth: egg on leaf, caterpillar, cocoon, moth. All occur in one apple tree. Teacher and children can make up their own descriptions to accompany the drawings. Use with a display of caterpillars and cocoons.

————. *The Chicken and the Egg.** New York, NY: Pantheon, 1969. A hen lays an egg, and the sequence of pictures shows the development of the chick until it finally hatches. This book can be used in studying growth cycles.

Miles, Betty. *Save the Earth! An Ecology Handbook for Kids.* New York, NY: Knopf, 1974. A useful and enjoyable book providing information and guidance for children in the areas of conservation and ecology.

Parker, Nancy Winslow, and Joan Richards Wright. *Bugs.* New York, NY: William Morrow, 1987. "What slippery bug made Doug say 'ugh'? A slug." Slugs, spiders, centipedes, and 13 other common creepy crawlers can be found in this informative book of insects. Labeled diagrams, charts, and brief descriptions provide basic information for the young entomologist. For example, the house centipede is born with only seven pairs of legs, a tiny flea can leap a foot or more, and the female moth lays 300 to 400 eggs. Colorful illustrations and lively rhymes will capture the interest of children ages 4–8.

Peters, Lisa Westberg. *The Sun, the Wind, and the Rain.* New York, NY: Henry Holt, 1988. This is the story of two mountains: The earth made one, and Elizabeth in her yellow sun hat made the other. The simple text and dramatically colorful two-page paintings illuminate and reinforce basic geological concepts by comparing the evolution of the mountain to Elizabeth's small-scale activities on the beach. This evocative first lesson in geology helps young children understand how a small sand hill and the majestic mountain are both transformed by the sun, wind, and rain.

Quinlan, Patricia. *Planting Seeds.* Toronto, Canada: Annick Press, 1988. The fact that people in today's world fight wars often makes children feel helpless and confused. Using Rachel's garden as a symbol, the text shows how a young child learns about the big and small ways people can use their creativity to work for peace by planting seeds of hope. Children from 3 to 7 years old can relate to this simple text.

Selsam, Millicent E. *Is This a Baby Dinosaur?* New York, NY: Harper & Row, 1972. Photographs stress the importance of careful observation. For example, the caption accompanying a photo of lentil seeds asks, "Are these pebbles?" This author produces consistently high-quality books on science concepts for the young child.

Stone, Lynn M. *Marshes and Swamps.* Chicago, IL: Children's Press, 1983. An examination of the ecosystems in wet, marshy environments.

Tafuri, Nancy. *Do Not Disturb.* New York, NY: Greenwillow, 1987. Each page of this lovely picture book shows a different animal's home that a family is inadvertently disturbing with its daytime camping activities. But other things happen at night. A good resource for ecology.

Tresselt, Alvin. *The Dead Tree.** New York, NY: Parents, 1972. The reader is helped to appreciate the natural cycle of life in the forest, where even a dead tree serves to enhance new growth. A good book for studying ecology.

Udry, Janice May. *A Tree Is Nice.* New York, NY: Harper & Row, 1956. An old favorite showing why trees are nice to have around. You can climb on them, eat their fruit, hang a swing on them, picnic in their shade, and plant your very own. The text encourages observation and appreciation of nature.

Wosmek, Frances. *The ABC of Ecology.* Los Altos, CA: Davenport Press, 1982. A guide to the subject of plant and animal relationships, written for preschool and early elementary school children. Available in both English and Spanish.

POETRY AND NURSERY RHYMES

Ciardi, John. *You Know Who.** Philadelphia, PA: Lippincott, 1964. A book of poems about children who pout, hide, misbehave, and are mischievous. Titles include "Someone Showed Me the Right Way to Run Away" and "Get Up or You'll Be Late for School, Silly!"

de Regniers, Beatrice Schenk, et al. *Sing a Song of Popcorn.* New York, NY: Scholastic, 1988. A stunning collection of poetry ranging from ancient to contemporary. Poems by Shel Silverstein, Robert Louis Stevenson, Ogden Nash, Emily Dickinson, and many others are gloriously illustrated in color by Caldecott Medal–winning artists.

Field, Eugene. *Wynken, Blynken and Nod.* New York, NY: Putnam's, 1986. Barbara Cooney's dream-like illustrations capture the mood of this classic children's poem.

Frank, Josette. *Poems to Read to the Very Young.* New York, NY: Random House, 1982. A selection of poems about common events and topics of interest to preschoolers.

Opie, Peter, and Iona Opie (eds.). *Tail Feathers from Mother Goose.* Boston, MA: Little, Brown, 1988. This important anthology is a collection of rhymes, songs, and riddles culled from thousands of items gathered over a period of more than 40 years. It includes such verses as "Mrs. Brown went to town, with her knickers hanging down. Mrs. Green saw the scene, and put it in a magazine." Creatively illustrated by more than 60 of today's most acclaimed artists, this collection of children's folklore is truly outstanding.

Pomerantz, Charlotte. *The Tamarindo Puppy.* New York, NY:

Greenwillow, 1980. A unique collection of poems in which English and Spanish words are interspersed quite naturally. The simple themes will be of interest to young children.

Prelutsky, Jack (ed.). *The Random House Book of Poetry for Children.* New York, NY: Random House, 1983. A wonderful anthology of poetry to delight children of all ages. Most are twentieth-century poems accompanied by Arnold Lobel's humorous illustrations. Poems, grouped by subject matter, include "City, Oh City," "I'm Hungry," "Some People I Know," and a wealth of the best in child-oriented verse.

Richardson, Frederick (illus.). *Mother Goose: The Original Volland Edition.* New York, NY: Derrydale Books, 1984. This wonderful collector's item is a republication of the 1915 edition, with faithful reproductions of the old illustrations. It includes a foreword that tells the history of Mother Goose.

Stevenson, Robert Louis. *A Child's Garden of Verses.* New York, NY: Random House, 1978. A classic combining poetry with storytelling, illustrated by Brian Wildsmith.

————. *The Land of Nod and Other Poems for Children.* New York, NY: Henry Holt, 1988. All the old favorites illustrated in colorfully imaginative style; easy to tell and look at. Included are such familiar poems as "In winter I get up at night, and dress by yellow candlelight. In summer, quite the other way, I have to go to bed by day."

Tripp, Wallace (illus.). *A Great Big Ugly Man Came Up and Tied His Horse to Me.* Boston, MA: Little, Brown, 1973. A compilation of silly verses accompanied by illustrations that tickle the reader's sense of humor.

Wildsmith, Brian (illus.). *Mother Goose.* New York, NY: Merrimack, 1982. Colorfully illustrated with pictures that have a more modern feeling than those in the traditional versions of Mother Goose.

BOOKS ABOUT CHILDREN WITH SPECIAL NEEDS

Aseltine, Lorraine, et al. *I'm Deaf and It's Okay.* Niles, IL: Albert Whitman, 1986. A young boy describes the frustrations caused by his deafness and the hearing aid he must wear. He receives encouragement from a deaf teenager and learns that he can lead an active life.

Braithwaite, Althea. *I Have Asthma.* Cambridge, Great Britain: Dinosaur Publications, 1982. A young boy explains what asthma is, discusses the medication and inhaler he uses, and helps remove the mystique from asthma.

This same company publishes other excellent books about children with special needs, such as *I Have Epilepsy, I Use a Wheelchair,* and *I Can't Talk Like You.*

Brightman, Alan. *Like Me.* Boston, MA: Little, Brown, 1976. "There's a word that is used to describe kids like us . . . though a kid is much more than a word. The word is RETARDED. It means SLOW TO LEARN." A child looks at his mentally handicapped friends and points out that everyone is the same, but some are slower. Appropriate for ages 3–7.

Cairo, Shelley. *Our Brother Has Down's Syndrome.* Toronto, Canada: Annick Press, 1985. Color photos of a Down's syndrome child and his family are accompanied by a simple text in which the child's siblings tell how he may be a little different, but mostly he's just like the rest of us. The description of the causes of Down's syndrome is a bit difficult for children, but useful for teachers.

Fassler, Joan. *Howie Helps Himself.* Chicago, IL: Albert Whitman, 1975. The story of a wheelchair-bound boy, Howie, and his efforts to push his wheelchair across the classroom by himself. We see pictures of Howie doing his exercises and lessons, preparing himself for this stupendous task. Children and adults will be touched by Howie's life.

Fort, Patrick. *Redbird.* New York, NY: Orchard Books, 1988. Redbird, a small airplane, encounters numerous hazards as it attempts to land at the airport. The text is in Braille and in clear black type; raised pictures can be both felt and seen. For sighted and blind to enjoy together.

Litchfield, Ada B. *A Button in Her Ear.* Chicago, IL: Albert Whitman, 1976. About 7 percent of school children have some degree of hearing loss, either from birth or due to illness or accident. The problems are not always identified. This story familiarizes the reader with how a young girl's hearing loss was discovered and what was done for her.

Peterson, Jeanne Whitehouse. *My Sister Is Deaf.* New York, NY: Harper & Row, 1977. A small deaf girl can understand by reading people's lips and eyes. She can say with her face and shoulders what many people cannot say with words. Soft charcoal sketches enhance this first-person text.

Rabe, Berniece. *The Balancing Girl.* New York, NY: E. P. Dutton, 1981. Despite being confined to a wheelchair, little Margaret earns money for the school and the respect of her classmates, by using her special skill. The positive aspects of a crippled child's creativity are emphasized.

———. *Where's Chimpy?* Niles, IL: Albert Whitman, 1988. Actual color photographs show a Down's syndrome child, Misty, and her father reviewing her day's activities in their search for her stuffed monkey. (The incidence of Down's syndrome is about one in 800 live births. The exact cause is not known, but most children can be mainstreamed.)

Rogers, Alison. *Luke Has Asthma, Too.* Burlington, VT: Waterfront Books, 1987. Asthma disrupts the living patterns of children because of its unpredictability. It can be frightening to a child and his or her friends. This story provides simple, basic information about the need for an asthmatic child to learn about self-care, taking medicine, breathing exercises, and staying overnight in the hospital at times. It conveys the message that asthma can be managed in a calm fashion. (Childhood asthma affects 5 percent of children. It is the leading cause of absenteeism among school children in the United States.)

Sargent, Susan, and Donna Aaron Wirt. *In Jimmy's Chair.* Nashville, TN: Abingdon, 1984. A boy has a disturbing dream that helps him understand what it would feel like to be confined to a wheelchair like his friend Jimmy. Good for developing empathy.

PICTURE BOOKS WITHOUT WORDS

The following are excellent lap books that encourage language development and use of the imagination. They are used most effectively with one child at a time.

Alexander, Martha. *Bobo's Dream.* New York, NY: Dial, 1970. Bobo is a dachshund whose master saves his bone from a large mongrel. Bobo dreams of returning the favor.

See also another of the author's wordless books, *Out! Out! Out!* (1968).

Anno, Mitsumasa. *Anno's Peekaboo.* New York, NY: Philomel, 1988. Peeking out from behind the pop-up hands in this innovative book are a rabbit, a clown, a baby, and even Santa Claus. A treat for ages 3 and under.

Goodall, John S. *The Adventures of Paddy Pork.* New York, NY: Harcourt, Brace & World, 1968. A charmingly illustrated book with detailed black-and-white line drawings of a pig who runs away to join the circus.

A second book without words by the same author is *The Ballooning Adventures of Paddy Pork* (1969), which has our hero saving a piglet from a band of gorillas. Good for use with children who have been exposed to many stories and will not be frightened by ferocious-looking animals.

———. *The Midnight Adventures of Kelly, Dott, and Esmeralda.* New York, NY: Macmillan, 1973. Soft, detailed watercolors without words tell the story of three toys—a koala bear, a doll, and a mouse—who wake up at midnight and begin their adventures by climbing into a landscape picture on the wall. The effective use of half-pages heightens the child's interest and challenges the imagination.

———. *The Surprise Picnic.* * New York, NY: Atheneum, 1977. This wordless book will allow even very young readers to follow the action entirely through its lovely, detailed pictures. It shows the suspenseful adventures of a mother cat and her two kittens and how they cleverly cope with catastrophe.

Hoban, Tana. *Look Again!* New York, NY: Macmillan, 1971. Look once, look twice, look again! A collection of black-and-white photos in an amusing format, showing that there is more than one way of seeing a picture. Children enjoy guessing the surprise answers. See other books by this author under Books about Concepts.

_____. *Round and Round and Round.* New York, NY: Greenwillow, 1983. Color photos feature objects that are round.

Mayer, Mercer. *A Boy, a Dog and a Frog.* New York, NY: Dial, 1971. A small book of delightful drawings of a boy and his dog and their attempt to catch a frog for a pet.

The sequel to this book, *Frog, Where Are You?* (1969), shows the frog escaping from a jar at night and the little boy and his dog finding their friend in the pond.

_____. *Bubble, Bubble.* New York, NY: Macmillan, 1980. A little boy buys a magic bubble-maker and blows bubbles in all kinds of shapes, including some scary animals. But he can always pop his bubbles—or can he?

Wezel, Peter. *The Good Bird.** New York, NY: Harper & Row, 1966. A large, colorfully illustrated book about a bird who makes friends with a fish in a goldfish bowl by sharing a worm. See also, by the same author, *The Naughty Bird* (New York, NY: Follett, 1967).

Bibliography of Language Activity Books for the Teacher

Anderson, Paul S. *Story Telling with the Flannel Board.* Minneapolis, MN: T. S. Denison, 1963. An old favorite with instructions for making flannelboards and many traceable patterns of figures that teachers can use to introduce beginning, traditional, and modern stories to young children.

Bauer, Caroline. *Handbook for Storytellers.* Chicago, IL: American Library Association, 1977. All phases of storytelling are covered in detail, including techniques for different age groups, exhibits, and the use of slides, films, and multimedia presentations. Sections are included on the use of flannelboards, chalkboards, puppetry, and magic.

_____. *This Way to Books.* New York, NY: H. W. Wilson, 1983. A collection of ideas, programs, techniques, and activities designed to involve children in books. Toys, puppets, crafts, music, costumes, and banners are used as devices to bring children and books together. Material suitable for preschool and up. Bibliographies throughout.

Beck, M. Susan. *Kidspeak.* New York, NY: Signet, 1982. The author of *Baby Talk* writes about the ways in which children develop language skills. Topics include the learning of concepts and relationships and the child as metaphor-maker and poet.

Boegehold, Betty D. *Getting Ready to Read.* New York, NY: Ballantine, 1984. This book, based on sound principles of how young children learn and develop, emphasizes the link between good reading skills and love of books. Topics include how to monitor TV watching, integrating readiness activities into daily life, age-appropriate books, and games and activities to promote reading skills.

Carlson, Bernice Wells. *Listen! And Help Tell the Story.* New York, NY: Abingdon, 1965. The emphasis is on encouraging children to listen and participate in telling a story. Included are sections on finger plays, action verses, action stories, poems, and stories with sound effects. Some can be easily memorized by the teacher.

Catron, Carol Elaine, and Barbara Catron Parks. *Super Story Telling with Reproducible Patterns.* Minneapolis, MN: T. S. Denison, 1986. A handy pattern book with finger plays, familiar stories, puppetry, and even a pattern for a storytelling apron.

Coody, Betty. *Using Literature with Young Children.* Dubuque, IA: William C. Brown, 1983. Written for teachers in early education to acquaint them with good literature for children, the book concentrates solely on literature for preschool and early primary years. Chapters cover such topics as books for reading aloud, poetry, dramatization, and puppetry.

Engler, Larry. *Making Puppets Come Alive: A Method of Learning and Teaching Hand Puppetry.* New York, NY: Taplinger, 1980. A useful resource for teachers who want to use puppets for storytelling. It includes directions for teaching children how to make and use puppets in the classroom.

Glazer, Susan Mandel. *Getting Ready to Read, Creating Readers from Birth through Six.* Englewood Cliffs, NJ: Prentice-Hall, 1980. For parents and teachers who want to help children develop a sound foundation for reading. Developmental charts provide guidance for adults in understanding learning behaviors at each age. There are many activities for adults to use with their children.

Gross, Jacquelyn. *Make Your Child a Lifelong Reader.* Los Angeles, CA: Jeremy P. Tarcher, 1986. A program for children of all ages who can't, won't, or haven't yet started to read. It includes many easily followed suggestions for involving youngsters in reading skills.

Hunt, Tamara, and Nancy Renfro. *Puppetry and Early Childhood Education.* Austin, TX: Nancy Renfro Studios, 1981. This text describes how to make and use puppets in all areas of the curriculum. (See the bibliograpy in the Music, Drama, and Movement section for descriptions of other puppetry books.)

Jacobs, Leland B. (ed.). *Using Literature with Young Children.* New York, NY: Teachers College Press, 1965. A well-known booklet of essays by various experts on such topics as presenting poetry to children, dramatizing literature, relating literature to other school learnings, reading aloud, and telling stories.

Kimmel, Margaret Mary, and Elizabeth Segel. *For Reading Out Loud!* New York, NY: Delacorte Press, 1983. This book stresses the importance of reading aloud during the early years, with descriptions of how to do it both at school and at home. A reading list is included mostly for kindergarten through elementary grades.

Lamme, Linda Leonard. *Growing Up Reading.* Washington, DC: Acropolis, 1985. Many ideas and activities for parents and teachers to use with children. Age-specific guidelines and recommendations for appropriate books are included.

Machado, Jeanne M. *Early Childhood Experiences in Language Arts.* New York, NY: Delmar, 1985. This well-written text for teachers in early education covers the language development of young children and ways the teacher can promote language skills. It includes many useful suggestions and activities for developing listening and speaking skills, as well as writing and reading readiness. The suggestions on planning the language arts area in a preschool classroom are excellent

Salinger, Terry. *Language Arts and Literacy for Young Children.* Columbus, OH: Merrill, 1988. A text by a teacher of young children, covering topics from the growth of oral language to the use of computers to enhance literacy.

Sawyer, Ruth. *The Way of the Storyteller.* New York, NY: Penguin, 1977. This is not a book on "how to tell stories and what to tell," according to the author, but every teacher should be familiar with Ruth Sawyer's philosophy on the creative art of storytelling.

Schickedanz, Judith A. *More Than the ABCs: The Early Early Stages of Reading and Writing.* Washington, DC: National Association for the Education of Young Children, 1986. A practical guide for parents and teachers on incorporating literacy skills into the informal daily activities of children from birth to first grade.

Schimmel, Nancy. *Just Enough to Make a Story: A Sourcebook for Storytelling.* Berkeley, CA: Sister's Choice Press, 1984. Tips on choosing, learning, and telling a story. Included are songs, finger plays, paper folding, and a selected bibliography.

Scott, Louise B. *Developing Communication Skills: A Guide for the Classroom Teacher.* New York, NY: McGraw-Hill, 1971. In addition to describing the stages of language development, this text offers teachers of young children a variety of activities, including some involving the use of poetry. Also offered are suggestions for helping children with speech problems and those for whom English is a second language.

_____. *Rhymes for Learning Times.* Minneapolis, MN: T. S. Denison, 1984. Many good ideas for finger plays and for acting out rhymes with patterns on the flannelboard. Other sections focus on holidays, numbers, active and quiet times, and more.

Trelease, Jim. *The Read-Aloud Handbook.* New York, NY: Penguin, 1985. This highly acclaimed best seller offers useful hints as to why the experience of reading aloud is so rewarding. It suggests how adults can improve children's language skills and awaken their imaginations. An annotated list of children's books for preschool through grade 6 is included.

PART FIVE

The Physical World

Introduction to the Physical World

A FOUNDATION FOR SCIENCE IN THE EARLY YEARS

A young child and her teacher watch in wonder as a spider deftly spins its silken web in perfect symmetry. By the next morning, the web is complete, with several insects already trapped in its sticky threads, ready for future meals.

Everywhere in the young child's environment are opportunities to establish a strong foundation for learning about the physical world. Watching birds build a nest, collecting a deserted spider's web, making footprints in the sand—these activities engage the natural curiosity of children, leading them to further exploration.

The teacher of young children is in a unique position to establish a firm basis for the scientific method. "How did the web catch the insects?" "Where do birds go when it rains?" "What makes footprints?" When children ask questions such as these, they are posing a problem. When the teacher says, "What do you think will happen if you stand in the dry sand? In the wet sand?" the children's guesses are predictions. The suggestion "Let's watch to see what happens when you pour water on the sand" leads children to conduct an experiment, observe what actually happens, and make conclusions about the results.

Youngsters watching the spinning of a web or observing the results of rain are engaged in *natural science*. When they participate actively in experiencing the effects of energy on matter (pouring water into the sand and making footprints), they are involved in *physical science*. It is important for teachers to differentiate between the two and to maintain a balance between them in curriculum planning.

HOW YOUNG CHILDREN LEARN

Experiences in the early years are the most powerful in forming adult intelligence. By the time a child is 6 years old, much of the groundwork has been laid for his or her future learning success. Thus, the teacher who understands how young children learn plays an important role in contributing to their later success.

The impressive work of Swiss psychologist Jean Piaget tells us much about how children think and perceive the world at different stages of their early development. (See the introduction to Part One.) Piaget provides evidence that children at the preoperational stage (about ages 2–7) base their thoughts primarily on immediate perceptions—that is, they are still misled by appearances.

For example, even though the child pours liquid from a short, squat glass into a tall, thin one, he or she believes that the tall glass has more liquid than the shorter one. Children at the preoperational stage are not yet capable of intellectualizing that the amount remains the same. And, more importantly for the teacher, they do not learn by being told. Thus, when physical science activities are presented, it is vital that children have many variables to manipulate so that they can see the cause and effect of their actions.

Active learning facilitates reasoning, which is how children construct their knowledge about the physical world.

GUIDING CHILDREN TO LEARN ABOUT THE PHYSICAL WORLD

Knowledge about the physical world grows out of a child's natural curiosity and urge to touch, see, hear, taste, and investigate. Through a variety of hands-on experiences, children develop their abilities to think and learn. The teacher acts as a facilitator by asking questions and providing guidance and encouragement.

What-if questions motivate children to *experiment* and to seek out answers:

What do you think will happen if you blow on the leaf? the piece of cotton? the rock?

Shall we try it and see?

By *hypothesizing* and *observing*, children gain knowledge about the physical world. They can see what happens as a result of what they do.

What happened when you blew on the leaf? the piece of cotton? the rock?

Which objects are easy to move by blowing?

Why do you think the rock is harder to move?

With the encouragement and modeling of the teacher, children learn not only that it is okay to ask questions, but also that they can help to find answers for themselves. Their observations may be inaccurate, but they are valid indications to the teacher of how the children are interpreting what they perceive.

By asking pertinent questions yourself, you can teach children to phrase questions that will help them make discoveries on their own. A teacher guides a child's action and thinking by the way a question is worded. When you ask:

What do you think will happen if you drop the ball?

a child will probably be inclined to drop it to see what happens (act on the object). When you ask:

What happened?

Does the ball always fall to the floor when you drop it?

the child's reply will give an indication of his or her level of perception.

If, however, you ask:

Why does the ball fall to the floor?

you are likely to mystify and confuse the child. Questions that are appropriately phrased lead children to think, reason, and construct their own knowledge.

Given a problem within their ability to solve, children will discover a need for certain scientific processes:

Look what's happening! (observing)

I wonder if . . . ? (hypothesizing)

How can we find out? (testing)

Maybe if we do this . . . (predicting)

These have six legs and those don't have any. (classifying)

The teacher who encourages curiosity and creativity will recognize that children need time and freedom to follow through with trial and error. Creative people are likely to give unconventional responses and offer unusual ideas. They also tend to have a higher tolerance for ambiguity and want to find out more about a topic. Rushing children or giving the "right" answers may stifle their creativity.

PLANNING THE CURRICULUM

The school is a natural laboratory for engaging the children in both the natural and the physical sciences. The teacher needs only to be alert to the chance to do some spontaneous teaching during the daily routine. A snail from the garden, a bird's nest a child has discovered, some seashells from a recent trip—all provide the teacher and the children with opportunities to learn more about the environment. When a school has many kinds of animals and plants, the children learn about living things and what they need to survive.

The outside environment is a rich laboratory for discovery: leaves change colors, die, and drift to the ground; a bud blossoms into a flower; rocks decompose into sand. The weather can also be discussed: rain falls from clouds, puddles dry up on a sunny day, the wind causes certain sensations and makes things move when it blows.

The classroom also offers many areas for discovery. A science center with a terrarium, a set of balance scales, and a display of rocks and plants offers interesting things for children to examine and experiment with. Children can be encouraged to bring their own contributions to share with others. Centering activities around a particular theme, such as Growing Things, How Different Things Feel, or Changes, can provide a useful focus.

For the theme Changes, you might do some of the following:

- Make cinnamon toast for snack time, and talk about how the bread changes to toast.
- Make body outlines to show how children change as they grow.
- Watch how cocoons and polliwogs change.
- Collect leaves to show how they change color with the changing seasons.
- Provide opportunities for children to manipulate and change materials in the science center—mixing colors, forming and reforming clay, dissolving salt and sugar, making and then melting ice.

Some of the activities may not lead to complete understanding. The fact that matter may change in form but continue to exist (as in dissolving, freezing, and melting) is a concept that preschoolers are not likely to comprehend fully. But their actions along with your questioning will lay a good foundation for understanding the principle of conservation.

Children's curiosity about the physical world provides a natural opportunity for teaching ecology and conservation. The damaging effects of litter, waste, and pollution can be demonstrated through curriculum activities. In areas where drought is sometimes a problem, young children can be made aware of the need to save water and to recognize some of the obvious ways to avoid waste. They can learn that it is not a good idea to leave the faucet running or to throw paper and soft drink cans out of the car, even though they may not be able to explain the logic of recycling.

Young children can be taught to save, to avoid pollution, and to value clean air and water. The central concept of ecology—that life forms depend on one another and on their physical surroundings—isn't something children are prepared to explain. But attitudes toward littering, wasting, and polluting can be learned and taught, and preschool is the time to teach them. For this generation of children, respect for the environment may be a matter of survival. In addition, the principles of cooperation and consideration for others that conservation and ecology embody are themselves well worth the effort required to include these topics in the curriculum.

Most of the activities in this section draw on resources that exist in the natural environment of the school or home. Adapt them as needed, keeping in mind that children are active investigators, not passive observers.

In the final analysis, it is the teaching strategies—the way you phrase your questions, your perceptiveness and enthusiasm—that will determine the quality of your science program. A popular quotation expresses well the way young children learn best:

I hear and I forget.
I see and I remember.
I do and I understand.

PLANNING THE SCIENCE CENTER

The science area in your school is where children can explore, experiment, and practice the skills of scientific investigation—observing, classifying, comparing, communicating, inferring, predicting, and concluding. It is also a place where materials from nature can be displayed and worked with, so that children can better understand the environment in which they live. (See Illustration 5.1.)

The materials in this area should be changed often to reflect current interests. If a child brings in some seashells to share, they should be displayed in a special place, along with appropriate tools and equipment for further studying the collection—magnifying glasses, books about shells and the seashore. The learning could possibly be

Illustration 5.1 **The science area**

extended to such concepts as sorting and grouping by texture (rough and smooth shells), weighing and balancing the objects, and so on.

A well-planned center enables children to be self-sufficient, with low shelves to keep equipment within easy reach. Label storage containers with pictures. Materials that need teacher supervision can be stored on higher shelves or in cabinets. In all cases, children should be familiar with proper usage and storage of materials and equipment. Post pictures as reminders, and talk to the children during group time about putting things back in their proper places and cleaning up when they have finished.

Depending on your outdoor facilities and the space available, you may want to include a sand and water table. Since activities involving water and sand require extra supervision and clean-up, locate the table near a sink. Provide waterproof aprons, short-handled mops, brooms, sponges, and dustpans. Ask for donations of old shower curtains to tape down around the table. A child-height counter with a sink is an excellent feature.

Situate in the science area display tables where theme materials can be exhibited and handled. Movable wallboard dividers provide excellent backgrounds for posters and pictures that tell about the materials on display.

In addition to the low storage shelves, have a bookcase where magazines like *Ranger Rick* and *National Geographic* and paperback guides to rocks, seashells, birds, and such can be readily available for reference.

Since science and math are closely allied, locate the two areas next to each other. That way, you will not need to duplicate such equipment as balance scales, containers, and other measuring tools.

Perhaps more than any other area, the science center needs plenty of storage space for collectible materials. Post or send home a list of items that parents and volunteers can donate, such as the following:

Display Containers

Styrofoam trays
clear plastic containers
aluminum pie pans

small cardboard boxes
cafeteria lunch trays
pieces of material

Storage Containers

cereal boxes (cut away one
    narrow side and use to store
    magazines upright)
milk cartons
baskets
sturdy carrying bags

shoe boxes
plastic dishpans
file boxes
large commercial cardboard ice
    cream cartons

Experimental Equipment

pails
plastic jars and containers
aquarium
coffee cans
food coloring
binoculars
egg cartons
tape measures
sponges
rubber tubing
potting soil
pitchers
measuring cups and spoons
pulleys
magnets
old sheets and pillow cases
cardboard tubes

milk cartons
juice cans
prisms
small cages
magnifying glasses
spools
scales
rulers
egg timer
candles
yarn
funnels
latches
locks and keys
flower pots
plastic bags

Natural Materials

rocks
plants
dried flowers
birds' nests
feathers
gourds

seashells
insects
fossils
pine cones
nuts and seeds

Physical World Activities

SENSORY PERCEPTION

Touch

How Different Things Feel

MATERIAL
Objects of different textures such as foam rubber, cork, cotton balls, pennies, velvet, satin, burlap, erasers, marshmallows, marbles

PROCEDURE
- Have the children examine one object at a time.
- Encourage them to talk about how each object feels, comparing textures and using descriptive words such as *smooth, hard, soft, spongy, rough*. Name the objects as you talk about them.
- When children are familiar with the objects, have them play a guessing game by either closing their eyes or wearing a blindfold while you or one of the children hands them an object to identify. Use descriptive words as clues to help children guess which objects they are holding.
- Talk about the importance of a sense of touch in our daily activities. Invite the children to give examples, like getting around in the dark, testing bath water, petting an animal, walking barefoot on different surfaces, holding hands, or fingerpainting.

VARIATION
Place several objects in a bag or box. Have each child in turn reach into the container and select an object. Before pulling it out, the child should describe and name the object. When the children are comfortable with the activity, vary it by placing items under a cloth and letting the youngsters identify the objects with their bare feet.

Taste

How Different Things Taste

MATERIAL
A variety of common foods, such as apples, popcorn, bread, dry cereal, bananas, oranges, peanut butter

PROCEDURE
- Show the children the different kinds of food you are using in the activity.
- Name the foods, and talk about how they taste: *soft, sweet, crunchy, salty, sticky, juicy, sour*.
- Blindfold the children or have them close their eyes while you place a small amount of food in their mouths. Let them guess what they are tasting.
- Ask them to describe how they arrived at their guesses.
- Repeat the procedure, having the children hold their noses while they taste.
- Talk about the importance of smell in helping us tell how something tastes.

Note: Some children do not like being blindfolded, so do not insist on it. They may enjoy using a Halloween mask with the eyes covered. The object is to have them focus on their sense of taste, even if they wish to keep their eyes open.

Sight and Touch

How Some Things Feel the Same but Look Different

MATERIAL   Objects that feel the same but look different, such as apples or crayons of different colors, cups and small table toys that are the same shape but different colors, paper with and without print or pictures

PROCEDURE   • After the children have had some experience describing how different things feel (see preceding activities), blindfold them or have them close their eyes while you hand them an object.
            • Let them examine and describe what they are holding. If they guess the object immediately, ask them to tell you how they arrived at their conclusion. If they need help, ask questions about the object, such as
            Is it rough or smooth? hard or soft? round or flat?
            What color is it?
            Does it have a design or picture on it?
            • Talk about how some things feel the same but look different. Our eyes tell us about some things that we cannot feel, such as color and design.

Smell

How Different Things Smell

MATERIALS   Babyfood jars
            Black paint, black paper, or dark contact paper
            Things that have an odor, such as cloves, mint, flower petals, onions, garlic, apples, orange peels, chocolate

PROCEDURE   • Let the children help place one ingredient in each jar.
            • Punch holes in the jar lids.
            • Let the children smell each jar and talk about the ingredients.
            • When they are familiar with the various odors, have them close their eyes and guess the contents of the jars.
            • After the children have become experienced with the activity, paint the jars with black paint (or cover the insides with dark paper), leaving the bottoms clear. Punch holes in the lids, and place new ingredients in the jars.
            • Introduce the painted jars as a further challenge. The children can check the contents by turning the jars over.
            • Talk about the importance of smell in warning us (smoke/fire) and in helping us to identify things and to taste foods. Encourage the children to observe how dogs and other animals sniff at things in their environment. Talk about noses—how they differ in size and shape, who or what has one.

VARIATIONS   Make a collage of magazine pictures of all kinds of human and animal noses.

         Saturate cotton balls with flavor concentrates for children to smell and identify. Have jars of scents for children to match.

Hearing

How Different Things Sound

MATERIAL   Common objects in the rooms

PROCEDURE

- Have the children close their eyes while you make various sounds by clapping hands, hitting a drum, opening and shutting a door, pouring water, ringing a bell, shaking a rattle, etc.
- Have the children guess what each sound is and describe how it is made.
- Let the children see how the sounds are made and make the sounds themselves.
- Have a child make some kind of sound for the others to guess.
- Talk about the importance of hearing in our daily activities: walking in traffic, listening to other people, following directions, enjoying music.

Note: Encourage lots of discussion and guessing. Praise the children, and reinforce their attempts to describe the properties of the objects they are naming. Encourage the children to work together and help each other. Correct answers should not be the goal of these activities.

Identifying Different Sounds

MATERIALS   8–10 Small plastic film or pill containers (available from photo shops or pharmacies)

Small items such as salt, rice, macaroni, popcorn, marbles, or beans

PROCEDURE

- Using two containers per item, let the children help fill each container about a quarter full. Secure the lids.
- Let them shake the cans and guess at the contents. Encourage the children to cooperate in their guessing, and let them look inside the cans to validate their answers.
- When they are familiar with the sound each item makes, have the children match the pairs of cans that sound the same.

Making a String Phone

MATERIALS   String or twine 10' or more in length

2 paper cups or empty frozen juice cans

Paper clips (optional)

PROCEDURE

- Thread each end of the string or twine through a hole in the bottom of a paper cup or juice can. Make a knot on the end of each string

(or tie the end of the string around a paper clip inside each can) so that it won't pull out of the hole.
- Have a child at each end of the string, holding the can so that the string is taut.
- Have one child talk quietly into one end of the "phone" while the other child listens by holding the can to his or her ear.

VARIATION   An extension can be made by looping a second set of phone lines over the first set.

Note: Waxing the phone strings with a candle or piece of paraffin will improve transmission of sound because the denser the material, the better it will carry sound waves.

You can talk about the sounds of voices being carried by the string, and how the cans help to make the sounds clearer by amplifying the vibrations. Although most preschoolers will not be able to understand that sounds are made by a vibrating object such as a string or wire, they will be interested to discover that when the vibrations are interrupted (as, for example, when someone holds the string or it touches an object), they cannot hear each other.

Making Stereo Sounds

MATERIALS   Metal coat hanger
2 Paper cups
String

PROCEDURE   • Tie a 12" piece of string to each end of a hanger. Insert the other end of each string through a hole in the bottom of a paper cup (as in making a phone).
- Have someone tap the hanger with a pencil or some other object while a child listens to the various sounds through one or both cups.
- Have the children compare the quality of sounds they hear using one cup to the stereo effect they get by listening through two cups.

Note: Encourage children to experiment by bending the shape of the hanger or by replacing the hanger with other objects, such as a metal grill from the stove or a paper clip.

Making Sounds Louder (Amplification)

MATERIALS   Cone-shaped paper cup
Emery board (a nail file)
Straight pin
2 Funnels
Plastic tubing to fit the funnels

PROCEDURE   • Have the children listen carefully while you scratch a pin over the emery board. Talk about the sound it makes. Show them how you can make the sound louder by putting a straight pin through the narrowest part of a paper cup. The cup amplifies the same way the cans did in the phone activity.

• Connect two funnels with a length of plastic tubing, and let the children talk and listen to each other through the funnels. They can even whisper and be heard.

Note: Children can experiment with sound amplification by making megaphones from construction paper rolled and stapled into cone shapes.

Making Sounds with Rubber Bands

MATERIALS   Metal loaf pan
Rubber bands of various colors

PROCEDURE   • Put rubber bands around the loaf pan, and let the children experiment with the sounds they can make by plucking on the bands.

VARIATIONS   Prop up the ends of varying lengths of 2 x 2 soft wood (such as redwood) with rolled up towels or cartons. Have the children make different sounds by hitting the pieces of wood with wooden spoons.

    Let the children pop balloons or squeeze plastic bubble packing material to experience the explosive sounds made by a sudden burst of air.

PHYSICAL PROPERTIES AND ENERGY

Air Moves Things

Making Things for Children to Blow

MATERIALS   Sturdy, bendable plastic straws
Ping Pong balls
Colored feathers
Foam packing materials
Leaves
Unsharpened pencils
Cone-shaped paper cups
Straight pins

PROCEDURE   • Talk about air and how we cannot see or touch it. Ask:
Since air is invisible, how do we know it is really there?
Discuss familiar experiences children have had with air, such as blowing out candles and inflating balloons.
• Let the children move light objects such as feathers, leaves, and foam packing materials by blowing at them through straws. Talk about how the children are using air to move things.
• Hold a Ping Pong ball over the end of a sturdy, flexible plastic straw that has been bent so that one end points up at the ball.

Demonstrate how you can keep the ball suspended and moving by blowing through the straw. Let the children try to do it.

- Help the children make weather vanes as follows: Cut a piece of paper in an arrow shape, and attach it with tape to one end of a straw. Attach a feather to the other end of the same straw. Stick a straight pin through the middle of the straw and into the center of the pencil eraser. The children can make the weather vane move round and round by blowing at it through a straw.
- Take the weather vane outside on a windy day to see if the wind will make it move. (You can make a sturdier weather vane by using a wooden dowel.) Ask:
  Can you tell the direction of the wind by using the weather vane? What else can you use or look at to tell the direction of the wind?
- Make 1" cuts around the edges of cone-shaped paper cups. After flaring out the cut edge, place each cup upside down on a pencil. Let the children make the cups go around by blowing on them through straws. Children can decorate the cups to take home for demonstrations of how they can use air to move things.

Note: Other activities showing that air is all around us include blowing bubbles, making blow-out pictures (see page 30), and feeling the wind and watching the things it blows (smoke, clouds, trees, clothes, kites, and flags).

Making More Air Toys

MATERIALS
Jumbo straws
Lightweight objects such as feathers, Styrofoam packing materials, lens tissues, paper, cotton, balsa wood, plastic caps, foil
Round objects such as beads, marbles, pencils, cardboard rolls, straws, Ping Pong balls
Heavy objects such as small blocks, scissors, books, playdough

PROCEDURE
- Select one or two objects from each of the three categories: lightweight, round, and heavy. Place them on a table, and ask the children which objects they can blow around the table.
- Ask questions such as
  What happened when you blew on the paper? the scissors? the Ping Pong ball?
  Why do you think this moved? (Point to a light object.)
  Why do you think this didn't move? (Point to a heavier object.)
  What do you think will happen if we stand this cardboard roll on end? Let's try it and see. Which way is it easier to move?
- Have the children talk about why they think some things move more easily than others when they are blown on. They may say things like "It's flat," "It's round," or "It's not heavy."
- Introduce other objects, and have the children predict whether they will be able to move them by blowing on them.
- Ask questions that begin with
  What if . . .
  What happened when . . .

What do you think will happen if . . .
Why do you think . . .

VARIATIONS   Have the children try blowing on objects without the use of straws. Ask them whether the straws make it harder or easier to move the object.

Let the children use straws to move objects such as balsa wood, Styrofoam, bottle caps, foil, Ping Pong balls, and feathers on water.

Delivering an Airmail Letter

MATERIALS   Balloon
Plastic straw
Twine or heavy string
Envelope
Masking tape

PROCEDURE
- Cut a length of twine 10–12' long.
- Thread the twine through a straw.
- Tape an envelope to the straw.
- Have two children hold the twine taut.
- Make a loop of tape, sticky side out. Stick the bottom of the loop to the straw, above the envelope.
- Inflate a balloon, holding the end so that no air can escape. Stick the balloon to the top of the loop of tape.
- Starting at one end of the twine, send the letter to the other end by letting go of the inflated balloon. The escaping air will push the straw with the envelope along the twine. The larger the balloon, the farther the envelope will travel through the air.

VARIATION   Hold one end of the twine, and affix the other end to a door. Turn off the lights, and attach a glow stick (available during Halloween season) to the straw. (Glow sticks will last longer if kept in the freezer.)

Note: To reinforce the notion that air moves things, let the children fly kites and balloons, squeeze bottles or bellows, or make fans by folding paper into accordion pleats.

Children will love surprising adults by making twine pop out of squeeze bottles. Simply insert knotted yellow or red twine into an empty plastic squeeze bottle for mustard or ketchup. After pulling the twine through the narrow dispenser tip, make another knot on the outside. When children squeeze the bottle, the colored twine will shoot out.

Lifting Things with Air

MATERIALS   Book
Balloon
Air pump

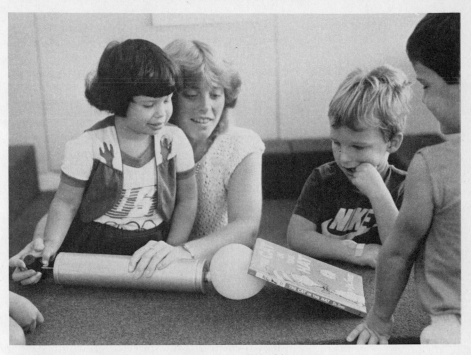

Illustration 5.2 Demonstrating that air can lift things

PROCEDURE
• Talk with the children about their experiences with air and about some of the things that air can do.
• Show them the book, the balloon, and the air pump. Ask if they can figure out a way to make the air lift the book.
• Let the children test their suggestions, even if they are not correct.
• If the children need help, suggest that they place the balloon under the book.
• After they have inflated the balloon with the air pump, talk about other experiences they have had with air lifting or moving an object. Let them try lifting other things with the balloon and the air pump. Concepts need to be reinforced in many different ways to be learned and retained.

Making Bubbles

MATERIALS
Water
Glycerin
White sugar
Dawn or Joy liquid detergent
Unbreakable containers such as empty juice cans
Bubble wands
Cut-out empty juice cans
Plastic six-pack holders
Coated wire
Jumbo straws
Bendable straws

PROCEDURE
- Make bubble solution by mixing together 2 quarts of water, 2 tablespoons of glycerin, 1 tablespoon of white sugar, and 1 cup of liquid detergent. Let the mixture sit for at least 3 hours. This bubble solution can be stored in the refrigerator for weeks and improves with age. (See the Art Recipes section for more bubble recipes.)
- Give each child a container half full of bubble solution.
- Provide a selection of objects that the children can use to make bubbles.
- Let the children experiment with twisting the coated wire to create different shaped bubbles.
- Suggest that they make a circle with the thumb and forefinger, dip it into the bubble solution, and blow.
- Talk about the shapes and colors of bubbles, what they look like in the sunlight and in the wind, why some are small and some are large, what happens when different kinds of straws are used, and what the children think will happen if they use different objects to make the bubbles.

VARIATION
Generally bubbles will float and blow away because they are lighter than air, but if you blow them into a container that has a piece of dry ice in the bottom, they will remain suspended. *(Caution: Do not let children come into contact with the dry ice.)* Because the carbon dioxide from the dry ice is heavier than air, it will stay on the bottom of the container and suspend the lighter bubbles. Although preschoolers are not expected to understand this concept, such activities—in addition to being fun—add to their total experience.

Making Person-Size Bubbles

MATERIALS
Small wading pool
Hula Hoop, large enough to fit around the child but small enough to fit inside the pool
Block
Bubble solution (See the preceding activity for recipe.)

PROCEDURE
- Cover the bottom of the wading pool with about ½" of bubble solution.
- Place a block or some other appropriate sturdy object in the middle of the pool, for a child to stand on.
- Let one child stand on the block. Dip the hoop in the bubble solution, and pull it straight up over the child's head to encase the child inside a huge bubble.

Capturing Snowflakes

MATERIALS
Piece of heavy acrylic or glass
Can of clear spray lacquer
Snow
Magnifying glass

PROCEDURE
- On a day when snow is falling, talk with the children about snow and how no two snowflakes are exactly alike. Explain that when the weather is very cold, water vapor high above the earth freezes around tiny dust particles to form snowflakes. Talk about how you might catch a snowflake and examine it more closely.
- Place the can of lacquer and the piece of glass in the freezer for 2 minutes, and then take them outdoors before they warm up.
- Spray a thin coat of lacquer on the glass. Be careful to point the spray so that the children do not inhale the fumes.
- Hold the glass so that snow falls on it, and then place the glass in the freezer for 15 minutes. The snowflakes will be "captured" on the glass.
- Let the children study the patterns of the snowflakes through a magnifying glass. Explain that the distinctive shapes are made when the snowflakes twist and spin while falling to the earth.
- Talk about the importance of snow to our environment—how it serves as a warm blanket to keep the soil from freezing, and how many plants and animals would die without a snow blanket.

Making Rainbows

MATERIALS
Garden hose
Small mirror
Glass container of water
Flashlight
Red, orange, yellow, green, blue, and violet construction paper

PROCEDURE
- Have the children make a rainbow outdoors by standing with their backs to the sun and turning a garden hose on to a fine spray. Ask them to identify the colors.
- Indoors, place a small mirror in a glass container of water. Position the glass so that the sun shines on the mirror. (If there is no sun, use a flashlight.) Turn the glass until a rainbow is reflected against the wall or ceiling. The colors of the rainbow will be clearest if they are reflected onto a white surface, such as a piece of paper. Have the children identify the colors.
- Let the children experiment with making rainbows. Ask:
  What happens if you take the light or water away?
  How does the light have to shine—around, under, over, or through the water?
  Talk about the conditions that are necessary to make a rainbow: light (sun) being reflected through water (rain). Note that you can see a rainbow only if the sun is at your back and it is shining through water.
- Have the children name the colors that they saw in the rainbows they made. Were the colors the same both indoors and out? Point out that the colors are always in the same order: the longest waves are red, followed by orange, yellow, green, blue, and violet.
- Let the children cut and paste colored strips of paper to make their own rainbows.

Note: Sunlight is made up of all the colors of the rainbow mixed together. When sunlight hits the water, the colors are separated. Although children at the preoperational stage are not likely to arrive at a correct conclusion about how rainbows are made, or even to recall the order of the colors, arousing a child's curiosity and sense of wonder is a worthwhile objective in itself.

Discovering Some Properties of Water

MATERIALS
Water table or large tub
Plastic aprons
Funnels of various sizes
Squeeze bottles
Pumps
Test tubes
Cups
Syringes
Plastic bottles with holes punched out at varying levels
Measuring spoons
Sponges
Syphons
Flexible and rigid tubing
Y fittings
Sieves or colanders
Small watering cans

Illustration 5.3 **Sand and water tables**

PROCEDURE
- Talk with children about water and how we use it: for drinking, washing, cooking, raising food, fighting fires, transportation, power, etc. Mention that water comes from rain, that we get it from rivers, streams, wells, and dams; and that people, animals, and plants can't live without it. Note that water's also fun to play and swim and splash in. Talk about different ways children are familiar with water.
- After they put on their plastic aprons, let the children help fill a water table or tub with water.
- Provide the children with water play equipment selected from the list of materials above. The amount of equipment should be determined by the amount of space and the number of children. Do not overcrowd the water table, but have enough materials that children can experiment with a variety of equipment.
- Begin with simpler materials, such as cups, squeeze bottles, and funnels. Gradually introduce more complex equipment over a period of days and weeks. Putting out too many things at one time may distract children from focusing on the properties of water.
- Establish ground rules about keeping the water in the tub or table, not on other people. Watch how the children play, and listen to each child. Very little direction is usually necessary. As children play, they will become increasingly aware of some of the properties of water.
- Encourage the youngsters to share their discoveries about how water squirts, splashes, and falls from different heights, and how it can be pumped, absorbed, and poured into different shapes. Whatever children do with intensity and interest will have meaning to them. Sometimes a simple observation by the teacher will help focus a child's attention on a new wonder.
  I see you discovered how to fill your pail with a syphon.
  Can you make the water come out one drop at a time?
- Talk about some properties of water that the children experienced: water has weight, it can change form, it can float some things, it can be absorbed by some things, it is transparent, it can dissolve some things, it flows and pours.

Note: Have mops and sponges nearby for children to help with clean-up.

Investigating Materials That Absorb Liquids

MATERIALS
Egg cartons
Small plastic containers
Eye droppers
Water
Food coloring
Assorted common materials that may or may not absorb liquids, such as cotton, sponges, sand, paper, wood, cloth, yarn, plastic, rocks, leaves, soil

PROCEDURE
- Talk with children about the word *absorb*, and demonstrate its meaning by showing how a paper towel or sponge soaks up water.

- Ask the children to think of other things that might absorb water.
- Provide each child with an egg carton. You may want to start with fewer than 12 egg cups.
- Let the children select from among an assortment of different materials, placing one item in each egg cup. As they make their selections, have them guess whether the item will absorb water.
- Give each child a container (such as a small plastic medicine bottle) of colored water and an eye dropper.
- Let the children test the items for absorbency by dropping water on each one.
- Have them observe and report which materials soaked up the water and which did not. Ask whether some soaked up the liquid quickly, some slowly, and some not at all.
- Suggest that children sort the items into two different groups— things that absorb and things that do not.
- Have them select new items, placing those that they think are absorbent on one side of the egg carton and those they think are non-absorbent on the other.
- Let them test their hypotheses and report their findings (or mark the egg cups).
- Have the children collect other kinds of materials to add to the selection.

Sinking and Floating

MATERIALS   Water table or large tub
Plastic aprons
Assorted light and heavy objects, such as corks, plastic containers, Styrofoam meat trays, wood, toy boats, metal objects, rocks, pebbles
Plastic containers with removable lids

PROCEDURE   • After the children put on their aprons, let them play at the water table with objects selected from among the materials listed.
- Call to their attention that some objects stay on top of the water (float) and others go to the bottom (sink).
- Ask how the children can make things float or sink.
  What do you think will happen if we put a lid on this empty cup with only air in it? Will it float or sink?
  When air is squeezed out of the bottle, what happens?
  What if you put a pile of rocks in the middle of your boat (Styrofoam tray)?
  What if you spread the rocks around evenly?
- Have the children compare the buoyancy (floatability) of objects having similar weights but different shapes.

Note: Relate new concepts to children's experiences. Even though the youngsters will not understand buoyancy, they can relate their experiences with sinking and floating to other properties of water if the teacher reinforces those experiences with stories, songs, and field trips.

Studying the Weather

MATERIALS   Tagboard sketches showing the sun, clouds, and rain, as well as perhaps lightning, snow, and wind

Books about weather[16]

Calendar and weather symbols

PROCEDURE

- Talk about the weather to determine how much the children know about the meaning of the word.
- Have the children name different kinds of weather.
- Show the tagboard picture of the sun, and talk about sunny days. Discuss how the children feel, what they wear, what they do, and how they cool off on such days. Ask:

  Is today a sunny day?

  Is it sunny every day?

  Does the sun shine at night?
- Show the picture of clouds and have the children identify it. Ask:

  What does a cloud look like?

  Do you see clouds every day?

  What are clouds made of?

  Where is the sun on a cloudy day?
- Show the picture of rain. Ask:

  How do we dress on a rainy day? Why?

  Where does rain come from?
- Do the same with any other sketches you have selected.
- Read aloud some books dealing with weather cycles. Explain how the sun heats air and water, causing water to evaporate, condense, and precipitate (rain). Young children cannot be expected to understand the intricacies of weather systems, but they can develop an awareness of some of the factors that determine weather: air, wind, sun, temperature, clouds, rain, and snow.
- Start keeping a weather calendar, and have the children help by selecting the appropriate symbols for each day.

Making a Thermometer

MATERIALS   Clear plastic bottles

Drinking straws (translucent plastic)

Playdough or clay

Red food coloring

2 Small buckets

Ice water

Hot water

---

[16]Suggestions: *The Cloud Book*, by Tomie dePaola (New York, NY: Holiday House, 1975); *Weather*, by Imelda and Robert Updegraff (New York, NY: Penguin Books, 1982); any of the fine selections from Thomas Y. Crowell Publishers' *Let's Read and Find Out Series*, including *Rain and Hail* and *Flash, Crash, Rumble and Roll*, both by Franklyn M. Branley, and *Water for Dinosaurs and You*, by Roma Gans. A book that is fun to read is *Cloudy, with a Chance of Meatballs*, by Judi Barrett (New York, NY: Macmillan, 1978).

PROCEDURE
- Have the children fill a bottle with red-colored water. Put a straw in the bottle, and secure it with clay wrapped around the neck of the bottle, making sure that the bottle is airtight.
- Put the bottle in a shallow bucket of hot water, and watch the red water rise in the straw.
- Put the bottle in a bucket of ice water, and watch the red water drop in the straw.
- Have the children talk about their observations. When the temperature is warm, the liquid in the "thermometer" goes up because warm things expand and take up more space. When the temperature is cool, the liquid drops because cool things contract.
- Talk about some different ways thermometers are used in their daily lives: to record the weather, to measure the temperature in their homes, to see whether they have a fever.
- Let the children use clear plastic bottles to make their own individual thermometers to test in hot and cold water.

Making a Rain Gauge

MATERIALS   Bucket
Ruler

PROCEDURE
- Talk with the children about people who report the weather on the radio and TV. Discuss how some people keep records of various aspects of weather, such as rainfall.
- On a rainy day, help the children make a simple rain gauge by placing a bucket outdoors. Leave it out overnight.
- The next day, have the children use a ruler to measure the rain collected in the bucket.
- Have them keep a record of the daily rainfall over a period of time.

MAKING BOBBLERS

Fill a tall glass or jar with 3 parts water to 1 part soda water or any other kind of clear carbonated beverage. Add a few drops of food coloring if desired. Place a few moth balls in the liquid, and watch them bobble up and down.

Another way to make a bobbler is to stir 2 tablespoons of vinegar and a few raisins into a jar of water. Add about 1 teaspoonful baking soda. Do not stir.

The dissolved carbon dioxide from the soda water or mixture of vinegar and baking soda will collect on the mothballs or raisins, lifting them to the surface. When the gas dissipates, the objects will sink. Add more soda as needed.

Young children will not understand the technical explanation about carbon dioxide, but have them notice the bubbles that collect around the mothballs or raisins and lift them up. This demonstration is interesting and fun to watch. Be prepared to explain to other adults how and why it works.

MAKING WAVES AND WHIRLS

2 Large, clear plastic soft drink bottles
2" Length of plastic PVC pipe (available in hardware stores), the same width as the mouth of the bottle (usually 1")
Mineral oil
Blue food coloring

Fill one bottle about two-thirds full of water. Add a few drops of blue coloring and about 2" of mineral oil. Attach the two bottles together at the mouth with the PVC pipe, making sure it is airtight.

    Holding the bottles sideways, twirl the bottle holding the liquid, and then immediately turn it upside down so that the liquid flows into the empty bottle. The more vigorously you twirl the liquid, the more it will whirl around when it passes through the narrow opening.

    You can make waves by tilting the bottle sideways and gently tipping the liquid.

THE DIVER

Fill a clear plastic bottle with water. Drop into the bottle a glass eye dropper partially filled with water. Replace the lid. When you squeeze the bottle, the eye dropper will rise to the top. (You might want to decorate the eye dropper to resemble a diver.)

Investigating Properties of Sand

MATERIALS   Sand table or sand box with sand
Sieves, including colanders, netting, and strainers
Funnels
Paper cups (some cone shaped)
Styrofoam meat trays
Straws
Hand-held magnifying glasses
Water

PROCEDURE   • Talk with the children while they play in the sand. Limit the kinds and pieces of equipment in order to encourage more direct interaction with the sand.
• Ask:
What is sand?
Can it be sorted into different sizes?
Where does sand come from?
Where do you usually find it?

What do you think will happen if you mix water with sand?
Will the sand melt?
How does wet sand look different from dry sand? How does it feel?
Does wet sand hold a shape better than dry sand?

• Set some wet sand shapes aside, and inspect them after they have dried. Talk about the properties of wet and dry sand. Ask:
Is one heavier than the other? How can we find out?

• Put a small amount of sand on several meat trays, and let the children take turns looking at the grains with magnifying glasses. Ask:
Are the grains of sand different sizes? colors? shapes?

• Let the children try blowing the sand through a straw. Ask:
Is it easier to move wet or dry sand?

• Have the children poke large holes in some cone-shaped paper cups and small holes in others. As they pour sand through the holes, ask them to compare the speed with which the sand flows through the cups with large and small holes. Ask:
Does sand have some of the same properties as water?
Can sand change shape as water does?
How can you stop the sand from flowing out of the cup?
Can you do the same thing with water?

• Later in the day, talk with the children about the things they did with the sand. Review and reinforce what they discovered about the properties of sand.

VARIATIONS   See the art activities in Part One for sand painting activities.

Sand paper can be made by applying a mixture of white glue and water to heavy paper, then sprinkling sand on top.

Sand sculptures can be made from a mixture of two parts sand, one part cornstarch, and one part water. Heat the mixture until the corn starch thickens. Cool until it is comfortable to handle. Colored tempera or food coloring can be added, or children can paint their sculptures when dry.

Poke a small hole in the bottom of a cone cup to make a one-minute timer

Investigating Properties of Soil

MATERIALS   Dirt
Bucket
Newspaper
Sifters, colanders
Magnifying glasses

PROCEDURE   • Dig up a small bucketful of dirt.
• Pour small amounts of the dirt onto some newspapers.
• Have the children examine the dirt with their fingers and describe how it feels; have them smell it and describe any odors. Ask them to look at the color and texture.

MAKING A VOLCANO

(for use with older preschoolers)

Build a sand mountain. Bury a large, empty juice can in the mountain peak to form an open crater. Have on hand the following mixture in a large jar:

½ cup dishwashing liquid
¾ cup vinegar
1 cup water
6 drops red food coloring

Put ¼ cup baking soda in the empty juice can. Slowly pour some of the red solution into the juice can. Carbon dioxide gas is created when the vinegar and baking soda mix, causing the volcano to "erupt." Add more baking soda and solution as needed.

Tell the children that the hole in the center of the mountain is called a crater. Explain that gases similar to the ones you have created are found deep inside a volcano. The gases push up the hot, melted rock, or lava, to cause an eruption. The March 1980 issue of *National Geographic* has an excellent article and photos of the eruption of Mt. St. Helens.

- Let them look more closely at the soil through magnifying glasses and discover that dirt is made up of pieces of small rocks (sand) and decaying matter from plants and animals.
- Collect some dirt from another part of the yard, and have the children look for differences in color, texture, odor, and composition.
- Encourage the children to explore further by mixing dirt, sand, water, and other materials in the yard.
- Have the children try growing plants in different kinds of soil to determine whether clay-like soil or sandy soil is better.
- Talk about how bugs and worms help to aerate the soil to improve drainage.

LEARNING ABOUT MACHINES

Using Levers, Wedges, and Wheels

MATERIALS   Examples of levers, such as a bottle opener, pliers, wrench, claw hammer, nut cracker
Wedges, such as a knife, doorstop, chisel
Wheels from small toys

PROCEDURE   • Show the tools one at a time, and ask the children if they know the names of the tools and how they are used.

- Demonstrate how levers are used to lift or pry, how wedges are used to hold things apart or to split things, and how wheels are round and are used to move things. If practical and safe, let them try each of the tools.
- Talk about how each of these tools makes work easier by helping us do things we are not strong enough to do ourselves.
- Have the children think of some experiences they have had with levers, wedges, and wheels (for example, using a hammer in carpentry, a knife in cooking, a wagon to pull a load).

VARIATIONS   Identify other familiar machines that help make our work easier: stapler, scissors, can opener, telephone, clock, typewriter, computer, record player, lawnmower, vehicle.

    Provide discarded appliances, such as telephones, radios, and clocks, for the children to take apart and examine.

    Whenever practical, plan activities that involve hands-on experiences for children rather than lecture/demonstrations.

Making Pulleys

MATERIALS   4–6 Empty thread spools (preferably wooden)
3–4 Thin rubber bands
4–6 Nails smaller in diameter than the holes in the spools
1 Nail with a large head
Small piece of colored tape
12" square of ¾" plywood or particle board

PROCEDURE
- Place three of the spools on the plywood, and nail them in place so that they still turn easily.
- Hammer the nail with the large head into the top of one of the spools, and cover the head with colored tape to make a handle.
- Let the children stretch rubber bands between the spools. (See Illustration 5.4.)
- Have the children turn the spool with the handle to see how a pulley works.
- Suggest that they rearrange the rubber bands to see what happens.
- Nail more spools onto the board to extend the pulley system.

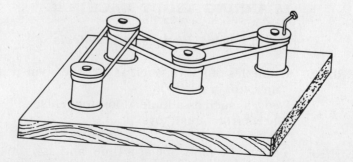

Illustration 5.4 **Pulleys**

- Have the children guess which way each spool will turn.
- Show pictures of other examples of pulleys (dump trucks, elevators, lifting cranes).

Note: Leave the pulley board in the science center for children to play with.

Making Pendulums

MATERIALS   Sand box or large flat container of sand
2 Chairs
Wooden dowel
String
Funnel with small hole
Colored sand

PROCEDURE
- Place a chair at either end of a box of sand.
- Suspend a dowel between the chairs.
- Use string to hang a funnel from the middle of the dowel. (You can make a funnel by rolling and taping paper into a cornucopia, leaving a small hole. If you use a regular funnel, you may need to tape part of the hole closed to slow the flow of sand.)
- Have the children fill the funnel with colored sand and then swing it like a pendulum, creating colored designs in the sand.
- Encourage the children to think of ways to vary the effects (lengthening or shortening the string, using greater or less force, making the hole larger or smaller).
- Talk about other kinds of pendulums familiar to children, such as swings and pendulum clocks. Point out that they are making their bodies into pendulums when they swing back and forth while hanging from a bar.

Note: Children can cooperate in setting up this activity. They can also build a smaller version by hanging a funnel or some other object from a ruler, yardstick, or dowel suspended between two blocks.

Exploring the Effects of Magnets

MATERIALS   Magnets of different shapes and sizes
3 Containers (such as Styrofoam meat trays), one labeled YES, one labeled NO, and the third containing assorted magnetic and nonmagnetic items, such as paper clips, nails, keys, bottle caps, plastic items, paper, rocks

PROCEDURE
- Let the children explore freely with the items, discovering for themselves which objects the magnets attract and repel.
- When they have had plenty of time to play with the magnets, remove the magnets and ask the children to sort the objects into the YES and NO containers according to their magnetism.

• Talk with them about their experiences, using the words *magnets*, *attract (stick to)*, and *repel (won't stick)*. Help the children to recognize that magnets will pick up some things but not others. Magnets do not pick up all metal; they pick up only those items that have iron or steel in them.
• Place a paper clip in a child's open palm. Approach the clip from above with a magnet, and show how you can make the clip jump out of the child's hand.
• Let the children explore other areas of the school to discover other magnetic objects.

Experimenting with Magnetic Strength

MATERIALS   Large, strong bar magnets
Large nails
Paper clips
Cardboard
Plastic container with lid
Empty tin cans

PROCEDURE
• Have the children hold a large nail in one hand and a strong magnet in the other, and then slowly bring the two together, feeling the force of the magnet.
• Ask the children if they think a magnet can attract a piece of cardboard. Have them try it. Then ask if they think a magnet can attract a paper clip through a piece of cardboard. Have them try it.
• Let the children experiment with magnetic force by picking up clips or nails through a plastic lid.
• Demonstrate magnetic force by using a magnet to make cans move or roll along a table.
• Scatter paper clips over an area, and have the children pick the clips up with large magnets.
• Encourage the children to try other possibilities to test magnetic force. Ask:
  If the magnet can attract the paper clip through the cardboard and the plastic lid, can it do the same through a person's hand? a piece of glass? water?

VARIATION   Make a small cork sail boat, attaching a tack to the bottom of the cork. Float the boat in some water in a glass baking pan. Run a magnet under the boat to move it around in the water.

Making Magnetic Puppets

MATERIALS   Shoe box or cigar box
2 Small, strong horseshoe magnets
2 Small puppets, one with paper clips or tacks for feet (Simple puppets can be made by dressing up bent wire figures.)

PROCEDURE
- Make a simple stage by inverting an empty shoe box and cutting out one of the long sides.
- Make up a story about two people who are doing something of interest to the children, such as getting ready for school.
- With the cut-away side of the inverted shoe box facing you, move the magnetic puppets around the stage by shifting the position of the magnets inside the box. The children should see that you are using magnets.
- Talk about how the puppet with the nonmagnetic feet simply "won't budge."
  Is [name of puppet] lazy? Why won't he [she] move? We'll all be late for school!
- Invite the children to figure out why the puppet won't move and to suggest what you should do. Do as the children suggest, even if it doesn't work.
- Have the children verbalize why you need to attach a paper clip or tack to the puppet's feet.

Note: Only the teacher should handle the tacks.

LEARNING ABOUT LIVING THINGS

Collecting Bugs and Insects

MATERIALS
Small juice or plastic containers
Fine netting or gauze
Rubber bands
Magnifying glasses
Sheet about 4' square

PROCEDURE
- Talk with the children about the kinds of bugs and insects that are familiar to them: ants, flies, bees, spiders, etc. Discuss where bugs live and how you might find some.
- Have each child prepare for a bug hunt by decorating and labeling a container with his or her name.
- Cut pieces of fine netting or gauze large enough to cover the containers.
- Select an area in the school yard or neighborhood in which to hunt for bugs.
- Let each child carry his or her container. Adults should carry the netting, rubber bands, magnifying glasses, and sheet.
- When children find a bug, let them study the natural habitat of the bug with a magnifying glass. Talk about the kinds of vegetation and the environment surrounding the bug's home.
- Help the child get the bug into the container, and secure a piece of netting over the top with a rubber band. Talk about the need to use netting in order to give the bug air.
- Place the sheet under a bush or plant where insects and bugs are likely to be found. Shake the bush, and look to see what collects on the sheet.

- Study the collection with the children, placing some of the insects into the children's containers along with bits of the vegetation from which the bugs and insects came.
- Upon returning to the school, have the children examine the collections more closely under magnifying glasses. Handle live bugs and insects gently.
- Talk about the different colors and shapes of the bugs.
  Do they have heads? eyes? ears?
  How do they feed themselves?
  Do some have antennae? If so, are they bent or straight?
  How many legs do they have?
- When the children have completed their investigations, have them help decide where the bugs and insects would be happiest living. Release the bugs to appropriate environments.

COLLECTING A WEB

Find a spider web that is no longer inhabited. Using a can of white spray lacquer, gently spray (at an angle) both sides of the web from a distance of about 8". (Have the children stand away from the fumes of the spray.)

While the paint is still sticky, collect the web by placing a large piece of black construction paper behind it and then cutting the web loose around the edges. You can protect the web by placing it under a glass frame or some clear plastic wrap.

Collecting Earthworms

MATERIALS
Large container of dirt
Small buckets
Garden tools for digging
Worm food made by mixing ½ cup raw oatmeal, ½ cup coffee grounds, and 1 tablespoon milk
Paper towels
Magnifying glasses
Flashlight

PROCEDURE
- Ask the children whether they are familiar with worms and whether they know how to find worms. Talk about how worms serve as food for birds and help farmers by keeping the soil aerated and fertilized. They swallow the dirt as they wriggle through it, thus helping to plow, cultivate, and fertilize the soil.
- Find a moist area of soil under some rotting leaves and plants, and dig for worms. (The best time to dig for worms is after a rain.)
- Collect the worms and soil in buckets. Then put them all together in the large container.
- Scratch some worm food into the soil in the large container.
- Put some of the worms onto paper towels for the children to study more closely with their magnifying glasses. Ask:

Do the worms have heads? (yes)
Do they have eyes? (no)
How can you tell which is the head and which is the rear?
What happens when you put them back in the soil?
Do they like moist or dry soil?
What do they do when you shine a flashlight at them?
- Explain that worms reproduce by laying eggs.

Collecting Caterpillars and Butterflies

MATERIALS   Caterpillars
Leaves
Large glass jars
Netting or gauze
Rubber bands

PROCEDURE
- Have the children collect some caterpillars and the leaves on which they are feeding.
- Place one or two caterpillars in each jar along with some leaves, and secure a piece of netting or gauze over the mouth of the jar with a rubber band.
- Have the children help clean the jar of wastes and dead leaves daily. They should pick a fresh leaf each day from the plant on which the caterpillar was originally feeding and place it in the jar.
- Soon the caterpillar will make a ladder and climb to the top of the jar. Have the children watch, and help them record the changes each day as the caterpillar spins its chrysalis. Point out how it first spins a pad and hangs by its feet, finally changing into a chrysalis. In a week or two, the chrysalis will split open and a butterfly will emerge.
- Do not touch the butterfly for at least 12 hours. When its wings are dry, release it.

Watching Birds

MATERIALS   Construction paper or felt pieces cut into shapes representing a bird's body, wings, feet, head, beak, and tail
Pictures of different kinds of birds
Flannelboard
Empty toilet paper rolls
Masking tape
Yarn or string
Collection of scraps suitable for birds' nests, such as colorful string, yarn, hair, bits of cotton, Christmas tree "icicles"

PROCEDURE
- Talk about the birds that the children may have seen in the trees, at the beach, and at the zoo.
- Show them pictures of different kinds of birds, and talk about the differences in size (for example, between an eagle and a hummingbird), color, and shape.

- Talk about the things birds have in common: they all use their beaks to eat (birds do not have teeth), and they all have wings.
- Have the children name the parts of a bird as they help put the felt pieces together on a flannelboard. Point out the bird's breast on the body.
- Ask the children to practice how they will move and sit quietly when watching birds outdoors.
- Have the children make "binoculars" by attaching two toilet paper rolls with masking tape. Punch a hole about ½" from the top of each roll on the outside edge, and attach some yarn or string to hold the binoculars around the child's neck. Tell the children that the binoculars they have made are pretend. You may wish to provide a few real ones for them to look through.
- As a group, sit quietly in an area where birds are likely to be and look through the binoculars for birds. (You may wish to try making rhythmic "pssh. . .pssh. . .pssh-pssh. . .pssh" sounds to attract large birds.)
- When the children spot a bird, encourage them to identify the colors and the markings on various parts of the bird's anatomy. Remind them to use the appropriate labels, such as beak, wings, feathers, tail, breast, and feet.
- During the spring season, hang a mesh onion bag filled with the nest-building scraps from the limb of a tree. Watch birds to take the materials for their nests. Go for a walk around the neighborhood to see if you can spot some of your materials in the nests.

Note: If you decide to build and stock a bird feeder, be sure you maintain it throughout the winter, because the birds become dependent on it for food.

BUILDING A TERRARIUM

A terrarium is simply a small environment for plants and animals. A terrarium can be constructed easily from a large glass jug, a plastic container, or even a glass baking pan covered with plastic wrap. One of the best containers for a terrarium is a discarded, leaky aquarium.

Line the bottom of the container with a shallow layer of pebbles for good drainage. Add 2–4" of a sand and soil mixture. Poke a small shallow dish of water into the soil so that the rim of the dish is level with the soil's surface. Add a few decorative rocks and some pieces of rotting tree or bark for the animals to hide under. Plant some small ferns and a little moss, and dampen the soil just until moist.

Cover the terrarium with glass or plastic, and place it in a location out of direct sunlight. If the glass or plastic fogs over, remove the cover partway to allow for evaporation. If the soil gets dry, spray with water. Stock your terrarium with salamanders, lizards, turtles, or baby toads. Research the kinds of food and environment each prefers, and adjust the terrarium accordingly.

Making Bird Feeders

MATERIALS   Flour
Water
Tongue depressors
Pine cones
Bird seed
Red ribbons or yarn

PROCEDURE   • Mix flour and water in a bowl to make a thick paste.
• Have the children spread the paste on pine cones with tongue depressors and then roll the pine cones in a container of bird seed.
• Help them tie a piece of red ribbon or yarn around the top of each pine cone. (The color red is often used to attract birds.) Hang the bird feeders on tree limbs.

Note: A tag with the child's name may be attached to each ribbon if desired.

GUINEA PIGS AS PETS

Guinea pigs make some of the best pets for young children. They are mild mannered, coy, and cuddly. They rarely bite, keep themselves clean, and are inexpensive to feed. With proper care and training, they can learn to do tricks, like standing on their hind legs for food or finding their way through an obstacle course.

Sanitation

Since guinea pigs are naturally clean and odorless, the most important part of caring for their homes is keeping the floor dry and the cage sanitary. Feeding dishes should be cleaned and washed daily. Depending on the number of animals and the size of cage, the flooring needs changing once or twice a week. Twice a year, the cage should be thoroughly scrubbed and disinfected.

Diet

Guinea pigs are vegetarians, and they like to nibble all day long. Though they act coy by running to the other side of the cage when you go to pick them up, they will come eagerly if you offer some lettuce or other veggies. Like humans, they are not able to manufacture vitamin C in their own bodies, so they need plenty of fresh fruits and vegetables every day. Their diet should include a daily bowl of guinea pig or rabbit pellets, which can be purchased at an animal feed store. They should be fed a variety of vegetables once or twice a day. Give only enough greens to last about 20 minutes— large rations of greens lead to loose bowels, causing the cage to become wet and soggy. Fresh vegetables can include lettuce, cabbage, carrots (with the tops), tomatoes, clover, outer leaves of broccoli and cauliflower, and celery. Small pieces of ripe apples and beets make good desserts. Fresh water should be in good supply at all times. Bread soaked in milk is a good addition to the diet of infants and pregnant mothers.

Breeding

Guinea pigs enjoy family life together, and they rarely fight. The father generally does not disturb the babies, although on rare occasions a jealous male will try to harm the youngsters.

The gestation period is from 63 to 70 days. A female can have as many as five litters a year, with an average of three offspring per litter. Several litters can live happily together in a cage of suitable size. It is a good idea to limit the handling of pregnant females, since they can be hurt easily.

Newborn babies are alert and wide-eyed within an hour after birth. At 3 days of age they can be held gently and can begin to nibble on soft vegetable leaves. When young ones are 28 days old, males and females should be caged separately to control breeding.

Illness

Like humans, guinea pigs catch colds, have coughs and runny noses, and wheeze. They should not be handled by people with colds or other illnesses. Sick animals should be isolated in their own disinfected cages and should not be handled by the children. Eliminate fruits and vegetables from the diet of any guinea pig with loose bowels. If the guinea pig does not respond to home treatment, take it to a qualified veterinarian.

Vacation Time

Guinea pigs should not be left alone for more than four days. Even with plenty of pellets and water, they will need fresh vegetables. Send along a copy of instructions for proper guinea pig care to the families willing to care for the animals during vacation. Include a brush and a wide-toothed comb for grooming.

Note: Gather information about other animals that your school might enjoy, such as hamsters, rabbits, turtles, snakes, mice, domestic birds, and gerbils. Caring for a pet is a wonderful way for young children to gain first-hand experience in taking responsibility and providing for the well-being of others.

Body Awareness

MATERIALS   Paper suitable for drawing children's body outlines
Felt markers

PROCEDURE   • Talk about living and growing things, and ask what plants and animals need to stay alive.
              • Discuss the different ways plants and animals get their food and the kinds of food they need. Ask:

In what ways are you like plants and animals?
How do you get your food?
What kinds of food do you need to grow?
How do you know you are growing?

- Talk about measuring people's height, weight, and size.
- Have each child take a turn lying on the paper while someone outlines his or her body with a felt marker, as shown in Illustration 5.5.
- Talk about the different parts of the body as the outlines are drawn.
- Let the children color in whatever parts of their bodies they like; print their names and ages and/or that day's date.
- Post the outlines, titling the display "I Am Special." Talk about how each one is different in size, shape, and height, just as each person looks different, has different coloring, and so on.
- Have each child look in a mirror and describe himself or herself. Invite the other children to add their observations.
- Talk about the ways in which all children are alike and the ways in which they differ. Note how plants and animals also share some basic characteristics, but differ in size, shape, and coloring.
- Take the opportunity to point out positive attributes of each child, stressing how unique and special each one is.

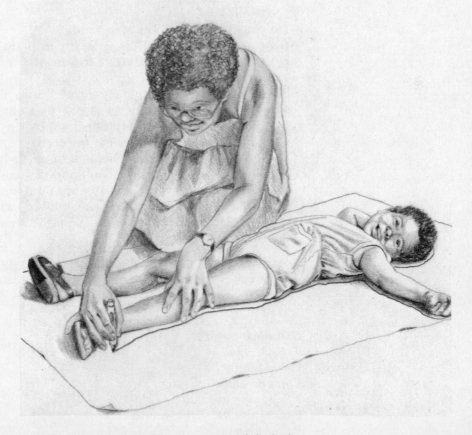

Illustration 5.5 **Learning about parts of the body**

- Combine this activity with a math activity involving recording weights and heights. Reinforce body awareness and the specialness of each child through activities described in the music section.
- Have children bring T-shirts, shoes, and other clothing they have outgrown; display these articles, sequenced from small to large to show how a child outgrows clothing.
- Make body outlines later in the school year, and compare them to the ones made earlier.

Learning About Seeds

MATERIALS   A variety of seeds, such as bird seed, beans, corn, peas, fruit and vegetable seeds, flower seeds

Pictures of plants pasted on a large cardboard chart

PROCEDURE
- Seat a group of children around a large table, and ask them if they know what a seed is. Cut an apple crosswise through the core and talk about the star shape; have them show you the seeds.
- Use other familiar foods such as grapes, melons, tomatoes, cucumbers, and pumpkins to investigate some of the properties of seeds. Note that some seeds are edible and others aren't.
- Show the children different kinds of seeds (beans, peas, corn, flower seeds) and ask:
  Do you think these are also seeds?
  Do you know what will happen if you plant the seeds?
  Do you know that different kinds of seeds grow into different kinds of plants?
- Seeds are actually completely formed little plants. Soak and dissect some lima bean or kidney bean seeds to see what the plants look like. Peanuts are a good choice for showing the beginnings of the stalk between the two halves of the seed.
- Let the children make a collection of seeds by shelling peanuts and peas in the pod. Cut open fruits and vegetables for them to dig out the seeds. Spread the various seeds out on a table; discuss their size, shape, and color, as well as what they will grow into.
- Have the children place the seeds on the chart next to the picture of the parent plant.

Note: A good book to use with this activity is *Seeds and Weeds*, by Joan Westley (Sunnyvale, CA: Creative Publications, 1988).

Growing Seeds

MATERIALS   Dried lentils

Lima or navy beans

A very ripe avocado

Glass jar with screw-on lid

Paper towels

Large toothpicks
Magnifying glasses

PROCEDURE
• Soak some of the lentils and beans overnight so that they will be soft.
• Let the children dissect the seeds and examine them with magnifying glasses.
• Reinforce some of the discoveries the youngsters have made in previous activities with seeds, stressing the fact that every seed is a tiny plant ready to grow.
• Talk about plants and how they have roots, stems, leaves, and flowers. Ask:
Do you think the seeds will grow into plants? How can we find out?
• Sandwich an assortment of 4 or 5 seeds between some paper towels and the inside of a glass jar. Pour just enough water into the jar to soak up into the towels. Screw the lid on and put the jar in a sunny place. Have the children check daily to see whether the seeds have sprouted. You might want to tape some sample seeds to the outside of the jar as a reminder of what you planted. (When bean seeds fail to germinate, it is usually because they are too old or have not been kept damp enough.)
• Cut open the ripe avocado, and remove the pit. Let the children examine the pit and, if it is already cracked, look for the beginning of the stalk.
• Dry the pit overnight, and have the children peel off the outer shell. (You may wish to have an extra pit already prepared before you start this activity.)
• Poke large toothpicks into three sides of the pit at its widest part.
• Rest the toothpicks on the rim of a jar, with the pointed end of the pit facing up.
• Fill the jar with water to cover the bottom of the pit. Set the jar in a dark place for 4 weeks, or until roots begin to grow from the bottom of the pit. Be sure to maintain the water level in the jar.
• Move the jar to a sunny location. In a few more weeks, the pit will crack and a small stem will appear at the top.
• Have the children watch for growth and note the directions in which roots and stem grow.
• When the stem is about 4 or 5" high, have the children plant the avocado in soil. Do the same with the bean plants.

VARIATIONS
Grow a small orchard from fresh grapefruit, apple, orange, and pear seeds as follows. Soak the seeds in water for a day or two, until they sink to the bottom of the container. Place a thin layer of pebbles in the bottom of a small container, and cover with some potting soil. Press the seeds gently into the soil, and cover with another 1/2" layer of potting mix. Place the container in a sunny place, watering daily to keep the seeds moist but not overly wet. In about 10 days, the seedlings will sprout. Transplant them to larger pots as they grow more leaves.

Try planting vines in the same way, using dry watermelon and pumpkin seeds.

For an interesting activity using wheat seeds, see Illustration 5.6.

1. Plant wheat in flower pots
2. Separate wheat from chaff
3. Grind the wheat into flour

Illustration 5.6 **Learning about planting, separating, and grinding wheat**

Sprouting Seeds

MATERIALS   Sandwich-size ziplock bags
Large needle
Sponges
Plastic cups
Potatoes
Pieces of bell peppers and other vegetables
Toothpicks
Bandannas
Egg cartons
Eggshell halves
Potting soil
Eyedropper or teaspoon
Mung bean, alfalfa, grass, and marigold seeds

PROCEDURE
- Invite the children to help pick an area in a sunny part of the classroom in which to display sprouts. Talk with them about the meaning of the word *sprout*.
  How can you make sprouts?
  What do they need?
  What do all plants need? (air, food, water)
- Explain that seeds are tiny plants complete with enough food to allow them to grow until they can put roots down into the earth to get more food (nutrients).
- Set up a sprouting table where children can start several kinds of sprouts. The children might decorate a chart on which to keep a record of the sprouting process.
- Use a needle to punch 10 to 12 holes in the bottom of the ziplock bags for drainage. Have the children make sprouts as follows. Fill each bag about a quarter full of mung bean seeds (available in health food stores). Zip the bags closed, and place them in a bowl of warm water. Soak overnight. The next day, drain the seeds well and place the bags containing the seeds in a light area, but not in direct sunlight. Rinse and drain the seeds daily for 3–4 days. (Be sure the children notice how the seeds are sprouting.) On the fifth day, place the bags of seeds in direct sunlight. The chlorophyll will turn the sprouts a bright green. They can now be eaten. Serve with a salad or sandwich. Sprouts can be stored in the refrigerator for up to a week.
- Select some potatoes with interesting shapes. Slice off the bottoms to provide a flat surface. Then slice off the tops, and scoop out 2–3" of potato. Have the children fill the potatoes with potting soil sprinkled with grass or alfalfa seeds, set the potatoes in the sun, and keep them moist. In about 7 to 10 days, the seeds will sprout a nice head of hair for the potato person. The children can use pieces of vegetables to make a face and bits of bell peppers to fashion a bow for the hair or a tie for under the chin. Have them fasten the pieces with toothpicks.
- Cut each sponge in the shape of a caterpillar (or a shamrock for St. Patrick's Day). Have the children sprinkle the sponges with grass or alfalfa seeds and keep them moist. If the plants are given sunlight after they sprout, they will turn bright green.

• Have the children fill plastic cups with potting soil and sprinkle the soil with seeds and water. The cups can be decorated with funny faces. When the seeds sprouts, the youngsters can wrap bandannas around the cups and tie them in a bow under the "chin."
• Fill an egg carton with eggshell halves. Let the children fill each shell with some potting soil and 2 or 3 marigold seeds. They should use an eyedropper or teaspoon to water the plants daily. The seeds will sprout more rapidly if you close the lid of the carton at night to keep them warm. When the seeds sprout, have the children transplant the eggshells into small pots or into the ground, where the plants will be able to get more nourishment. By leaving the plants in the eggshells, you will avoid disturbing the new roots.

Growing Plants from Vegetables

MATERIALS   Jars, flat dishes, empty containers of various shapes and sizes
Potting soil
Pebbles
Wire, toothpicks, pipe cleaners
Potato peeler
Empty spray bottles
Small watering cans
Food coloring
Vegetables such as potatoes, yams, carrots, beets, onions, parsnips, celery

PROCEDURE   • Select potatoes and yams with many eyes and, preferably, with sprouts already starting.
• Have each child place a potato, narrow end down, into a jar containing 2" of water; or stick three toothpicks into the sides of each potato so that it can be balanced on top of a full jar of water, with about 2" of the potato submerged in the water. Have the children set the jars in a cool place and maintain the water level. After 10 days, they should move their jars to a warm, light spot. Potatoes grow well in water and do not need to be transplanted. The water should be changed once a week and weaker shoots removed to encourage faster and stronger growth of the larger shoots. (Note: Sweet potatoes and yams tend to be slower growing than white potatoes.)
• Cut the tops off carrots and beets, leaving 1" of the vegetable. Then have the children make a colorful centerpiece as follows. Trim away all the leaves, leaving 1–2" of stem. Layer the bottom of a pie pan or wide dish with pebbles and water. Bury the vegetable ends of the carrots and beets in the pebbles. Place the dish in a light place. Pour in water up to the top of the vegetables, but do not cover the stems. Add fresh water every 2 to 3 days. Sprouts will appear in about a week. Carrots will produce feathery green foliage, and beets will have dark green leaves with red veins and stalks. The centerpiece will last about 3 to 4 weeks. Stake the foliage by tying soft pipe cleaners to the upper part of the stems for support.
• Select a large, firm carrot. Cut off the bottom third, and use a potato peeler to scoop out the inside. Push a piece of thin wire through the

carrot, and hang it with the scooped-out part facing up and the top facing down. Trim off some of the heavy leaves. Have the children keep the scooped-out part filled with water, checking on it several times a day. In about a week, the green foliage will begin to grow upward and cover the carrot. Carrot ferns last about a month.

• Peel the outer layer of dry skin from an onion. (Try to find one that is already sprouting.) Using three toothpicks, suspend the onion over a jar of water so that the water covers the bottom of the onion. The onion stems will be yellow if kept in a dark place and will be bright green if kept in a sunny place.

• Cut parsnips and place them in pebbles like the carrot and beet tops, or suspend one in a jar like the onion and potato. Parsnips produce lovely green leaves. Children like using spray bottles to give the leaves a shower. Talk about the importance of plants' receiving air through their leaves.

• Demonstrate how plants get their food and water through their roots and veins by placing a stalk of celery in a glass of colored water. (You can also use white flowers, such as daisies, Queen Anne's lace, or chrysanthemums, for this project. Cut the stems of the flowers at an angle, place them in colored water, and watch the blossoms gradually take on a pastel shade of the water's color.)

Note: Growing plants in glass jars with water enables the children to see the roots, making it easier for them to understand the parts of a plant and how it gets food. Point out the parts that can be eaten and how sunlight affects the colors of the leaves.

ECOLOGY ACTIVITIES

Cooking with the Sun

MATERIALS   Empty aquarium or other large glass container
Piece of glass to cover the aquarium
Insulation, such as sheets of thick plastic, roofing insulation, or corrugated cardboard
Sheets of aluminum foil
Glass jar with lid
2 Clear plastic cups
Thin slices of apple
Plastic wrap
Piece of black paper
Paper towel
Tape

PROCEDURE   • Have the children help build a solar unit as follows. Line the inside of an empty aquarium or other large glass container with insulation material. Cover the insulation with foil so that the shiny side of the foil faces the inside of the container. (See Illustration 5.7.)

• Have a group of children fill a glass jar with water, add two tea bags, put the lid on, and place the jar in the solar unit.

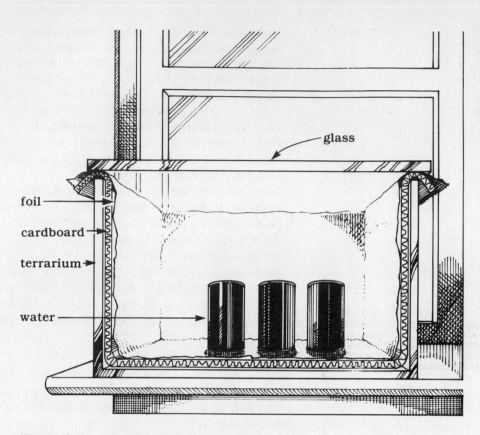

glass

foil

cardboard

terrarium

water

Illustration 5.7 **Heating water in a solar unit**

- Have another group of children place one or two thin slices of apple in a plastic cup, wrap the cup tightly in plastic wrap, and tape a piece of black paper around it. After lining a second cup with a paper towel to provide insulation, they should put the first cup inside the towel-lined cup and place the two cups inside the solar unit.
- Cover the solar unit with a sheet of glass, and place it in a spot where it will collect the maximum amount of sunlight. If the sun is at an angle, remove the insulation and foil from one of the sides so that the sunlight can enter.
- Explain that the solar cooker is collecting heat from the sun and that some people use solar units to heat their water.
- After an hour or more, check the tea and apples. Let the children feel the heat and taste the food. Ask them to suggest other things they might try to cook with the sun's heat.

Illustrating a Food Chain

MATERIALS   Mural-size sheet of paper
Blue, green, and brown paint
Construction paper in various colors
Glue
Paintbrushes

PROCEDURE
- Have the children paint a backdrop for a mural for the classroom, using blue for the sky and green and brown for the earth.
- Discuss things they might add, such as the sun, clouds, rain, lakes, trees, and plants. Have them make some of these things from construction paper and glue them to the mural.
- Talk about the necessities for life: sun, air, water, and food.
- Ask the children to name some of the foods they eat. Add to the mural a selection of these foods, such as chickens, fish, fruits, and vegetables.
- Ask the children to name the things fish and chickens eat. Depict some of these foods on the mural: worms, insects, grains, vegetables.
- Picture some of the sources of food for insects (plants, nectar from flowers) and plants (sun, rain, decomposed plants).
- Talk about the interdependence of life forms and how the destruction or interruption of one link in the chain eventually affects the rest of the chain.
- Refer to the mural to reinforce other teachings in ecology and conservation.

Note: This activity is adaptable for use with a flannelboard.

Conserving Water

MATERIALS
Bucket or pitcher
Garden hose or faucet
Display of plants and animals

PROCEDURE
- Ask the children to name some things around the school that must have water to live.
- Talk about the importance of conserving water and using it in ways that are not wasteful.
- Introduce them to the word *drought*. Explain that when there isn't enough rain, all living things suffer from the drought. Stress that it is especially important to conserve water during times of drought.
- Leave a pitcher or bucket under a dripping faucet or at the end of a dripping hose. After a time, observe how much water has collected in the container. Have the children use the water that was collected to replenish the animals' water dishes, water the plants, or mix juice for snack time. Note how just a few continuous drips can add up to a lot of useful water.
- Invite suggestions about ways everyone can help prevent waste of water: shutting faucets tightly, flushing toilets only when necessary, using a stopper in the sink, taking brief showers.
- Talk about ways to save water: collecting rain water for plants, saving water that was used to wash fruits and vegetables for use in the garden.
- Over wash basins and faucets, post illustrations showing a child turning the faucet off.
- Ask the children questions about their daily routines, such as
Do you leave the water running when you brush your teeth?

Ask them to explain why they shouldn't. Praise them for correct answers.

• Explain that water is needed not only for drinking, washing, and growing food, but also for working (power), cooling, transportation, and playing (swimming, boating).

Conserving Paper and Paper Products

MATERIALS   Disposable paper goods—cups, plates, napkins, towels, wax paper, newspaper, paper bags

Reusable counterparts to the above—ceramic and plastic dishes, cloth napkins, glasses, towels, lunch boxes, reusable shopping bags

PROCEDURE   • Ask the children what each of the paper items is used for. Ask what happens to each item after it has been used.

• Talk about how paper is made by cutting down trees.

• Ask the children to suggest alternatives for each of the paper items. Have the reusable items in sight to give them ideas.

• Ask about other things we can all do to save paper: not waste toilet paper or tissues, recycle newspapers, use both sides of art papers, reuse paper bags.

VARIATION   Discuss other types of conservation, such as energy conservation (turning lights off, walking rather than driving) and food conservation (saving scraps for animals or compost).

Making a Compost Pile

MATERIALS   Sheet of plastic
Grass clippings and leaves
Food scraps, eggshells, fruit and vegetable peelings
Animal manure
Weeds and wilted plants
Wood shavings

PROCEDURE   • Select an isolated place in the yard for your compost pile. A shaded area near a deciduous tree is a good spot. (A small fenced area, a large container like a barrel, or a shipping crate would also be appropriate.)

• Let the children help layer grass clippings and other organic compost materials with dirt. The ideal time to start a compost pile is in the fall or spring. Mix leaves and grass with wood shavings; each layer should be no more than 6" thick. Droppings of rabbits, guinea pigs, ducks, and chickens can be added.

• Sprinkle the compost pile with enough water that the moisture content of the pile is like that of a wrung-out sponge. Cover the pile with plastic. The material will take several weeks to "cure." Have the children turn and mix the compost as more organic materials and dirt are added.

- Each time the children add to the pile, have them examine how the previous materials are breaking down. The smaller the pieces of material, the more quickly they will break down. Compare compost with nonorganic materials (such as plastic), that do not decompose.
- Have the children use the compost in their gardening potting soil.

Note: To illustrate the value of compost, plant quick-sprouting seeds, like beans, in four separate pots containing clay, sand, rocky soil, and composted soil. Have the children label each pot and compare the growth of the plants.

SAFE INSECT REPELLENT

6 garlic cloves
3 hot chili peppers (dried or fresh)
6 cups water

Place garlic, peppers, and 1 cup water in a blender. Blend until finely ground. Let the mixture stand 10 minutes; strain through cheesecloth. Add the remaining 5 cups water. Mix well and pour into spray bottles. Shake well, then spray plants and vegetables as necessary to repel insects. Makes 1½ quarts. (Do not let the children handle peppers when making this recipe.)

Creating a Miniature Ecosystem

MATERIALS
Babyfood jars with lids, or clear plastic cups and clear plastic tape
Gravel
Potting soil
Wood shavings
Tap water that has been sitting 24 hours or longer
Small terrarium plants
Snails

PROCEDURE
- Let each child fill a babyfood jar or plastic cup about a third full of potting soil and gravel.
- Pour in enough aged water to barely cover the gravel mix.
- Let each child select a small plant and put its roots into the gravel. A few wood chips can be added for landscaping.
- Have the children put a small snail in each container. Seal each jar with a lid; seal the rim of each cup to that of an empty cup with tape.
- Label each ecosystem with the child's name. Ask the children to monitor the changes as water evaporates, condenses, and rains on the plants and snails.

VARIATION
Ecosystems can also be created for ants, praying mantises, ladybugs, sowbugs, and spiders.

Note: *Ecology* is derived from a Greek word meaning "house." Earth is our house, and we share it with every other living thing.

A BREEDING BOX

Cut out one or two large windows on the sides of a large empty oatmeal box. Cover the windows with clear plastic, attached with tape. Line the bottom of the box with aluminum foil to prevent moisture from weakening it.

Introduce larvae of insects such as moths, butterflies, beetles, and caterpillars. Include some of the plants and leaves they thrive on. Snails, slugs, and pillbugs will feed on lettuce leaves, raw apple, or raw potato. Add a small container of water to provide moisture. Don't forget to keep the lid on!

Collecting Litter

MATERIALS
Paper bags, tissue boxes, small cartons, and other such containers
Art materials
Plastic or canvas gloves for each child

PROCEDURE
- Ask the children:
  What is litter? (anything that is out of its proper place)
  Should candy wrappers be in the street?
  Where do they belong?
  Should soft drink cans be out in the yard?
  Should your sweater be on the floor?
  Should your toothbrush be in the basin?
  Children enjoy ridiculous questions, such as:
  Should your hat be in the guinea pig cage?
  Should your toothpaste be in the car?
- Let the children decorate some litter containers (bags, boxes, and cartons) with the art materials.
- Have the children put on gloves. Then take a walk around the school grounds and help them identify and pick up litter.
- When the children become competent at identifying litter, let small groups take a few minutes each to collect as much litter as they can find.
- Look at the collections together, and discuss where each item of litter should be placed: back on the toy shelf, on a table, in the garbage, in a recycling bin.
- Talk about the ways each person can help clean up after litterbugs at home and at school.

Note: Have the children wash their hands thoroughly after collecting and examining litter, even if they wore gloves.

Field Trips

Carefully planned field trips can add a great deal to a young child's knowledge about the world. Trips offer opportunities for children to see for themselves some of the things they may have only heard or read about.

When youngsters actually see what the farmer and the grocer do to supply the food they eat, they are more likely to understand and appreciate the roles of these workers in the community. When they visit a junior museum or explore a tidepool, they experience firsthand the joy of discovering new things about their environment. Reading stories and looking at pictures of a dentist is quite different from seeing a real dentist's office and maybe even sitting in the dentist's chair!

Children have different levels of understanding about their world. Field trips enable them to use all their senses to reinforce and, in some cases, revise and correct their perceptions.

Seeing something new and interesting also sparks children's imaginations and sharpens their observation skills. They are often impressed with some details of a trip that adults might overlook. Sociodramatic play tends to take on new dimensions after children have been on field trips, especially those involving community workers.

Young children respond best to field trips that are short and close to home. Extensive trips requiring long bus rides, a lot of walking, and staying together in a group can be very tiring—for the teacher as well as the children.

Start with walks around your own school, looking at details of the buildings and grounds. Encourage the children to take plenty of time to explore and examine the environment. Be a good model yourself by looking closely at and listening to things around you. Call the youngsters' attention to details, and use statements and questions such as **I wonder why the bark on this tree is rough and on that one is smooth. Can you feel the difference?**
Do you hear birds singing? I wonder how many different songs we can hear.

Gradually extend your trips to the neighborhood, taking an after-the-rain walk, or a let's-look-for-shadows walk. You can revisit many of the same sites, either with different goals in mind or simply to give youngsters more time to reinforce their perceptions and add to their knowledge.

PLANNING FIELD TRIPS

Give thought to the interests and abilities of the children. Would a trip to the planetarium help expand their knowledge about outer space? Can you relate such a trip to current activities in the classroom? A field trip is more effective and meaningful when children can relate what they see to experiences both before and after the trip.

Whenever possible, visit the site yourself before taking the class. Imagine your group of children in the particular environment. If it is a building, note the locations of exits, drinking fountains, restrooms, and parking facilities.

Talk with the people in charge. Give them information on your children's ages, levels of understanding, and attention span, and describe the kinds of questions they might like to have answered. Let the people know how they might help to expand on concepts that are already familiar to the children. Adults who have had only limited experiences with young children will particularly welcome your suggestions. Let them know that they are not expected to give a long lecture, and that the youngsters like to have the opportunity to touch things.

Ask for their suggestions based on previous visits by groups similar to yours.

Tell the children what to expect. Describe what they will see and do. Invite comments about their expectations, and correct any misinformation.

Plan related experiences in your school before and after the trip. Incorporate as many areas of the curriculum as possible. Have books, posters, and related materials on hand to reinforce information gained from the field trip. You may want to take pictures of the trip and let children dictate stories to make a book for the school.

SOME PRACTICAL GUIDELINES

- Inform parents of the place you are visiting and the times of departure and return.
- Have on file release forms signed by the parents.
- Invite parents to accompany the group; orient them to safety procedures.
- Be sure that there are extra adults along in case some child needs special attention.
- Take along a first aid kit; attach a list of emergency phone numbers.
- Depending on the size and experience of the children, you may find it useful to walk with a knotted rope (one knot for each child to hold onto) or to use a whistle or some other special signal when you want the children to congregate.
- Have alternative plans for care of children who prefer to remain at school.
- Take along a "security bag" of food (such as crackers and raisins), some crayons and paper, tissues, wet wipes, extra clothing, and plastic bags.

SOME IDEAS FOR FIELD TRIPS

There are many exciting things for youngsters to discover and explore right under their noses. Here are some suggestions for short excursions on or near the schoolgrounds:

Hunting insects
Collecting leaves
Exploring a tree
Looking for birds' nests
Observing an anthill
Digging for worms
Looking for animal tracks

Collecting and studying rocks
Looking for the effects of erosion
Looking for colors
Going on a listening walk
Visiting a nearby construction site
Looking for worms and snails

Possibilities for trips that are a bit more extensive include visits to a

Duck pond (take along plenty of bread and crackers to feed the ducks)
Public park
Pet shop
Veterinary hospital
Produce market
Fire station
Police station
Service station
Forest ranger station
Garbage dump
Junior museum
Planetarium
Wildlife refuge
Bird sanctuary
Natural science center
Youth science institute

There may be local nature conservation or bird-watching groups that would be willing to visit the school. Some children are more comfortable when community workers such as doctors, dentists, police officers, and firefighters come to the school. In many communities, public service agencies have educational programs and are pleased to accept invitations to visit area schools.

Bibliography of Resources

(See the Language Arts section for children's books.)

Althouse, Rosemary. *Investigating Science with Young Children.* New York, NY: Teachers College Press, 1988. A guide to help teachers understand the process approach to implementing a science program for children 3–5 years old. Includes such activities as exploring water, mixing colors, and setting objects in motion.

Brown, Sam (ed.). *Bubbles, Rainbows and Worms.* Mt. Rainier, MD: Gryphon House, 1981. Activities designed to allow adults to help preschool children gain experience in science through practical hands-on experiments. Children learn by doing rather than by being shown.

Carmichael, Viola. *Science Experiences for Young Children.* Saratoga, CA: R & E, 1982. Sections of this book are devoted to plants, animals, weather, the human body, cooking, machines, and developing concepts. Each section provides the teacher with background information, suggested class projects, arts and crafts ideas, and book lists.

Cornell, Joseph Bharat. *Sharing Nature with Children.* Nevada City, CA: Ananda Publications, 1979. Nature games designed to emphasize the development of intuitive qualities, including patience, trust, and empathy for nature.

Follman, Ilene, and Helen Jackson. *Science in a Nutshell.* Long Branch, NJ: Kimbo Educational, 1977. Activities for young children, covering five major areas: plants, animals, our bodies, the physical world, and food experiences. Most are open-ended and drawn from the child's daily environment.

Forte, Imogene. *Science Fun: Discovering the World Around You.* Nashville, TN: Incentive Publications, 1985. Simple activities designed to encourage young children to investigate, explore, and experiment with common materials in creative ways.

Forte, Imogene, and Marjorie Frank. *Puddles and Wings and Grapevine Swings.* Nashville, TN: Incentive Publications, 1982. Interesting ways to use nature's materials. Clear directions are provided for outdoor and indoor projects and adventures. The book includes crafts for all seasons, games, weather and ecology experiments, and recipes for fun and food.

Gale, Frank C., and Clarice W. Gale. *Experiences with Plants for Young Children.* Palo Alto, CA: Pacific Books, 1975. The pages are filled with ideas to help teachers and parents provide young children with sensory experiences and guide them in exploring, comparing, and seeing relationships. The experiences are designed to enlarge children's understanding of the world in which they live.

Harlan, Jean. *Science Experiences for the Early Childhood Years.* Columbus, OH: Merrill, 1988. This edition examines new research evidence that suggests the need to modify Piaget's description of reasoning during the early years and supports efforts to nourish children's curiosity with science experiences during early childhood. Direct and indirect techniques for discovery science are stressed.

Harrah, David F., and Barbara K. Harrah. *Conservation—Ecology: Resources for Environmental Education.* Metuchen, NJ: Scarecrow Press, 1975. Offers numerous activities and crafts, as well as sources of teaching aids and support in the field of ecology.

Hibner, Dixie, and Liz Cromwell. *Explore and Create.* Livonia, MI: Partner Press, 1979. In the belief that adults can extend children's curiosity by providing an environment that encourages observation and exploration, the book offers a variety of experiences to foster discovery and learning. Hands-on activities are designed to increase awareness by means of observation, discussion, and experimentation.

Holt, Bess-Gene. *Science with Young Children.* Washington, DC: National Association for the Education of Young Children, 1977. Helps the teacher understand why science is important in the curriculum. The book provides suggestions for setting up activities, including a section on ecology.

Jorgensen, Eric, et al. *Manure, Meadows and Milkshakes.* Los Altos Hills, CA: The Trust for Hidden Villa, 1986. Gives teaching ideas for sharing the natural world with children. The book is an outgrowth of activities developed by the Hidden Villa Nature Center, a 2,400-acre preserve dedicated to promoting an appreciation of the earth's resources and an understanding of our dependence on them.

Katz, Adrienne. *Naturewatch, Exploring Nature with Children.* Menlo Park, CA: Addison-Wesley, 1986. Activities involving looking at plants, insects, birds, and seeds and using natural dyes and herbs.

Knight, Michael E., and Terry Lynne Graham. *Leaves Are Falling in Rainbows.* Atlanta, GA: Humanics, 1984. Science activities to teach children concepts and properties of water, air, plants, light, shadows, magnets, sound, and electricity.

Levenson, Elaine. *Teaching Children about Science.* New York, NY: Prentice-Hall, 1985. A book for parents and teachers, with activities involving weather, electricity, animals, plants, ecology, volcanoes, rocks, sound, light, air, and water.

National Wildlife Federation. *Ranger Rick's Nature Magazine.* This monthly magazine presents simply written and informative articles about wildlife. The lovely photographs in every issue make it a particularly valuable resource. Order from 1412 16th St. NW, Washington, DC 20036.

Nickelsburg, Janet. *Nature Activities for Early Childhood.* Menlo Park, CA: Addison-Wesley, 1976. A book of activities for adults to use with young children. It covers outdoor group projects (looking for spiders), projects with insects and small animals, indoor projects (making an aquarium, keeping mice), hatching chickens, looking for things in the ground, and projects with plants.

Redleaf, Rhoda. *Open the Door, Let's Explore: Neighborhood Field Trips for Young Children.* St. Paul, MN: Toys 'n Things Press, 1983. This guide to inexpensive activities for 2- to 8-year-old children tells what they can learn from neighborhood walks and field trips. A special section for teachers and group leaders is included.

Rockwell, Robert E., et al. *Hug a Tree, and Other Things to Do Outdoors with Young Children.* Mt. Rainier, MD: Gryphon House, 1986. Learning experiences (with suggested age levels) include such activities as "Where Do Things Go at Night?," "Take a Bird to Lunch," and "Spyglass Treasure Hunt." The suggested activities help youngsters appreciate their environment through simple observations and more complex identification.

Strongin, Herb. *Science on a Shoestring.* Menlo Park, CA: Addison-Wesley, 1985. A program designed for K–7 teachers with little or no science background, few supplies, and limited budgets. Many of the simple activities can be adapted for the preschooler.

Ticotsky, Alan. *Who Says You Can't Teach Science? (Grades K–6).* Glenview, IL: Scott-Foresman, 1985. Many of the activities are easily adaptable for younger children. They include experiences with air, water, dirt, rocks, the sun, motion, sound, light, color, simple machines, plants, animals, and the human body.

Westley, Joan. *Seeds and Weeds.* Sunnyvale, CA: Creative Publications, 1988. This is one of a series called *Windows on Science: Active Learning for Young Children (Grades PreK–2).* Detailed instructions and illustrations are provided for activities using simple materials. Five other books in the science series are

Water and Ice; Insects and Other Crawlers; Light, Color, and Shadows; Rocks, Sand, and Soil; and *Constructions.*

Williams, Robert A., et al. ***Mudpies to Magnets, A Preschool Science Curriculum.*** Mt. Rainier, MD: Gryphon House, 1987. Simple hands-on experiments grouped under curriculum units, including such activities as "Ocean in a Jar," "Put a Rock to Bed," and "Puddle Walk."

PART SIX

Health and Safety

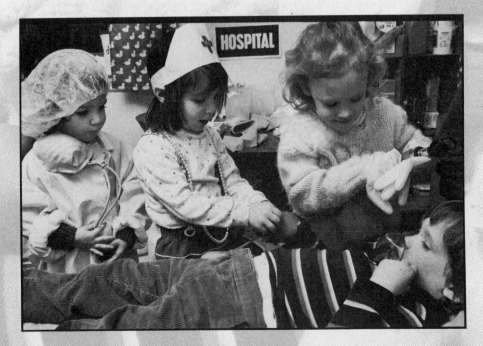

Introduction to Health and Safety

At one time, health and safety issues such as brushing teeth, toilet training, and learning to avoid strangers were the exclusive purview of the child's parents. Today, when many youngsters spend most of their waking hours in day care situations, teachers are expected to assume many of these responsibilities.

THE IMPORTANCE OF HEALTH AND SAFETY

The areas of health and safety are especially important at the preschool level. Young children are susceptible to colds and other infections and are more vulnerable than older children to many kinds of accidents. Teachers are in a unique position to observe the health of young children and to ensure their physical safety. They are with the children long hours and often are more attuned to subtle changes in a child's physical and emotional state than parents can be. Frequently the teacher is the first to suspect the onset of an illness or to sense from a change in a child's behavior that the child may be having emotional problems.

EFFECTS ON CLASSROOM BEHAVIOR

Teachers realize that health is not an objective or static condition. A child's state of health is continually changing and affects the way he or she behaves at a particular moment, especially the way the child learns and socializes. Health is not simply the absence of illness. Rather, health is a state of being that can be viewed as a continuum, with varying degrees of fitness and vitality at one end and illness and abnormal functioning at the other. As any teacher can verify, the degree of health and well-being of a child can dramatically affect his or her attention span and attitude toward others—and, in fact, the mood of the entire classroom or day care center.

FOUR ASPECTS OF HEALTH AND SAFETY

Teachers of young children need to be concerned about four aspects of health and safety:

1. Prevention of illness and injury
2. Detection of illness
3. Knowledge of first aid
4. Promotion of good health and safety habits

Prevention

Because children spend long hours in child care facilities, teachers need to emphasize the importance of good hygiene in order to prevent the spread of infection. A highly contagious infection like *giardiasis* spreads so quickly that health departments must frequently intervene and close afflicted facilities. (See the activity on washing hands, page 281, for further information about this disease.) Practicing the basic principles of good hygiene can prevent such occurrences. The activities offered in this section are designed not to frighten youngsters, but to help them develop good health habits.

Many injuries can be prevented by teaching children the proper ways to use toys, ride tricycles, climb gym equipment; how to use swings and slides without hurting others; when it is safe to run; and other safety measures.

Stress management and personal safety are also important aspects of an effective preschool curriculum. Emphasis on early achievement places undue stress on young people, often resulting in regression, anger, frustration, and lowered self-esteem. Children lack the experience and wisdom to put their fears and frustrations into a realistic perspective; teachers can help by being sympathetic listeners and by giving them some techniques for stress reduction.

The increase in the numbers of child abduction and molestation cases has given parents and children cause for much concern—sometimes leading to suspicion and mistrust of the school. Teachers are in a good position to allay some of the parents' fears by working closely with parents and children to teach youngsters how to take responsibility for their own personal safety.

Detection

A good detection program in the school includes screening for dental, vision, hearing, and speech problems. Professionally trained technicians are generally available through the local health department. In some cases, teachers and parents can be trained to do screening by the Red Cross, the community day care association, or a local college or university.

Successful early learning depends on a child's ability to see and hear accurately. The learning of speech patterns, interactions with others, and the development of a healthy self-concept are all affected by how well a child's senses function. Many children suffer from some degree of hearing loss, which often goes undetected. Sadly, children who have problems hearing are sometimes labeled slow learners or retarded. Early detection can prevent such unfortunate mistakes.

One out of every four children of school age has some degree of vision impairment. With early detection (between the ages of 3 and 6), disorders such as *amblyopia*, or "lazy eye," can be corrected. Often it is the alert teacher who notices clues in the child's behavior that indicate a possible vision problem. (See Where to Write for More Information at the end of this section.)

Knowledge of First Aid

Teachers have many opportunities to provide children with information about first aid and basic treatment of simple injuries. For example, when a child suffers minor bruises, the teacher can talk about how to report an accident (describe how and where it happened, the extent of the injury, and so on) and can discuss hygienic measures, as well as methods for preventing future accidents. The attitude the teacher conveys about health and self-care can go a long way in influencing children to take responsibility for their own well-being.

Promotion of Good Health and Safety Habits

Good health and safety habits can be promoted most effectively throughout the curriculum by offering appropriate dramatic play materials in the dress-up area, having the children help prepare nutritious foods, reading appropriate stories, and using music to reinforce the concepts being taught. [Try Hap Palmer's recording on health and safety: *Learning Basic Skills Through Music* (AR526).] Daily activities can be planned with long-range goals in mind, and topics selected that correspond to the children's immediate needs and ability levels. Isolated facts unrelated to a child's life and interests are quickly forgotten. The teacher needs to adapt curriculum activities to make them age-appropriate, always using simple, clear explanations stressing *why* health and safety practices are important and beneficial to the child. "When you blow your nose, you are helping your body to get rid of the germs that make you sick."

The school setting offers many natural opportunities to teach safety and health. Teaching other topics such as using seat belts, telephoning for help in an emergency, and reporting abuse and molestation requires the cooperation of both teachers and parents. An effective way to approach these topics is to invite speakers from some of the agencies listed at the end of this section. See also Personal Safety, later in this section.

AIDS

Recent figures on the alarming growth of AIDS (Acquired Immune Deficiency Syndrome) among young children indicate a need for teachers to be informed about the disease and how to get more information. The Centers for Disease Control report that the rate of AIDS in children will increase from 300 reported cases in 1986 to more than 20,000 by 1991. Surgeon General C. Everett Koop has called for mandatory AIDS education beginning with 8-year-olds (*Surgeon General's Report on Acquired Immune Deficiency Syndrome*, Washington, DC: U.S. Government Printing Office, 1986).

In the majority of pediatric AIDS cases, a pregnant woman with the disease transmitted the antibodies to the fetus. The virus may also be transmitted through breast milk. Babies cannot be tested for the virus until they are about 15 months old. Some who test positive may eventually turn negative once the mother's antibodies are cleared from the infant's system. The mortality rate is high, not because of the virus itself, but because the victim's immune system is so weakened that he or she is highly vulnerable to infections and other illnesses. It appears that the greatest risk of having a child with AIDS in the classroom is to that child rather than to his or her classmates.

AIDS is not contagious. It cannot be spread through coughing, sneezing, kissing, touching, or hugging. Although no known cases have been transmitted in schools or day care settings, any theoretical transmission would most likely involve exposure of open skin lesions or mucous membranes to blood or possibly other body fluids of an infected person. Precautions that teachers need to take with AIDS children include wearing gloves to change diapers and being careful to bandage any bleeding cuts or wounds on the child.

A more common problem than having a child with AIDS is having a child whose parent or relative has AIDS, in which case the teacher's role is one of support and understanding. It is vital for the teacher to know how much the child has been told about the disease and to help the child cope with the likely death of a loved one. The Surgeon General's report emphasizes that children under age 8 generally have little concept of sexuality, death, or the notion of infected blood. Such information can be confusing, frightening, and misconstrued.

Education about AIDS is the teacher's best protection.

INFORMATION ABOUT CHILDREN WITH AIDS*

- In 1988 there were 833 known cases of AIDS in children under age 5 in the United States.
- Although a pregnant woman with AIDS always passes the antibodies to the baby, the actual AIDS virus gets passed on to the baby in about half the cases.
- Doctors cannot tell if the AIDS virus is present in a baby until the baby reaches about 15 months of age.
- Some babies who test positive for the AIDS virus may eventually test negative once the mother's antibodies have been cleared from the infant's system.
- It is common for children with AIDS to be developmentally delayed.
- The AIDS virus has never been transmitted via food and drink and cannot penetrate intact human skin.
- Precautions that teachers need to take with AIDS children include wearing gloves to change diapers and being careful to bandage any bleeding cuts or wounds on the child.
- For more information, write Children's Hospital of New Jersey, AIDS Program, 15 S. Ninth St., Newark, NJ 07107.

*Data from U.S. Centers for Disease Control.

PLANNING THE CURRICULUM

However the topics are approached, attitudes about health and safety are best taught by the important adults in a child's life. Learning is most effective when both teachers and parents reinforce the same concepts consistently and encourage children to ask questions and communicate about how they feel. It is particularly important that teaching strategies help youngsters to see health care professionals as helpful, not frightening, individuals and to see safety rules as beneficial precautions, rather than restrictive measures.

The following health and safety activities are not intended to be taught as isolated concepts, since children have difficulty integrating such information into their daily lives. It is important to limit the number of ideas and to offer them in many different contexts. The open classroom is an ideal setting in which to reinforce concepts through dramatic play, field trips, stories, posters, art, music, and so on. Habits are developed slowly and often only after much repetition.

Activities in this section that relate to daily occurrences—handwashing, sneezing, coughing, brushing teeth—are best taught through active involvement within the context of a child's daily experiences. Children are most likely to understand and retain information when the teacher relates facts to actual experiences. There are many opportunities to reinforce the importance of cleanliness, exercise, and other good health habits throughout the day. The teacher needs only to be alert and responsive to those teachable moments.

The books in the bibliography at the end of this part can help you to expand the ideas presented here to fit the individual needs of your classroom. Use the list of addresses to write for more materials. See also health-related food activities in Part Seven, Cooking and Nutrition.

Health Activities

Seeing What Bacteria (Germs) Look Like

MATERIALS
1 Envelope unflavored gelatin
2 Cups water
2 Small clean containers (such as cottage cheese cartons)
Masking tape
Marking pen
Soap and water

PROCEDURE
- Dissolve the gelatin in hot water, and pour 1 cup of the dissolved gelatin into each of the clean containers.
- When the gelatin is cool, have a child with dirty fingers touch the surface of the gelatin in one of the containers. Label this container "Dirty Fingers."
- Wash the same child's hands well with soap and water. (See the next activity, Practicing Washing Hands.)

- Have the child touch the surface of the gelatin in the second container with clean fingers. Label this container "Clean Fingers."
- Cover the containers and place them in a warm, dark place (near a heater or in an oven with a pilot light).
- Check the containers in 5 days. In the dirty-fingers container, colonies of bacteria will be visible. In the clean-fingers container, few or no bacteria colonies will be visible.
- Explain that the growths in the dirty-fingers container are called *bacteria*. Bacteria are very tiny plants that are found everywhere. Some bacteria are good for us and help us to stay well; others can make us sick. Most of the time we can't see bacteria, but with food (like the gelatin) and warmth they divide and grow to create more bacteria. Bacteria grow on food that is not properly refrigerated and on damp towels, handkerchiefs, and clothes. Thorough washing removes most bacteria.

Practicing Washing Hands

MATERIALS   Dispenser or bar soap
2 Wide plastic tubs filled with warm water
Paper towels

PROCEDURE
- Teach the children the "Rub-a-Dub-Dub" song with handwashing motions (sung to the tune of "Twinkle, Twinkle, Little Star"):
Rub-a-dub-dub, rub-a-dub-dub,
Ten little fingers, scrub, scrub, scrub.
Inside, outside, fingers too,
Rinse them off and dry them too.
Rub-a-dub-dub, rub-a-dub-dub,
Ten little fingers, clean and scrubbed.
- Talk about the importance of washing with vigorous rubbing motions, making sure to wash the palms, backs of hands, wrists, between the fingers, and under nails (use a brush if one is available).
- Choose a child to wash hands with your help while you all sing the song.
- Have the child rinse hands in a second tub of clear water, dry hands with a paper towel, and discard the towel in a wastebasket.
- Change the water for each child.
- Talk about how germs (bacteria) get on our hands when we handle things, go to the bathroom, blow our noses, and so on. Explain that germs are invisible, but they can make us sick.
- Ask the children when they think we should wash hands. Stress both *before* and *after* eating, toileting, and preparing food.

Note to the teacher: Be aware that germs hide in jewelry and chipped nail polish.

VARIATION   Use a puppet to reinforce the importance of frequent and thorough handwashing. Have the puppet help clean the animal cage, help cook, go to the toilet, play in the sand, sit down to eat, and so on, forgetting to wash hands each time. Let the children "remind" the puppet to wash hands. Have the puppet inspect the children's hands periodically and give children lots of praise for remembering to wash.

Note: In recent years the highly contagious infection giardiasis has forced the closing of many child care centers. It is caused by an intestinal protozoan, *giardia lamblia*, which can be spread by people who do not have the symptoms themselves. The onset of this illness may be gradual or sudden, and is characterized by diarrhea, abdominal cramps, loss of appetite, nausea, and sometimes vomiting and fever. Transmission of the disease is by the fecal-oral route (usually by putting contaminated food, hands, or other objects into the mouth). Therefore, thorough handwashing with soap after bowel movements, after changing diapers, and before handling food is extremely important.

Activities about bacteria and handwashing are not intended to make children fearful of germs. They are meant for the teacher to use as guides in teaching the beginnings of good hygiene and self-responsibility. The success of such activities depends on the teacher's modeling behavior and the appropriateness of the material for the child's age and ability to understand.

HELPFUL HINTS

- Be especially careful to disinfect toys and equipment such as stethoscopes and listening stations with alcohol or bleach mixed with water.
- All sleeping cots should be wiped with a sponge dipped in disinfectant every day.
- Remove and clean all hats from dramatic play and dress-up areas if there is an outbreak of lice in the school.

Learning the Correct Way to Sneeze and Wipe the Nose

MATERIALS
Photo or sketch of a person sneezing, showing explosive spread of droplets
Box of tissues
Puppet

PROCEDURE
- Have the puppet sneeze at the children while it is talking to them.
- After you tell the puppet to cover its nose and mouth and turn away from others when sneezing, have the puppet ask "Why?"
- Show the puppet and the children the photo of a person sneezing, and ask what is happening in the picture. Let the children help the puppet answer.
- Talk about things the puppet and the children can do to prevent the spread of droplets and germs when they sneeze.
- Ask:
  What can happen if you cover your nose and mouth with your hands, but don't wash your hands?

What can happen if you use a tissue and then put it into your pocket?

- Talk about other ways germs are spread: coughing, touching, kissing, sharing the same eating and drinking utensils.
- Have the puppet and the children practice using tissues to wipe their noses, then discarding the tissues and washing their hands.

Learning How Germs Are Spread by Sneezing and Coughing

MATERIALS   Tissues

Confetti

Storybooks such as *Morris Has a Cold*, by Bernard Wiseman (New York, NY: Dodd, Mead, 1978); and *Germs Make Me Sick*, by Parnell Donahue (New York, NY: Knopf, 1975)

PROCEDURE

- Read the books to the children.
- Talk about how colds are spread by sneezing and coughing.
- Sneeze into a handful of confetti to demonstrate how far the germs can spread.
- Do the same by coughing into the confetti.
- Ask the children what they think you could do to prevent the germs from spreading.
- Repeat the sneezing and coughing using tissues.
- Discuss what happens when someone sneezes or coughs without covering the nose or mouth.
- Discuss how coughing and sneezing are the body's way of getting rid of germs.
- Encourage children to share experiences they have had with coughs and colds.

Learning About Dental Health

MATERIALS   Storybooks such as *How Many Teeth?*, by Paul Showers (New York, NY: Crowell, 1962); and *A Trip to the Dentist*, by Margot Linn (New York, NY: Harper & Row, 1988)

PROCEDURE

- Read the stories to the children (or tell them with the flannelboard).
- Talk about the things the children will see and do when they visit a dentist. Reinforce the concepts of dental health as presented in the stories.
- Have the children describe some ways they can promote dental health.
- Talk about the functions of teeth—that is, chewing, making word sounds, shaping the jaw and face, smiling.
- Identify foods that promote healthy teeth, especially raw fruits and vegetables.
- Identify foods that are bad for the teeth. Caution children to avoid chewing on nonfood items like pencils, toys, eating utensils, and crayons.
- Have the children help plan some nutritious snacks that are good for their teeth.

MORE INFORMATION ON DENTAL HEALTH

- Sugary foods cause fewer cavities when eaten with meals than when eaten between meals.
- Sticky foods such as peanut butter with jelly or honey, dried fruits, gum drops, and caramels stay in contact with the teeth longer and thus are more likely to produce cavities.
- Saliva is reduced during sleep; thus when children are given bottles at bedtime, liquid from the bottles may collect around the front teeth, causing decay.
- Fluoride significantly decreases cavities.

SAVING A KNOCKED-OUT TOOTH

- Find the tooth.
- Hold the tooth by the crown, not the root.
- Rinse the tooth gently in tepid tap water. *Do not scrub the tooth*! Be careful not to injure the surface root tissue, which is needed for successful replantation.
- Call the dentist to advise him or her of your emergency and ask if you should insert the tooth in its socket.
- If the dentist recommends reinsertion, place the tooth in the socket and then have the child bite down firmly on a clean piece of cloth to seat the tooth properly. The child should continue to bite down with moderate pressure until he or she gets to the dentist's office.
- If reinsertion is not possible but the child is able, have him or her hold the tooth gently under the tongue or inside the cheek, keeping it bathed in saliva.
- If the child is so young that he or she might swallow the tooth, transport it in a plastic cup or bag filled with milk or tap water and a pinch of salt.
- There is a 50 percent chance of successful replantation if the child gets to the dentist within 30 minutes.

Practicing the Correct Way to Brush Teeth

MATERIALS   One toothbrush and paper cup for each child (Use small toothbrushes with soft bristles that are straight across the top.)
Disclosing tablets
Unbreakable hand mirrors
Oversized model of teeth and toothbrush (optional; often available on loan from the local American Dental Association)
Toothpaste
Styrofoam egg carton
The story *D Is for Dentist* and the film *Tooth Brushing with Charlie Brown*, both available from the American Dental Association

(Contact the American Dental Association, Bureau of Audiovisual Service, 211 East Chicago Ave., Chicago, IL 60611. Also available from this address is a large, colorfully illustrated flip chart, published by the American Society of Dentistry for Children and titled "Tooth Talk; A Teacher's Guide—Flip Chart for Use with Grades K–3.")

PROCEDURE
- Read the story and show the film to the children.
- Use the oversized teeth and toothbrush to demonstrate correct brushing methods. Show children how to direct the bristles at a 45-degree angle where the teeth and gums meet. Use a circular scrubbing motion.
- Hand each child a toothbrush and have them copy your technique, using dry brushes.
- Follow a systematic routine. Brush the outside surfaces of the top teeth first, and work from left to right. Follow the same system for the inside surfaces. Then brush the chewing surfaces. Repeat the same procedure for the bottom teeth, stressing the importance of following a consistent pattern rather than brushing haphazardly.
- Label each toothbrush with a child's name, and store them by poking the handles through the bottom of an overturned Styrofoam egg carton. (See Illustration 6.1.)
- After the children have practiced brushing with dry brushes, have them chew half of a disclosing tablet and then rinse their mouths. Explain that the red spots left on their teeth show where germs remain. Let them look in the mirror to see the red spots. **Caution:** Be sure to check with parents before introducing this exercise, to see if any children are allergic to red dye. Also, let parents know that the child's tongue will be red for a day.

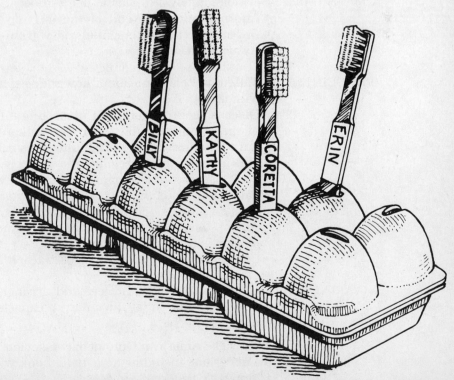

Illustration 6.1 **Holder for children's toothbrushes**

• Have the children brush their teeth the way you showed them, using a small amount of toothpaste, until all the red color is gone. Have them brush their tongues as well (the red dye will remain to some extent, however).

• Suggest that after the children have brushed their teeth at home, they should ask their parents to brush them again.

• Share this teaching activity with parents, and ask their assistance in reinforcing dental hygiene habits at home. It is especially important that children brush before bedtime, because bacteria are more active when the mouth is quiet.

HELPFUL HINTS

• The use of disclosing tablets enables children to see in vivid detail where bacteria reside in their mouths.

• Use correct terms, such as *plaque* and *bacteria*. (Plaque is the by-product of bacteria feeding on food in the mouth.)

• Teaching how to floss the teeth may not be a practical activity for the preschool. However, this essential part of cleaning the teeth can be taught to parents in a parent education meeting.

• Invite a local dentist to visit the children at school and to talk to parents during a parent meeting.

Developing Good Eye-Care Habits

MATERIALS   Seymour Safely, the plastic-bag puppet (See Where to Write for More Information at the end of this section for information on how to order this and other materials from the American Optometric Association.)

PROCEDURE   • Talk to the children about how they use their eyes and what they see with them.

• Discuss the importance of protecting the eyes and taking good care of them (not rubbing them; protecting them from dirt, sand, and harmful objects; not staring into the sun).

• Talk about eyeglasses and the purposes they serve. Mention that dark glasses protect against the sun's rays.

• Talk about watching TV and the importance of sitting at a distance of least five times the width of the screen. If you have a TV in the school, ask the children to help measure the proper distance and mark where they should sit.

• Use the Seymour Safely puppet to teach the six eye safety tips.

VARIATION   Call the local Braille Society and arrange to borrow some copies of books in Braille to let the children experience how blind people read and communicate.

Note: The American Optometric Association also publishes other useful materials, including an activity book with vision games that can be adapted for different age groups.

SOME SIGNS OF POTENTIAL VISION PROBLEMS

- Unusual redness of eyes
- Unusual redness of eyelids
- Crusted eyelids
- Styes or sores on lids
- Excessive tearing
- Unusual lid droopiness
- One eye turns in or out with fatigue
- Excessive rubbing of eyes
- Avoidance of bright light
- Keeping eyes closed much of the time

HELPFUL HINTS

- Supply medical equipment in the dramatic play area.
- Refer to the annotated bibliography "Books About Children with Special Needs" in Part Four for storybooks about medical situations.
- Invite a medical worker to visit the school and talk to the children about the work he or she does.

Understanding the Need for Medical Care

MATERIALS Large doll
Medical equipment, such as stethoscope, tongue depressors, thermometer, hypodermic syringe without the needle, small flashlight, and doctor's coat

PROCEDURE
- Dramatize a situation in which the doll is not feeling well.
- Say:
  My doll (or the doll's name) **is sick. Do you know what it means to be sick?**
- Let the children volunteer information from their own experiences.
- Use their information to describe symptoms of illnesses (headache, sleepiness, fever, stomachache, sore throat, and so on).
- Ask them to help you decide what to do with your sick doll.
- Emphasize that the doll should describe to the adult (parent, teacher, or medical worker) the physical symptoms, showing where the body aches.
- Encourage the children to be aware of physical discomfort, and praise their ability to describe it.

Developing an Awareness of Appropriate Clothing

MATERIALS A selection of children's clothing, including jackets, sweaters, hats, shoes, thongs, and other items suitable for different kinds of weather

Illustration 6.2 **Using a doll is a good way to help children understand medical care.**

A flannelboard story or book such as *How Do I Put It On?* by Shigeo Watanabe (New York, NY: Collins, 1979); or *What Should I Wear?* by Helen Olds (New York, NY: Knopf, 1961)

PROCEDURE
- Talk about the different seasons, and invite children to describe how they feel when the weather is warm, hot, chilly, cold, comfortable, uncomfortable.
- Describe a variety of weather conditions, and ask the children to select appropriate clothing for each situation.
- Reinforce the importance of each child's taking responsibility for seeing that his or her need for appropriate clothing is met.
- Have the children practice dressing skills such as using zippers, buttoning, snapping, tying, putting on and taking off clothing, hanging items in their proper places.
- Talk about ways the children and their parents can help the teacher—by choosing clothes that are appropriate for the weather, labeling jackets and sweaters with the child's name, and so on. Make copies of the following lists and send them home to parents.

Children's Clothing That Makes Life Easier for Teachers

Pants with elastic waistbands
Shoes with Velcro fasteners
Clothes with pockets
Hooded jackets or sweaters

Clothing that is clearly labeled with the child's name
Shoes with nonskid soles
Clothing appropriate for the weather
Clothing that children can put on and take off by themselves
Mess-proof clothing

Children's Clothing That Makes Life Harder for Teachers

Clothing with zippers that don't work
Shoes with laces that are frayed, too short, or too long
Cowboy boots (they're too hard on balls and on other children's shins)
Shoes with slippery soles
Long dresses and frilly clothes
Jewelry
Barrettes that do not grip the hair
Thongs or sandals
Crotch-snap jumpsuits
Improperly sized clothing
Clothes the child is afraid to get dirty

Identifying and Reducing Stress

MATERIALS   Storybooks such as *It's Not Fair!* by Anita Harper (New York, NY: Putnam, 1986); *It's Mine! A Fable*, by Leo Lionni (New York, NY: Knopf, 1986); *Boy, Was I Mad!* by Kathryn Hitte (New York, NY: Parents' Magazine Press, 1969); and *Alexander and the Terrible, Horrible, No Good, Very Bad Day*, by Judith Viorst (New York, NY: Atheneum, 1972)

Recordings of music such as Vivaldi and Mozart, or tapes appropriate for stress reduction, such as those by Steven Halpern or Daniel Kobialka (available from Li-Sem Enterprises, 1775 Old County Rd., #9, Belmont, CA 94002)

PROCEDURE   • Read the books aloud, and encourage the children to relate the feelings described in the stories to their own experiences.
• Role-play how children react to frustrating situations.
• Discuss the ways children can identify and label stressful feelings. Ask questions like
  Does that bother you?
  How do you feel when that happens?
  What do you feel like doing?
  What else can you do?
• Present hypothetical situations such as fighting over a toy, being bothered by too much noise, disagreeing over TV, worrying about a parent's not returning, being rejected by friends. Ask children to identify, label, and deal with reactions to such situations.
• Practice these stress-reducing exercises: rubbing each other's backs, breathing deeply, closing the eyes and imagining a safe and comfortable place, lying down in a darkened area and listening to some restful music.

```
┌─────────────────────────────────────────────────────────┐
│  EXERCISE CONTRIBUTES TO GOOD HEALTH                      │
│  • Good exercise habits should be developed early.        │
│  • The strongest influences on a child's exercise habits  │
│    are the important persons around him or her.           │
│  • Exercise should be fun.                                │
│  • Emphasize activities in which the child competes       │
│    against himself or herself rather than against others. │
│  • Emphasize improvement as a reward in itself.           │
│  • Running, in moderation, is a good aerobic activity     │
│    for young children.                                    │
│  • Teachers set the best example by participating along   │
│    with the children.                                     │
│  • Plan a balanced curriculum, setting aside time each    │
│    day for some type of aerobic exercise.                 │
│  • Make sure to include in your exercise program          │
│    children who are overweight or lethargic. (Refer to    │
│    the Bibliography of Resources at the end of this       │
│    section for a description of The Stoplight Diet for    │
│    Children, by Leonard Epstein.)                         │
└─────────────────────────────────────────────────────────┘
```

Becoming Aware of the Special Health Needs of Some Children

MATERIAL   A book such as *The Balancing Girl* or *In Jimmy's Chair* (about children in wheelchairs); *Our Brother Has Down's Syndrome; I'm Deaf and It's Okay; I Have Asthma; Why Are People Different?*; or one of the other selections listed in the Bibliography of Books for Children in Part Four

PROCEDURE   • Read the story aloud.
            • Engage the children in discussion about the story and how some people have special needs.
            • Stress that children with special needs have the same feelings we do, enjoy the same things, and are more like us than different from us.
            • Emphasize some of the special benefits and challenges facing people with special needs.
            • If appropriate, involve children in the classroom who have special needs by having them share their feelings and experiences with the rest of the class.

Safety Activities

Identifying Poisonous Materials

MATERIALS   Empty, clean containers of poisonous items found in the home, such as cleaners, polishes, perfumes, paints, bug sprays, aspirin, and medicines
            Posters and stickers (such as the skull in Illustration 6.3) from a poison control center. (*Note*: There is a nationwide network of regional

---

INFORMATION ABOUT CHILDREN WITH SPECIAL NEEDS

- About 7 percent of school children have some degree of hearing loss either from birth or due to illness or accident.
- Childhood asthma affects 5 percent of young children and is the leading cause of absenteeism among preschool children in the United States.
- An epileptic seizure can be alarming, but most epilepsy can be controlled with medication. It is often the reaction of people who do not understand that creates the real handicap.
- About 3 percent of all children born in the United States are of mixed racial and ethnic heritage.

---

poison control centers. Look in the phone book under "Poison Control Center" for the office nearest you.)

PROCEDURE
- Show each container to the children, and ask if they know what is in it.
- Talk about how the contents of the containers are used.
- Ask the children:
  Should you play with what's in here?
  pour it out? touch it? put it in your mouth?
  Why not?
- Talk about poisons and what poisons can do.
- Discuss ways of reminding everyone that something is poisonous.
- Show the warning stickers and tell the children that the stickers mean the contents are poisonous.
- Also, emphasize that some poisonous materials are not labeled.
- Put a sticker on each of the containers.

Note: Keep syrup of ipecac on hand, but out of the children's reach. Syrup of ipecac can be purchased at any pharmacy without a prescrip-

Illustration 6.3 **The Poison Control Center skull indicates contents are poisonous.**

tion and is a safe means of inducing vomiting when recommended by a doctor or the poison control center.

Learning How to Telephone for Help

MATERIALS   Telephone with push-button numbers
Brightly colored adhesive tape
Adhesive labels with small pictures of familiar animals such as dogs and cats.[17]

PROCEDURE   • Color-code the operator button of the telephone with a piece of adhesive tape labeled "O."
• Fasten one dog label next to the "9" button.
• Put two cat labels next to the "1" button. (See Illustration 6.4.)
• Talk to the children about emergency situations, such as a fire, illness, or physical injury. Allow time for each child to share personal experiences.
• Talk about the importance of calling for help when there is an emergency.
• Show the children the telephone with color-coded labels.
• Explain that if they need to call for help, it is important that they know who to call and what to say.
• Teach the use of the telephone to small groups of children at the same level of ability. Very young children can learn to push the "O"

Illustration 6.4 **"911" identified with dog and cat labels**

[17]Children who cannot identify numbers can recognize and name animals. Stress "911" as children become more familiar with the location of the numbers on the phone.

button; older preschoolers (ages 4 and 5) will be able to learn to call 911 by pushing "doggy, kitty-kitty."

- Ask each child to push either O or 911 and pretend that he or she is calling for help. You or another adult can play the role of the operator.
- Have each child practice giving his or her name, the address (especially the city), and the nature of the emergency.
- Very young children can practice pushing O, saying "help," and leaving the phone off the hook.
- As children become more familiar with the procedure, have them role-play emergency situations. Pretend, for example, that a baby-sitter has fallen and is unconscious, a parent is too sick to get help, a sibling has swallowed too many pills, and so on.
- Explain to the children that they should run to a neighbor's house for help if there is a fire in the house.
- Repeat the role playing frequently. When children are familiar with the routine of calling for help, remove the labels from the telephone and have them practice pushing O or 911 without the aids. Remind the children that they are not to practice on a phone that is operational, because operators, police, ambulance drivers, and fire fighters cannot help people who really need them if they receive a call that is not a real emergency.
- Enlist the help of parents to reinforce learning to phone for help from home. (Although dialing is more difficult for little fingers, this activity can be adapted for use with a rotary telephone dial.)

Note: The emergency number 911 is in effect in most areas. If possible, children should learn to call 911 rather than O, because 911 will immediately place the phone line on hold, with ring-back capabilities if the caller should hang up. The address of the caller will flash on the screen of the operator's terminal, enabling the operator to dispatch help.

If the child dials O, the computerized capabilities of the 911 code are not functional, so it is important that the child then ask for help, give the address—especially the city—and leave the phone off the hook so that the operator can trace the location.

Becoming Aware of Appropriate Ways to Use Play Equipment

MATERIALS Collection of unsafe toys: toys with sharp or jagged edges; small toys; toys with small parts; stuffed toys with poorly constructed seams; loud noise-making toys; toys with sharp points, pins, staples, and wires; and toys that propel objects (such as dart guns and bows and arrows)
Story about safety

PROCEDURE • Read a story emphasizing toy safety to the children.
- Talk about safety, encouraging the children to share their experiences.
- Show unsafe toys one at a time, and ask the children to help explain why each toy is unsafe.

• Discuss what children can do to help identify, call attention to, and avoid unsafe toys.

Note: Write the U.S. Consumer Product Safety Commission, TOYS, Washington, DC 20207, or call toll-free 800-638-2666 for information on toy safety.

Learning Proper Use of Swings, Slides, and Climbing Apparatus

MATERIAL   A series of sketches, photographs, or film slides showing staged sequences of proper and improper ways to play on swings, slides, and climbing apparatus

PROCEDURE   • Use the following guidelines in preparing a series of sketches, photographs, or slides:[18]

Swings

Sit in the center of the swing; never stand or kneel.
Hold on with both hands.
Stop the swing before getting off.
Walk way around a moving swing—not too close to the front or the back.
Never push anyone else in the swing or allow others to push you.
Have only one person in one swing at a time.
Never swing empty swings or twist swing chains.
Avoid putting your head or feet through exercise rings on the swing sets.

Slides

Hold on with both hands as you go up the steps of the slide, taking one step at a time; never go up the sliding surface or the frame. Keep at least one arm's length behind the person in front of you.
Slide down feet first, always sitting up, one at a time.
Be sure no one is in front of the slide before sliding down.
Be patient, do not push or shove, and wait your turn.
Leave the front of the slide after you have taken your turn.
Never use a metal slide that has been sitting out in the sun.

Geodesic Domes or Arches and Jungle Gyms

Use the correct grip; use fingers and thumbs (lock grip) for climbing and holding; use both hands.
Watch carefully when climbing down, and avoid those climbing up.
Avoid having too many people using the equipment at once.

Horizontal Ladders and Bars

All start at the same end of the equipment and move in the same direction, using the lock grip.
Stay well behind the person in front, and avoid swinging your feet.

[18]From *Play Happy, Play Safely: Playground Equipment Guide* (U.S. Consumer Product Safety Commission, Washington, D.C. 20207).

Never use equipment when it is wet.

Avoid speed contests or trying to cover too large a distance in one move.

Drop from the bars with your knees slightly bent, and land on both feet.

• Show a picture of an improper way to use a swing (for example, standing up or not holding on with both hands). Ask the children if this is the right way to use the swing. Identify what is wrong, and describe what should be done instead. Then show a picture of the correct way to use the swings.

• Do the same for other areas of the playground, following each example of incorrect use of equipment with a picture of correct use.

Learning to Listen and Look for Cars

MATERIALS Tape recorder

PROCEDURE • Tape-record sounds of cars approaching and driving by on the street. Include silent pauses between each car or group of cars.

• Talk to the children about listening for cars in the street. Tell them they can sometimes hear a car before they see it.

• Take them into the playground and mark a path so that they can pretend they are crossing the street.

• Have them stand at the "curb" and listen while you play the tape recorder from behind them, varying the directions from which the sounds emanate.

• Have each child point and look in the direction of the sound.

• Talk about the fact that sounds are softer when the cars are farther away and get louder as the cars get closer.

• Have the children practice listening and looking for cars on the street.

Note: The teacher can use other opportunities to teach safety on the streets. Short walks in the neighborhood or field trips are times to practice what the children have learned in school.

The American Automobile Association publishes an excellent series of booklets designed for adults who work with preschool children. Titles include "Preschool Children in Traffic," "When I Go Outside," "I Listen and Look for Cars Coming," "How I Cross a Street," and "Traffic Signal Lights." Contact your local AAA for ordering information.

Learning About Pedestrian Safety

MATERIALS Flannelboard circles in red, green, and yellow
Pictures of stop signs
Paper and crayons
Appropriate storybooks, such as "How I Cross a Street," available from the American Automobile Association

PROCEDURE
- Read the story (or tell it with the flannelboard).
- Have children identify the various traffic signals and what they mean.
- Ask questions like
  How do you use your eyes before you cross the street?
  How do you use your ears?
  Should you cross in the middle of a block?
  Where should you cross the street?
  Should you cross the street by yourself?
  What if your favorite ball rolls out into the street and you really want to get it right away? What should you do?
- Have the children make traffic signs similar to the ones in the neighborhood, and role-play traffic safety with them in the school yard.
- Take small groups of children on a walking field trip, emphasizing traffic safety.
- Invite a safety patrol officer or crossing guard to visit the school and talk with the children about pedestrian safety.

Understanding the Importance of Using a Safety Car Seat

MATERIALS
Child's safety car seat
Large building blocks
Discarded seat belts or canvas straps
The recording "Buckle Your Seat Belt", by Hap Palmer in *Learning Basic Skills Through Music—Health and Safety, Vol. III* (AR 526)

PROCEDURE
- Build a car with the blocks.
- Attach a seat belt to one of the blocks to make a back seat, making sure that the belt is designed to restrain the child across both the lap and the shoulder.
- Have the children take turns riding in the safety car seat.
- Make seat belts for the driver and other passengers.
- Play the recording "Buckle Your Seat Belt."
- Let the children help each other into the car seat.
- Discuss the importance of buckling up, with the shoulder straps across the shoulder, not the neck.
- Ask what can happen if the car has to stop suddenly.
- Display posters showing children in car seats and adults wearing seat belts.

Learning to Stop, Drop, and Roll

MATERIAL
None

PROCEDURE
- Tell the children that you are all going to practice how to stop, drop, and roll in case your clothing should catch on fire.
- Talk about the importance of rehearsing safety practices, such as through fire drills and earthquake drills (duck and cover).
- Remind the children that these events are not likely to occur, but that it is important to practice what to do in case they should happen.

INFORMATION ABOUT CAR SAFETY

- Automobile accidents are the leading cause of death and serious injury for children over 6 months old.
- All states now require children to ride buckled up, yet surveys show that many children travel without any restraints at all.
- The combination of lap and shoulder straps is most effective.
- Use booster seats to raise the children so that the shoulder straps cross their chests, not their necks.
- Information about car seat loan programs is available from state and regional offices of the National Child Passenger Safety Association. Call Information for your local number.
- For information about proper safety seats, send for the free booklet "Child Safety Seats for Your Automobile" from the U.S. Government Printing Office, Washington, DC 20402-9325.

- Act out pretend situations with them—for example, they are outdoors cooking hot dogs over an open fire, when suddenly their pants catch on fire.
- Practice *not running*, but instead stopping, dropping to the ground, rolling over and over, and yelling for help.
- Praise them for being calm and not running.
- Practice these kinds of incidents repeatedly so that the children develop a sense of what it feels like to stop, drop, roll, and yell for help.

Personal Safety

The increasing numbers of child molestation, kidnapping, and abuse cases and the resultant media coverage have made parents and teachers fearful for their children. The responsibility for educating youngsters about such matters lies primarily with the parents; yet so many children are under the care of teachers for a large part of the day that it would be remiss to ignore the importance of both the school and the home in teaching children about personal safety. Many teachers are reluctant to take on such an awesome task for fear of offending the parents, perhaps saying the wrong things, or simply frightening the children unnecessarily. Following is some helpful information provided by experts in child-abuse prevention.

- Children learn best from their parents and other important adults in their lives, including their teachers.
- The most effective learning takes place when parents and teachers agree on what is to be taught and how each will reinforce and support the other so that the child receives consistent information. (Suggestions: Have parent education meetings, provide speakers and data from the Child Advocacy Council, devise a cooperative plan for teaching personal safety, and keep one another informed of progress.)

- Traditional ways of teaching children about personal safety have been through warning and instilling fear. Although these may be strong motivators, they are not always constructive or healthy.
- Young children have short attention spans and are not likely to integrate isolated facts into other aspects of their lives. They may misinterpret or forget what they hear. Thus, personal safety is best taught to young children as part of their daily routines.
- Promoting self-esteem in young children is one of the best deterrents to vulnerability. See books such as *How to Boost Your Child's Self-Esteem: 101 Ways to Raise a Happy, Confident Child,* by A. Price and J. Parry (New York, NY: Golden Press, 1984).
- Keep communication open by encouraging children to share their fears, thoughts, ideas, and experiences with the adults they love.

As teachers, we recognize how important it is for young children to develop a strong sense of self-worth. The activities we plan are geared toward helping children gain confidence and a healthy curiosity. We relate to youngsters in ways that let them know it is okay to trust us and the environment of the school. It is on a strong basis of trust that they develop a sense of security and self-esteem. Thus, it can be very confusing when the child gets messages on the one hand to love and trust, and on the other hand to be wary of others.

The prospect of molestation or abduction is frightening indeed, and as caring adults, we want to protect our children's safety. But *equally important* is the protection of their emotional health and well-being.

In practicing the personal safety activities, use good judgment about the child or children with whom you are working. Will you be telling them too much too soon? Will they be burdened with the fear that "something" might happen to them? Is the child's healthy sense of self sufficiently developed that he or she can integrate such information into his or her life?

The following activities are intended to provide ideas for teachers to adapt. They are designed not to be taught only once or twice in a formal setting, but rather to be kept in mind for those times when they can be integrated into the child's daily activities and reinforced. Children learn best through play, not through lectures or warnings.

- Keep instructions simple.
- Use short sentences.
- Teach at a time when the children are receptive, not tired or distracted.
- Limit the number of facts presented.
- Be concrete, and use correct labels.
- Make eye contact; look for understanding and wait for feedback.
- Repeat the lesson under many different conditions.
- Be a good model; be confident and relaxed.

Children learn and retain best when they are actively involved, using their senses of sight, hearing, touch, and motion. They respond well to puppetry and play acting. Have them rehearse such activities as saying "no!" emphatically or yelling loudly for help. Give them many opportunities to practice what they are to say and do.

When practicing the activities, create an atmosphere of fun and confidence, rather than fear. Most importantly, as pediatrician T. Berry Brazelton says: "Whatever we teach our children to prepare them for an unsafe world had better come *after* they've developed a sense of inner security."

Learning to Say No to Strangers

MATERIALS

Puppets or dolls
Toys
Gift-wrapped box
Coins
The book *It's O.K. to Say No!* by Robin Lenett and Bob Crane (New York, NY: Tom Doherty, 1985)

PROCEDURE

- Talk about the meaning of *stranger* with the children, and have the children give examples of strangers.
- Ask a series of what-if questions appropriate to the ages of the children, such as
  What if a stranger [someone you don't know] said, "Come here and have some candy." What would you say?
  Other situations might include a stranger's offering to take the child to his or her "sick" parent, an invitation to enter a car or house to see some kittens, or a plea for help.
- Tell the children you want to play pretend with them by being a stranger. Act out the part dramatically, approaching each child with a toy, some coins, candy, or a gift and giving different compelling reasons why the child should go with you.
- Each time a child says "no!" emphatically and with confidence, give him or her a lot of praise.
- If a child should accept one of your offers (the other children will probably correct him or her), ask why the child should have said no. Give the child more opportunities to play-act saying no.
- Use puppets or dolls to dramatize the same and similar situations, asking the children to help you come up with other possibilities.
- Read the book *It's O.K. to Say No!* to expand on the topic.

Note: Most molestation cases are committed by people known to the child.

Important: *Teachers and child-care workers are mandated by law to report suspected cases of child abuse.*

Recognizing a Bribe

MATERIALS

Enticing gifts such as stuffed toys, candy, items popular with the children
The book *It's O.K. to Say No!* by Robin Lenett and Bob Crane (New York, NY: Tom Doherty, 1985)

PROCEDURE

- Say something like

  Sometimes people try to trick you into doing something you don't want to do. Remember when we played pretend and I was a stranger? What did the stranger try to get you to do?

- Talk about people who use tricks and bribes. Say:

  Sometimes it isn't only strangers who try to trick us. Sometimes the people we know might try to trick or bribe us.

- Use what-if situations such as

  What if your babysitter said, "I'll let you stay up late if you'll take off your clothes and let me touch your bottom"?

- The object of this type of activity is to teach the children not to be tricked into doing something they don't want to or ought not to do. The notion of bribery is difficult for children to comprehend. Use actual scenarios to relate the concept of bribery to experiences that are familiar. For example, say:

  I'll let you play with my toy if you'll promise not to play with anyone else.

  I'll give you this candy if you'll invite me to your birthday party.

- Read the book aloud, and discuss the situations cited in the story.

Learning the Difference Between a Secret and a Surprise

MATERIALS

The books *The Trouble with Secrets*, by Karen Johnsen (Seattle, WA: Parenting Press, 1986); and *Sometimes It's O.K. to Tell Secrets*, by Amy C. Bahr (New York, NY: Grosset & Dunlap, 1986)

PROCEDURE

- Ask the children to recall a surprise, such as opening a present and being surprised at the contents; having a surprise party; making a surprise picture for mom or dad; hiding and surprising someone. Make sure they notice that a surprise is generally something nice and is eventually revealed.

- Ask the children to recall a secret—something they didn't tell someone.

- Use what-if situations to help the children understand the difference between a *surprise* and a *secret*. Since children are usually asked to keep secrets when they are being molested, stress what-if situations referring to private body parts. Explain that it is not okay, for example, for an adult to say, "This is our little secret; don't ever tell."

- Read the books aloud, and discuss how the children would feel and what they would do in the given situations.

Learning to Yell for Help

MATERIAL

None

PROCEDURE

- Tell the children the first thing they need to do is learn how to yell loudly. Have them take a deep breath, hold it, and then let out a loud "help!" Let them practice yelling "help" several times, praising them for doing it loudly and effectively.

- Play a pretend game in which you are a potential abductor. Invite the children to get into your car, go see some lost kittens, have some candy, etc. Each time, have them give out a yell for help and run away. (Puppets or dolls can be used to enact pretend scenes if you prefer.) Be sure to run away when the children yell for help so that they can see that what they are doing is effective.
- Have the children tell someone about the incident after it has occurred.

Note: Make this a fun activity in which the child's confidence and assertiveness are praised. If appropriate, have the children practice giving descriptions of the abductor.

Learning About Good Touches and Bad Touches

MATERIAL The storybooks *Talking About Touching, for Parents and Kids*, by Kathy Beland, and *Loving Touches*, by Lory Freeman (See the Bibliography.)

PROCEDURE
- Read the stories aloud (or tell them using the flannelboard).
- Engage all the children in answering the questions raised by the stories.
- Stress the following:
  Your body belongs to you.
  There are good touches, like hugs, kisses, and back rubs, that make you feel good.
  There are bad or confusing touches that make you feel "icky" or "squishy" like touching your private parts or any place you don't like to be touched. Sometimes you like or love the person, but not the way he or she touches you.
  Say "No!" or "Stop it! I don't want you to touch me!"
  Tell someone you trust about what happened and how it made you feel. Who are some of the people you trust? (parent, teacher, principal, police, friend)
  If you tell someone and that person does not believe you, go tell another person you trust and keep telling people until someone believes you.
  It is not your fault, and you are not to blame for what an adult does to you.
- Acknowledge that sometimes it is hard to say no to grownups. Have children practice saying "no!" using firm voices and making eye contact. Use questions and comments like
  Let me have your toy.
  Let's hide in your closet.
  Can I wear your hat?
  Let's play with your mom's purse.
  I'll give you some candy if you give me a kiss, okay?

• Role-play other possible problem situations, using the resources listed in the bibliography at the end of this section.

Identifying Private Body Parts

MATERIAL   Anatomically correct dolls

PROCEDURE
- Tell the children you want to see how much they know. Begin by asking them to identify parts of your body. For example, point to your nose and ask them to tell you what that part of your body is called.
- Do the same with their body parts.
- Then point to various parts of a child's body, such as the ear, and say:
  Whose ear is this?
  Can I have your ear?
  Can I touch your ear?
- Stress over and over that these body parts belong only to him or her and no one has the right to touch them without his or her permission.
- As the game progresses, include names of body parts that may be unfamiliar to them, such as *anus, penis, vagina, vulva,* and *breasts.* (It is a good idea to let parents know you plan to use this activity and ask for permission to teach the names of private body parts.)
- Be sure to do this activity in a relaxed and fun-loving atmosphere.
- Talk about some parts of our bodies that are private, such as the penis, anus, vagina, vulva, and breasts. (Sometimes it is helpful to refer to parts of the body that are covered by bathing suits.)
- Remind the children to tell an adult they trust anytime someone touches their private parts without their permission.
- Use the anatomically correct dolls to identify and talk about private body parts.

Bibliography of Resources

Adams, Caren, and Jennifer Fay. *No More Secrets.* San Luis Obispo, CA: Impact Publishers, 1981. An excellent book designed primarily to help parents protect their children from sexual assault. Chapters cover strategies for teaching children what to do and say to protect themselves, how to listen and watch for behavior signals, and games to teach prevention of assault. Community action suggestions and a list of resources make this a valuable book for parent education.

Bahr, Amy C. *Sometimes It's O.K. to Tell Secrets.* New York, NY; Grosset & Dunlap, 1986. This is a book for parents and children to read together, expanding on the various situations. This book is intended not to frighten, but to educate, and is based on the premise that children need to learn and practice phrases in order to be comfortable using them.

Bassett, Kerry. *My Very Own Special Body Book.* Redding, CA: Hawthorne Press, 1981. A simply written and illustrated book to be read aloud to 3- to 6-year-olds. Its messages are (1) your body is very special and it's yours; (2) if someone touches you in a way you don't like, say no and always tell someone (your mom or dad or another person) about it.

Beland, Kathy. *Talking About Touching, for Parents and Kids.* Seattle, WA: Committee for Children, 1988. This is an excellent resource for preschoolers, parents, and teachers. Simply illustrated and clearly written, it discusses aspects of safety, touching body parts, and secrets. A parent guide accompanies the text.

Brenner, A. *Helping Children Cope with Stress.* Lexington, MA: Lexington Books, 1984. A review of current literature about stress and its effects on children from infancy to age 12. Death, divorce, separation, abuse, neglect, parental alcoholism, and other related topics are discussed.

Curran, D. *Stress and the Healthy Family: How Healthy Families Control the Ten Most Common Stresses.* Minneapolis, MN: Winston, 1985. A useful resource book for parents and teachers, with examples of ways in which families successfully deal with common stresses.

Dayee, Frances S. *Private Zone.* New York, NY: Warner Books, 1982. A well-illustrated book appropriate for children between the ages of 3 and 9 years old. The purposes of this read-aloud book are to create an atmosphere in which a delicate subject can be discussed openly in a nonfrightening way; to give children tools to use as preventive measures against sexual assault and to help them recognize trouble signs; to offer ways of guarding against repeated assaults; and to teach children recognition and reporting skills in case sexual assault occurs.

Elkind, David. *Miseducation, Preschoolers at Risk.* New York, NY: Knopf, 1987. The thesis is that schools and homes are using inappropriate educational programs, not recognizing differences between the minds of preschoolers and school-age children. Pressure to learn and the resultant stress are treated as important issues affecting preschoolers today.

Epstein, Leonard, and Sally Squires. *The Stoplight Diet for Children: Eight Week Program for Parents and Children.* Boston: Little, Brown, 1987. Children learn to classify foods by colors of traffic lights to help them remember that red foods, such as ice cream and potato chips, are high in calories and should be avoided. Yellow foods, such as lean meats and bread, can be eaten in moderation, whereas green foods, such as vegetables, are low in calories and can be eaten in larger quantities.

Fleisher, Gary R. *Barron's First Aid for Kids.* New York, NY: Barron's Educational Series, 1987. Written by a professor of pediatrics at Harvard Medical School, this guide is a handy, colorful, indexed reference for the teacher or parent. The laminated heavy cardboard pages are designed to be hung in the classroom for easy access. The text covers such common problems as fever, cuts, nosebleeds, insect bites, stings, burns, major accidents, choking, and CPR. Actions are suggested for each situation. Very practical.

Freeman, Lory. *It's My Body.* Seattle, WA: Parenting Press, 1984. A book for 2- to 5-year-olds, with excellent pictures and text about body ownership. A parents' guide is included. The publisher also has books on health and first aid for children who are home alone. Some titles are available in Spanish.

————. *A Kid's Guide to First Aid.* Seattle, WA: Parenting Press, 1983. Designed to be read and acted out by adult and children, this book is based on the premise that telling the child what to do in an emergency is not necessarily transferable to action in a real situation. Emergencies covered include fire, bleeding, and touching an electric outlet.

————. *Loving Touches.* Seattle, WA: Parenting Press, 1986. Offers positive ways for children to get gentle, truly loving touches, which are necessary to human existence. This positive approach can be used to lead into the topic of good and bad touches.

Green, Martin I. *A Sigh of Relief.* New York, NY: Bantam, 1984. Easy-access index with large print. Simple instructions for every common childhood illness and injury are accompanied by step-by-step illustrations. Tips on accident prevention are also included.

Johnsen, Karen. *The Trouble with Secrets.* Seattle, WA: Parenting Press, 1986. Helps children learn when to share and when to keep a secret. Children are asked how they feel and what they would do in different situations.

Kersey, Katharine. *Helping Your Child Handle Stress.* Washington, DC: Acropolis Books, 1986. Children are more vulnerable to stress because they have no past history to help them put life into perspective. Uncertainty, strangeness, or anything that happens for the first time to a child can trigger stress responses. How children respond and the attitudes of adults affect future coping skills. This guide to normal and abnormal stresses for different ages is a helpful resource for parents and teachers. It describes symptoms, how to listen, how to clear up misconceptions, how to encourage verbal expression, and other healthy ways to deal with stress.

King County Rape Relief. *He Told Me Not to Tell.* Renton, WA: King County Rape Relief, 1979. A collection of suggestions for parents and teachers on talking to children about sexual assault. The booklet includes suggestions for teaching prevention and reporting.

Leach, Penelope. *Your Baby and Child from Birth to Age Five.* New York, NY: Knopf, 1978. A very helpful resource covering common concerns such as feeding, toilet training, causes and cures of crying, loving and spoiling, and beginning school.

Lenett, Robin, and Bob Crane. *It's O.K. to Say No!* New York, NY: Tom Doherty, 1985. Short, simple stories of kids faced with potentially dangerous situations. Cartoon-type illustrations encourage adult-child play-acting.

Lorin, Martin I. *The Parent's Book of Physical Fitness for Children: From Infancy Through Adolescence.* New York, NY: Atheneum, 1978. A pediatrician explains exercises, nutrition, and health-promoting programs geared to different developmental stages of children.

Lovejoy, Frederic H., and David Estridge. *The New Child Health Encyclopedia: The Complete Guide for Parents.* New York, NY: Dell, 1987. A 740-page resource for parents and teachers, covering every aspect of child health, including sound health practices, finding good health care, handling emergencies, and diagnosing childhood diseases and symptoms.

Morgan, Marcia. *My Feelings.* Eugene, OR: Migma Designs, 1984. An activity book designed for children ages 4–10. Deals with feelings and saying no to inappropriate touch.

Palmer, Pat. *Liking Myself.* San Luis Obispo, CA: Impact Publishers, 1977. Helps children ages 5–9 to build self-esteem, acknowledge feelings, and deal with emotions.

Prudden, Bonnie. *How to Keep Your Child Fit from Birth to Six.* New York, NY: Ballantine, 1986. A series of illustrated exercises adults can use with young children.

Reinisch, Edith H., and Ralph E. Minear, Jr. *Health of the Preschool Child.* New York, NY: Macmillan, 1978. Covers nutrition, infections, behavioral problems, first aid, and accident prevention and gives an overview of the preschool health program, with sample forms for the teacher to use with parents.

Samuels, Mike, and Nancy Samuels. *The Well Child Book: Your Child from Four to Twelve.* New York, NY: Summit Books, 1982. A sensibly written book explaining common illnesses of children. It discusses dental health, eating sensibly, stress, and relaxation exercises.

Sanford, Linda T. *The Silent Children: A Parent's Guide to the Prevention of Child Sexual Abuse.* New York, NY: McGraw-Hill, 1982. A helpful resource that takes a positive approach to warning children of all ages about sexual abuse.

Seuling, Barbara. *Stay Safe, Play Safe.* Racine, WI: Western Publishing, 1985. Playing is fun, but accidents are the leading cause of death among children. Short, interesting situations are presented in a clear, nonfrightening manner, with basic safety rules for the playground, street, water, bicycle riding, and the home.

Strong Kids, Safe Kids. This home videotape, produced by Henry Winkler in 1984 for Paramount Pictures, is available from video stores or local libraries.

U.S. Department of Health and Human Services. *Coping with AIDS: Psychological and Social Considerations in Helping People with*

HTLV-III Infection (DHHS Publication No. ADM 85-1432). Washington, DC: U.S. Government Printing Office, 1986.

————. *Surgeon General's Report on Acquired Immune Deficiency Syndrome.* Washington, DC: U.S. Government Printing Office, 1986.

Wachter, Oralee. *Close to Home.* New York, NY: Scholastic, 1986. For children ages 5–10. Relates stories such as that of a baby sitter who breaks the rules, a boy who almost follows a security guard, a noncustodial father who tries to take his children. The message is that sometimes the hard and fast rules don't apply.

Where to Write for More Information

American Academy of Pediatrics, 1125 A St., San Rafael, CA 94901. Publishes "Guidelines for the Management of Infectious Diseases in Day Care for California."

American Automobile Association, 8111 Gate House Rd., Falls Church, VA 22042. Provides an excellent series of booklets designed for parents and teachers to use with young children. Each booklet is written and illustrated in story form, to be shared with the child. Titles include "I Listen and Look for Cars Coming," "Traffic Signal Lights," "When I Go Outside," "How I Cross a Street," and "Preschool Children in Traffic: Parents' Guide for Action."

American Optometric Association, 243 N. Lindberg Blvd., St. Louis, MO 63141. Supplies materials suitable for use with young children, including safety puppet shows.

American Speech and Hearing Association, 9030 Old Georgetown Rd., Washington, DC 20014. Provides free information and materials about various hearing impairments and testing procedures.

Analeka Industries, P.O. Box 141, West Linn, OR 97068. Supplies anatomically correct dolls that can be used to help teachers, parents, police, and counselors talk with young children about abuse prevention.

CAPP—Child Abuse Prevention Project, 1017 University Ave., Berkeley, CA 94710. Provides workshops and publications for parent and teacher groups concerned about child abuse.

Child Care Information Exchange, C-44, Redmond, WA 98052. Publishes "Infection and Day Care" and "Health Policies and Procedures."

Child Protective Services. Every state has at least one agency that receives and investigates complaints about child abuse and neglect. Look in the phone book under Juvenile Probation, Department of Protective Services, or simply call the police for information about the protective service in your city or state. Teachers and child care workers are required by law to report suspected cases of child abuse. Protective services can provide the child care center and parents with brochures and other resources. The school should have phone numbers and names of contacts on hand at all times.

Committee for Children, 172 20th Ave, Seattle, WA 98122. Publishes an excellent book for preschoolers and their parents, *Talking About Touching, for Parents and Kids,* by Kathy Beland, 1988. This simply illustrated resource explains safety, touching body parts, and secrets. There is an accompanying parent guide.

Kemper Insurance Co., Long Grove, IL 60049. Publishes an excellent series of colorfully illustrated booklets for teachers and parents to read to young children about such topics as playing with matches, keeping trash cleaned up, touching electrical plugs, flying kites, playing in the street, and riding bikes.

National Association of Speech and Hearing, 919 18th St. NW, Washington, DC 20006. Provides helpful information about speech and hearing impairments for use in the classroom.

National Child Abuse Hotline. For referral services, call 1-800-422-4453.

National Child Identification Center, P.O. Box 5839, Fresno, CA 93755. Provides parents with suggestions on how to help keep children from becoming victims of abduction. Children's identifying data are kept on file by this nonprofit organization, and in the event of an emergency, computers and other electronic equipment assist in searching for the lost child. Bumper stickers and window decals are available.

National Committee for Prevention of Child Abuse, 332 S. Michigan Ave., Chicago, IL 60604-4357. Write for brochures, books, and information about child abuse.

National Society for the Prevention of Blindness, 79 Madison Ave., NY 10016. Supplies a home version of the Illiterate E test, entitled "Home Test for Preschoolers."

Rape Crisis Center of Syracuse, 423 W. Onondaga St., Syracuse, NY 13203. For a nominal fee, you can order *Sometimes I Need to Say No!,* by Lisa W. Strick—a series of short skits designed for children, using songs and humor. The concepts are based on a privacy continuum, moving from general to specific issues of sexual assault. Included are supplemental activities for teachers, parents, and children. Send for a price list.

U.S. Consumer Product Safety Commission, Division of Consumer Response and Information, 5401 Westbard Ave., Bethesda, MD 20207. Write for a free copy of *Listing of Education Materials for Use by Schools.* The agency will provide up to 10 free copies of any of the materials listed in the booklet. Some of the educational materials deal with bicycle safety, child and infant safety, consumer products, fire, kitchen safety, playground safety, poison prevention, and toy safety. An excellent source of well-designed materials for the school and for parent workshops.

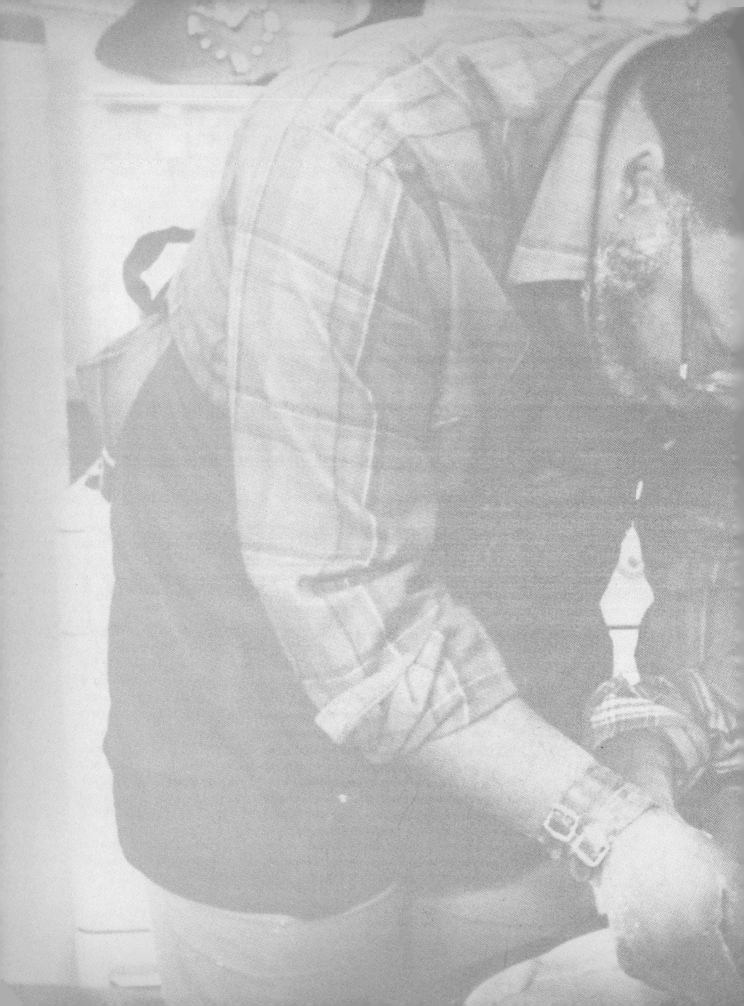

PART SEVEN

Cooking and
Nutrition

Introduction to Cooking and Nutrition

Cooking with young children offers many opportunities to attain several quite different objectives. It is an intrinsically exciting experience. Children love to do things they see adults doing, and cooking offers them the chance to do something "grown-up." It provides a way for youngsters to gain a sense of mastery, feel important, and achieve a sense of accomplishment.

But cooking can be more than fun. With the proper selection of recipes and use of materials, cooking offers many opportunities for cognitive, social, and cultural learning.

COGNITIVE AND SENSORY EXPERIENCES

You can use cooking to expose children to a variety of cognitive and sensory experiences. Let them *see* how the food changes before their eyes—how brittle noodles become soft and slippery after boiling, how an egg becomes hard when it is cooked. Let them *smell* the aroma of foods: bread baking, apples simmering, pancakes browning. Let them *feel* the different textures of food, like the squishiness of bread dough oozing through their fingers, the roughness of nut shells. Call their attention to *hearing* the different sounds of foods, such as corn popping or the crunch of celery when it is chewed. Note the colors, shapes, and sizes of foods—the black, shiny seeds of the papaya next to the bright orange of the fruit, the white of the coconut meat and the rough, hairy brown shell surrounding it. And, of course, let the children enjoy *tasting* the food.

With guidance and encouragement, the children begin to learn about units of weights and measures (1 teaspoon oil, 3 cups milk, ½ pound flour, 2 drops vanilla) and how these units relate to one another (3 teaspoons equals 1 tablespoon, 1 cup equals ½ pint, 16 ounces equals 1 pound). They learn to use the proper tools to achieve the best results—measuring cups for liquids, spoons for powders and for solids such as shortening. Successful experiences enhance their manual dexterity and help them gain confidence in working safely with tools. They also learn the meanings of new words: *dice* the carrots, *fold in* the egg whites, *grate* the lemon rind.

The children learn why liquid must be added gradually and why greens must be dry for salad. They watch physical and chemical changes take place as bread rises, whipping cream solidifies into butter, and peanuts are ground into peanut butter. They become aware of the need to learn about time: mixing for 2 minutes, waiting for the timer to ring, looking at the clock to see when the muffins will be ready.

SOCIAL AND CULTURAL GAINS

There are also social and cultural gains to be made through cooking activities. The child learns and feels the importance of sharing in a group project and realizes the need for cooperation. Planning the project, taking turns at stirring and pouring, and talking about the ingredients all require individual contributions to a group effort. Language skills are enhanced, and the joy of accomplishment is shared with others.

The common appeal of the foods of various ethnic groups provides opportunities to illustrate cultural differences. Some of the recipes in this section have been selected to emphasize these contrasts: rice balls from Japan, Chinese won tons, Mexican tortillas. Food is generally a topic of interest to all the parents in a school, regardless of language barriers, and many adults will be eager to contribute their favorite ethnic recipes. This kind of involvement on the part of parents allows them to contribute something unique and worthwhile to the program and exposes the children to food tastes and flavors from a variety of cultural and ethnic backgrounds. Stories and songs can be incorporated into the preparation and serving of foods, to celebrate customs or holidays. Special dishes can be planned and selected to fit into a schedule that allows plenty of time for preparation and eating. Keep in mind, though, that elaborate dishes requiring a great deal of adult preparation (and therefore much waiting by the children) should be discouraged.

LEARNING WHERE FOODS COME FROM

In addition to tasting new flavors and learning about other cultures, the children can learn about how others live and why they eat the things they do. For example, because corn grows well in warm climates, masa and tortillas are staples of the Mexican diet. Japan has very little land for animals to graze on, so meat is not a major part of the daily diet; however, fish is plentiful. The environment and climate in the countries of Asia are conducive to growing grains; thus rice and millet constitute a major part of the daily diet. Asian children are often allergic to milk and milk products because they and their ancestors are not accustomed to a diet of dairy foods.

Children can learn to identify and label plants and their parts—root vegetables such as potatoes and carrots, leafy foods such as lettuce and chard, flowering vegetables such as broccoli. Show the children how seeds contain enough nutrients to sprout new and larger growths. You can use alfalfa seeds or legumes to demonstrate that sprouts are only the beginnings of plants. If left to grow larger, they develop stems and leaves and need to have soil, light, air, and water to continue growing.

NUTRITION

Good nutrition should be a key objective in any preschool curriculum. Children need to be educated about food—what it is for, how it is related to health and well-being, and how it is produced and consumed.

Health Benefits

In 1988 the First Surgeon General's Report on Nutrition and Health strongly recommended that Americans

- Reduce their intake of fat by eating less meat and saturated fats. Fat makes up 37 percent of the American diet.
- Eat more fish, lean poultry, whole grains, vegetables, fruits, and low-fat dairy products.
- Increase fiber by eating more dried beans, peas, oat bran, and whole grains.
- Limit intake of sodium and sugar.
- Get sufficient exercise to burn off the calories they consume.

Many modern-day illnesses, including heart disease, cancer, and diabetes, can be related to poor nutrition. Even though Americans have the most food on earth, they are still unhealthy because they eat the wrong foods.

Eating habits are developed early in life and often have emotional overtones that continue into adulthood. Think about your favorite foods, why you like them, and what you associate them with. Do you often turn to food when you feel depressed or angry? What foods do you dislike and why? Many adults can vividly recall incidents in their early years when they learned to associate a food with an emotional situation: a special soup they ate when they were ill, a favorite cake of mom's they got for being good, vegetables they were punished for not eating.

As teachers, we need to be aware of our own eating habits and strive to be good models for our children to emulate. Your attitudes and enthusiasm for nutritious foods have a strong influence on the children. If you show that you are willing to try something new and encourage them to take just one taste, they are more likely to be open-minded to new foods. One teacher cooked oatmeal in apple juice every morning; although many of the children refused it at first, by the end of several weeks they were all eating and enjoying it. She invited the children to try a small amount but never pressured them. She encouraged them to help with the cooking and praised them for their cooperation. She also ate with the children. Learning to like something new or different takes time. Often children have limited opportunities to taste a variety of foods because they come from families that favor only a few foods. Sometimes parents are too busy to shop for and prepare fresh vegetables and grains, so fast foods may be their mainstay. Although nutritious foods will not do a child any good if he or she refuses to eat them, the positive results of good eating habits make it worthwhile to continue offering healthful foods in the curriculum.

Consumer Awareness

Perhaps more than any other age group, preschoolers are susceptible to television commercials touting highly sugared foods, such as cereals, candy bars, and fruit-flavored drinks. Young children have no way of knowing that the cartoons on the television screen are attempts to sell products and are not necessarily factual. Even adults are misled by commercials advertising "all natural" ingredients or the addition of vitamins and minerals to products that are low in fiber and high in salt, sugar, saturated fats, modified starches, and fillers.

As consumers, we should be informed about what we are buying. Make it a habit to read labels carefully when grocery shopping. Ingredients are listed in descending order according to their amounts, but some manufacturers list several ingredients such as sucrose, maltose, and dextrose separately in order to avoid having to list sugar first.

Reading labels, however, will not tell us if our foods are safe from pesticides. Though the FDA (Food and Drug Administration) has banned certain poisonous pesticides like DDT, there are less stringent controls on foods imported from other countries. Thus, when we insist on having fruits and vegetables out of season (peaches and strawberries in December, tomatoes in January), we can be sure that they were grown in some country where the pest-control laws are more lenient than our own. The more out-of-season the food and the better it looks the more drastic the measures taken to preserve it. Tomatoes that are shipped long distances are picked when they are bright green, stored, and then artificially ripened with diethylene gas. Apples and cucumbers are waxed to make them last longer and look pretty, but we do not always know what is in the wax. Some growers use wax made from petroleum, insects, and beef tallow. The FDA has never made a ruling on wax because it is considered to be a by-product, not a food; so we eat waxy foods without knowing what we are eating.

In 1989 the National Resources Defense Council (NRDC), an environmental group, released a study titled "Intolerable Risk: Pesticides in Our Children's Food." The report provided data on the eating habits of infants and children through age 5, along with figures on the amounts of pesticides found in 27 different crops. The study assessed the long-term risk of cancer and neurological problems in these children. Eight of the pesticides are believed to be human carcinogens; all are used on fruits and vegetables frequently consumed by children, including peas, carrots, fruit juices, and applesauce.

Daminozide (trade name: Alar), a chemical used to retard ripening in apples, is the greatest cancer hazard. Public concern about the pesticide resulted in the apple industry's pledge to stop using daminozide. Yet the company producing the chemical continues to sell the product outside the United States. Since more than 50 percent of the apple juice concentrate in the United States is imported, the public may still be exposed to dangerous levels of the chemical. It is a systemic poison that cannot be peeled, washed, or cooked away. Pesticides are more toxic to young children because their bodies are still maturing and their organs, like the liver, are not as efficient as an adult's in removing toxic chemicals. They also consume more food for their body weight than adults do. Preschoolers eat 6 times as many grapes and 7 times as many apples as their parents do. The typical preschooler drinks 18 times as much apple juice as the average adult does. Thus the child's ingestion of pesticides is likely to be much greater.

Teachers need to remain alert to information about potential health hazards and take an active part in lobbying for a safer environment for our children. Preschoolers are not too young to understand that we are fighting to have foods that are clean and safe to eat.

We are accustomed to seeing such a large variety of foods in grocery stores all year round that we often forget to consider whether they are in season and locally grown. One good yardstick is price. Generally foods that are in season are lower in price; again, the more out-of-season a food, the more drastic the measures taken with pesticides and preservatives. Many consumers, such as Concerned Citizens for Safe Food, are insisting that stores label organically grown fruits and vegetables. Local farmers' markets are a good source of fresh produce.

Maintaining Good Health

We seldom stop to consider how much fat is used to prepare some of our favorite foods. Flaky croissants, hot dogs, French fries, potato chips, gravies, sauces, salad dressings, and rich ice creams all contain hidden fats. Sometimes 50 percent or more of what we eat is pure fat. Although many adults crave such foods, young children usually prefer bland foods. They only learn from adults to develop a taste for fats.

The preference for salt in our foods is another highly developed taste. Many of our processed foods—canned soups, cookies, cakes, quick breads, and cereals—contain salt. Excess salt (which is 40 percent sodium and 60 percent chloride) has been linked to high blood pressure, migraine headaches, and kidney damage.

Today a large proportion of the food Americans eat is processed. Often this processing is done to prolong shelf life. White bread, for example, is made from flour that has had the fiber-rich bran removed, as well as the wheat germ, which contains 20 different nutrients. In an attempt to restore some of the lost vitamins and minerals, the flour is "enriched" with about 5 synthetic nutrients, and salt and sugar are added for flavor. The resulting bread has less fiber, fewer vitamins, and more sodium and sugar than whole grain bread.

Foods are processed because the public prefers to buy products that require less time to prepare, such as Minute Rice, instant breakfast cereals, and pancake mixes. As a result there are more than 1400 additives, preservatives, artificial flavors and colors, emulsifiers, and other chemicals approved for use in the United States. By contrast, there are only 7 approved food additives in France and 11 in Germany. In recent years more than 70 additives formerly approved as safe by the FDA have been banned because they have been found to be harmful. These chemicals have the potential to accumulate in the body resulting in serious illnesses later in life.

Salt and sugar are the additives most widely used in food processing. Although sodium is necessary for many body functions, there is more than enough naturally present in our foods to supply the requirement. The National Academy of Sciences recommends about 1100 milligrams (about ½ teaspoon) of salt a day. The average American consumes 8000 milligrams (4 teaspoons) a day.

In 1977 Congress formed the Senate Select Committee on Nutrition and Human Needs. The committee studied the role of diet and nutrition in health and issued a set of guidelines intended to reduce the incidence of many of the nation's leading degenerative diseases. The Committee recommended that Americans eat more fruits, vegetables, and whole grains and less fatty foods, sugar, salt, processed foods, and foods high in cholesterol, such as eggs and red meat. They also suggested eating more complex carbohydrate foods and more fiber.

Most vegetables and whole grains contain complex carbohydrates, including cellulose, which is often called fiber. Fiber is the structural part of plants, which is basically indigestible. The skin of an apple is made up of a cellulose fiber called lignin. The flesh of the apple contains another kind of fiber called pectin. There are different kinds of fiber in grains such as oats and wheat. Because fiber cannot be digested, it has no nutritional value, but it is essential to proper digestion. Fiber soaks up liquids, provides bulk, and aids the movement of food through the digestive process. It acts like a broom on the intestinal walls and absorbs toxins on its way through the system. Children do not appear to need as much fiber as adults do; however, it is probably a good idea to peel their fruits to eliminate surface poisons and waxes.

Teaching young children to practice good nutrition and to be wise consumers is not an easy task. They must learn to make difficult judgments about when to trust others and when to be skeptical. And although teaching good health habits is definitely worth the time and effort, it does not necessarily alter behavior rapidly. We know only too well how difficult it is for adults to change their diets, even though they know that the foods they are consuming are not conducive to maintaining good health. Perhaps young children will be less resistant because their eating patterns have not yet become well established.

PLANNING THE CURRICULUM

The teacher has a unique opportunity to involve youngsters in learning about nutrition and foods, as well as to introduce and expose children and their parents to healthy foods and good eating habits. Talk with the children and send notes home about the foods you plan to prepare and serve in school. Emphasize that you will choose recipes that avoid salt, refined sugars and flour, and ingredients with little food value. Instead, you will introduce recipes that require whole grains, dried or fresh fruit, wheat germ, seasonal vegetables, nuts and seeds—all of which are tasty and healthful.

Involving the children in planting a garden of easy-to-grow foods such as carrots, radishes, spinach, and chard is an exciting and rewarding project. It is one of the most effective and successful ways to give children firsthand experiences in learning how food grows, how to nurture and care for plants, and how to harvest and prepare nutritious foods.

Remember too that if you convey enthusiasm and a genuine interest in maintaining good health through good nutrition, children are more likely to do the same. Positive experiences help reinforce your comments about selectivity and skepticism in selecting foods. Teachers are among the most important adults in a young child's life, and their attitudes about food and nutrition can be an important influence on a youngster's thinking and behavior.

PLANNING FOR SUCCESSFUL COOKING PROJECTS

Children learn best when they participate in an activity. Thus, the recipes in this section were chosen to allow children to discover and learn through involvement. Most recipes can be prepared by a group of children, providing good opportunities to teach cooperation and teamwork. However, there will be times when you may want to encourage children to work individually simply because they will benefit from doing something all by themselves.

Individual Portions

Several recipes have been adapted to accommodate individual portions—pancakes, Raggedy Ann salad, deviled eggs, muffin pizzas, and baked apples. In other recipes, the number of servings is based on child-size portions; these recipes can be adapted for single servings as needed. See the bibliography at the end of this section for books with more individual-portion recipes.

Some teachers like to use prepared mixes for such foods as gingerbread, pancakes, and muffins in order to simplify the individual cooking procedures. Then illustrated directions (see Illustration 7.5) can be used. The directions for gingerbread, for example, would tell students to measure 3 tablespoons mix into a cup, add 1 tablespoon water, stir, and bake in an electric frypan for 15 minutes. Ideally, however, the child should be learning good nutrition and preparing healthful foods while learning to cook by himself or herself. Thus, the use of prepared mixes should be kept to a minimum.

Guidelines for Cooking Projects

As much as possible, projects should be planned and presented so that the children do the majority of the work—measuring, pouring, sifting, cracking eggs, cutting, peeling, kneading, and mixing. This calls for preplanning on the part of the teacher. If possible, try recipes at home before using them in the classroom. You may find it helpful to measure the dry ingredients in advance and to set out only the amount needed.

There will be times when you will want to use cooking as an activity to serve a special need, such as language development or engaging a shy child in a group experience. In such cases you might decide to select children who are more competent to help those with less experience.

Following are some guidelines to keep in mind:

• Preplan the steps of a cooking project, and discuss the plans with the children before beginning. They should be clear about what they are expected to do and what the adults will do before the cooking materials are made available to them.

- Identify children with food allergies. Post a list of the names of children who have allergies, along with the foods they cannot eat. Some of the more common substances to which young children are allergic are milk and milk products, juices with high acid content (such as orange and grapefruit), chocolate, eggs, nuts, food additives, wheat, and food coloring.
- Have the children wash their hands thoroughly before beginning any cooking project.
- Use low work tables and chairs.
- Use unbreakable equipment whenever possible.
- Have extra tools and utensils on hand, as well as extra ingredients in case of spills and for touching and tasting.
- Have only the necessary tools, utensils, and ingredients at the work table. Remove materials as soon as they are no longer needed.
- Have beginners use serrated plastic knives to cut such foods as bananas and cooked potatoes and carrots. As the children become more experienced, let them use small paring knives that are just sharp enough to do the job at hand. (Try the knives first.) Before letting children cut foods that are likely to roll around (potatoes, apples, carrots), slice off a portion to make a flat surface; this makes the food easier and safer for them to manage. The tops of handles of sharp knives can be color-labeled to remind children to hold the knives correctly. Take the child's hand to show how to make a sawing, slicing, or grating motion. Children can learn to bend their knuckles under while holding a food for slicing. Individual cutting boards are useful to help define the space in which a child can cut. Let the children use vegetable peelers only after you have demonstrated their use. (See Illustration 7.1.) Supervise the children carefully, especially when they are using a utensil for the first time.
- Limit the number of children to avoid crowding and to allow for adequate participation by each child.
- Long hair should be pulled back and fastened. Floppy clothing and cumbersome jackets should be removed. Aprons, although not essential, are helpful.
- Match the task to the child. Inexperienced children should begin with simple recipes that involve little cooking.
- Plan the project so that you do not have to turn your back on the children or leave them unattended at any time during the preparation process.
- Never let children stand on chairs to reach the top of the stove. Adults should do the cooking over burners. Turn pot handles away from the stove edge. Whenever possible, use electric frypans or pots on a table at the child's level, so that he or she can help with the cooking. Be sure to remind children that these utensils are hot. A picture of a flame placed by the appliance provides a visual reminder that it is hot.
- Allow plenty of time for discussing, looking at, touching, tasting, smelling, and comparing. Use every step of the cooking project as an opportunity for the children to expand their learning.

Illustration 7.1 **Ask children to use vegetable peelers only after you have demonstrated—and supervise the children carefully.**

- Be very cautious when serving or preparing foods that might cause choking (see Prevention of Choking, page 319). Children should always sit down to eat. Remind them to chew food thoroughly.
- Clean-up should be part of the total project. Children enjoy wiping, sweeping, and washing and they will participate in these activities as readily as they do in the cooking—especially if you provide small brooms, dustpans, sponges, aprons, and soapy water in a sink or basin that the children can reach.
- Send recipes home with the children, emphasizing the nutritional values of the foods served at school and how the children participated. Because of busy work schedules, many parents do not have the time to cook at home with their youngsters and are pleased to know what their children are capable of doing. Invite suggestions, comments, and participation from the parents. Suggest that they reinforce some of the concepts, skills, and new words the children learned during the cooking experience. Each time a child repeats a recipe, he or she gains more confidence and independence in performing the task. A sample note to be sent home to parents is shown in Illustration 7.3.
- Picture recipes are helpful for children to look at while cooking; they also provide a good prereading exercise.

Illustration 7.2 **It is essential to observe safety precautions when cooking with young children.**

PREVENTION OF CHOKING

- The following foods have caused choking in children, especially those under age 3: hot dogs, candy, nuts, grapes, bananas, raw carrots, corn, peas, peanut butter, popcorn.
- Avoid feeding very young children nuts and candies, including gumdrops, jelly beans, and cough drops.
- Cut foods into thin strips so that they cannot block the windpipe.
- Cook and mash foods such as carrots, corn, and peas; cut grapes into fourths.
- Avoid feeding raw carrots, whole peas, corn, grapes, and popcorn to children under age 3.

Dear Parents:

DID YOU KNOW THAT . . .

1. almost 90 percent of the mothers in a survey reported that they let their five- to seven-year-old children select the breakfast cereal?
2. television program content can have a negative effect on children's behavior?
3. watching aggressive and violent programs tends to increase aggressive behavior in young children?
4. as many as two-thirds of the commercials associated with children's TV programs are for sugared snacks?

HOW CAN WE IMMUNIZE OUR CHILDREN AGAINST TV COMMERCIALS?

What we plan to do at school:

1. The teachers are going to help the children identify commercials on TV.
2. We are going to talk about commercials and why the cereal and snack food companies show them.
3. We are going to let children test the claims that some TV ads make about certain products.
4. We will present our own "commercials" for nutritious foods — fresh fruits, vegetables, dairy products.

What you can do at home:

1. Watch TV with your children. See if they can tell the difference between a commercial and the program.
2. Show them that what they see is not always what they get.
3. Teach them what is good for their teeth and what is bad for their teeth.
4. Reinforce what we are doing at school and *share your good ideas with us.*

Illustration 7.3 **A sample note you can send home to parents**

Food Activities Children Can Do

The activities in the following lists are in approximate order of difficulty. The lists are intended as very general guidelines. An individual child's skills will depend on his or her level of ability and experience.

2- and 3-Year-Olds:

Wash vegetables
Shuck corn
Snap beans
Tear lettuce
Roll dough
Fold tortillas
Peel bananas (if top is cut)
Place things in trash
Clear place setting
Slice bananas
Spread soft substances

3- and 4-Year-Olds:

Break eggs into a bowl
Pour ingredients into a cup

Open packages
Knead and shape dough
Shape meatballs
Turn pancakes with help
Pour cereal and liquids
Apply spread to make sandwiches
Toss salads
Stir batter
Use serrated plastic knives
"Wash" cooking utensils (water play)

5-Year-Olds and Older:

Squeeze and juice fruit
Cut with table knives
Mash fruits and vegetables
Use an eggbeater or whisk
Grate (using large pieces of food)
Crack eggs neatly
Use peeling tools
Use baking mixes
Make pancakes, scrambled eggs, hot cereal, with supervision
Set and clear the table
Help load the dishwasher

GUIDELINES FOR FEEDING YOUNG CHILDREN

- Serve meals at the same time each day. Children thrive on regularity and routine.
- Seat the children at a table to eat meals and snacks. Discourage them from eating while walking or standing.
- Use unbreakable bowls and dishes when children first start to feed themselves.
- Encourage finger feeding by serving julienne strips of steamed vegetables, bread, cheese, and other foods that are easy to handle.
- Have nutritious snacks available throughout the day. Children need to eat more frequently than adults because they have smaller stomachs.
- Clean children's teeth or at least have them rinse their mouths out after eating. Frequent snacking contributes to tooth decay.
- Children will be more enthusiastic about eating and trying new foods if they are involved in meal preparation.
- Children's appetites may suddenly slow down around age 2 because of a slower growth rate and/or expression of autonomy.
- Children enjoy brightly colored fruits and vegetables.
- Children around age 4 and older enjoy raw vegetables with their own bowl of dip.
- Serve small portions; do not insist that a child finish all of his or her food.

Note: Adults should not assume that a child will outgrow baby fat. An increasing number of young children are suffering from hypertension and overweight. A major contributor to weight gain in young people is television viewing. Not only are the children bombarded with commercials about high-calorie foods, but they are forming sedentary habits. Children need to watch TV less and exercise more.

HELPFUL HINTS ABOUT SWEETENERS

Refined sugar, or *white sugar*, is the processed by-product of sugar cane. The cane is chemically stripped of its minerals and bleached. White sugar lacks fiber and is quickly absorbed into the bloodstream. *Brown sugar* is simply white sugar flavored with molasses.

Turbinado sugar is slightly less processed than white sugar in that it is steam cleaned rather than bleached. It is sometimes labeled raw sugar.

Fructose is extracted from refined sugar by breaking down the sucrose molecule into fructose and glucose. Fructose reaches the bloodstream more slowly than other sugars, so it does not affect blood sugar levels as dramatically. It is about 60 percent sweeter than sugar, but its sweetness is greatly reduced when it is cooked.

Honey, raw and unfiltered, is a whole, unprocessed food. It is twice as sweet as sugar, and since it needs the least amount of refining, it is most deserving of the often misused label "natural." A word of caution: Honey can cause infant botulism in babies under the age of 18 months. It often contains spores of bacteria that can grow in an infant's intestine. Don't add it to a baby's food or formula.

Molasses is the thick, dark liquid produced during the refining of white sugar. *Blackstrap molasses* is the liquid remaining after all the sucrose crystals have been removed and contains a significant amount of minerals. Look for molasses that does not contain sulfur as a preservative.

Maple syrup is a whole food made by the minimal process of boiling maple sap. When purchasing maple syrup, be sure that it is pure and not just a maple-flavored sweetener with additives.

Fruit juice concentrates offer good flavor, high fiber (pectin), slower and more uniform digestion, and added nutrients. There are cookies, jams, cereals, and juices on the market (especially in health food stores) that use fruit juice concentrates—primarily apple and white grape—as sweeteners.

Sucanat is made from the juice of organically grown sugar cane. Nothing is added; only the water is removed. Sucanat contains the natural complex sugars, molasses, and up to 30 percent vitamins and minerals. It is comparable to white sugar in sweetness and in use.

Artificial sweeteners such as aspartame (Nutrasweet) and saccharin are 200 times as sweet as sugar. Although aspartame is advertised as a natural product, its two ingredients—phenylalanine and aspartic acid—are not found combined in nature as they are in the laboratory. Some people have complained of headaches, depression, irritability, or dizziness after using artificial sweeteners. Long-term effects are not known.

Although natural sweeteners are more appealing and healthier than chemically refined sugars, the fact remains that *all* sweeteners are basically antinutrients and their use should be limited. Sugar crowds out more nutritious foods by using up valuable nutrients during sugar metabolism, thereby causing a dietary imbalance.

MORE INFORMATION ABOUT FOOD AND HEALTH

- Hot dogs, bacon, and most lunch meats are about 85 percent fat. In addition to a great deal of salt, they contain nitrates and nitrites, which are known cancer-causing preservatives.
- Some cheeses are fattier, saltier, and more caloric than red meat.
- Some cereals, like S'mores Crunch, derive more than half their calories from sugar.
- Use low-fat and powdered skim milk in place of regular milk. Look for reduced-calorie margarines.
- The main ingredients of most granola bars are fat and sugar.
- Although margarines and polyunsaturated oils have no cholesterol, they still have the same number of calories as butter and other oils. Use all fats sparingly.
- Encourage children to play outdoors and be physically active all year long. Do not carry a child who can walk.
- Introduce small amounts of new foods to children when they are hungry.
- Offer children a variety of foods from several different food categories every day.

HELPFUL HINT

Microwave ovens can produce significant heat absorption of deeper materials, with minimal heating of outermost structures. Thus, a baby's formula can be scalding hot when the bottle merely feels warm to the touch. If you heat bottles in a microwave, remember that the liquid continues to heat after the oven is turned off, so be sure to shake the bottle and test some of the liquid on your forearm before giving it to the child.

SOME COMMENTS TO THE TEACHER

Most of the recipes that follow were included for their nutritional value and ease of preparation by young children. There are a few recipes calling for sugar and ingredients that are high in calories and cholesterol, such as the butter making and egg recipes. As the teacher, you must make the final selection in light of your classroom—the concepts you want to teach and the ability levels of your children.

Whenever possible, choose foods that are low in fat, sodium, and sugar and high in carbohydrates and fiber. Fresh or frozen fruits and vegetables are preferable to processed foods. With whatever recipes you use, you can reduce calories substantially by substituting such ingredients as low-fat milk and cottage cheese, reduced-calorie margarine, vegetable oil spray for coating pans. Reserve rich foods like ice cream and butter for special occasions, and use them infrequently. Browse through the health foods section of your grocery store, or spend some time looking at health foods and books to broaden your knowledge about nutrition. (Not *all* products in health food stores are healthful!) Ask questions about how foods are prepared. Read labels. Talk with the parents in your school who are from ethnic and minority cultures about their foods, and learn more about the ingredients they use that may be strange to you.

The activities and recipes you choose will be determined by your knowledge about the youngsters with whom you work. If you have a great cooking project one day, evaluate why and how it was successful. If you have a terrible day, ask yourself, Was what you chose to do age-appropriate? Were there too many or too few children? Did you take enough time to plan? The fact that the food turned out okay does not necessarily mean that a cooking project was successful. Did the children learn something new and useful about foods? Were social interaction and language enhanced? Were cognitive skills reinforced? In other words, was the *process* as well as the *product* successful?

One way to increase your success rate is to read the recipes before you use them. Making chicken soup with rice requires quite different skills than does making won ton. Some recipes call for more adult help, in which case you may wish to involve some parents in planning and carrying out the activity. Other recipes are most successful with small groups of children. The list of Food Activities Children Can Do, presented earlier in this section, is only a rough guide. You know best what *your* children are capable of doing.

In the final analysis, your interest in nutrition and your good judgment, based on knowledge about young children, will be the biggest determinants of success in cooking activities. Good luck, good eating, and have fun!

Healthful Food Activities

Learning What the Body Needs to Be Healthy

MATERIALS   Flannelboard
Pictures of fruits, vegetables, and whole grains
Pictures of processed foods that are high in sugar, salt, and fats
Pictures of dairy products, such as milk, eggs, cheese, and yogurt

PROCEDURE
- Talk about healthful foods such as fresh fruits, fresh vegetables, and grains. Show pictures of these foods, and explain how the body needs them to stay healthy and to grow.
- Show pictures of milk products, and explain that these foods supply calcium for strong bones and healthy teeth. Point out that some children cannot eat milk products because they are allergic, so they have to get calcium from other foods like leafy green vegetables.
- Show pictures of processed foods, such as candy, sodas, potato chips, fried potatoes, and hot dogs. Explain that these foods do not help the body to grow and be healthy.
- Divide the flannelboard, to display healthful foods on one side and processed foods on the other. (See Illustration 7.4.) Hold one picture up at a time and ask:
  Does your body need this to be healthy?
  Let volunteers place each picture on the proper side of the board.
- Ask children to cut out and bring in other pictures to share.
- Explain that eating too much sugar can hurt the teeth and make a person unhealthy and eating too much salt and fried and fatty foods is harmful to the heart. People should eat foods that help keep them healthy and not eat if they are not hungry. The body and heart have to work extra hard when a person eats more than he or she needs.

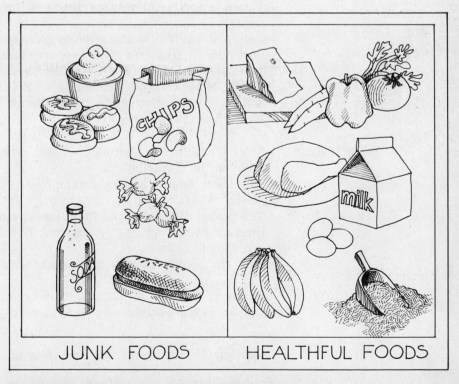

Illustration 7.4 Flannelboard with food illustrations

Identifying Fresh Foods

MATERIALS   Variety of fresh fruits and vegetables, such as an orange, apple, pear, zucchini, squash, potato, lettuce, and broccoli

Canned and frozen foods, such as frozen orange juice, frozen vegetables, and canned fruits

PROCEDURE   • Show each food item, and ask the children to identify it.
• Give the children time to talk about the foods they eat.
• Talk about fresh foods and how they grow.
• Show one item at a time, and ask if that food is fresh. Ask how they know (it is not wrapped in a package or in a can).
• Explain that fresh foods have to be washed carefully before they are cooked or eaten because they have been sprayed with chemicals that kill bugs.
• Talk about processed foods and how they have to be handled much more and often need more chemicals in order to be preserved.
• Talk about fresh foods being better for our bodies.
• Hold up a fresh food in one hand and a processed food in the other, and ask the children to tell you which is better to eat.
• Visit a grocery store, and have the children identify fresh and processed foods.

Learning Where Food Comes From

MATERIAL   Flannelboard

Pictures of foods, including vegetables, meat, fish, seeds, grains, and fruits

Pictures showing how these foods grow in their natural habitats (fish in the ocean, fruit tree in an orchard, animals on a farm, and so on)

The Carrot Seed, by Ruth Krauss (New York, NY: Harper & Row, 1945); *More Potatoes*, by Millicent Selsam (New York, NY: Harper & Row, 1972); and *Apples*, by Nonny Hogrogian (New York, NY: Macmillan, 1972)

PROCEDURE   • Ask the children to identify the pictures of various foods as you place them on the flannelboard.
• Talk about where the foods come from.
• Match the foods with pictures of their natural habitats.
• Talk about the amount of time, labor, water, and energy required to produce foods. Discuss waste and how children might help avoid throwing food away.
• Read the books and talk about them with the children.

VARIATION   Take the children on a field trip to an orchard or a farm, or grow some of the foods from seeds.

Learning About Vegetables and How to Grow Them

MATERIALS   Root foods such as potatoes, carrots, beets, onions, radishes, and turnips

Stem foods such as asparagus, celery and rhubarb
Leafy foods such as lettuce, spinach, and cabbage
Flowers such as broccoli, cauliflower and artichokes
Seeds for vegetables selected by the children
Pots, potting soil, and plant food

PROCEDURE
- Show the children one food at a time. Talk about each food and how the children like to eat it (raw, cooked in dishes).
- Let the children select one or two vegetables from each group to grow, and buy those seeds to plant.
- Discuss how the seeds will grow and what they need (water, plant food, removal of weeds, protection from bugs).
- Ask the children to tell what they think the plant will look like, and whether it will grow above or below the ground.
- As each plant grows, have the children examine the vegetable, tell how it grows, and name the part that they eat (the root, stem, leaves, or flowers).
- Remind the children that there are many poisonous leaves and flowers and that they should not eat plants without permission.

Note: Children will take a more active interest in this project if each child is assigned to a particular plant. Put the child's picture on a post next to the plant. Let the children help prepare their vegetable to eat after harvesting.

TABLE OF EQUIVALENT MEASURES

1 teaspoon	= 60 drops
1 tablespoon	= 3 teaspoons
1/8 cup	= 2 tablespoons
1/4 cup	= 4 tablespoons
1/3 cup	= 5 1/3 tablespoons
1/2 cup	= 8 tablespoons
1 cup	= 16 tablespoons
1 lb. margarine/butter	= 4 sticks = 2 cups
1/2 lb. margarine/butter	= 2 sticks = 1 cup = 16 tablespoons
1/4 lb. margarine/butter	= 1 stick = 1/2 cup = 8 tablespoons
1 medium egg	= 4 tablespoons (for easier measuring, add 1 teaspoon water and mix well)

METRIC CONVERSION

1 teaspoon	= 5 ml	1/4 cup	= 60 ml
1/8 teaspoon	= 0.6 ml	1/3 cup	= 80 ml
1/4 teaspoon	= 1.2 ml	1/2 cup	= 120 ml
1/2 teaspoon	= 2.5 ml	3/4 cup	= 180 ml
1 tablespoon	= 15 ml	2/3 cup	= 160 ml
1/2 tablespoon	= 7.5 ml	1 cup	= 240 ml

Learning About Seeds

MATERIALS   A variety of seeds, such as pumpkin, sesame, sunflower, corn, fresh string beans, peas in the pod, and peanuts in the shell
Pots, potting soil, and plant food
A story such as *The Carrot Seed*, by Ruth Krauss (New York, NY: Harper & Row, 1945); *The Tiny Seed*, by E. Carle (New York, NY: Crowell, 1970); or *Seeds and More Seeds*, by M. Selsam (New York, NY: Harper & Row, 1959).

PROCEDURE   • Show a variety of seeds.
• Let the children name the seeds and eat them.
• Read the story aloud.
• Plant some of the seeds and watch them grow.
• Explain to the children that seeds are very nutritious and contain enough nutrients to help the plants get a good start in life. Seeds contain important vitamins, minerals, and protein that help our bodies grow strong and healthy. (See also Sprouts, page 340.)

Note: In connection with this activity, you might want to make peanut butter, toast pumpkin seeds, or make sesame sticks (recipes follow).

BAKING BREADS

Playdough Biscuits

2 cups whole wheat pastry flour, sifted	**1 teaspoon salt**
	⅓ cup oil
3¾ teaspoons baking powder	**¾ cup milk**

• Let the children measure and sift the dry ingredients.
• Stir in the liquids gradually, and mix lightly.
• Using as little flour as possible on the table top, have the children knead the dough and roll it out about ¼" thick.
• Cut to any desired size or shape.
• Cook in a lightly greased electric frypan on top of a table on low heat. Let the biscuits brown and rise.
• Turn and cook on the other side. (Packaged refrigerated biscuits also cook up nicely.)

Children tend to overhandle the dough at first, but soon learn to knead lightly. Makes about 20 small biscuits.

Quick Bread

3¾ cups whole wheat flour	**2 teaspoons soda**
¼ cup wheat germ	**pinch of salt**
1 cup molasses	**raisins and chopped dates**
2 cups buttermilk or plain yogurt	(optional)

- Preheat oven to 375°.
- Mix all the ingredients together.
- Bake in one large or several small greased loaf pans for 30–40 minutes.

Brown Bread

2 cups whole wheat flour
1 cup unbleached flour
2 teaspoons baking powder
½ teaspoon salt

½ cup molasses
2 cups plain nonfat yogurt
  or 2 cups buttermilk
½ cup raisins

- Preheat oven to 325°.
- Stir all the dry ingredients together in a large bowl.
- Add the molasses, yogurt or buttermilk, and raisins. (Buttermilk can be made by adding 1 teaspoon vinegar or lemon juice to 1 cup regular milk.)
- Stir the batter until thoroughly blended.
- Spoon into one or more greased and floured loaf pans.
- Bake in one large loaf pan for 1 hour or in individual loaf pans for 30–40 minutes.

HELPFUL HINT

Use cookie cutters to cut bread into different shapes. Spread the bread with low-fat Neufchatel cheese or imitation cream cheese (it has about half the calories of regular cream cheese). Supply small containers of raisins, alfalfa sprouts, shredded carrots, and so on, for children to use to create faces on their sandwiches.

Steamed Monk's Bread

1 cup corn meal or corn flour
1 cup whole wheat flour
¼ cup soy flour
¼ cup bran (moistened with water)

2 tablespoons wheat germ
1 teaspoon baking powder
1 egg
1 tablespoon honey
1 cup buttermilk

- Mix all the dry ingredients, including moistened bran, together.
- Mix the egg, honey, and milk together and add to the dry mixture. Stir until well blended.
- Shape into a round loaf.
- Line the bottom of a steamer with wax paper or banana leaves.
- Steam the loaf over high flame for 20 minutes.
- Serve warm.

Note: This is an adaptation of an ancient recipe from China; it is excellent for making bread without an oven. Children can participate in every part of the preparation.

Soft Pretzels

4 teaspoons fast-acting yeast
3 cups warm water
1 teaspoon salt
2 tablespoons plus 2 teaspoons sugar

8 cups flour
1 egg
grated parmesan cheese
vegetable oil spray for coating pan

- Dissolve the yeast in the warm water.
- Add the salt, sugar, and flour. Stir well.
- Cut the dough into 32 pieces.
- Roll the pieces of dough into ropes, and shape as desired.
- Place the pretzel shapes onto cookie sheets that have been lightly coated with vegetable oil spray.
- Beat the egg with a fork.
- Using a pastry brush, brush each pretzel with beaten egg, then sprinkle with cheese.
- Bake in a 425° oven for 15–20 minutes.
- Allow the pretzels to cool before eating.

Note: This project requires only about 10 minutes to prepare, since there is no need to wait for the batter to rise. Children can participate in all phases of preparation except for putting the pretzels into the oven and taking them out. Because it is very elastic, the dough does not fall apart or stick, which makes it easy for children to handle.

Graham Crackers

1 cup graham flour
1 cup whole wheat flour
½ teaspoon baking soda
¼ cup apple juice concentrate (unsweetened)

¼ cup vegetable oil
1 banana, sliced
1 teaspoon vanilla
1 teaspoon cinnamon

- Stir the graham flour, whole wheat flour, and baking soda together in a large bowl.
- Blend the remaining ingredients in a blender or beat thoroughly with an eggbeater.
- Add to the dry ingredients and mix well.
- Divide the dough in half, and let the children roll each half out with a rolling pin on a floured surface. Roll to the thickness of a cracker.
- Poke the dough with a fork and cut into 2" squares.
- Bake on a nonstick cookie sheet at 350° for 6–8 minutes.

Makes 3 dozen.

Tortillas

⅔ cup warm water

1 cup **Masa Harina** (corn flour)

- Gradually stir water into the Masa Harina until the dough can be worked into a smooth ball.

- Let the children take a small handful of mix, form it into a ball, and roll it into a circle with a rolling pin or by hand (or use a tortilla press).
- Bake about 2 minutes on a hot griddle, turning frequently.
- Eat with butter and a little salt.

These tortillas are also delicious with grated cheese.

Muffins

2 cups whole wheat flour, sifted	1/4 cup molasses
1/4 cup wheat germ	1 cup milk
1 tablespoon baking powder	1 egg, beaten
1/2 teaspoon salt	1/4 cup melted margarine

- Preheat oven to 400°. Mix together the dry ingredients.
- Combine the milk and egg and stir into the dry ingredients.
- Add the margarine, and stir until moistened but still lumpy.
- Fill greased muffin tins about 3/4 full.
- Bake 10–15 minutes.

Makes 2 dozen small muffins or 1 dozen regular size.

HELPFUL HINTS ABOUT SUBSTITUTING FOODS

Remove 2 tablespoons coarse ground flour for every cup of white flour. Omit sifting.

3/4 cup of honey equals 1 cup sugar; reduce the liquid in the recipe by 1/4 cup for every cup of honey used. In recipes where no liquid is called for and where crispness is important, add 4 tablespoons flour for every cup of honey. When using honey, reduce the baking temperature by 25°.

3 tablespoons of carob powder plus 2 tablespoons of water or milk equals 1 square of chocolate.

Fruity Muffins

1 cup oat bran	2 large egg whites, lightly beaten
1/2 cup rolled oats	1 apple, peeled and grated
1/4 cup whole wheat flour	1/2 ripe banana, mashed
1 1/2 teaspoons cinnamon	1 small peach, pear, or other fruit in season, peeled and and chopped
1 teaspoon baking soda	
1/2 teaspoon nutmeg	
1/2 cup buttermilk	

- Preheat oven to 400°.
- Mix the dry ingredients.
- Combine the liquid ingredients.
- Add the liquids and fruit to the dry ingredients; stir until just moistened.
- Divide the batter among 12 paper-lined muffin cups.
- Bake for 25 minutes.

Popovers

4 eggs	**2 cups flour**
2 cups milk	**1 teaspoon salt**
2 tablespoons oil	

- Preheat oven to 475°.
- Beat the eggs well with an eggbeater or wire whisk.
- Add the milk and oil and mix well.
- Sift the dry ingredients together; gradually add the liquid mixture. Beat until smooth.
- Fill well-greased muffin tins ⅓ full.
- Bake for 15 minutes.
- Reduce the heat to 350° and continue baking for 20–25 minutes.
- Serve with margarine or honey.

Makes approximately 24 popovers.

Note: This is a good recipe to use if you have an oven with a glass door so children can watch the batter rise.

French Toast

2 eggs	**1 tablespoon oil**
⅔ cup skim or low-fat milk	**6 slices bread**
½ teaspoon vanilla extract	
1 teaspoon grated orange or lemon rind	

- Beat the eggs, milk, vanilla, and rind together, and put the mixture in a shallow, flat dish.
- Heat the oil in a frying pan (an electric skillet at the table works well).
- Cut the bread in half, soak it in the mixture, and brown it on both sides.
- Serve with orange-honey syrup (recipe follows) or a little warm applesauce.

Note: To cut down on oil, use a nonstick skillet and simply wipe it with a small amount of oil or spray it with a vegetable coating before cooking.

Orange-Honey Syrup

1 cup orange juice	**2 teaspoons grated orange rind**
5 tablespoons honey	

- Blend all the ingredients, and stir over low heat until the honey and juice are well combined. A small amount of arrowroot or cornstarch may be added as a thickener if desired.
- Serve warm or cold over French toast or pancakes.

Pancakes

2 cups whole wheat flour
2 teaspoons baking soda
½ cup wheat germ

2 eggs
2½ cups milk
2 tablespoons oil

- Let the children measure and sift the flour and baking powder.
- Stir in the wheat germ.
- In a separate bowl, beat the eggs, then stir in the milk.
- Combine all the ingredients and mix until smooth, but do not over-mix.
- Add the oil.
- Lightly grease an electric skillet at the table and heat to medium high. The skillet is hot enough when drops of water thrown on the surface "dance."
- Drop batter by the spoonful onto the hot pan. When bubbles appear on the surface, the pancakes are ready to be turned.
- Serve hot with orange-honey syrup or applesauce.

Makes 3 dozen small pancakes.

Note: To make buttermilk pancakes, replace baking powder with 1 teaspoon baking soda and substitute buttermilk for the regular milk.

Let the children vary the recipe by selecting other ingredients to add to the batter, such as blueberries, chopped nuts, diced apples, or raisins. This is a good opportunity to introduce children to new tastes. Suggest that they put a dab of yogurt and fruit on a bit of pancake. In this way they learn that certain foods do not always have to be prepared in exactly the same way. They can experiment with different tastes in small portions and discover the fun of creating their own recipes.

A good storybook to read before this cooking project is *Pancakes, Pancakes!* by Eric Carle (New York, NY: Knopf, 1970). Bright collage-type illustrations show where the flour, eggs, milk, and butter come from; the text explains how to cook pancakes. Another popular selection is Tomie dePaola's wordless book *Pancakes for Breakfast* (San Diego, CA: Harcourt Brace, 1978).

CUP COOKING

In "cup cooking," or individual-portion cooking, each step is illustrated on a separate card and the card is placed next to the appropriate materials or ingredients. Cards and accompanying materials are arranged in numbered sequence, and the child is instructed to follow each in turn, matching what he or she is doing to the picture on the card. Spring-type clothes pins make good stands for holding cards upright.

Illustrations 7.5 and 7.6 depict this procedure. Illustration 7.5 shows actual cards that might be used; Illustration 7.6 shows a child following the steps to make a salad.

Illustration 7.5 **Individual portion cooking cards**

Following is a pancake recipe that might be used for cup cooking.

1. Wash hands.
2. Take one bowl.
3. Measure 10 tablespoons flour into the bowl.
4. Measure 1 teaspoon baking powder into the bowl.
5. Measure 1 tablespoon wheat germ into the bowl.
6. Stir and mix all the dry ingredients well.
7. Add 3 tablespoons egg.
8. Add ½ cup milk.
9. Add 1 teaspoon oil.
10. Mix until smooth.
11. Ask the teacher to help cook the pancakes.

     Many of the other recipes in this handbook can be adapted for use in cup cooking. Refer to the Table of Equivalent Measures at the beginning of this section to determine quantities of the various ingredients for individual portions. See the Bibliography of Resources at the end of this part for additional books on cup cooking.

Illustration 7.6 **Child following individual portion cooking cards to make a chef's salad**

MAKING SPREADS

Sweet Butter

1 pint whipping cream   **small jars with tops**

- Let the cream stand out overnight.
- Fill each jar with about ⅓ cup cream. Screw the lids on tightly.
- Have the children take turns shaking the cream and watching how it thickens and begins to solidify.
- When butter has formed, pour off the buttermilk and let the children taste it.
- Rinse the butter with cold water, and press out excess milk with a spoon.
- Serve with warm sourdough bread.

Compare the taste of fresh sweet butter with that of the salted kind.

Peanut Butter

4 cups roasted peanuts, in the shell   **2 tablespoons salad oil**

- Let the children shell the peanuts. (Make sure there are enough that they can taste some during the process.)
- Put the peanuts through a hand grinder or blender. If a grinder is used, you may need to put the peanuts through twice.
- Add oil.

Any leftover peanut butter should be refrigerated because no preservatives have been added.

Strawberry Jam

1 pint fresh strawberries   **1 envelope** (4 servings) **straw-**
1 cup water   **berry gelatin dessert mix**

- Let the children help wash and hull the strawberries.
- Cut the berries up into a saucepan.
- Mash them and add the water and gelatin mix.
- Cook over medium heat, stirring until the mixture boils.
- Simmer 2 minutes, cool, and pour into small glass jars (babyfood jars are excellent).

Pineapple-Orange Marmalade

1 envelope unflavored gelatin   **1 20-oz. can juice-packed,**
1 6-oz. can unsweetened frozen   **crushed pineapple, undrained**
orange juice concentrate, thawed   **3 teaspoons grated orange rind**

- Combine the gelatin with the orange juice concentrate in a saucepan.
- Cook over medium heat.
- When the gelatin softens (after about 10 minutes), add the remaining ingredients.
- Cook, stirring, for 2 minutes.
- Taste for sweetness; add honey if desired.
- Cool and store in glass jars in refrigerator.

MISO SPREAD

Miso is a naturally fermented soybean paste. According to the Japanese, miso was a gift from the gods to assure health and long life to the people who ate it. It is gaining popularity in the West and can usually be found in Japanese and health food stores. The mellow white miso resembles peanut butter in color and consistency. Miso is worth introducing to young children as a healthy substitute for high-calorie spreads. It contains living enzymes, which aid digestion, and provides a nutritious balance of natural carbohydrates, essential vitamins, minerals, and protein.

Miso's salty taste makes it a popular base for soup and other vegetable dishes. It is delicious spread on toast or combined with peanut butter or tahini (sesame butter) to make sandwiches. Because it contains living enzymes, miso should be refrigerated and never boiled.

To learn more about miso, refer to *How to Cook with Miso*, by Aveline Tomoko Kushi (Tokyo, Japan: Japan Publications, 1978).

TOFU

Available in produce or refrigerated departments of most supermarkets, health food stores, and Asian groceries, tofu has been a staple of Asians for thousands of years. It is just being discovered as the "superfood of the future" in the West, however. Tofu is made from soybeans, contains no cholesterol, and is one of the highest nonmeat, nondairy sources of protein, calcium, iron, and potassium.

Tofu must be kept under refrigeration. After purchasing it, drain off the water, re-cover with cold water, and refrigerate. If you change the water daily, it will keep about 10 days.

Although tofu is bland tasting, like pasta, it is delicious when combined with the flavors and textures of other foods. It can be sauteed with vegetables; grilled or fried with meats; crumbled, mashed, tossed, or diced in salads and grain dishes; pureed as part of a dip; or even frozen into an ice cream–like dessert. A delicious nonmeat sauce can be made by crumbling a cup or more of tofu into a basic tomato sauce for lasagne or spaghetti. The following recipe is excellent for introducing children to an eggless sandwich spread.

Eggless Tofu Spread

1 lb. firm tofu	2 tablespoons sunflower seeds
2 green onions	2 tablespoons pickle relish
3 tablespoons mayonnaise	1 teaspoon cumin
2 tablespoons canned diced chilies	½ teaspoon turmeric
	½ teaspoon garlic powder

- Drain the tofu well to remove as much of the liquid as possible.
- Dice the green onions, including the green parts.
- Mash the tofu to the consistency of mashed hard boiled eggs.
- Combine all ingredients, and serve on whole wheat or pita bread with lettuce and tomatoes.

MAKING SALADS

Fruit Salad

Invite parents to contribute whatever fresh local fruits are available for children to bring to school. In addition, have on hand such colorful fruits as

bananas	apples
oranges	peaches
pears	strawberries
fresh pineapple	seedless grapes

Whenever possible, introduce some less common varieties of fruits:

mangoes	papayas
figs	kiwi
Asian pears	tangelos

In season, use a variety of melons and berries for a colorful contrast and a delicious mixture.

Depending on age and ability, let the children wash, peel, and/or cut the fruit. Preparation of a community fruit salad is an excellent social experience for adults and children. This should be a relaxed, unhurried project, with plenty of time for discussion about colors, contrasts, taste, and how and where different fruits grow. Some of the adults might be asked to take responsibility for looking up information about the various fruits before the salad preparation. Others might bring pictures of fruits and the many ways they are prepared. Learning can be reinforced and made enjoyable by having the adults and children share information.

VARIATION   Try threading fruit and pieces of cheese onto wooden skewers to make *fruit kabobs.* Or fill scooped-out pineapple or melon shells with fruit to make *fruit boats.*

Super Salad

6 medium carrots	⅓ cup raisins
2 apples	½ cup chopped nuts

1 large orange
2 small stalks of celery
¾ cup pineapple bits

¾ cup plain low-fat yogurt
3 tablespoons honey

- Wash, scrape, and grate the carrots; wash, peel, and cut the apples into small pieces; peel and cut the orange; wash, string, and dice the celery; and cut the pineapple as needed.
- Add raisins and nuts.
- Combine the yogurt and honey, and stir into the salad mixture.

This is a good opportunity for children to practice a variety of manual skills. Be careful that they do not get their fingers too close to the grater. Adults should finish the grating while children cut the fruit and prepare the dressing. Makes 12–14 small servings.

Orange Yogurt Sauce

1 cup low-fat yogurt
2 tablespoons honey

2 tablespoons grated orange rind

- Blend all the ingredients.

Makes 1¼ cup sauce. Great as a fruit dip or salad dressing.

Raggedy Ann Salad

peach or pear halves
celery and carrot sticks
cottage cheese
raisins or prunes
pimento

cheese, shredded
carrots or red cabbage, shredded
lettuce leaves

- Provide each child with a peach or pear half for Raggedy Ann's body and a scoop of cottage cheese for her head.
- Set the other ingredients on the table in muffin tins so that children can create their own Raggedy Ann salads. Arms and legs can be celery or carrot sticks; raisins, pimentos, or prunes can be eyes, nose, shoes, and buttons. The shredded cheese, carrots, or cabbage can be used for the hair, and lettuce leaves for the skirt.

HELPFUL HINTS

- Give each child a serving of cottage cheese or yogurt. Supply containers of fresh fruit, such as small pieces of pineapple, banana, grapes, pears, oranges, and apples. Let each child select fruits to stir into the cottage cheese.
- Avoid foods that spoil rapidly. Keep sauces, meats, and dairy products refrigerated.
- Serve cheese, raw vegetables, and fresh fruits for snacks.
- Save pumpkin seeds from your jack-o-lantern. Soak them in water, then toast them in the oven for a taste treat.

Cinco de Mayo Salad

1 head lettuce
½ lb. cheddar cheese
2 tomatoes
1 red onion
1 6- or 8-oz. package corn chips
1 lb. lean hamburger
1 small package taco seasoning
  mix (1¼ oz.)

1 15-oz. can kidney beans,
  rinsed and drained
1 12-oz. bottle low-calorie
  creamy thousand island
  dressing, or 1 14-oz. can of
  tomato sauce mixed with
  powdered taco seasoning

• Shred the lettuce, grate the cheese, cut up the tomatoes, chop the onions, and crumble the corn chips.
• Saute the hamburger together with the taco seasoning.
• Mix all the ingredients in a large salad bowl, and toss with the dressing.

Avocados, mushrooms, and a dash of hot sauce can be added if desired. Serves 25–30.

SPROUTS

Soak about 1 teaspoon alfalfa seeds or a small handful of soy or mung beans overnight in a jar of warm water. Drain. Cover the top of the jar with cheesecloth, and secure with a rubber band. Put the jar on its side in a dark place or inside an open paper bag. Rinse and drain well three times a day for 3 days. On the fourth day, place the jar in direct sunlight. As chlorophyll develops, the sprouts will turn green. (Mung beans and soybeans will take 2 to 3 days longer than alfalfa seeds to sprout.)

This project is a good example of how Mother Nature works miracles through the germinating process, in which a dormant seed springs back to life, the seed's vitamin and mineral content increases, and the proteins and carbohydrates become more digestible.

Sprout Salad

4 cups mixed sprouts
2 small carrots, shredded
1 apple, pared, cored, and
  shredded
½ cup sunflower seeds

½ cup raisins
½ cup plain low-fat yogurt
1 tablespoon honey
2 tablespoons apple juice

• Combine the sprouts, carrots, apple, seeds, and raisins in a salad bowl.
• Mix the yogurt, honey, and apple juice together and toss with the salad.

Makes 12 servings.

Carrot Salad

4 medium carrots
⅓ cup raisins
½ cup pineapple bits
sunflower or sesame seeds
  (optional)

6 tablespoons plain yogurt
2 teaspoons honey
juice of ½ lemon

- Wash and scrape the carrots.
- Shred finely with a grater.
- Add the raisins, pineapple, and seeds.
- Stir the honey and lemon juice into the yogurt.
- Mix thoroughly with the carrot mixture.

Makes 8 servings.

HELPFUL HINTS

- In selecting a cooking project, consider all the possibilities it provides children for learning concepts through active involvement (washing, scrubbing, peeling, cutting, comparing shapes, textures, and colors).
- Keep cooking projects simple. Shelling peas, shucking corn, and washing vegetables are educational and fun activities.
- Help the children plant a vegetable garden to provide food for cooking projects.
- Very young children can help wash vegetables, scrub potatoes, tear lettuce, and shell peas.
- Older children can help grate, measure, beat, and grind.
- Adults should do the sharp cutting and the more difficult peeling.
- Make vegetable kabobs by cutting a variety of vegetables into squares, triangles, and circles.
- Serve fresh orange sections with green leafy vegetables. Vitamin C from the fruit helps increase iron absorption.

Chinese Workingman's Salad

4 cups bean sprouts (about ½ lb.)
2 cups cooked chicken, shredded
3 cups lettuce, shredded
⅓ cup coriander (Chinese
  parsley) or parsley, chopped

⅓ cup toasted sesame seeds
3 tablespoons sesame oil
4½ tablespoons vinegar
2 tablespoons soy sauce
½ teaspoon Five Fragrant Spices

- Combine the sprouts, chicken, lettuce, coriander, and sesame seeds in a salad bowl.
- Mix the remaining ingredients, and pour over the salad.
- Toss lightly.

Makes about 25 small servings.

Note: Five Fragrant Spices, available in Oriental food stores and most supermarkets, is a cocoa-colored powder that is a blend of star anise, cloves, fennel, anise, and cinnamon. Let the children sniff the fragrant spices and experience the new taste when it is mixed with the salad.

Potato Salad

4–6 medium potatoes, boiled and cooled
2 hard boiled eggs

1 small can pitted olives (optional)
½ cup mayonnaise
1 carrot, grated

• Peel and dice the potatoes and eggs, peel and grate the carrot, and cut the olives into small pieces.
• Mix all together.

(Other ingredients such as green pepper, tuna, celery, and onions can be added and olives eliminated to cut down on sodium. To cut down on the fat and cholesterol, instead of ½ cup mayonnaise, make a paste of 3 tablespoons dried skim milk and 3 tablespoons buttermilk and stir in thoroughly with 2 tablespoons mayonnaise.)

Makes 12–15 small servings.

Note: This is a good recipe for beginners because the ingredients are easy to peel and cut. Serrated knives work well in this project. Children who have never cut with knives enjoy the success they have in cutting boiled potatoes. The salad is made fairly quickly, and the children can taste the results of their work without having to wait too long.

Macaroni Salad

2 cups macaroni, cooked
2 hard boiled eggs
½ cup celery, diced
½ cup pitted olives, diced
1 cup cheddar cheese, shredded

6 radishes
4 tablespoons parsley, chopped
½ cup mayonnaise or substitute (See the preceding recipe for Potato Salad.)

• Let the children peel and cut the eggs, dice the celery and olives, and shred or grate the cheese. Adults can slice the radishes and chop the parsley.
• Mix all with the mayonnaise or substitute.

Makes 15–20 small servings.

COOKING EGGS

Scrambled Eggs

6 eggs
⅓ cup low-fat milk

vegetable oil spray

• Break the eggs into a large bowl.
• Beat with an eggbeater; add milk.

- Spray a nonstick frypan with vegetable oil spray and pour in the egg mixture. If you are using an electric pan, set the temperature at low so that the eggs will cook slowly.
- Use a wooden spoon or spatula to pull the cooked egg away from the sides of the pan.
- Have the children stir and move the mixture around so that the uncooked portions get cooked.

Makes 10 small servings.

HELPFUL HINTS

- Sit down and eat with the children. Show them that you enjoy food.
- Talk about different kinds of foods.
- Notice whether young children are influenced in their eating habits by TV commercials.
- Offer new foods more than once.
- Send notes home about good nutrition and the new foods each child has helped prepare in school.
- Invite parents to share their recipes with the school.

HELPFUL HINTS ABOUT EGGS

- The dietary cholesterol in eggs, meat, and dairy products contributes to high levels of blood cholesterol and increases the rate of arteriosclerosis. Egg yolks are especially high in cholesterol. When cooking, use 2 egg whites to replace 1 egg.
- Provide a variety of ingredients for children to add to their scrambled eggs, such as mushrooms, onions, minced green and red peppers.
- When recipes call for eggs, children experienced in cracking eggs can take advantage of the opportunity to practice separating the yolk from the white, since a mistake won't matter.
- Have children break the eggs into small bowls first; then eggshells can be removed before the eggs are poured into a larger bowl.
- A paper plate placed under the egg bowl makes for easier clean-up and prevents egg from falling on the floor.
- Discuss the various ways eggs can be cooked—poached, baked, hard boiled, soft boiled, fried sunny side up, and so on. What happens to the whites and yolks during cooking? What is an egg? What are some different kinds of eggs? What do they hatch into?

Deviled Eggs

6 hard boiled eggs
1 tablespoon mayonnaise
2 tablespoons plain low-fat yogurt

1 teaspoon prepared mustard
celery or onion powder

• Peel the eggs and cut them in half lengthwise.
• Place the yolks in a bowl and mash them.
• Mix in the mayonnaise, yogurt, and mustard, and season to taste.
• Let the children stuff the egg whites with the yolk mixture, using small spoons, forks, or cake decorators.

Deviled eggs can be decorated with sprigs of parsley, stuffed olives, pimento, or paprika.

PREPARING GRAINS AND LEGUMES

Steamed Rice

2 cups brown rice   3 cups water

• Put the rice and water in a large pot. Cover the pan with a tight-fitting lid.
• Cook the rice on high heat until most of the water has been cooked away.
• Turn the heat down as low as possible, and steam the rice for about 30 minutes.
• Fluff the rice with a fork or chopsticks before serving.

Makes 20 servings.

Note: Wheat berries cooked along with the rice add a delicious contrasting texture. Use about ¼ cup.

Fried Rice

2 eggs
2 green onions (scallions)
½ cup cooked meat, such as
chicken, pork, or beef

4 cups cooked rice (leftover
day-old rice works best)
2–3 tablespoons soy sauce
1 tablespoon vegetable oil

• Scramble the eggs and set aside.
• Clean and dice the green onions, including the green stems.
• Stir-fry the onions and the cooked meat in a nonstick pan until heated through. Set aside.
• Heat the vegetable oil in the pan and then add the cooked rice.
• Stir and cook until the rice is heated through. If the rice is very dry, add a little water and cover the pan in order to thoroughly heat the rice.
• Add all other ingredients, including soy sauce.
• Stir until the meat, onions, and eggs are evenly distributed.

Makes 10–12 servings.

Chicken Soup with Rice

2 cups chicken stock   **2" square of tofu** (optional)
½ cup cooked rice

• Bring the chicken stock to a boil; add ½ cup rice (more or less as desired).
• A good way to introduce tofu is to cut a small piece into tiny squares and simmer it along with the rice for 5 minutes.

Makes 4 small servings.

HELPFUL HINT

Read Maurice Sendak's *Chicken Soup with Rice* (New York, NY: Harper & Row, 1962) to the children.

Rice Balls

1 cup short grain brown rice   **sesame seeds, toasted, or nori,**
1½ cups water   **cut into 3" squares***
salt   **parsley**

• Cook the rice in water on high heat in a pan with a tight-fitting lid.
• When most of the water has been cooked away, lower the heat and steam the rice for about 30 minutes, then fluff with a fork.
• Turn off the heat and let the rice sit for about 10 minutes.
• Transfer the hot rice to a large bowl.
• Hands should be slightly damp, not wet, when rice is rolled, so set out a bowl of tap water into which the children can dip their hands and paper towels they can use to blot the moisture.
• Sprinkle a little salt onto the palms of the children's hands.
• After testing to be certain that it is not too hot for children to handle, give each child a warm scoop of rice.
• Have them shape the rice into balls, triangles, or squares. Keep the rice as warm as possible while the children are making the shapes.
• Roll each piece in the toasted sesame seeds, or wrap in nori squares.
• Serve as snacks on a large platter decorated with sprigs of parsley.

Oatmeal

1 cup water   **⅛ teaspoon ground ginger**
1 cup unsweetened apple juice   **1 cup oatmeal or other whole**
½ teaspoon cinnamon   **grain cereal**

Nori is a highly nutritious sea vegetable which is made into thin flat sheets and roasted. It is used as a garnish or to wrap around rice balls as in sushi. Nori can be purchased in most grocery stores selling Japanese foods. It comes in thin black or dark purplish sheets packaged in cellophane. Nori is high in vitamins A, B, C, and D, protein, phosphorus, iron, and trace minerals.

- Combine the water, apple juice, and spices.
- Bring to a boil.
- Stir in the cereal.
- Cook for 1 minute, continuing to stir.
- Reduce the heat and stir occasionally until the liquid has been absorbed.

(If desired, add raisins, bananas, dates, or chopped fruits in season.) Makes 6 small servings.

Note: Different types of cereals require different cooking times. Follow the directions on the package.

Muesli

1½ cups rolled oats, uncooked
1½ cups fruit juice
2 tablespoons wheat germ
½ cup dried fruits, chopped fine
  (apricots, raisins, peaches, pears, apples, prunes)

½ cup chopped toasted almonds (optional)
1 tablespoon honey
2 tart apples, peeled, cored and shredded

- Combine the oats and juice in a large bowl.
- Cover and refrigerate 8 hours or more.
- Before serving, add wheat germ, fruits, nuts, and honey. Stir well.
- Top with freshly shredded apples, and serve with milk if desired.

Makes 8–10 servings.

Note: Children can help with most of the preparation.

Buckwheat Burgers

1 cup buckwheat groats (kasha)
2¼ cups water
1 small onion, minced
¼ cup parsley, minced
½ lb. firm tofu, drained and mashed

½ cup mushrooms, finely diced
1 teaspoon soy sauce
arrowroot or flour
1 tablespoon oil

- Bring the buckwheat groats and water to a boil in a pan with a tight-fitting lid.
- Lower the heat and simmer 30 minutes.
- When the buckwheat is cooked, add all other ingredients except the arrowroot and oil.
- Remove the pan from the heat, and mix thoroughly.
- When cool enough, form the mixture into small patties. Add a small amount of arrowroot or flour to thicken the mixture if patties do not hold their shape.

• Heat the oil in a skillet, and fry the patties over medium heat until lightly browned—about 5 minutes on each side.
• Serve like burgers—on small buns with lettuce and tomato.

Makes 12 small patties.

Split Pea Soup

2 cups split peas, rinsed
10 cups water
2 tablespoons oil
1 cup carrots, chopped
1 cup celery, sliced

1 medium onion, chopped
2 cloves garlic, minced
½ teaspoon marjoram
½ teaspoon basil
½ teaspoon cumin

• Rinse the split peas; place them in a large kettle with the water and bring to a boil.
• Lower the heat and simmer.
• Meanwhile, let the children chop and slice carrots and celery (steamed and cooled carrots are easier to chop). Adults can chop and mince the onions and garlic.
• Saute the vegetables in oil for about 5 minutes.
• Add the herbs, and saute another 5 minutes.
• Add the cooked vegetables to the split peas, and continue cooking for 1½ hours, stirring occasionally.
• The soup can be thickened by mashing the cooked peas or putting the soup through a blender.

Makes about 15 servings.

Upama

1 cup cream of wheat
1 tablespoon butter or
  margarine
1 cup onions, finely chopped
½ teaspoon mustard seeds
½ cup peas

½ cup carrots, diced
⅓ cup raisins (optional)
⅓ cup chopped cashew
  nuts (optional)
2 cups water

• Melt the butter or margarine in a saucepan. Stir in the mustard seeds and chopped onions. Saute for 5 minutes.
• Stir in the peas, carrots, raisins, and nuts.
• Add the cream of wheat and mix thoroughly.
• Stir in the water, cover and simmer until all the water has been absorbed.

Makes 10 small servings.

Note: This is a favorite recipe among Hindu families.

HUMMUS

Hummus is a delicious high-protein, high-fiber bean spread from the Middle East. Serve it as a spread for pita bread or as a dip with carrot, celery, or jicama sticks. All ingredients are available from major supermarkets.

1 15-oz. can garbanzo beans (chick peas)
1 garlic clove, minced, or ½ teaspoon garlic powder
4 tablespoons tahini (sesame seed butter) or peanut butter
1 tablespoon parsley, finely chopped
½ teaspoon cumin
¼ teaspoon paprika
2 tablespoons lemon juice
3–5 tablespoons water

Drain and mash the beans. Add the remaining ingredients and mix well. The dip will be much smoother if you use a blender. Add more liquid as needed to achieve the desired consistency for dipping. A dash of cayenne is optional.

FALAFEL

Falafel balls, shaped like small meatballs, are a traditional filling for Arab bread. Falafel is high in protein and low in fat.

1 15-oz. can garbanzo beans (chick peas)
⅓ cup mashed potatoes (instant mashed potatoes work well)
1 small onion, chopped
¼ cup parsley, minced
1 clove garlic, minced
1 teaspoon ground cumin
1 package whole wheat pita bread
alfalfa sprouts
shredded lettuce
1 medium tomato, chopped
plain low-fat yogurt

Preheat oven to 350°. Combine the garbanzo beans, potatoes, onion, parsley, and garlic. Put the mixture through a food processor or mash it to a medium texture. Add cumin and mix well. Shape the mixture into 1" balls. Place on a lightly greased cookie sheet, and bake about 5 minutes on each side. Cut each pita bread in half to form pockets. Layer lettuce, sprouts, and tomatoes into each pocket, and top with 4 or 5 falafel balls and a dab of yogurt. Makes enough for 6 small pita pockets.

Note: The small size (about 6" in diameter) pita pockets are best for young children. They hold sandwich fillings securely and are suitable for many creative combinations of food.

COOKING MEAT, POULTRY, AND FISH

Meatballs

1 lb. lean ground beef, or a mixture of ½ lb. each of beef and turkey
½ cup bread crumbs

½ cup canned evaporated skim milk
¼ cup wheat germ

- Mix all the ingredients together, and form into small balls.
- Cook in a lightly greased electric frypan at the table, browning the meatballs on all sides.
- Serve plain or over hot noodles or rice, with a simple tomato sauce.

Makes about 2 dozen small meatballs.

Note: Add Italian seasonings such as garlic powder, oregano, and thyme to the tomato sauce, or stir in a spoonful of plain low-fat yogurt for a creamier sauce.

Canned evaporated milk in a ground meat recipe serves the same function as eggs, binding the ingredients together without the added cholesterol.

Pasties

½ lb. ground turkey
½ lb. ground beef
1 cup onions, finely chopped
½ cup wheat germ
3–4 cloves garlic, crushed
1 teaspoon oregano
4 8-oz. packages refrigerator biscuits

grated cheese, grated carrots, chopped eggs, chopped mushrooms, diced cooked potatoes, chopped parsley (optional)
1 egg
1 teaspoon water
flour

- Preheat oven to 375°.
- Mix together the meats and seasonings.
- Stir-fry over medium high heat until the meat is cooked through. Drain off any grease, and let cool.
- Meanwhile, let the children help prepare plates of cheese and the optional ingredients.
- Let each child roll out or flatten 2 individual biscuits (use a little flour as needed to prevent sticking).
- Spoon about 1 teaspoon or less of meat onto a biscuit, and let the children select optional ingredients to add to their pasties.
- Cover the filling with the other flattened biscuit.
- Moisten the edges of the two biscuits, and pinch them together with the fingers or the tines of a fork to make crescent shapes.
- When ready to bake, place the pasties on a lightly greased nonstick baking sheet; brush each with a mixture of 1 egg beaten with 1 teaspoon water.
- Perforate each pastie with a fork.
- Bake 10–12 minutes.
- Cool slightly before eating.

Makes 48 small pasties.

Teriyaki Meatballs

½ lb. lean ground beef
½ lb. ground turkey
½ cup bread crumbs
½ teaspoon garlic puree

4 tablespoons light soy sauce
½ teaspoon powdered
   ginger
¼ cup water

- Mix all the ingredients together and form into small balls.
- Cook in a lightly greased skillet, browning the meatballs on all sides.
- Serve with rice.

Makes about 24 small meatballs.

Won Ton

½ lb. ground lean meat such as
   pork, chicken, beef, turkey, or
   some combination of these
2 green onions
¼ lb. shrimp (raw or cooked)
6–8 water chestnuts (fresh or
   canned)

1 tablespoon light soy sauce
¼ teaspoon ground ginger
2 teaspoons cornstarch or
   arrowroot
1 tablespoon water
1 package won ton skins
chicken broth (½ cup per
   serving)

- Place the meat in a mixing bowl.
- Clean and finely chop the green onions, including the green stems.
- Clean, devein, and finely chop the shrimp.
- Chop the water chestnuts.
- Add all ingredients except the won ton skins and broth to the meat. Mix well.
- Place 1 teaspoon of meat mixture in the center of each won ton skin.
- As shown in Illustration 7.7, bring up the two sides of the skin to fold won ton in half. Dampen the edges with a little water to make the skin stick together. Pinch around the meat to seal it. Pull the two bottom edges together and pinch firmly to seal, using a little water again if necessary.
- Place the individual won ton on a platter and cover with a damp cloth to prevent them from drying out.
- While children are wrapping the won ton, bring several quarts of water to a boil in a large pot.
- Add the won ton to rapidly boiling water.
- When the water returns to a boil, add ½ cup cold water and let it come to a boil again. The won ton are cooked when they float to the top.
- Heat the chicken broth in a pot.
- To serve, place 3 or 4 cooked won ton in individual bowls and ladle broth over them.

Finely minced green onion tops and slivers of meat or eggs can be used for garnish. Makes about 50 won ton.

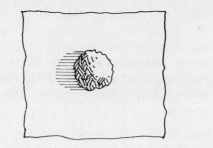

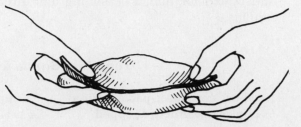

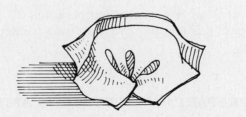

Illustration 7.7 **Folding and forming won ton**

Muffin Pizzas

8 whole wheat English muffins
toppings such as grated mozzarella
  cheese, ground beef or turkey,
  chopped onions, chopped olives,
  chopped peppers, sliced
  mushrooms

1 15-oz. can tomato sauce
1 teaspoon garlic powder
1 teaspoon Italian seasoning

- Preheat oven to 450°.
- Add the garlic powder and Italian seasoning to the tomato sauce in a pan and heat through.

- Toast the muffins lightly.
- Spread about 2 teaspoons of the tomato sauce on each muffin half, and let the children select ingredients to put on each pizza. Use a small amount of meat so that it will cook thoroughly.
- Bake on a cookie sheet until the meat is cooked, or place under the broiler for a few minutes. Watch carefully to avoid burning the pizzas.

Note: Oregano, thyme, and garlic powder in equal amounts can be substituted for Italian seasoning. Pita bread is a good substitute for muffins.

Tuna Pita Sandwiches

1 6½-oz. can water-packed tuna	⅓ cup plain low-fat yogurt
⅓ cup celery, finely chopped	4 tablespoons mayonnaise
¼ cup onions, chopped	1 cup fresh alfalfa sprouts
¼ cup water chestnuts or jicama, chopped	1 package whole wheat pita bread

- In a large bowl, break the tuna into coarse flakes with a fork.
- Add the chopped ingredients.
- In a separate bowl, combine the yogurt and mayonnaise.
- Mix well and combine with the tuna mixture.
- Cut the pita bread in half and fill the pockets with the tuna mixture.
- Top with alfalfa sprouts.

Makes about 6 regular size or 10 small pita sandwiches.

Note: Water-packed tuna contains 20 percent more protein and 160 fewer calories per can than tuna packed in oil.

PREPARING VEGETABLES AND DIPS

Vegetable Soup

variety of chopped vegetables: carrots, potatoes, celery, tomatoes, onions, peas, beans	alphabet noodles or rice (optional)
soup stock made with meat bones or instant soup base and water	seasoning to taste

- Plant a garden outdoors and have the children harvest the vegetables, or invite children to bring vegetables from home.
- Talk about colors, textures, and tastes while children help to wash, scrape, and peel the vegetables.
- Make soup stock in a pressure cooker or electric pan. (A simple soup base can be made by browning lean hamburger with minced onion and adding tomato sauce, bouillon cubes, and water.)
- Let the children add their vegetables.

• Add a handful of alphabet noodles or rice if desired.
• Season with salt, oregano, herbs, and other spices to taste.

Note: Read the book *Growing Vegetable Soup*, by Lois Ehlert (New York, NY: Harcourt Brace, 1987). Brightly illustrated pictures tell the simple story of a father and child who select and grow vegetables for their soup.

Minestrone Soup

1 tablespoon olive oil
1 clove garlic, minced
½ onion, chopped
3 cups tomato juice
3 cups water
2 carrots, peeled and diced
1 stalk of celery, diced
1 tablespoon chopped parsley
½ lb. potatoes, diced
1 teaspoon basil
1 medium zucchini

½ cup whole wheat pasta shells
1 cup cooked green beans or any suitable leftover vegetables
2 cups chopped greens such as chard, spinach, romaine, or chicory
grated parmesan cheese (optional)

• Saute the onion and garlic in olive oil until soft and golden.
• Place these ingredients in a large pot along with the tomato juice, water, carrots, celery, potatoes, parsley, and basil.
• Bring to a boil, then simmer and cook 20 minutes.
• Meanwhile, prepare the rest of the vegetables.
• Add these vegetables along with the pasta, to the soup.
• Cook another 20–30 minutes.
• Serve with grated parmesan cheese if desired.

Makes about 15 servings.

Note: This soup takes about 1 hour to cook, but allow plenty of time for preparing all the vegetables that go into it.

Glazed Carrots

4 medium carrots
2 teaspoons butter or margarine

1 tablespoon honey
¼ cup orange juice

• Scrape the carrots and slice them into thin strips.
• Melt the butter or margarine in a large electric frypan.
• Add the carrots and stir to coat.
• Add the orange juice.
• Cover and simmer for 5–7 minutes. Add more juice if necessary to keep the carrots moist.
• Cook until just tender.
• Stir the honey into the remaining liquid.
• Leave the pan uncovered and stir, coating all the carrots, until the liquid is reduced.

Makes 6–8 servings.

Latkes (Potato Pancakes)

2 medium potatoes   ¼ cup flour
1 egg   vegetable oil

- Peel and coarsely grate the potatoes.
- Mix with the beaten egg and flour.
- Fry tablespoon-size pancakes in hot vegetable oil. Brown on both sides.
- Serve with applesauce.

Makes 10-12 small latkes.

Spaghetti Squash

1 spaghetti squash, about 3 lb.   1 15-oz. jar spaghetti sauce
1 medium red or green bell   ½ teaspoon Italian seasoning
  pepper   mix
¼ lb. mushrooms   grated parmesan cheese
1 4-oz. can diced green chilies   ½ lb. ground turkey (optional)

- Rinse and pat the squash dry.
- Pierce the shell with a fork in several places.
- Bake in 350° oven about 1½ hours or until the shell gives way when gently pressed. Turn the squash over halfway through the baking. (Baking can be done by the teacher in advance of the cooking project if time is limited.)
- Let the children dice the bell pepper and mushrooms.
- If you are using turkey, brown the meat in a pan.
- Put the diced vegetables in the pan, and stir until the peppers are cooked through, about 10 minutes.
- Add the chilies, spaghetti sauce, and seasoning mix.
- Simmer gently for 10 minutes.
- Cut the cooled squash in half; let the children scrape out the seeds.
- Pull the spaghetti-like squash from the shell, and place it on a large platter.
- Spoon the sauce over the squash, and serve with grated parmesan cheese.

Makes 10–12 servings.

Raw Vegetable Platter

- Provide a variety of raw vegetables, such as carrots, tomatoes, bell peppers, radishes, celery, cauliflower, and cucumbers.
- Wash and cut into bite-size pieces.
- Arrange attractively on a platter at each lunch or juice table.

Note: Introduce new foods such as fresh peeled water chestnuts, Jerusalem artichokes, and jicama.

Dilled Yogurt Dip

1 cup low-fat yogurt	**½ teaspoon dill seeds**
2 tablespoons vinegar	**¼ teaspoon dry mustard**
½ small yellow onion	**¼ teaspoon minced garlic**

• Mix all the ingredients, and use as dip for fresh vegetables.

Note: Talk about the different odors of the various ingredients. Discuss what each ingredient tastes like by itself and when mixed with the others. Ask the children if they can still detect the taste of the individual ingredients after they have been combined.

Buttermilk Dip

½ cup dry low-fat cottage cheese (Farmer's cheese)	**2 cups buttermilk**
4 cups cheddar cheese, shredded	**1 clove crushed garlic**
½ teaspoon nutmeg	**3 tablespoons cornstarch**

• Let the children help shred the cheese.
• Mix the cottage cheese and cheddar cheese with the cornstarch and nutmeg.
• Heat the buttermilk with garlic over low heat until just hot to the touch.
• Add the cheese mixture, stirring constantly until the cheeses are melted.
• Serve warm as a dip for fresh vegetables or bite-size pieces of sourdough bread.

MAKING DESSERTS AND SNACKS

Coconut Apricot Candy

1 cup dried apricots (or pears)	**½ teaspoon grated orange rind**
½ cup nuts	**1 tablespoon lemon juice**
½ teaspoon vanilla	
1 cup shredded coconut	

• Let the children help wash the dried fruit.
• Steam the fruit for 5 minutes.
• Put the apricots, coconut, and nuts through a food chopper or processor.
• Add the grated orange rind and lemon juice.
• Knead the mixture until well blended.
• Add small amounts of orange juice to moisten as necessary.

Makes 1 dozen small candy balls.

Note: Be very certain that children's hands and nails are scrubbed clean before they help with this project.

Natural Finger Jello

3 cups fruit juice (not pineapple)   **4 packets plain gelatin**

- Pour half the fruit juice (1½ cups) into a medium-size bowl.
- Sprinkle gelatin over the juice. Let stand for 1 minute.
- Heat the remainder of the juice to boiling and add it to the first mixture, stirring until the gelatin is completely dissolved.
- Pour into a 9" square baking pan, and chill until firm.
- Cut into 1" squares.

This gelatin is firm enough for children to pick up with their fingers.

Toasted Pumpkin Seeds

- Save the seeds from a jack-o-lantern.
- Wash, drain, and spread the seeds on an ungreased cookie sheet.
- Bake in a 350° oven.
- Stir to dry out, and toast lightly on all sides.
- Show the children how to crack and eat the toasted seeds.

Mashed Pumpkin

- Steam or bake pieces of pumpkin until tender.
- Mash the cooked pumpkin, and use for cookies.

Pumpkin Cookies

½ cup (1 stick) **butter or margarine**
1¼ cups brown sugar
2 eggs
1½ cups cooked mashed pumpkin
½ teaspoon salt
½ teaspoon ginger

½ teaspoon nutmeg
½ teaspoon cinnamon
2¼ cups flour, sifted
4 teaspoons baking powder
1 cup raisins
1 cup walnuts (optional)
1 teaspoon vanilla extract

- Preheat oven to 375°.
- Cream together the butter and sugar.
- Add the eggs, pumpkin, salt, and seasonings. Mix well.
- Sift the flour and baking powder together; stir in the raisins and nuts.
- Add the flour mixture slowly to the creamed mixture and blend well.
- Stir in the vanilla.
- Drop the batter by the teaspoonful onto greased cookie sheets.
- Bake about 15 minutes or until lightly browned.

Makes about 3 dozen cookies.

Puddle Cake

1 ½ cups unbleached white or whole wheat pastry flour, sifted
3 tablespoons cocoa or carob powder
½ teaspoon salt
1 cup brown sugar

1 teaspoon soda
6 tablespoons salad oil
1 teaspoon vanilla
1 tablespoon vinegar
1 cup cold water

- Preheat oven to 350°.
- Sift all the dry ingredients into an ungreased 8" x 8" x 2" pan.
- With a mixing spoon, make a well in the center of the pan.
- Make a puddle in the well by pouring the liquid ingredients into it.
- Stir with a spoon until the mixture is smooth.
- Bake 35–40 minutes.

Makes 12–15 servings.

Vegetable Cookies

2 cups flour
1 ½ teaspoons baking powder
¾ teaspoon salt
1 ½ teaspoons cinnamon
¼ teaspoon nutmeg
1 cup wheat germ
¾ cup butter or margarine
1 cup dark brown sugar, firmly packed

1 large egg
1 teaspoon vanilla
¾ cup milk
1 cup zucchini, finely grated, or 1 cup carrots, grated
½ cup raisins

- Preheat oven to 375°
- Stir together all the dry ingredients.
- Cream the butter and sugar; beat in the egg and vanilla.
- Add the flour mixture alternately with milk.
- Stir in the vegetables and raisins.
- Drop the batter by the teaspoonful onto lightly greased cookie sheets.
- Bake 12–14 minutes.

Makes about 50 small cookies.

Melon Finger Food

1 ripe melon (cantaloupe, honeydew, or casaba)

- Cut the melon in half and remove all seeds.
- Cut the halves into eighths and remove the peel.
- Cut the meat into slices, sticks, or chunks, or use a small melon scoop to make melon balls.

Makes 8–10 servings.

Applesauce

6 tart apples
1¼ cups water

3–4 tablespoons honey
cinnamon

- Let the children help peel, core, and slice the apples.
- Cook them in water, covered, until tender (approximately 20–30 minutes).
- Add honey and cinnamon to taste.

Makes 12 small servings.

Baked Apple

1 small apple for each child
variety of nuts

variety of dried fruits
honey

- Remove apple cores to within ½" of the bottom of the apple.
- Let the children select nuts and dried fruits to fill the hollow apples.
- Moisten the centers with a small amount of honey, and place the apples in a baking dish.
- Add water or fruit juice to a depth of ½" to prevent sticking and promote steaming.
- Cover with foil, and bake at 375° for 40 minutes or until tender.
- Serve warm or chilled.

Apple Fritters

4 small pippin apples
⅓ cup lemon juice
1 teaspoon cinnamon

1 cup graham cracker crumbs,
   finely ground

- Preheat oven to 400°.
- Peel, core, and slice the apples into rings ¼" thick.
- Combine the graham cracker crumbs with cinnamon.
- Dip the apple slices in lemon juice, then coat both sides with the crumb mixture.
- Place on lightly greased cookie sheet, and bake for 15 minutes.
- Serve plain or with orange-honey syrup (p. 332).

Makes 8 servings.

Celery Crunch

1 stalk of celery
1 cup crunchy peanut butter
¼ cup coconut

⅓ cup Grape Nuts cereal
¼ cup wheat germ
dash nutmeg (optional)

- Trim and wash the celery.
- Let the children mix the remaining ingredients, stuff the celery, and cut it into bite-size pieces.

This snack has a delicious, nutty flavor.

Apple Honey Nutters

6 apples
½ cup crunchy peanut butter
¼ cup wheat germ

¼ cup nonfat dry milk
2 tablespoons honey

• Wash and core the apples.
• Combine the remaining ingredients, and stuff the mixture into the center of the apples.
• Slice into round pieces 1" thick.

Makes 12–18 servings.

Sesame Sticks

1 cup cornmeal
¼ cup wheat germ
4 tablespoons sesame seeds
(the brown seeds with hulls are more nutritious than the white)
2 teaspoons sea salt

3 teaspoons vegetable herb seasoning
3 tablespoons safflower oil
1 tablespoon sesame oil
4 oz. plain low-fat yogurt
2 sheets waxed paper, 12" x 15"

• Preheat oven to 375°.
• Let the children measure the dry ingredients into a mixing bowl.
• Stir the safflower and sesame oil into the yogurt until well blended.
• Add the yogurt mixture to the dry ingredients. Mix well.
• Divide the dough into three balls.
• Place one ball at a time on a sheet of waxed paper. Cover with the second sheet, and roll the dough with a rolling pin to make a 12" x 15" rectangle.
• Remove the top paper, and let the children help cut the dough into 1" x 2" strips.
• Invert onto a nonstick cookie sheet. Remove the paper.
• Bake 15–20 minutes.
• Cool.

Makes 10–12 servings.

Note: Vegetable herb seasonings are available at most health food stores. A mixture of onion, garlic, and celery powders can be substituted.

Banana–Wheat Germ Snacks

bananas
milk

honey
toasted wheat germ

• Let the children peel and cut the bananas into bite-size pieces.
• Dip each piece into a mixture of half milk and half honey.
• Drop the pieces of banana into a plastic bag filled with wheat germ, and shake until well coated.
• Serve on a tray with colored toothpicks.

Crunchy Snacks

3 cups old-fashioned oatmeal
1 cup unsweetened shredded
coconut
1 cup toasted wheat germ

½ cup blanched almonds,
chopped
½ cup honey
2 tablespoons water
¼ cup toasted sesame oil

- Preheat oven to 250°.
- Combine the oatmeal, coconut, wheat germ, and almonds in a bowl.
- Warm the honey, water, and oil in a saucepan, and pour over the oat mixture.
- Stir well to coat all particles.
- Spread in a thin layer on a cookie sheet, and bake in the oven for 20 minutes, stirring occasionally to toast evenly.
- Serve in small quantities as a snack.

Won Ton Crispies

1 package won ton skins
1 6–oz. container of grated
parmesan cheese

vegetable cooking spray

- Preheat oven to 350°.
- Spray individual won ton skins lightly with the cooking spray, and sprinkle a small amount of grated cheese on each.
- Place on nonstick baking sheet, and bake in the over 5–7 minutes or until lightly browned and crisp.
- Cool.
- Serve as a snack or in place of crackers.

Popcorn

corn for popping
vegetable oil
grated parmesan cheese

condiments such as onion
powder, ground sesame
seeds, or powdered herbs

- If available, use a hot-air, no-oil corn popper. Follow the directions for popping.
- Have small bowls or baskets handy so that the children can sprinkle herbs and cheese over the warm popcorn.
- If an electric popper is not available, pour about ¼ cup vegetable oil (just to cover the bottom) into a heavy pan large enough to accommodate the popping of the corn. Heat the oil over medium heat for 2 minutes; add just enough popcorn to cover the bottom of pan. Cover the pan securely, and shake the pan occasionally as the corn pops. Adjust the heat to avoid burning the corn.

Note: Popcorn is an excellent high-fiber, low-calorie food. It is only when people add lots of salt and butter that popcorn becomes less healthy.

Remind the children to chew the popcorn thoroughly and to remain seated while eating.

HELPFUL HINTS ABOUT POPCORN

- Let the children examine the kernels of corn before they are popped. Explain that this is a special kind of corn grown just for popping and that it is different from the kind we eat off the cob. Each kernel of popcorn has moisture (a drop of water) inside of it, and when the popcorn gets hot, the moisture turns into steam and causes the kernel to explode.
- Place an electric popper without the top on a large sheet spread on the floor. Have the children sit back and watch how far the corn can pop.
- Play "Popcorn" by Hot Butter (Stereo MS3242—Musicor Records, A Division of Talmadge Productions, Inc., 240 W. 55th St., New York, NY 10019).

Rice Pudding

2 cups cooked brown rice
1 egg
1 cup plain low-fat yogurt
1 cup low-fat milk

5 tablespoons honey
1 teaspoon vanilla
1 teaspoon cinnamon
½ cup raisins

- Preheat oven to 350°.
- Beat the egg; stir in the yogurt, milk, and honey.
- Add the remaining ingredients, and mix well.
- Pour into a 1½-quart casserole dish.
- Bake for 40 minutes.

Makes 12 servings.

Note: Rice becomes a complete protein when combined with dairy products.

Indian Custard

1 quart low-fat milk
¼ cup water
½ cup molasses
½ cup stone-ground cornmeal
1 tablespoon honey

¼ teaspoon each: nutmeg, ginger, and cinnamon
1 egg

- Preheat oven to 350°.
- Scald the milk in a saucepan.
- Mix together the water, molasses, and cornmeal.
- Stir this mixture into the milk and bring to a boil.
- Remove from heat; add the honey and spices.
- Cool.
- Beat the egg, and blend it into the cooled cornmeal mixture.
- Pour into a 1½-quart casserole.
- Bake 1 hour.

Makes 12 servings.

Strawberry Yogurt

1 cup fresh strawberries   **1 cup plain low-fat yogurt**
¼ cup powdered skim milk

- Mash the strawberries.
- Beat in the powdered milk; add the yogurt.
- Stir well.
- Serve in small cups.

Makes 6–8 servings.

Melon Slush

3 cups melon cubes (cantaloupe,   **2 cups crushed ice**
crenshaw, honeydew)   **fruit garnish** (optional)
1 cup low-fat milk
6 tablespoons frozen orange
juice concentrate, thawed

- Place all the ingredients except the fruit garnish in a blender, and blend until just slushy.
- Serve immediately with sliced strawberries or orange slices for garnish.

Note: It may be necessary to divide the ingredients into several batches to fit them into the blender.

Fruit Smoothies

1 banana, cut into pieces and   **handful of fresh or frozen**
frozen   **berries**
½ cup plain low-fat yogurt   **vanilla extract** (optional)
1¼ cups fruit juice or milk

- Whip all the ingredients in a blender until smooth and creamy thick. Using frozen bananas creates an ice cream–like texture. This method also works with other frozen fruits such as apricot halves, sliced peaches, whole strawberries, raspberries, or grapes. A bit of vanilla extract adds to the flavor of the smoothie.

Note: To freeze the banana, peel, slice into 1" pieces, lay on a cookie sheet, and put in the freezer. When frozen, store the fruit in ziplock bags.

Fruit Shake

2 cups cold juice (orange,   **½ cup powdered milk**
pineapple, or grape)   **1 drop vanilla extract**

- Combine all the ingredients in a 1-quart plastic container.
- Add crushed ice and shake until mixed.

Serves 4–6.

Frothy Fruit Drink

2 oranges, peeled
2 bananas, peeled
2 cups apple juice

½ teaspoon cinnamon
2 cups crushed ice

• Blend the oranges, bananas, and juice in a blender until frothy.
• Gradually add the crushed ice while still blending.
• Serve with a sprinkle of cinnamon on top.

Makes 15 small servings.

Fruit Sorbet

1 cup fresh strawberries
1 banana

¼ cup unsweetened apple juice

• Wash and hull the strawberries. Cut into halves.
• Slice the banana.
• Place the fruit in an airtight container and freeze.
• When frozen (or partially frozen), place the fruit and juice in a blender and blend until the mixture is the consistency of ice sorbet. Add more juice if needed.

Makes 4–6 small servings.

Fruity Yogurt Pops

1 cup fresh fruit, finely chopped or crushed (strawberries, raspberries, bananas, peaches, or pineapple), or 1 can frozen orange juice concentrate (12 oz.)

4 cups plain yogurt
honey (optional)

• Blend the fruit with the yogurt.
• If the fruit is tart, add honey to taste.
• Pour into 3-oz. paper cups.
• Place a popsicle stick in the center of each cup and freeze.

Makes 15 servings.

Yogurt Creamsicles

6 oz. orange juice concentrate
1 cup plain yogurt
1 tablespoon honey

6 oz. water
1 tablespoon vanilla extract

• Blend all ingredients.
• Pour the mixture into ice trays.
• When partially frozen, insert popsicle sticks and complete the freezing.

Bibliography of Resources

The following books will be helpful to teachers who wish to use additional resources to enhance their knowledge about cooking and nutrition.

Albright, Nancy. *The Rodale Cookbook.* New York, NY: Ballantine Books, 1982. A comprehensive book of recipes using natural foods. It includes a useful listing of natural food stores in the United States, the nutritional content of many foods, a food substitution table, a cost table, and a section of cooking hints.

Brody, Jane. *Jane Brody's Nutrition Book.* Des Plaines, IL: Bantam Books, 1987. A well-researched book, with general information on all aspects of nutrition from abortion to zinc.

Endres, Jeannette Brakhane, and Robert E. Rockwell. *Food, Nutrition, and the Young Child.* (New York, NY: Merrill, 1985. A useful text for teachers who want to learn more about nutrition for young children. It covers food needs from infancy through age 5 and food service management for day-care settings.

Estella, Mary. *Natural Foods Cookbook.* New York, NY: Japan Publications, 1985. Features over 200 easy-to-prepare recipes with an international flair; all are dairy-, meat-, and sugar-free.

Gooch, Sandy. *If You Love Me Don't Feed Me Junk.* Reston, VA: Reston Publishing, 1983. Personal accounts and stories of eating with children. Recipes included.

Goodwin, Mary T., and Gerry Pollen. *Creative Food Experiences for Children.* Washington, DC: Center for Science in the Public Interest, 1980. A comprehensive book of food experiences designed to teach young children how the food they eat affects their growth and development. Useful information is provided with each recipe to educate children to make good food selections. Included are many excellent ideas for the teacher to incorporate into the curriculum.

Greene, Karen. *Once Upon a Recipe.* New Hope, PA: New Hope Press, 1987. Fantasy recipe titles are based on favorite children's fables. This is a good book to share with children of all ages. It includes many hints for healthful eating.

Gross, Joy. *The Vegetarian Child.* Secaucus, NJ: Lyle Stuart, 1983. The vegetarian alternative and how to make it healthy. Recipes included.

Isaac, Katherine, and Steven Gold. *Eating Clean: Overcoming Food Hazards.* Washington, DC: Center for Study of Responsive Law, n.d. This consumer's guidebook of selected readings is published by Ralph Nader and has an introduction by him. The readings cover pesticides and chemicals in food, sweeteners, irradiated food, organic foods, and other topics relating to healthy eating.

Jenkins, Karen S. *Kinder-Krunchies.* Pleasant Hill, CA: Discovery Toys, 1982. Has picture recipes children can follow to make such foods as banana bread. This colorful and simple book answers such questions as "How are raisins made?"

Johnson, Barbara, and Betty Plemons. *Cup Cooking, Starter Set: Single Step Charts for Child-Portion Picture Recipes.* Lake Alfred, FL: Early Educators Press, 1985. Single-portion recipes that young children can use to learn how to measure, mix, count, and cook.

Kamen, Betty, and Si Kamen. *Kids Are What They Eat: What Every Parent Needs to Know About Nutrition.* New York, NY: Arco Publishing, 1984. Advice on coping in the supermarket, planning menus, and maintaining health. A bibliography of books, organizations, and filmstrips is included.

Lappé, Frances Moore. *Diet for a Small Planet.* New York, NY: Random House, 1982. A classic book which has sold more than 2 million copies since its first publication. This tenth-anniversary edition updates the original philosophy, which impressed on Americans the social and personal significance of a new way of eating. Simple guides and recipes for healthy eating are provided.

McAfee, O. *Cooking and Eating with Children: A Way to Learn.* Washington, DC: Association for Childhood International, 1974. Gives the rationale for cooking with children. Both group and individual recipes are included.

McWilliams, Margaret. *The Parents' Nutrition Book.* New York, NY: Wiley, 1986. This basic nutrition text, simply written, contains chapters on preschool children's nutritional needs.

Marbach, Ellen S., et al. *Nutrition in a Changing World.* Provo, UT: Brigham Young University Press, 1979. This preschool curriculum guide stresses the importance of nutrition education for young children. Written for teachers with little or no training in nutrition, the guide offers preschoolers many opportunities to experience a wide variety of foods through sight, sound, taste, smell, and touch.

Palmer, Michele, and Arline Edmonds. *Vegetable Magic*. Storrs, CT: Connecticut State Board of Education, 1981. Simple stories, games, and activities accompany illustrated recipes involving all kinds of wonderful vegetables.

Richert, Barbara. *Getting Your Kids to Eat Right.* New York, NY: Cornerstone, 1981. Practical planning with recipes from a mother. Information is provided on additives, reading labels, analyzing nutrient needs, and combining foods for complete proteins.

Robertson, Laurel, et al. *The New Laurel's Kitchen.* Berkeley, CA: Ten Speed Press, 1986. More than 500 recipes with good health as the main concern. Guidelines are included for making daily food choices and for feeding children, pregnant mothers, athletes, and the elderly. Excellent vegetarian recipes.

Satter, Ellyn. *Child of Mine.* Palo Alto, CA: Bull Publishing, 1986. This guide to nutrition for children espouses a philosophy of moderation, feeding with love, and good sense. This same author covers healthful eating in another publication, *How to Get Your Kids to Eat . . . But Not Too Much* (1987). In both books, she offers a new way to look at feeding and presents guidelines for encouraging children from newborns to teens to have healthy attitudes toward food.

Smith, Lendon. *Feed Your Kids Right.* New York, NY: Dell, 1982. A pediatrician approaches total health, both mental and physical. He explains how problems can be treated with good eating and vitamins. The author covers many other food-related topics in a 1987 publication, *Foods for Healthy Kids* (Berkeley Publishing).

Stori, Mary T. *I'll Eat Anything If I Can Make It Myself.* Chicago, IL: Chicago Review, 1980. Simple recipes for healthful foods that children can prepare themselves.

Veitch, Beverly, and Thelma Harms. *Cook and Learn*. Menlo Park, CA: Addison-Wesley, 1981. Single-portion cooking presented through pictures. The recipes use nutritious foods from various cultures. Accompanied by a teacher's guide.

Wanamaker, Nancy, et al. *More Than Graham Crackers.* Washington, DC: National Association for the Education of Young Children, 1979. An educational guide for adults who want to help young children learn about cooking and nutrition. Recipes for snacks and main dishes are included.

Warren, Jean. *Super Snacks/Sugarless*. Everett, WA: Warren Publishing, 1982. Written for parents and teachers of young children who want to offer alternatives to sugary foods, it contains suggestions and recipes for special-occasion foods containing no sugar, honey, or artificial flavorings.

Weiner, Michael A., and Kathleen Goss. *The Art of Feeding Children Well.* New York, NY: Warner Books, 1982. A nutritionist's guide for adults who want to give children the best nutrition possible. It informs on the benefits and dangers in foods and offers advice on the treatment of sick children through diet and herbs. Recipes are included for wholesome dishes that children like better than junk food.

Winick, Myron. *Growing Up Healthy: A Parent's Guide to Good Nutrition.* New York, NY: William Morrow, 1982. A book by a nutritionist for parents and parents-to-be. Topics include the importance of breast feeding, infant obesity, snack foods, hyperactivity diets, and other aspects of nutrition for young children.

Wishik, Cindy S. *Kids Dish It Up Sugar-free.* Port Angeles, WA: Peninsula Publishing, 1982. Beginner cooks learn their way around the kitchen and about nutrition, arithmetic, planning, cooperation, timing, and the satisfaction of creating a product for others to enjoy.

PART EIGHT

Computers for Preschoolers

Introduction to Computers for Preschoolers

YOUNG CHILDREN AND COMPUTERS

Computers have become a part of the lives of many young children and their families. A number of the daily routines in our society rely on computers—checking out library books, totaling purchases at the grocery counter, withdrawing money from the bank teller machine. Even some of our watches and bathroom scales are computerized.

Many families who own computers report that once their youngsters discover how to press the keys and make things happen on the screen, they want equal time at the machine. Parents want to know what teachers of young children think about encouraging youngsters to use the computer. Is it good for them? What kinds of limits should be set? Does the teacher have recommendations for choosing software? Does the school plan to have a computer for children to use?

Parents rely heavily on teachers' expertise and judgment. Whether or not you have computers in your classroom, you will find it useful to give some thought to the pros and cons of including computer activities in your curriculum.

ARE COMPUTERS GOOD FOR YOUNG CHILDREN?

Teachers of young children recognize the value of encouraging children to be creative, to socialize with their peers, and to enhance their language development. Computers appear to discourage such creative, artistic, and linguistic expression. Some critics argue that computers in a preschool classroom will decrease social interaction among the children. They note that young children need to be physically active, not sit passively in front of a keyboard.

Advocates, on the other hand, point to studies indicating that mastery and control over computers bolsters a child's self-concept. Furthermore, they point out that, when introduced and used properly, computers increase thinking, memory, reasoning, and problem-solving skills. They make a case for introducing computers early so as to develop competence and positive attitudes; this is especially important in helping girls to overcome potential sex-role stereotyping.

RESEARCH STUDIES

Muhlstein and Croft compared language usage and cooperative play among a group of 3- to 5-year-old boys and girls when they were working at the computer and when they were engaged in four noncomputer activities: playdough, blocks, art with coloring pens, and a fishing game.[19] Counts were made of language events and cooperative play at all activities.

Children at the computer talked twice as much (in words per minute) as those at the other activities and played more cooperatively. The researchers concluded that the computer enhanced the language experiences and cooperative play of the preschoolers. Muhlstein and Croft's findings are borne out by several other research studies indicating that computers encourage social interaction. These studies stress the importance of having children work in pairs at the computer.

Robert D. Hess, research professor emeritus at Stanford University, states: "We have found children interact *more* with each other [at the computer] than they do around most other activities in the preschool. They talk, point, explain and encourage, taking an active role in the educational process. The idea that the child is going to become an isolated hacker has absolutely no foundation in any of the data."

Brawer compared the effectiveness of television and the computer in teaching basic relational concepts to preschoolers.[20] The children, ages 2½–4 years, were given pretests to determine their basic knowledge of concepts such as *above, below, over,* and *under.* They were then divided into three groups: the control group (which would receive no further training or information), the television group, and the computer group. Each child in the television group spent 8 minutes watching an animated cartoon developed by the makers of "Sesame Street." Each child in the computer group played for a maximum of 8 minutes with a game from Juggles Rainbow, developed by the Learning Company.

Posttest scores of the television group were 23 percent higher than pretest scores. The computer group's scores improved by 27 percent, and there was no significant improvement in the scores of the control group. A second posttest administered 3 to 5 days later showed that the children had retained the knowledge they had gained.

Like any other curriculum material, the computer (along with developmentally appropriate software) can serve as a resource to stimulate the imagination, enhance social interaction, and develop language and problem-solving skills.

[19]Eleanor A. Muhlstein and Doreen J. Croft, "Using the Microcomputer to Enhance Language Experiences and the Development of Cooperative Play Among Preschool Children," ERIC document #269–004, 1986.

[20]Jennifer Brawer, "The Effectiveness of the Computer and Television in Teaching Basic Relational Concepts: A Comparative Study" (paper presented at the International Communication Association Conference, San Francisco, CA: May 27, 1984).

Illustration 8.1 From all indications, computers are neither monsters depriving children of valuable playtime nor miracle workers replacing classroom teachers.

THE TEACHER'S ROLE

If you do decide to use computers and haven't had experience with them, how should you go about getting started?

One of the best ways to learn more about computers is to talk with other teachers who use them. Most computer users are enthusiastic about the capabilities of the machines and are pleased to share their knowledge.

Another excellent way to get an introduction to the computer is through workshops at early education conferences. One teacher was delighted to learn that more than half the registrants at a workshop had never had any prior experience with computers. She was encouraged to hear others asking the kinds of questions she wanted to ask. Moreover, there were dozens of computers and a variety of software programs for the teachers to play with. This kind of "safe" environment made it possible for her to overcome some of her reservations.

Other resources include local adult education classes and lessons offered through computer and software sales companies.

Learning the technicalities of operation—how to turn the machine on, insert a disk, bring up a program—is quite simple and does not require any extended instruction. More important is learning about software—that is, the games and activities you choose for the children to use.

Whenever any new technology is introduced, teachers need to consider its effects on their teaching methods. Computers offer new ways of thinking and learning. If you are to make the best use of this new tool, you must make sure that the children's lives are truly enriched. Your knowledge of how children learn and what is developmentally appropriate must be exercised in planning and selecting computer activities.

Selecting Appropriate Software

Perhaps more than any other single criterion, the appropriateness of the software determines the effectiveness of computer use with young children. Unless you are able to spend the time initially to learn about good-quality software, there is little use in investing in a computer. It is essential that you select wisely.

Fortunately, there are resources available to help you make good choices of software. One of the best resources is other teachers who have purchased programs. You might want to observe how their children use the computer in order to assess whether the programs are enhancing the skills you have in mind.

It is also a good idea to refer to some of the software guides that evaluate children's programs. One of the best is High/Scope's *Survey of Early Childhood Software*. (See the bibliography at the end of this section.) Otherwise, the quantity and variety of available software can be confusing. Do not rely on computer stores to be of much help; most do not carry a good selection of software for young children, and the clerks often are not familiar with a developmental approach to learning.

Depending on your location, there may be schools or libraries that can provide software programs for you to evaluate before making a purchase. Some stores are willing to order your requests for preview with the hope that you will buy from them. Many software companies will ship programs on request for review, especially if you write them using your school's letterhead. Finally, conferences and workshops offer exhibits and demonstrations that are worthwhile resources.

GUIDE TO SELECTING SOFTWARE

Ideally, a program should be previewed with the children before it is purchased, and then the teacher should practice using it before it is introduced in class. Remember that each computer has its own specific operating system; be sure the program is designed to operate on your particular computer.

Software programs, like phonograph records, often have several games on one disk. You will find that some are more useful or appealing than others.

In selecting software, look for the following characteristics:

1. **Ease of use:** Directions are simple, precise, and easily understood by adults and children.
2. **Clear objectives:** The program does what it is supposed to do.
3. **Age-appropriateness:** The content is related to the child's culture and level of understanding.
4. **Interactive style**: The pace is set by the child, not the program. Children can initiate and determine the sequence of events, with a variety of options.
5. **Process orientation**: Children learn through discovery rather than simply giving right and wrong answers. The program offers many opportunities to test alternative responses.

6. **Challenge:** The program expands in complexity, challenging children to continue to explore as their knowledge increases.
7. **Staying power:** The program holds the child's attention with a minimum of assistance from an adult.
8. **Positive reinforcement:** The program is so enticing that children enjoy doing it for the process alone, rather than for some superficial reward. It does not use loud buzzers, negative graphics, or violence.
9. **Good technical quality:** The graphics and sound are realistic; the software runs smoothly and fast enough to maintain children's attention; disks are sturdy enough to withstand much handling.
10. **Colorful and fun graphics:** Graphics are colorful and playful and are entertaining for the child.

The rating sheets shown in Illustrations 8.2 and 8.3 are based on this list of criteria. You can use the first sheet when evaluating software on your own; the second sheet is designed to be used when you preview a program with children. Adapt the sheets as necessary to suit your own priorities.

EVALUATING SOFTWARE FOR PRESCHOOL CHILDREN

Evaluator _____   Date _____

Name of Program _____

Name of Publisher _____

Name of Game _____

The evaluator may want to use a letter or number rating scale.

	Rating	*Comments*
1. Clear objectives		
2. Colorful graphics		
3. Positive reinforcers		
4. Absence of violence		
5. Patient approach		
6. Pace determined by child		
7. Adequate repetition		
8. Interactive style		
9. Lets child make decisions		
10. Requires thinking; challenges		
11. Staying power		
12. Ease of use		
13. Standard commands		
14. Appropriate content		
15. Is fun to use		

Illustration 8.2 **Rating sheet for software for preschoolers**

EVALUATING SOFTWARE WITH PRESCHOOL CHILDREN

Evaluator _____ Date _____

Name of Program _____

Name of Publisher _____

Name of Game _____

The evaluator may want to use a letter or number rating scale.

	Rating	Comments
1. Is the program easy for the child to use?		
2. Can the child understand the commands?		
3. Is the feedback appropriate and effective?		
4. Is the program "patient"?		
5. Is the pace determined by the child?		
6. Is the program interactive?		
7. Does it let the child make decisions?		
8. Is it challenging?		
9. Does it hold the child's attention?		
10. Is it fun for the child to use?		

Illustration 8.3 **Software rating sheet to be completed with preschoolers**

Setting Up the Computer Center

The following suggestions are designed to help the teacher set up a computer center in the classroom. (See Illustration 8.4.)

1. Identify the grounded electrical outlets in the classroom. Select a location near one of the outlets where the computer is protected from direct sunlight and extreme hot or cold temperatures.
2. Place the computer where it can be supervised easily from any part of the classroom.
3. Place the computer near an activity area that is relatively quiet and requires a minimum of supervision, but do not isolate it from other activities. A location adjacent to the listening or storybook area is good.
4. If you have more than one computer, place them at right angles to each other so that children can converse and compare.

Illustration 8.4   **The computer area**

5. Position the monitor so as to minimize glare and reflection on the screen.
6. Place the computer on a table large enough for two children to sit side by side facing the keyboard. Allow enough room for an adult to sit beside them. (It may be practical to place the computer on a portable cart so that it can be used in other areas of the classroom.)
7. Be sure the table is at a height that puts the keyboard at a comfortable level for the children.
8. Tape down the electrical cords so that children won't trip on them.
9. Place materials meant to be used by children within easy reach.
10. Provide a shelf out of the reach of children for storage of extra disks and other support materials.
11. Provide wall space or another suitable area in which to display children's work.
12. Read the user's manual and follow the directions for proper care of the computer.

HELPFUL HINTS

- On a wall near the computer, display charts listing the procedures to follow when operating the computer system. The charts will be helpful to adult volunteers and others who may not be familiar with the procedures. (See Illustration 8.5.)
- Using picture representations, identify each software program on an index card attached to the disk jacket so as to extend above it. Punch holes in the card, and hang each disk from a pegboard.
- Provide picture directions to help children use the disks independently.
- In a binder, keep an experience log where you record each child's reactions and progress.
- Place a sign-up sheet on a clipboard so that children (or the teacher) can sign or print their names for a turn at the computer.
- Color-code the "hot," or most-used, keys to help children locate them on their own.

Introducing Children to the Computer

Introduce the computer to groups of about 3 to 5 children, selected according to their ability levels. Even children with previous computer experience will need to become familiar with your rules. Once they know the procedures, however, they can be called on to help others.

Depending on your teaching style, you may find it most effective to demonstrate the basics of operating the computer to the group and then provide more individual instruction and hands-on experience to one or two children at a time. Some teachers prefer to incorporate the introduction into precomputer activities, such as those listed on the following pages. Still others are most comfortable giving brief instructions as children show interest in the activity.

In order to encourage independent use of the computer, you will need to provide the children with instruction in such basic operating procedures as turning the computer on, loading (booting) the disk, handling a disk properly, and accessing (getting to) the game or program they want to use. You will also want to discuss the importance of keeping the disks and computer clean and free of liquids, food, and other materials that will damage the equipment. Ground rules about the general care and maintenance of the computer can be reinforced at various times, such as large-group sharing time. The necessity of taking turns and the proper way of selecting and loading a program can be reinforced as necessary when individuals or small groups use the computer. Colorful picture displays and reminders posted near the equipment are also effective.

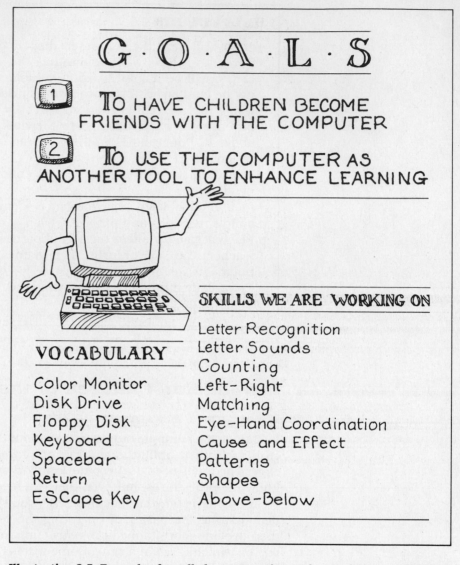

Illustration 8.5 **Example of a wall chart presenting goals, vocabulary, and skills**

As with other equipment in the school, children will need occasional reminders about proper usage of the computer. It is not realistic to expect young children to remember all the operating procedures and rules after one session; nor is it advisable to introduce everything at once. The younger and less experienced the children, the simpler and shorter the introduction should be. In most cases, children's natural curiosity and eagerness to help one another make introducing the computer a fairly simple task.

The software programs used in the activities that follow are merely examples; no endorsements are intended. Teachers need to make their own selections based on the needs of the curriculum and the children's ability levels. In fact, the selection of software for the classroom should precede the purchase of a computer. The Bibliography of

Resources for Teachers at the end of this part lists some excellent guides, as well as the addresses of software companies.

The dialogue accompanying the activities is intended to provide a very general guide to helping children learn the mechanics of each game. As children become more adept at using the computer, they will need less supervision and you will be able to add programs of increasing complexity. You will find that once the children become familiar with the procedures, there is much latitude for spontaneity and exploration. At that point, children enjoy working together while the teacher functions as a resource.

For those who remain skeptical about computers for preschoolers, take a look at some of the available programs, talk with colleagues who are using computers, attend workshops, keep an open mind, and ask a lot of questions. You may come to appreciate the computer as a tool that can, when linked to other activities, enhance your curriculum.

Computer Activities

Demonstrating How to Load Disks into the Disk Drive (for no more than 3 children)

MATERIALS   Computer
Computer disks

PROCEDURE   **Cold Start** (when the computer is off):

- Open the disk drive door.
- Hold the disk with fingers on the label only. Avoid touching any exposed part of the disk.
- Insert the disk with the label facing up, as in Illustration 8.6.
- Close the disk drive door.
- Turn on the computer and the monitor (or TV).
- The in-use light will go on, and the drive will make a whirring sound. Wait.
- When the in-use light goes off and the whirring stops, the computer is ready to use.

Warm Start (when the computer is on and you want to change disks):

- Be sure the in-use (or "busy") light on the disk drive is off.
- Open the disk drive door.
- Remove the disk, holding it by the label.
- Return the disk to the proper disk sleeve.
- Insert the new disk with the label facing up.
- Press the special loading keys specified for your particular computer. (On the Apple IIe, press CONTROL, OPEN APPLE, RESET.)
- The in-use light will go on, and the drive will whir. Wait.
- When the in-use light goes off and the whirring stops, the computer is ready for use.

Illustration 8.6 **Demonstration for children of "booting the disk"**

Note: You may prefer to turn computers on and off yourself, since many have controls in the back of the machines or in other places that are difficult for the children to reach.

Remember to ask about the availability and cost of back-up disks when purchasing programs.

Reinforcing Concepts Helpful in Using the Computer

MATERIAL   Selected activities from Part Four, Language Arts

PROCEDURE   • Give the children experience with the following language activities before they start working with the computer:

Listening to and Following Directions, page 174.
Learning Directional Words, page 177.
Learning Relational Concepts, page 178.
Matching and Naming Letters of the Alphabet, page 178.

- Adapt these activities so that they relate specifically to the computer—for example, following directions in proper sequence when loading a program disk, pressing certain keys to get to a particular program.
- Provide many physical activities in directionality, sequencing, and following directions that children can experience with the whole body.

Becoming Familiar with the Meaning of Menu

MATERIAL
Restaurant menus
Magazine pictures of food
Tables and chairs
Eating utensils
Napkins
Small pads and pencils for taking orders
Make-believe food (optional)

PROCEDURE
- Set up an area to look like a restaurant.
- Talk with the children about their experiences in restaurants to determine whether they are familiar with how to order food and what a waiter or waitress does.
- Make a menu, using pictures of food.
- Have some children play the role of waiter or waitress. Explain to them how they are to take food orders.
- Have some children be the customers at the restaurant and order from the menu.
- Talk about the menu and its purpose. Mention that there all kinds of menus, including the kind the children might see posted on the walls in fast-food restaurants.
- Point out that another kind of menu is the one the computer shows us so that we can select an activity of our choice. You may want to show the children an example of a computer menu at this time.

Becoming Familiar with the Keyboard

MATERIAL S
Pegboard, about 30" square
Cardboard replica of a computer keyboard
Construction paper or index cards
Enough pegs for each symbol plus 12 extra

PROCEDURE
- Make an enlarged cardboard replica of the computer keyboard, about 20" square.
- Attach the replica to the pegboard, leaving space at the top of the pegboard for a row of 12 pegs. Insert a push pin or peg into the top center of each symbol on the keyboard.
- Cut 3 to 6 copies of each of the keyboard symbols out of construction paper or index cards, and punch a hole in the top center of

each; hang these extra keys on the corresponding pegs of the keyboard.

- Across the top pegs, place a wide strip of construction paper containing symbols from the keyboard for children to match. You can use this keyboard activity to give children practice in finding the "hot" keys, such as the return, space bar, enter, shift, and delete. The children can also select letters from the keyboard to spell their names and other words.

Note: You may wish to color-code special keys on the practice keyboard as well as on the computer keyboard to help children locate the most frequently used keys.

Another activity for familiarizing the children with the computer keyboard is to play Bingo, using copies of the keyboard as the cards to be filled.

Practicing Using the Computer

MATERIALS　Apple computer, color monitor, disk drive
Muppetville program (Sunburst Communications) or other appropriate software (See Computer Programs for Young Children later in this section for other suggested selections.)

PROCEDURE
- Have one or two children seated in front of the computer.
- Demonstrate how to load the disk (see Illustration 8.6). Get the children to help determine the proper sequence of steps to take in order to turn the computer on and load the disk.
- Explain that the disk tells the computer what games you want to play.
- Listen for the whirring sound. Say:
The disk drive is now loading our game into the computer.
- When the picture menu appears on the monitor, explain that the children can use the menu to choose the game they want. (Muppetville has six activities on one disk, and the children can make selections by pressing the appropriate keys on the keyboard or by using the mouse—a separate hand-held attachment.)
- After the children make their choice, help them find the correct key to press. Listen again for the whirring sound that tells them to wait while the game is being loaded into the computer.

Note: Give the children ample time (15–20 minutes) to work at the computer, to explore, and to try various ways to respond to the activities.

Charlie Brown's ABC's

PURPOSE　To provide familiarity with the keyboard
To provide experience in letter recognition, letter matching, and letter sounds

MATERIALS Computer, color monitor, disk drive

Charlie Brown's ABC's program (Random House)

This game is suitable for ages 3 through 6. Large upper- and lower-case letters are presented along with colorful graphics and sound effects. When a letter is pressed, a large picture of an object whose name begins with that letter appears on the screen. Pressing that same letter key again animates the object. (Some helpful precomputer activities emphasizing upper- and lowercase letters can be found in Part Four, Language Arts.)

PROCEDURE • Load Charlie Brown's ABC's. Say:

This is a game about letters and the way we sound them. Press any letter key and let's see what happens.

• Assuming the child presses the L key, when the picture appears on the screen, say:

Do you know what letter that is?

Child responds:

L.

Say:

Yes.

Point to the picture of the lipstick and ask:

What is that?

Child responds:

Lipstick.

Say:

Yes. What letter do you think lipstick begins with?

Child responds:

L.

Say:

That's right. What do you think will happen if you press the L again?

(When the child presses the L key, Lucy puts on her lipstick. When the key is pressed again, Lucy puts on her lipstick again.)

• Here are some typical comments from children:

Watch! Watch this! I'm going to do it again!

See? Do you want to do it again?

Look! Let's take the lipstick off and put it on again!

• Encourage the children to press letters at random and to name the letter and the corresponding picture they see on the screen. Let them explore the keyboard and discover the results at their own pace.

• Record their reactions, progress, and language development in the log.

Note: Peanut's Maze Marathon is another colorful game from Random House. The program works best when a joystick is used to move an object through the maze from one picture to another. The cartoon characters animate themselves at the end of each maze. This game is good for developing eye-hand coordination, directionality, and eye-tracking.

Reader Rabbit

PURPOSE

To develop visual memory

To provide experiences in matching objects and taking turns at the computer

To provide opportunities for language development

MATERIALS

Computer, color monitor, disk drive

Reader Rabbit program (The Learning Company)

This game is appropriate for ages 3 and up. Colorful pictures are hidden under boxes, and the arrow keys are used to move the cursor to the box the child wants to look under. The child presses the space bar to reveal the object under the box. The purpose of the game is to match pairs of pictures that are alike. One reinforcing precomputer activity is playing the board game Concentration. Another is playing "What's Missing," by presenting several objects, removing one, and having the child recall the missing object. There are seven levels of difficulty in this game of Concentration. The program offers three other games using more than 200 lowercase three-letter words. The Apple IIGS version will say the words.

PROCEDURE

• Load the program. When the menu appears on the screen, say:
There is a picture-matching game on this program that is a lot of fun. If we press the letter A and then the number 4, we will get that game. Can you press A4?

• After the child presses A4 and the disk drive begins loading the program, say:
Listen; now the computer is loading the picture-matching game.

• When objects appear on the screen, say:
These are the things we are going to see in our game.

• After giving the child time to study and name the objects on the screen, say:
It says to press SPACEBAR. Can you do that?

• After the spacebar has been pressed, say:
All the things we just saw are hiding under here. (Point to the boxes.) **Let's see how we can find them. See this cursor?** (Point to the cursor on the screen.) **You can move it around with our arrow keys** (or joystick, or other peripheral).

• Invite the child to experiment with the arrow keys for a while. Then say:
You can look under the box where the cursor is by pressing the spacebar.

• Invite the child to press the spacebar. When a picture appears, say:
Now, there is another picture just like this one under one of the other boxes. Let's see if you can find it. Where would you like to look?

• Assist the child in noting which direction the cursor needs to go and which arrow keys will get it there, with comments such as
Yes, you want the cursor to move down. Which arrow key points that way?

• Play the rest of the game with the child, showing enthusiasm and excitement at each accomplished match. This is a good game for encouraging cooperation and taking turns.

The Learning Line

PURPOSE To reinforce letter matching

To provide experiences in eye-hand coordination, visual discrimination, cause-and-effect relationships, and directionality

MATERIALS Computer, color monitor, disk drive

Joystick (optional)

The E Game, on The Learning Line program (D. C. Heath)

This easy-to-use program requires no reading and is appropriate for ages 3–6. The E Game is a colorful, animated, letter-matching game which shows letters hanging on a clothesline between two palm trees. When a letter appears at the top of the screen, a joystick or arrow keys are used to move a monkey to the matching letter on the clothesline. (See Matching and Naming Letters of the Alphabet and Matching Letters and Words with Objects in Part Four.)

PROCEDURE • Load the program. When the picture menu appears (a clothesline hanging between palm trees, with six items pinned to the clothesline), say:

This is the picture menu. We use it to choose the game we want. Which game would you like to play?

• Assuming the child picks the letter game, say:

Can you show me a letter on the clothesline? (Run your finger along the line.)

• If the child points to the letter E, say:

Okay. Let's use the joystick (or arrow keys) **to move the monkey up to the letter E.**

• When the game appears, say:

See this letter? (Point to the letter appearing at the top of the screen.) **Can you find the same letter on the clothesline?**

• Have the child point to the matching letter on the clothesline. Say:

Yes! Now, can you move the monkey to that letter?

• When a correct response is made, the letter comes down off the line with the monkey, and the monkey pushes it away.

• Here are some typical children's comments:

Oh! I can find that one!

Let's make him push the letter.

Oh, I can do that!

I'm going to get them all!

• Record and log the child's reactions.

Note: Other games on the same disk are the Shirt Game (matching articles of clothing), the Cat Game (word matching with picture clues), the Face Game (matching details on faces), the Ten Game (number matching), and the Bouquet Game (classifying objects).

The Sweet Shop

PURPOSE
To provide counting experiences
To reinforce number recognition
To provide experiences in eye-hand coordination and directionality

MATERIALS
Computer, color monitor, disk drive
Joystick (optional)
The Sweet Shop program (D. C. Heath)

This program is appropriate for ages 3–7. It includes the Jelly Bean Game, for counting; the Popcorn Game, for simple addition; and the Ice Cream Game, for simple subtraction. In the Jelly Bean Game, children count jelly beans falling from a jar. Next, from a row of balloons they select the number that tells how many jelly beans fell. A joystick or arrow keys are used to move a friendly character to the correctly numbered balloon. Colorful graphics make this an enjoyable game for reinforcing number experiences.

PROCEDURE
- Load the program. When the picture menu appears, say:
  This is the picture menu. You can use it to choose the game you want to play. Which game would you like?
- Assuming the child points to the Jelly Bean game, point to the friendly character and say:
  Let's use the joystick (or arrow keys) **to move Mr. Jelly Bean to the game you want to play.**
- When the child has selected the game and the game has appeared, a jar full of jelly beans will tip over, spilling some of the jelly beans. Ask:
  How many jelly beans fell out of the jar?
- Have the child count the jelly beans, using a finger to point if necessary. After the child announces the number, say:
  Yes. Now can you find that number up here? (Run your finger along the row of numbers on the screen.)
- Have the child point to the number. Then say:
  Yes. Now let's see what happens when you move Mr. Jelly Bean to that number. (A happy face made of jelly beans appears with each correct answer.)
- Record and log the child's reactions. Children enjoy watching the jar tip over and the jelly beans spill out.
- To return to the menu, press ESC.

Note: The Grabbit Factory, another program published by D. C. Heath, also has number matching and simple addition and subtraction games that use colorful, animated graphics and sound effects. It is suitable for ages 3–8.

Creating Graphics with the Koala Pad

PURPOSE
To provide experiences in sequential procedures, eye-hand coordination, directionality, decision making, fine motor skills, and visual discrimination and tracking

MATERIALS   Apple IIe computer, color monitor, disk drive
              Koala pad touch tablet
              Micro Illustrator program (supplied with the Koala pad) (See Illustra-
              tion 8.7.)

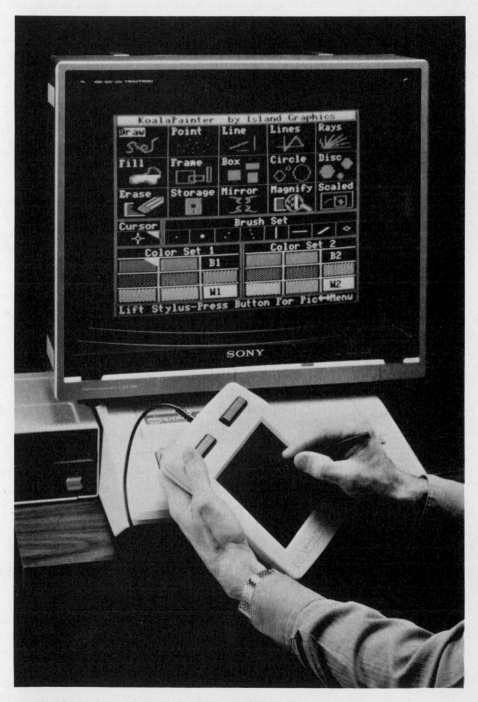

Illustration 8.7 **Koala Pad+ (Used by permission of Koala Technologies Corporation)**

This activity is appropriate for ages 3 and up. The Koala pad touch tablet is a 5" x 9" touch-sensitive pad with two buttons at the top. Graphics and some game commands are controlled on the monitor by moving a finger or stylus across the surface of the Koala pad. It takes some practice for children to master the mechanics involved in operating the Koala pad. Free-form drawing (using the draw option) is easiest for preschoolers. Give them plenty of time to practice. Children may be most successful if they master the use of one button at a time. Starting with the left button, explain how the cursor will leave a line if they hold that button down; if they do not want to leave a mark on the screen, they must release the button.

Once they have mastered the use of the draw option and the left button, children can learn to use the fill option. The fill option enables the child to select a color with which to fill in any of the spaces with the cursor. If your computer has a printer hooked up to it, you may print out the graphics designs created by the children.

PROCEDURE

- Load the program.
- When the title page appears, push the left button on the Koala pad.
- When the picture menu appears, say:
  This is the picture menu. We use it to choose what we want to make and the color we want to use. Today we are going to draw. (Point to the draw option.)
- Give these instructions:
  Use your stylus to put the cursor on "draw."
  While your stylus is on "draw," press the left button.
  With the stylus, put the cursor on the color you want.
  Now press the left button.
  Lift the stylus up.
  Push the button (to get to the screen).
  Place the stylus on the pad.
  Hold the button down while you move the cursor. Now you are drawing!
  If you want to move the cursor without drawing, do not push the button.
- To return to the menu, lift the stylus and push the button.
- To erase the graphics, return to the menu, use the stylus to choose "erase," and follow the erase instructions.

Computer Programs for Young Children

The following list is a limited sampling of software programs available for use with young children.[21] It is included to give you an idea of some of the many programs available. The titles were selected to provide a cross section of activities designed to promote different concepts and to reinforce various areas of the curriculum. For more complete

[21] Adapted from *Survey of Early Childhood Software,* by Warren Buckleitner (Ypsilanti, MI: High/Scope Press, 1989).

guides, refer to the Bibliography of Resources for Teachers at the end of this section.

Charlie Brown's 1-2-3's

Company: Random House Software
Computer: Apple
Ages: 3–7

The child selects a numeral, then uses the spacebar or number keys to count out the number. A correct response produces an animated Peanuts scene on the monitor. Another title, Charlie Brown's ABC's, provides practice with alphabet letters, again using animated Peanuts characters. Good sound and graphics make these fun programs to use.

Colors and Shapes

Company: Hartley Courseware, Inc.
Computer: Apple
Ages: 3–6

The child uses picture menus to select from among four activities involving matching colors and shapes. Options for speed, sound, and level of difficulty.

Counting Critters 1.0

Company: MECC
Computer: Apple (64K)
Ages: 3–6

Five games provide practice in counting and early math concepts. The child uses the arrow and number keys to match numerals from 1 through 20, match sets, create sets to correspond to given numerals, and fill in dot-to-dot designs. Good graphics and sound. Allows for teacher modification.

Explore-a-Story: A Great Leap

Company: D. C. Heath & Company
Computer: Apple (128K)
Ages: 5–10

The child uses a mouse, Koala pad, joystick, or arrow keys to move objects, words, or characters in a story (a mouse is recommended). Children can also type their own words. Stories can be saved and printed in color. Good for language development and creative expression.

Fun from A to Z

Company: MECC
Computer: Apple (64K)
Ages: 3–6

The child uses arrow keys to play three games: Birds (matching letters), Dots (using alphabet letters to complete dot-to-dot pictures), and Runners (selecting the missing letter in a sequence). Allows for selection of upper- and lowercase letters.

Kid's Stuff

Company: Stone & Associates
Computer: IBM, Apple, Atari ST
Ages: 3–8

An easy-to-use picture menu offers three activities in counting and letter recognition. An entertaining program with animation and sounds.

Magic Crayon

Company: C&C Software
Computer: Apple
Ages: 4–6

A simple program in which the child uses the arrow keys to draw in 16 different colors at three levels of difficulty. Good recordkeeping and management are available to the teacher. Stickers are included for labeling the keys.

Muppet Word Book

Company: Sunburst Communications, Inc.
Computer: Apple
Ages: 3–6

This disk offers six games that provide practice with upper- and lower-case letters, beginning consonants, and word endings. One of the activities provides large letters children can use for word processing. Can be used with a mouse, touch window, Muppet learning keys, or the regular keyboard. (See the Glossary for descriptions.)

Muppetville

Company: Sunburst Communications, Inc.
Computer: Apple
Ages: 4–6

Six games dealing with classifying and memory skills give practice with shapes, colors, and numbers. Options allow for different levels of difficulty. Can be used with a mouse, touch window, Muppet learning keys, or the regular keyboard.

Not Too Messy, Not Too Neat

Company: D. C. Heath & Company
Computer: Apple
Ages: 4–10

The child can use a mouse, joystick, Koala pad, or arrow keys to select and move objects, backgrounds, words, or characters in a story. The child can also type in his or her own words. Stories and pictures can be saved and printed in color. The design is good and the program is fun to use.

Observation and Classification

Company: Hartley Courseware, Inc.
Company: Apple
Ages: 3–5

In four classification activities, the child selects which object is different from the others, which is the same size as the one shown, or which belongs to the same class (for example, "all animals"). Options allow control over sound, movement of the cursor, and number of plays per game. The child can select the difficulty level.

Patterns and Sequences
Company: Hartley Courseware, Inc.
Computer: Apple
Ages: 3–6

Four clearly designed activities provide practice with matching and discrimination of large objects. The program gives positive feedback and has multiple skill levels. No reading is required.

Note: When evaluating and purchasing programs, remember to note the minimum amount of memory required (for example, Apple 128K). When the program is described as having the capability to save and print in color, you must have an appropriate color printer in order to do so.

Glossary of Computer Terms

Back-up copy   An extra copy of a program, to use in the event the original is damaged. Some software companies include a back-up copy with each program; others provide means for making a copy or will provide one at a reasonable cost.

Boot   To start up a computer by loading a program into memory from an external storage medium such as a disk (for example, inserting into the disk drive the disk that tells the computer what you want it to do). The program is said to "pull itself in by its own bootstraps," hence the term *bootstrapping* or *booting*.

Cable   Round or flat wires that connect the different parts of the computer.

Chip   A small piece of semiconducting material (usually silicon) on which an integrated circuit is fabricated. The word *chip* refers to the piece of silicon itself, but is often used to refer to an integrated circuit.

Cold start   The process of loading the operating system into memory when the power is first turned on. (Compare with *warm start.*)

Command   A communication, usually typed on the keyboard, from the user to a computer system, directing it to perform some action (that is, telling it what you want it to do).

Computer   An electronic device for performing predefined (programmed) computations.

Computer system   A computer and its associated hardware and software.

Connector   A physical device, such as a plug, socket, or jack, used to connect one hardware component in a system to another.

Control character   A character that controls or modifies the way information is printed or displayed. Some commands require that the user hold down the CONTROL key while typing some other character.

Crash   To cease operating unexpectedly, possibly damaging or destroying information in the process.

Cursor   A symbol on the screen that marks where the user's next action will take effect or where the next character typed from the keyboard will appear. (In LOGO, the cursor is called a *turtle*.)

Digit   One of the characters from 0 through 9, used to express numbers in text form.

Disk   An information storage medium consisting of a flat, circular magnetic surface. Information can be recorded on a disk in the form of small magnetized spots, much as sounds are recorded on tape. There are hard disks and flexible, or floppy, disks.

Disk drive   A device that writes and reads information on the surface of a magnetic disk. In some computers, the disk drive is built into the unit itself; in others, the external disk drive is a box with an opening into which a disk can be inserted.

Diskette   A term sometimes used to refer to the small (5¼" or 3") floppy disk.

Disk operating system (DOS)   A software system that enables the computer to control and communicate with one or more disk drives.

Disk sleeve   The paper pocket in which the disk is stored.

Display   Information exhibited visually, especially on the screen of a display device such as a TV set or monitor.

Escape mode   A state of the computer, entered by pressing the ESC key, in which certain keys on the keyboard take on special meanings with respect to positioning the cursor and controlling the display of text on the screen.

Execute   To carry out a specified action or sequence of actions, such as those described by a program.

Graphics   Information presented in the form of pictures or images; the display of pictures or images on a computer's display screen.

Hardware   Those components of a computer system consisting of physical (electronic or mechanical) devices, such as the monitor, computer, keyboard, and printer. (Compare with *software*.)

Icon   A picture or symbol that stands for a word. Icons are often used in menus to make programs usable by nonreaders.

Imagewriter   A printer designed for Apple computers. The Imagewriter II can print in color if it is loaded with a special ribbon.

Joystick   A computer attachment with a handle that can be moved up, down, left, or right to make an object or cursor on the display screen move in the corresponding direction. A button on the joystick may be used to stop or start action or to pick up an object.

Keyboard   The set of keys, similar to a typewriter keyboard, used for typing information into the computer.

Koala pad A book-size touch-sensitive pad that allows the user to enter information into the computer by drawing with a stylus or finger on the pad. A Koala pad is often used for drawing or moving a cursor on the screen.

Load To transfer information from a peripheral storage medium (such as a disk) into main memory for use; to copy a program's instructions from a disk or tape into the computer's memory.

LOGO A programming language designed to teach programming to children, making use of the computer's graphic display capabilities.

Memory A component of a computer system that can store information for later retrieval.

Menu A selection of choices on the display screen.

Microcomputer A desktop-size computer with many of the capabilities of a larger computer.

Modem A device enabling the computer to transmit and receive information over a telephone line.

Monitor The visual display for a computer, like a television screen without a channel tuner.

Mouse A hand-held computer attachment that, when moved left, right, up, or down, moves an object or a cursor on the display screen in the same direction. A button on the mouse may be used to start or stop action or to pick up an object.

Muppet learning keys A separate keyboard that plugs into a joystick port. It contains the numbers 0–9 in left-to-right order, the letters in alphabetical order, plus eight color keys. It requires specially designed software.

Operating system A software system that organizes the computer's resources and capabilities and makes them available to the user or to application programs running on the computer.

Output Information transferred from a computer to some external destination, such as the display screen, a disk drive, a printer, or a modem.

Peripheral devices Additional devices such as a monitor, disk drive, printer, modem, joystick, touch pad, or mouse. Such accessories are often physically separate from the computer, but connected to it by some means such as wires or cables.

Program A series of commands or instructions written in computer language, describing actions for a computer to perform. Programs are referred to as *software*.

Prompt A reminder or signal to the user that some action is expected. Typically a distinctive symbol, message, or menu of choices is displayed, or a particular sound is made.

Rebus Picture clues given in place of words, for nonreaders to interpret and follow.

Software A set of instructions used to direct a computer to perform some activity. For example, software may be stored on a disk which is loaded into the computer to tell it what to do.

Startup disk   A disk containing software recorded in the proper form to be loaded into the computer's memory to set the system into operation; sometimes called a *boot disk.*

User   The person operating or controlling a computer system.

Video monitor   A display device (often resembling a TV screen) capable of receiving video signals by direct connection only. It cannot receive broadcast signals such as commercial television waves.

Voice synthesizer   A device that enables the computer to synthetically create the speech sounds of a human voice.

Warm start   The process of restarting the computer with the power already on, without reloading the operating system into main memory and often without losing the program already in main memory. (Compare with *cold start.*)

Word processing   Using the computer to record and print words in much the same way as a typewriter is used. Word processing programs enable the user to enter, edit, save, recall, and print text.

Bibliography of Resources for Teachers

Brenner, Barbara, with Mari Endreweit. *Bank Street's Family Computer Book.* New York, NY: Ballantine, 1984. This book was written as an introductory guide for the whole family. Filled with anecdotes and comments from parents, teachers, and children, it provides information about how computers work, overcoming computer fear, ways in which computers serve children, and more. The appendix includes a list of selected software, books and magazines about computers, and addresses of software review sources.

Clements, Douglas H. *Computers in Early and Primary Education.* Englewood Cliffs, NJ: Prentice-Hall, 1985. This book was written for the preservice or inservice teacher. The author discusses educational principles of computers in early and primary education, as well as computer literacy issues, curricula, and activities. The appendix includes a list of software producers, magazines, and organizations dedicated to software evaluation.

Davidson, Jane Ilene. *Children & Computers Together in the Early Childhood Classroom.* New York, NY: Delmar, 1989. This excellent text comes complete with theory and detailed suggestions on the use of computers with young children. Topics range from the selection of hardware and software to integrating the computer into the early childhood program. There are practical suggestions on developing skills for computer use with supporting child-centered activities. Includes an annotated list of software and addresses of software manufacturers.

Education News Service, P.O. Box 1789, Carmichael, CA 95609. Publishes an annual guide, *Only the Best: The Discriminating Software Guide for Preschool–Grade 12,* based on the idea that the "wise buyer should not rely on just one favorable review or evaluation." The editors sift through evaluations published by education magazines, various state agencies, and many well-known evaluation services to find a consensus on the best educational software. To be included in the guide's "most highly rated" ranks, a program must receive a certain number of excellent and/or good ratings and no negative reviews. The program listing includes information on curriculum area, appropriate age level, price, and computer compatibility. Cost: about $24.

EPIE (Educational Products Information Exchange) **Institute,** P.O. Box 839, Water Mill, NY 11976. Publishes *The Educational Software Selector*, a comprehensive directory of more than 7700 software programs. Each entry provides a brief description of the program, with required computer components, appropriate grade levels, and price. Every other month this nonprofit institute also publishes *PRO/FILES*, which provides in-depth reviews of various software packages. Cost: about $60 for the directory, $33 for annual supplements. Write for the cost of *PRO/FILES*.

ERIC/EECE Clearinghouse (The Educational Research Information Center Clearinghouse for Elementary and Early Childhood Education), University of Illinois, 805 W. Pennsylvania Ave., Urbana, IL 61801-4897. Provides monthly indexes of documents and journal articles pertaining to computers and young children. ERIC documents are abstracted and indexed in *Resources in Education* and may be read on microfiche at libraries housing ERIC materials. This resource center also publishes *Micro Notes on Children and Computers,* a newsletter costing about $8 a year for four issues. A short report summarizing current practice and research, called *Microcomputers and Young Children,* is available at no charge.

High/Scope Press, 600 N. River St., Ypsilanti, MI 48198. Has been studying the use of computers with young children since the 1970s. Each year this nonprofit educational research foundation announces the recipients of the High/Scope Award of Excellence in Computer Software for Young Children. One of the ways High/Scope shares its findings is through its *Survey of Early Childhood Software.* The survey is referred to by its author, Warren Buckleitner, as the "original consumer's report" of computer programs for 3- to 6-year-olds. It is by far the most helpful of guides specifically geared to the needs of teachers of young children. It includes descriptions of programs, with listings by content areas. Cost: about $20. The foundation also publishes a monthly newsletter on early childhood education called *Key Notes,* which includes software reviews. Ten issues cost about $57.

The International Council for Computers in Education, University of Oregon, 1787 Agate St., Eugene, OR 97403. Publishes *The Educational Software Preview Guide,* an annual listing of over 600 recommended programs, with information on content, grade level, and instructional mode for each. From a data base of over 3000 titles, a consortium of agencies and committee members selects those that have received the most positive reviews. Cost: approximately $13.

PART NINE

Themes

Introduction to Themes

A theme is a central idea or subject on which units of activities throughout the curriculum can be focused. For example, the theme Colors of the Rainbow might be carried out in a wide range of activities in art, math, science, music, and cooking. The theme approach is often taught in curriculum courses and is very popular among teachers of young children.

BENEFITS OF THEMES

Themes are usually preplanned to encompass enough activities for one week, although a theme can be carried out in a day or over a period of a month or more. Because a theme provides a common thread throughout the different areas of the school, it gives teachers and children a focus.

Focusing on the theme Colors and Shapes, for example, serves as a reminder to teachers to plan activities that reinforce those concepts. The art area might include a color wheel and papers of different shapes. In the woodworking area, the teacher could call children's attention to the different shapes of blocks and woodworking supplies. Math activities might include exercises in sorting different shapes and colors.

A theme plan outlining activities for the week or month provides a degree of predictability and security for teachers, leaving them freer to assist children in experiencing the activities, which have been researched and preplanned.

Themes also provide an efficient way to collect, plan, and prepare curriculum materials. It is easier to be selective in gathering information when you have a specific topic in mind; the materials can be catalogued and set aside for future use, thus saving time and energy later.

Centering activities around a specific theme provides continuity and consistency. Children have more opportunities to be exposed to a particular concept if it is offered throughout the curriculum. A child who does not choose to participate in weighing and measuring objects at the science table, for example, may still be exposed to some of the same concepts if they are emphasized in the course of cooking, playing with clay, feeding and caring for animals, or harvesting vegetables from the garden. Thus children can explore and experience theme concepts freely at their own pace while choosing activities that interest them. Children are likely to retain more information about a particular subject if they experience that subject under many different conditions. Also, children learn from one another when they share common experiences.

LIMITATIONS OF THEMES

One of the biggest criticisms of using themes is that the teacher may come to rely on them as a crutch and risks losing the flexibility to incorporate age-appropriate activities into the curriculum. Relying on a preplanned program can inhibit the evolution of spontaneous activities. Because of time constraints, teachers may be less flexible about revising or discarding some of their plans, thus leaning toward a more rigid, teacher-directed program.

There is also the danger that the theme itself will become the primary emphasis rather than the developmental abilities and interests of the children. Once the "hard work" of collecting materials has been done, the teacher may be reluctant to critically analyze and revise the activities.

Many commercially prepared theme materials are available to assist the teacher in planning. Those materials, however, may not be developmentally appropriate for individual children. The teacher must be cautious in making choices and resist the temptation to adopt attractively packaged materials simply because they appear to be fun.

PLANNING THE CURRICULUM

Given the teachers' busy schedules and the many demands placed on their time, it is not surprising that prepackaged materials can be appealing. Any program, however, should be based on the observed interests of the children. Flexibility is essential in order to create and capitalize on "teachable moments." Themes exist to serve the unique needs of the children, not to serve as rigid programs to which everyone must adhere.

The themes offered in this section are intended to provide ideas for expanding your curriculum. Be careful not to let a theme dictate your choice of activities to the detriment of the curriculum. Do not include a weak activity simply because it is theme-related.

Use the suggested materials to enhance your program, revising and adapting them to suit the unique geographic, socioeconomic, and cultural aspects of your classroom. Take special care to plan themes that do not perpetuate stereotypes of other cultures. (For example, remember that not all Indians live in tepees or hogans; modern-day Indians live and work much like other people.) Above all, evaluate your plans in light of your children and their social, emotional, and cognitive needs. Leave room for innovation and creativity, and let your themes serve those goals.

This section suggests a number of themes that can be developed over a five-day week. They are categorized by the four seasons for ease of reference. You may prefer to use some other method that is better suited to your needs.

The first theme, The Forest in Fall, is summarized in chart form in Illustration 9.1 to show how a week might be organized. The activities are then described in greater detail in the following lists. The projects and materials listed are merely suggestions to inspire other related ideas. There is no need to do one activity from each subject area per day. It is often a good idea to repeat activities throughout the week; or you may find the interests of the children leading to something you had not planned. The important thing is to carry on relevant and meaningful activities, using themes as very general and flexible guides.

Feel free to alter, depart from, or embellish the resources offered here to suit the needs and interests of your children. Select topics that are relevant. Usually the simple, familiar themes work best with young children. The blank chart in Illustration 9.2 may be reproduced for use in planning other themes.

You may find it useful to post your theme charts so that parents can contribute related resources and reinforce the concepts at home.

Additional ideas for themes are listed at the end of this section.

Autumn

THE FOREST IN FALL

Art and Woodworking

- To make torn-paper trees, have the children tear up scraps of red, brown, orange, and yellow paper and paste them onto a large mural of trees in a forest.
- Collect bark and twigs for gluing and woodworking; make a nature hanging (see pages 30 and 61).
- Spatter paint over leaves (see Spatter Painting, page 29).
- To make a bear-cave diorama, staple a crumpled brown paper bag onto a small cardboard box or a Styrofoam meat tray. Children can add bits of pine needles, twigs, moss, sawdust, straw, and rocks. A tiny scrap of furry cloth tucked in the cave to represent the bear is the final touch.
- Fingerpaint, using fall colors.

Music, Drama, Movement

- Refer to *Mostly Movement, Book II (Accent on Autumn)*, by Edith Wax and Sydell Roth, for drama and movement activities.
- Read *I'm Going on a Bear Hunt*, by Sandra Stroner Sivulich (New York, NY: Dutton, 1973). This story can be chanted, to the accompaniment of body percussion, such as slapping thighs.
- Records:

"Sleepy Bear" from *People and Animal Songs*, by Nancy Raven (Pacific Cascade Records).

"Teddy Bear's Picnic" from *There's a Hippo in My Tub*, by Anne Murray (Capitol).

"Teddy Bear, Teddy Bear" from *Songs and Games for Toddlers*, by Bob McGrath and Katharine Smithrim (Kids' Records).

Math Experiences

• Provide an assortment of fall leaves for children to classify, sort, match, and count.
• Use an assortment of nuts to practice matching items.
• Sort by common characteristics objects relating to the forest in fall (page 137).
• Provide containers of various sizes and shapes that children can fill with playdough.
• Use fall objects (leaves, nuts, pine cones, etc.) to compare sizes and weights.

Language Arts

• Stories:

Bellamy, David. *The Forest*. New York, NY: Clarkson N. Potter, 1988.

Carlstrom, Nancy White. *Jesse Bear, What Will You Wear?* New York, NY: Macmillan, 1986.

Haseley, Dennis. *My Father Doesn't Know About the Woods and Me*. New York, NY: Atheneum, 1988.

Martin, Bill, Jr. *Brown Bear, Brown Bear, What Do You See?* New York, NY: Holt, 1967.

Titherington, Jeanne. *Pumpkin, Pumpkin*. New York, NY: Greenwillow, 1986.

Turkle, Brinton. *Deep in the Forest*. New York, NY: E. P. Dutton, 1976.

Udry, Janice May. *A Tree Is Nice*. New York, NY: Harper, 1956.

• Have a teddy-bear day, when children bring their teddy bears or other stuffed toys to share.
• Collect words about the forest in fall, and let the children make sentences to print out and display next to a mural.
• Plan, discuss, and act out a story such as "The Three Bears."

The Physical World

• Go for a nature walk; collect leaves, explore a tree.
• Provide rakes and baskets for raking leaves.
• Start a compost pile (see page 264).
• Collect materials from trees and shrubs for a science display. Provide magnifying glasses to inspect objects.
• Talk about conservation: making paper from trees; using wood for building; how long it takes for trees to grow big enough to provide wood for a house; what happens when we cut down too many trees.
• Display pictures and objects made from trees: furniture, houses, pencils, paper bags, napkins, paper towels, toothpicks, cardboard boxes, blocks, etc.
• Plant a tree in the school yard.

Theme: THE FOREST IN FALL

	Art & Woodworking	Music, Drama, Movement	Math Experiences	Language Arts	The Physical World	Cooking & Nutrition
M	Make a torn-paper tree, using apple/pumpkin colors.	Do *Mostly Movement* activities.	Sort and classify leaves.	Discuss teddy-bear or stuffed-toy day. (Kids bring them in on Friday.)	Take a nature walk; collect leaves.	Take a field trip; pick or buy apples and pumpkins. Display and taste a variety of apples.
TU	Use materials from a nature walk to make a nature hanging.	Listen to "Bear Hunt" or "Sleepy Bear."	Sort and match nuts by color and shape.	Read *Brown Bear* or *Deep in the Forest*.	Start a compost pile with stuff from the field trip. Discuss.	Discuss gourds. Make squash soup.
W	Spatter paint leaves.	Listen to "Teddy Bear's Picnic," and repeat Monday's movement activities.	Sort nature materials by common characteristics.	Use puppets to act out "The Three Bears."	Collect things from the yard; rake leaves; discuss conservation.	Cook and mash the pumpkin. Wash the seeds and leave them out to dry. Crack and taste nuts.
TH	Make a bear-cave diorama.	Act out/dance to "Teddy Bear's Picnic."	Use containers of various sizes and shapes with playdough.	Repeat Monday's activity. Tell *Pumpkin, Pumpkin, Pumpkin* using the flannelboard.	Take another nature walk. Use magnifying glasses.	Toast the pumpkin seeds. Taste a variety of seeds.
F	Fingerpaint	Do creative movement with teddy bears and/or scarves.	Compare the sizes and weights of fall objects.	Have teddy-bear or stuffed-toy day.	Discuss the week's activities.	Make pumpkin cookies to serve at the teddy-bear party.

Illustration 9.1 A sample theme chart for The Forest in Fall

Theme: _____

	Art & Woodworking	Music, Drama, Movement	Math Experiences	Language Arts	The Physical World	Cooking & Nutrition
M						
TU						
W						
TH						
F						

Illustration 9.2 A blank theme chart designed to be used with An Activities Handbook for Teachers of Young Children by Doren J. Croft

Illustration 9.3 **A nature walk can be used as an opportunity for children to learn about the seasons and about growing things.**

Cooking and Nutrition

- Make applesauce (see page 358).
- Display dried gourds and a variety of squashes, apples, and other fall produce.
- Make mashed pumpkin, pumpkin cookies, and toasted pumpkin seeds (see page 356).
- Take a field trip to an apple orchard or a produce market to select a variety of apples and other fall produce to cook at school.
- Collect materials about harvests in other parts of the world, and introduce children to foods from other cultures.

HALLOWEEN

Art and Woodworking

- Make orange and black playdough.
- Use paper plates to make masks, cutting out eyes, nose, and mouth. Punch holes in each side and attach yarn or elastic to hold the mask on. Let the children color and decorate the masks with crayons, cloth scraps, feathers, and other costume decorations.
- Make trick-or-treat bags by decorating grocery bags with paper cutouts, scraps, and felt markers. Attach sturdy handles made of construction materials.

• Make costumes with large grocery bags, old sheets, pillowcases, and cardboard cartons.

Music, Drama, Movement

• Records:

"Halloween Sounds," "I'm a Witch," and "Three Black Cats" from *The Small Singer* (Bowmar Records).
"March of the Ghosts" from *The Small Player* (Bowmar Records).
Witches' Brew, by Hap and Martha Palmer (Educational Activities).
"Have a Good Time on Halloween Night" from *Holiday Songs and Rhythms,* by Hap Palmer (Educational Activities).

• Have a Halloween parade.
• Act out a Halloween story.
• Set up a display table with a collection of nonscary masks.

Math Experiences

• Carve jack-o-lanterns; talk about circles, triangles, and other shapes.
• Count and sort the pumpkin seeds into sets for each child to clean and wash.
• Compare sizes and shapes of pumpkins. Weigh each one, and make a chart listing them from heaviest to lightest, largest to smallest.

Language Arts

• Stories:

Adams, Adrienne. *A Woggle of Witches.* New York, NY: Macmillan, 1971.
Balian, Lorna. *Humbug Witch.* New York, NY: Abingdon, 1965.
Bright, Robert. *Georgie's Halloween.* New York, NY: Doubleday, 1971.
Calhoun, Mary. *Wobble, the Witch Cat.* New York, NY: William Morrow, 1958.
Kroll, Steven. *Amanda and the Giggling Ghost.* New York, NY: Holiday House, 1980.

• Make flannelboard figures for one of the above stories, and let each child take a turn telling part of the story to a group.
• Make an audio tape of children telling about their Halloween experiences.

The Physical World

• Visit a pumpkin patch.
• Sprout and plant some pumpkin seeds (see page 256).
• Hide small pumpkins, and have a pumpkin hunt.
• Discuss fire safety when lighting jack-o-lanterns.

Cooking and Nutrition

• Wash and dry the seeds scooped out of the pumpkins; bake them and then eat them during snack time.
• Make pumpkin cookies (page 356).

• Wrap individual packs of raisins for treats.
• Have the children create eatable faces with ingredients such as those in the Raggedy Ann Salad (page 339).

THANKSGIVING

Art and Woodworking

• Make a mural showing the Pilgrims' first Thanksgiving, or the Mayflower crossing the ocean from England to Plymouth Rock.
• Make collages with dried seeds, grasses, and materials in fall colors.
• Make Indian necklaces with colored macaroni.
• Make Indian headbands with tie-dyed cloth or decorated construction paper.
• Glue small pine cones, twigs, seeds, and nuts to wood; attach a candle and use as centerpiece.

Music, Drama, Movement

• Records:

"Things I'm Thankful For" from *Holiday Songs and Rhythms*, by Hap Palmer (Educational Activities).
"Five Little Pumpkins" from *Singable Songs for the Very Young*, by Raffi (A&M Records).
"A Song of Thanksgiving" from *Autumn* (Bowmar Records).
"Thanksgiving" from *Holiday Rhythms* (Bowmar Records).

Math Experiences

• Plan a Thanksgiving "dinner," and count the number of people invited to attend.
• Have the children set the table, practicing counting and one-to-one correspondence.
• Provide Thanksgiving items such as small gourds, cranberries, and nuts for the children to measure, weigh, and "sell" in dramatic play.
• Have the children help estimate the amounts of some of the foods they will need to feed everyone dinner.
• Make pretend playdough pies, and have the children decide how many pieces they will need to cut in order to feed everyone.

Language Arts

• Stories:

Bunting, Eve. *How Many Days to America? A Thanksgiving Story*. New York, NY: Clarion, 1988.
Dalgliesh, Alice. *The Thanksgiving Story*. New York, NY: Macmillan, 1954.

• Use a puppet to tell the story of the first Thanksgiving.
• Have children retell the story, referring to the mural made in art activities.

- Talk about giving thanks and what being thankful means, and ask the children to share the things they are thankful for.
- If there are immigrant families in your class, relate their experiences to the story *How Many Days to America? A Thanksgiving Story.*
- Have families from other cultures talk about their thanksgiving ceremonies.

The Physical World

- Plant corn seeds.
- Collect autumn leaves, and talk about colors, textures, and why leaves fall.
- Visit a turkey farm.
- Visit a junior museum or a center featuring Indian artifacts.
- Collect natural materials, and add dried gourds, fruits, and vegetables to fill a cornucopia for a display.
- See Native Americans theme (next subsection) for additional ideas.

Cooking and Nutrition

- Make a pumpkin pie, pumpkin cookies, or cornbread.
- Talk about the ingredients, where they come from, and how they are important for good health.
- Grind up fresh cranberries and oranges to make relish. Use 1 orange (wash and remove seeds; do not peel) to 4 cups cranberries and 1 cup sugar (or its equivalent in honey). Pack in small, scalded baby-food jars and use as gifts.
- Plan a Thanksgiving feast, and invite friends and parents to participate.

NATIVE AMERICANS

Art and Woodworking

- Make pottery using the coil method, as follows. Flatten out a ball of clay or baker's dough for the base. Roll more dough into a snake shape and coil it around the base, building up the sides by winding it around and up. Smooth the inside of the pot with damp fingers. The pot can be painted when dry.
- Make sand paintings (see page 33).
- Make Indian necklaces with colored macaroni.
- Make totem poles by cutting egg cartons in half lengthwise; or use lengths of wood in carpentry. Decorate with colorful paints, and attach construction paper for the crossarms. Corks, spools, and Styrofoam can also be used.
- Display posters and pictures of Indian crafts and totem poles.
- Make other ornaments, including rattles, belts, head bands, wrist bands, masks, and hair ornaments.
- Make drums out of empty cardboard containers.

Music, Drama, Movement

- American Indian Day is celebrated in many states on the fourth Friday in September. Write to Canyon Records, 4143 N. 16th St., Phoenix, AZ 85016, for a catalog of records, cassettes, slides, posters, and bibliographies about Native Americans.
- Have children play tom-toms and drums to "Kaluba, Beat the Drum" from *I Know the Colors in the Rainbow,* by Ella Jenkins (Educational Activities).
- Dance to "Powama" (Cachuilla Indian dance) from *Cloud Journeys,* by Anne Barlin and Marcia Berman (LTM).
- Do creative movement activities to *Indian Dances and Folklore,* by Carole Howard (Kimbo Educational Records).
- Learn the "Maori Indian Chant" from Ella Jenkins's *You'll Sing a Song and I'll Sing a Song* (Educational Activities).

Math Experiences

- Have the children measure each other's heads and wrists to make head and wrist bands.
- Plan construction of an Indian tepee village; measure the height, width, and space needed for the tepees and totem poles.

Language Arts

- Stories:

Aliki. *Corn Is Maize.* New York, NY: Crowell, 1976.

Baker, Betty. *Little Runner of the Longhouse.* New York, NY: Harper & Row, 1962.

Beatty, Hetty Burlingame. *Little Owl Indian.* Boston, MA: Houghton Mifflin, 1951.

Miles, Miska. *Annie and the Old One.* New York, NY: Atlantic Monthly Press, 1971.

- Talk about the way Indians used to live and how they live today.
- Write the Navajo Film and Media Commission, The Navajo Tribe, Window Rock, AZ 86515, to request a list of films for young children. Show the films and talk about the topics. Plan some story-acting or puppetry activities.

The Physical World

- Use boxes to make pueblos and cave dwellings.
- Plan a tepee village outdoors.
- Talk about how the Indians kept warm, the kinds of food they planted, and the animals they hunted to feed themselves. Have the children imagine what it would be like not to have electricity, supermarkets, TV, and all the comforts of home today.
- Make a chart showing the basic necessities for survival; show how nature, plants, and animals were essential to Native Americans for food, clothing, and shelter.

Cooking and Nutrition

• Make Indian custard (page 361).
• Plant a variety of seeds, and talk about their importance to all people as a source of food and good nutrition.
• Make popcorn.
• Show pictures of foods that were common to various tribes of Native Americans.

Winter

WINTER WEATHER

Art and Woodworking

• Make a snowman with soap snow (see page 38).
• Make a weather wheel by scoring a cardboard circle into sections, as shown in Illustration 9.4. Have the children draw or paste on an umbrella, sun, clouds, kite, snowman—whatever is appropriate for local weather. Attach a pointer in the center of the circle with a brad. Each day, observe the weather and move the pointer to the appropriate section. Children can make their own wheels or cooperate to make one large one for the classroom.
• Invite the children to paint with white liquid tempera on blue paper. Use cotton balls for cloud pictures.

Illustration 9.4 **Weather wheel**

• Make bird feeders by spreading the crevices of pine cones with peanut butter or dough and then dipping the cones in bird seed. Hang them outdoors with red ribbons to attract birds. Or fill scooped-out orange rinds with bread crumbs and bird seed, and hang them inside a mesh vegetable bag.

Music, Drama, Movement

• See Clare Cherry's book *Creative Movement for the Developing Child* for the Big Snowman activity. (Refer to the annotated list on page 121).
• Records:

Rainy Day Dances, Rainy Day Songs by Anne Barlin (Educational Activities).
"It's Raining" from *Rainy Day Record,* by Henry "Buzz" Glass and Rosemary Hallum (Educational Activities).
"It Won't Rain, It Won't Rain" from *I Know the Colors in the Rainbow,* by Ella Jenkins (Educational Activities).
"Raindrops" from *Perceptual-Motor Rhythm Games,* by Jack Capon and Rosemary Hallum (Educational Activities).
Sky Bears, A Winter Festival of Children's Music from Around the World, by Nancy Raven (Pacific Cascade Records).
Health and Safety, by Hap Palmer (Educational Activities).

• Make a rain puddle game by cutting rain puddles of different sizes and shapes from blue contact paper. Have the children take turns following your directions to walk *around,* jump *over,* stomp *through,* or tiptoe *into* each puddle.

Math Experiences

• Set out pans to collect rain or snow. Mark and record each day's collection, and then compare (*more than, less than*) rainfall amounts for the week. Keep a chart.
• Read the temperature on an outdoor thermometer, and keep a record.
• Cut geometric forms out of folded paper to make snowflakes.

Language Arts

• Stories to read, discuss, adapt to flannelboard and act out:

Burton, Virginia. *Katy and the Big Snow.* Boston, MA: Houghton Mifflin, 1943.
Garelick, May. *Where Does the Butterfly Go When It Rains?* New York, NY: Young Scott, 1970.
Keats, Ezra Jack. *The Snowy Day.* New York, NY: Viking, 1962.
Tresselt, Alvin. *Hide and Seek Fog.* New York, NY: Mulberry, 1965.
_____. *Rain Drop Splash.* New York, NY: Lothrop, 1946.
Welber, Robert. *Song of the Seasons.* New York, NY: Pantheon, 1973.
Wolff, Ashley. *A Year of Birds.* New York, NY: Puffin, 1984.

• See page 283 for an activity and children's books about germs and how colds are spread.

• Make flannelboard figures with a variety of clothes. Let the children help decide what clothing is appropriate to wear in different kinds of weather.

The Physical World

• See Capturing Snowflakes (page 236) for a winter weather activity.
• Place a slightly dampened baking sheet in a freezer overnight. Remove it from the freezer, and let the children use a magnifying glass to observe the crystals that have formed.
• Make crystals by putting ½ teaspoon alum and ¼ cup hot water in a glass and inserting a pipe cleaner. Crystals will form on the pipe cleaner overnight. Provide a magnifying glass for children to use to study the crystals.
• After a rain, look for signs of how plants, insects, and birds are affected by the weather.
• Read about ways animals keep warm in cold weather.
• See pages 241–242 for instructions on making a thermometer and a rain gauge.
• Go for a "sky walk" and look for the different ways the sky behaves. Note whether clouds are light or dark, move fast or slow, etc.
• Observe how the wind moves things. Track wind patterns with maple seeds and leaves.

Cooking and Nutrition

• Make snow cones by pouring concentrated fruit juice over crushed ice.
• Make soup with vegetables that grow in the winter.
• Prepare food for an indoor picnic on a rainy day.

CHANUKAH

Art and Woodworking

• Sponge paint holiday shapes in white, royal blue, and orange.
• Make the Star of David by cutting out two triangles and inverting one over the other to form a six-pointed star.
• Use clay to make a menorah. A menorah should have spots for eight candles, plus a raised spot to hold the *shamash,* a ninth candle that is used to light the others.
• Make dreidels out of cardboard or oaktag and wooden dowels, as shown in Illustration 9.6.

Illustration 9.5 **Star of David**

Illustration 9.6 **Pattern for making a dreidel**

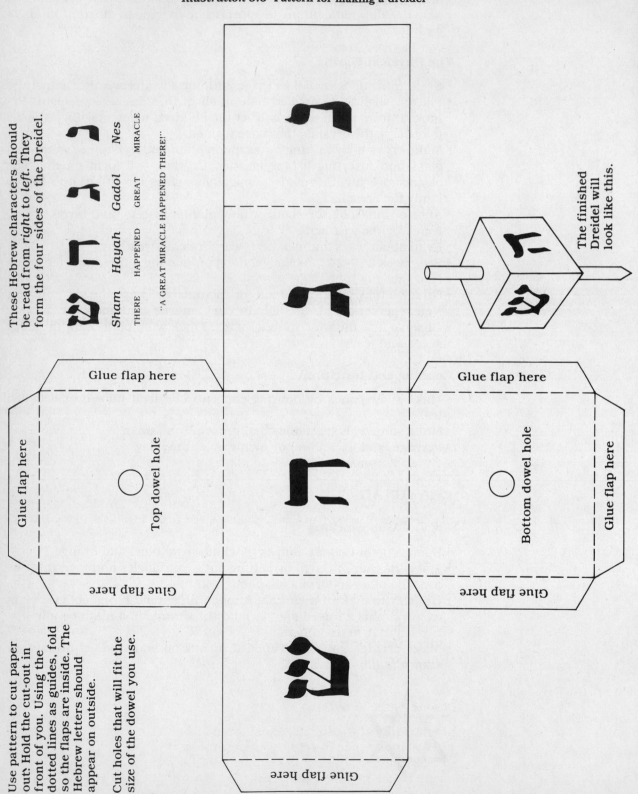

These Hebrew characters should be read from *right to left*. They form the four sides of the Dreidel.

Sham   Hayah   Gadol   Nes
THERE HAPPENED GREAT MIRACLE

"A GREAT MIRACLE HAPPENED THERE!"

Use pattern to cut paper out. Hold the cut-out in front of you. Using the dotted lines as guides, fold so the flaps are inside. The Hebrew letters should appear on outside.

Cut holes that will fit the size of the dowel you use.

Glue flap here

Glue flap here

Top dowel hole

Glue flap here

Glue flap here

Glue flap here

Bottom dowel hole

Glue flap here

Glue flap here

The finished Dreidel will look like this.

Music, Drama, Movement

• Records:

"Hanukkah" from *Holiday Songs and Rhythms*, by Hap Palmer (Educational Activities).
Israeli Children's Songs, by Ben-Ezra (Folkways).
"O Hanukkah" from *Folk Songs of Israel* (Bowmar).
"Eight Candles" from *rabbits dance and other songs for children*, by Marcia Berman (B/B Records).
"My Dreydl" from *Songs for the Holiday Season*, by Nancy Raven (Pacific Cascade Records).
"My Dreydl" from *Singable Songs for the Very Young*, by Raffi (A&M Records).
"Hanuka Dance" by Woody Guthrie from *Singing, Prancing & Dancing*, with Nancy Raven (Pacific Cascade Records).
Chanukah at Home (Rounder). Features some top children's performers, including Dan Crow, Marcia Berman, and Fred Sokolow.

Math Experiences

• Use triangle-shaped templates to make triangles for the Star of David. Talk about size, shape, and creating new shapes by combining two triangles.
• Count out the correct number of candles to use in a menorah.
• Read the book *Rainbow Candles, A Chanukah Counting Book*, by Myra Shostak (see page 198). Use colored playdough to make candles to count.

Language Arts

• Use the annotated list of books on pages 197–198 to find Chanukah stories to read to the children, and engage them in conversation.
• Invite a parent to tell the story of Chanukah to the children.
• Make a dreidel and play the game, using nuts and small toys for tokens.

The Physical World

• Make sand sculptures (page 244) and candles.
• Talk about the properties of sand and how it feels when wet and dry. Use sifters and talk about the coarseness of the grains. Study the grains under a magnifying glass.
• Talk about safety precautions to take when lighting and burning candles.

Cooking and Nutrition

• Make *latkes* (potato pancakes), page 354.
• Make applesauce to serve over the *latkes*.
• Make cookies with cookie cutters in Chanukah shapes. Discuss the reasons for the different shapes.
• Talk about foods and how different people use special foods for holidays.

CHRISTMAS

Art and Woodworking

• Make red and green playdough. Use cookie cutters in Christmas shapes.
• Make tree decorations with construction paper, Styrofoam, scraps of foil, and tinsel.
• Collect small pine cones, and decorate them with soap snow.
• Have the children make Christmas cards and send them to friends and family.
• Make the children's handprints from heavy construction paper or plaster of Paris for gifts.

Music, Drama, Movement

• Records:

Songs for the Holiday Season, by Nancy Raven (Pacific Cascade). This album has several Christmas songs.
Holiday Songs and Rhythms, by Hap Palmer (Educational Activities). This album includes "What a World We'd Have if Christmas Lasted All Year Long" and "We Wish You a Merry Christmas."

Math Experiences

• Carry out measurement activities in preparing Christmas snacks and treats.
• Frost windows with Glass Wax on stencils of geometric forms (see Matching and Pairing Geometric Forms, page 50).
• When making tree ornaments, have the children match and pair different objects, such as a candy cane with each boot or two tinsels for every star.
• Measure and wrap small gifts for children in hospitals. Count the number needed to represent each child in the class.
• Make a calendar of the 12 days of Christmas.

Language Arts

• Story:

Ets, Marie Hall, and Aurora Labastida. *Nine Days to Christmas.* New York, NY: Viking, 1959. This story tells how Christmas is spent in modern-day Mexico. Refer to the annotated list of stories on page 198.

• Use the wordless book *The Christmas Gift,* by Emily Arnold McCully (New York, NY: Harper & Row, 1988), to engage the children in telling the story. If possible, make slides from the illustrations and project them on a screen so that all the children in a group can see the pictures easily. Then act out the story, either in pantomime or using words, depending on the children's abilities.

The Physical World

- Visit a tree farm or a Christmas tree lot, and collect branches and greenery.
- Talk about the importance of trees in maintaining the balance of nature.
- Smell the pine needles, and talk about the colors, textures, and shapes of leaves, needles, and branches.
- Talk about safety measures to be taken with tree lights and candles.
- Talk about the importance of conserving and recycling paper. Have the children save their Christmas wrappings and cards to bring to school for art projects.

Cooking and Nutrition

- Use bread dough to shape and bake Christmas wreaths.
- Make a hearty holiday meal of split pea soup (page 347), vegetables with dip (page 354), and coconut apricot candy (page 355).
- Talk about other countries that celebrate Christmas and some of the foods the people prepare.
- Make special treats for the school's animals based on foods that are nutritious for them. For example, the children can bring bits of apple and carrot for the rabbits or guinea pigs.

AFRO-AMERICAN HISTORY

Art and Woodworking

- Make a mural with pictures from magazines such as *Ebony* and *Ebony, Jr.* showing children and families of Afro-American heritage.
- Display posters such as "Children of Africa," available from the Society for Visual Education, 1345 Diversey Parkway, Chicago, IL 60614.
- Write to Dial/Delacorte, School and Library Services, 750 Third Ave., New York, NY 10017, for free posters and bookmarks illustrating black culture.
- Make tie-dyed materials; show pictures of tie-dyed materials from Nigeria.

Music, Drama, Movement

- The following records by Ella Jenkins (Folkways) all include African songs and rhythms for movement:

African Songs and Rhythms for Children
Call-and-Response Rhythmic Group Singing
Jambo and Other Call-and-Response Songs and Chants
Rhythms and Chants

- Other records:

"Africa Thanksgiving" from *Sky Bears, A Winter Festival of Children's Music from Around the World*, by Nancy Raven (Pacific Cascade Records).

Step It Down, by Bessie Jones (Rounder Records).

Cloud Journeys, by Anne Lief Barlin and Marcia Berman has two African dances: "Shoo Lie Loo" and "Old Tar River." In *Dance-a-Story Sing-a-Song* (Educational Activities) Barlin and Berman perform an African rhythmic game for naming body parts titled "Kye Kye Kuli," as well as the Afro-American song "Oh, John the Rabbit." Have the children use drums to follow along in beating out some of the rhythms and chants.

Math Experiences

• Some Afro-American families celebrate Kwanza from December 26 to January 1 in recognition of traditional African harvest festivals. Kwanza means "fresh fruits," and the holiday stresses the unity of the family. Use this occasion to have children cooperate in preparing a celebration by bringing in fresh fruits of the season. In addition to matching, pairing, and counting the fruit, the children might prepare juice as an illustration of conservation of volume.

• Practice one-to-one correspondence by having the children set tables for the harvest dinner.

Language Arts

• Stories:

Adoff, Arnold, *Big Sister Tells Me That I'm Black.* New York, NY: Holt, Rinehart, Winston, 1976.

Greenfield, Eloise. *Africa Dream.* New York, NY: Crowell, 1977.

Refer to the bibliography of multi-ethnic books in Part Four for other stories appropriate to the theme. Books by John Steptoe and Ezra Jack Keats are excellent choices to share with children.

Illustration 9.7 **Celebrating Martin Luther King Day**

• Celebrate Martin Luther King Day on January 15 by displaying King's picture along with his famous quotation: "I have a dream that my four little children will one day live in a nation where they will not be judged by the color of their skin but by the content of their character." Talk about Martin Luther King, Jr. with the children, sharing simple facts about equality and prejudice at their level of understanding. Use *Why Are People Different? A Book About Prejudice,* by Barbara Shook Hazen (New York, NY: Western, 1985).

The Physical World

• Plan a field trip to a museum displaying African art objects.
• Talk about how the climate and environment have an effect on the food, clothing, and cultural patterns of African people.
• Write to the Institute for Positive Education, 7528 Cottage Grove Ave., Chicago, IL 60619, for information about activities suitable for preschool children.

Cooking and Nutrition

• Have a Kwanza party, serving fresh fruits, corn, and molasses bread.
• Make pecan pralines, molasses pudding, or a recipe using fresh fruits. Recipes can be found in such cookbooks as *Joy of Cooking,* by Irma S. Rombauer and Marion Becker (Indianapolis, IN: Bobbs-Merrill, 1988).
• Invite Afro-Americans to provide recipes and ideas to use in the curriculum.

CHINESE NEW YEAR

Art and Woodworking

• Asian families display pink and red blossoms in their homes during the new year. Have the children tear and crumple bits of pink and red tissue paper to attach to twigs or small branches. Poke the branches into a base of clay or spackle.
• Adults give children "lucky" money in small red envelopes for the new year. Make and decorate small red envelopes, and put a coin in each to give to the children.
• Make a papier-mache dragon head and attach it to bedsheets for use in a dragon dance.
• Make scrolls with wooden dowels (see page 61).

Music, Drama, Movement

• Write to China Books and Periodicals, 125 Fifth Ave., New York, NY 10003, for children's records.
• Do a dragon dance through the school, letting some of the children be the inside of the dragon while others play gongs, cymbals, drums, and other percussion instruments.
• Records:

"Feast of Lanterns" from *Sky Bears, A Winter Festival of Children's Music from Around the World,* by Nancy Raven (Pacific Cascade).

"In the People's Republic of China: A Train Ride to the Great Wall" from *I Know the Colors in the Rainbow,* by Ella Jenkins (Educational Activities).

Math Experiences

• Have the children help count and identify denominations of coins to place in red envelopes for lucky Chinese New Year money.

• Invite adults familiar with paper folding (origami) to show the children how to fold paper into different shapes involving triangles, rectangles, and squares.

• Let the children practice one-to-one correspondence by putting coins into envelopes.

Language Arts

• Read *The Chinese New Year,* by Hou-tien Cheng. See other listings under Multi-Ethnic Books at the end of Part Four for stories about Japanese, Vietnamese, and other Asians. Another helpful book with black-and-white photos and simple text explaining some of the activities and customs of the new year is *Chinese New Year,* by Tricia Brown (New York, NY: Holt, 1987).

• Have Asian families share their holiday traditions with the class by telling the children stories about their childhood memories of the holidays.

• Have Asians speak in their native tongues to let children hear the sounds of other languages.

• Teach the children how to say "Happy New Year" in Chinese. There are many different Chinese dialects. The Cantonese say *gung hay fot choy.*

The Physical World

• Refer to books listed in Part Five, The Physical World, to illustrate that although faces are different, they all have some things in common. Especially relevant is *Faces,* by Barbara Brenner. Another useful resource is Roma Gans's *Your Skin and Mine.*

• Bring in pink and red flowering plants, such as azaleas, for the children to enjoy and care for. Talk about watering and feeding live plants and deciding where to place them in a room. Later, when the weather is warmer, let the children help transplant the potted plants into the ground so that the roots can grow better.

• Display posters and pictures showing how Asian children live in their native countries. Write to School Products Division, 850 N. Grove Ave., Elgin, IL 60120, for *Mainland China—Today,* a set of 16 large pictures with a teacher's manual (order no. 68528).

• Display Asian artifacts, and talk about the materials that were used to make them.

Cooking and Nutrition

- Make rice cakes with puffed rice or crispy rice baked with honey.
- See Part Seven, Cooking and Nutrition, for ideas on making Chinese foods.
- Learn to use chopsticks.
- Invite Asian families to provide recipes and ideas for foods that the children can help prepare.
- Display oranges and tangerines (with some stems and leaves still attached).

VALENTINE'S DAY

Art and Woodworking

- Make red and white playdough.
- Make valentines with red construction paper, fabric doilies, lace, and other trim.
- Make a valentine mobile to hang in the school.
- Staple valentine folders together for the children to decorate and use for carrying valentines.
- Build a large valentine box of wood, or glue decorations onto a cardboard box for valentines.
- Make a loving branch by painting a branch white and securing it to a base of clay or spackle. Let the children hang valentine ornaments made of paper, Styrofoam, clay, and doilies on it.

Music, Drama, Movement

- Records:

"Valentine's Song" from *Songs for Learning Through Music and Movement,* by Hap Palmer (Alfred Publishing Company). This song is also on Hap Palmer's record *Holiday Songs and Rhythms* (Educational Activities).

"Will You Be My Valentine?" by Betty Ruth Baker, from *Piggy Back Songs,* by Jean Warren (Warren Publishing House).

Math Experiences

- Let the children practice writing the numbers in their home addresses, in preparation for sending valentines to family members.
- Use activities during snack time to teach one-to-one correspondence, sets, and grouping.
- Have the children count out a specific number of valentines that each one can deliver to others in the class.
- Use the book *One Zillion Valentines,* by Frank Modell (New York, NY: Greenwillow, 1978), to start a discussion about numbers and counting.

Language Arts

• Stories:

Adams, Adrienne. *The Great Valentine's Day Balloon Race.* New York, NY: Macmillan, 1980.

Balian, Lorna. *A Sweetheart for Valentine.* Nashville, TN: Abingdon, 1979.

Cohen, Miriam. *Be My Valentine.* New York, NY: Greenwillow, 1978.

Gibbons, Gail. *Valentine's Day.* New York, NY: Holiday House, 1986.

Greydanus, Rose. *Valentine's Day Grump.* Mahwah, NJ: Troll, 1981.

Modell, Frank. *One Zillion Valentines.* New York, NY: Mulberry, 1987.

Pretlutsky, Jack. *It's Valentine's Day.* New York, NY: Scholastic, 1983.

Schulz, Charles. *Be My Valentine, Charlie Brown.* New York, NY: Scholastic, 1985.

Zolotow, Charlotte. *Some Things Go Together.* New York, NY: Harper, 1969.

• Make a mailbox in which children can deposit their valentines. Help each child address valentines.
• If age-appropriate, have the children address and mail valentines to their families.
• Use books by Joan Walsh Anglund: *A Friend Is Someone Who Likes You* (1958) and *Love Is a Special Way of Feeling* (New York, NY: Harcourt Brace Jovanovich). Talk about feelings, friends, and expressing love.
• Talk about the meaning of *valentine,* whom the children want to remember, and why.

The Physical World

• Prepare a red ocean in a jar (see page 243). Talk about the properties of liquids.
• Pick flowers or have children bring some from home to make valentine bouquets for teachers or a special adult.
• Use a book such as *The Reason for a Flower,* by Ruth Heller (New York, NY: Putnam's, 1985), to express the wonder of nature.
• Place some of the valentine art materials in a box for sensory perception activities. Let the children feel the objects, describe their textures, and guess what they are.

Cooking and Nutrition

• Using different kinds of red foods—such as apples, strawberries, and red cabbage—to prepare snacks.
• Use beet juice or vegetable food coloring to make red designs on baked cookies.
• Dip pears into red vegetable coloring and fill them with cottage cheese.
• Use heart-shaped cookie cutters to make sandwiches for snacks.
• Talk about the importance of brushing teeth after eating valentine candies or other sweets.

SPRING

SPRING AROUND THE WORLD

Art and Woodworking

- To make a cherry tree, straw-blow branches with black or brown paint; use a finger dipped in pink paint to finger-dot blossoms on the branches. (See also the Japanese Cherry Blossom Festival activities described later in this section.)
- Do some of the Cinco de Mayo activities described later in this section.
- Make a piñata, tape on some small trinkets, and hang it in the classroom.
- Celebrate *Holi*, the Hindu spring festival. Using cut potatoes or felt shapes glued to wood blocks, print Indian motifs of fish, elephants, or paisley on paper. Use the *Holi* colors or red and yellow.

Music, Dance, Movement

- Records:

"Robin in the Rain" from *Singable Songs for the Very Young*, by Raffi (Shoreline Records).
"Dulce, Dulce" from *You'll Sing a Song and I'll Sing a Song*, by Ella Jenkins (Folkway Records).
- Select songs with multicultural themes to introduce children to songs from around the world.

Math Experiences

- Talk about shapes and forms as you fold accordion-pleated paper fans.
- Have the children help count the number of people in the class and select a corresponding number of trinkets to place inside a piñata.
- Provide experiences in weighing and measuring with cooking activities.

Language Arts

- Use the series of filmstrips or cassettes titled "Fall," "Winter," "Spring," "Summer," "A Child's Eye-View," by Doreen Rappaport and Susan Kempler, to engage children in talking about the wonders of the changing seasons (available from Linden Tree, Los Altos, CA 94025).
- Using a globe or world map, locate and talk about places where particular springtime customs are celebrated.
- Select stories from the bibliography in Part Four, Language Arts, such as *Umbrella*, by Taro Yashima (New York, NY: Penguin, 1977), and *Gilberto and the Wind*, by Marie Hall Ets (New York, NY: Puffin, 1978).

The Physical World

- Make kites in art and woodworking to demonstrate how air moves things (page 233).
- Have an international parade featuring the different cultures represented in the class. Display and talk about the different materials used in clothing from various parts of the world.
- Collect and display blossoms from various trees and plants.

Cooking and Nutrition

- Make latkes (see page 354).
- Use fresh spring vegetables to prepare recipes for salads and soups.
- Bring in an assortment of spices that come from India—for example, curry, cinnamon, dill, and coriander. Let the children smell the spices; use a small amount of curry to season cooked potatoes.

SEEDS AND GROWING THINGS

Art and Woodworking

- Use a variety of seeds and beans to make a collage.
- Glue seeds and beans to a chart; use corresponding pictures to show what the plants look like when the seeds sprout.
- Make prints with fruits and vegetables (see page 28).
- Cut and paste pictures to make a mural of things that grow, including human and animal babies.

Music, Drama, Movement

- Records:

Everything Grows, by Raffi (A&M Records).
"The Garden Song" from *10 Carrot Diamond,* by Charlotte Diamond (Hug Bug Records).

- Sing "Oats, Peas, Beans, and Barley Grow."
- Sing and act out "Growing" from *Learning Basic Skills Through Music, Vol. I,* by Hap Palmer (Educational Activities).
- Use the book and recording of *The Carrot Seed,* by Ruth Krauss (New York, NY: Harper, 1945), to act out the story.

Math Experiences

- Make sequence cards showing the development of a plant from seed. Have the children put the cards in correct order.
- Plant grass and other seeds in small containers. Measure and keep records of growth each day.
- Sort and match a mixture of beans by color and shape.
- Maintain records of changes in height and weight for each child.

Language Arts

• Stories:

Gans, Roma. *How a Seed Grows.* New York, NY: Crowell, 1962.
Hutchins, Pat. *Titch.* New York, NY: Macmillan, 1971.
Krasilovsky, Phyllis. *The Very Little Girl.* New York, NY: Doubleday, 1953.
Krauss, Ruth. *The Carrot Seed.* New York, NY: Harper, 1945.
Mari, Iela, and Enzo Mari. *The Apple and the Moth.* New York, NY: Dial, 1970.
The Chicken and the Egg. New York, NY: Pantheon, 1969.
Quinlan, Patricia. *Planting Seeds.* Toronto, Canada: Annick Press, 1988.
Titherington, Jeanne. *Pumpkin, Pumpkin.* New York, NY: Greenwillow, 1986.

The Physical World

• Refer to pages 256–260 on growing and sprouting seeds.
• Prepare ground, and plant a garden.
• Discuss a plant's needs for soil, water, and sun.
• Refer to *Seeds and Weeds,* by Joan Westley (Sunnyvale, CA: Creative Publications, 1988).

Cooking and Nutrition

• Shell and grind peanuts to make peanut butter.
• Display pictures of a variety of fruits and vegetables from seed to edible plant.
• Discuss whether we eat each plant's root (carrot), leaf (spinach), stalk (celery), or flower (broccoli).
• Roast and eat pumpkin, sesame, or sunflower seeds.
• Make popcorn.

EASTER

Art and Woodworking

• Decorate hard boiled eggs by dyeing, painting, gluing on decorations, or using crayon-resist (the wax in crayon designs will resist dyes). (See page 43 on dyeing eggs.)
• Make an egg tree by decorating blown-out eggs and hanging them on a branch that has been secured in a can of plaster of Paris. [Refer to *The Egg Tree,* by Katherine Milhous (New York: Macmillan, 1981).] To blow an egg, poke pencil-tip-size holes in both ends of a raw egg. Blow through one end. (Inserting a sharp object to break up the yolk makes ejecting the egg easier.)
• Make Easter bonnets with cardboard, ribbons, lace, and flowers.
• Make bunny puppets out of white paper bags, using thin strips of black construction paper for whiskers, cotton for tails, and pink and black paper for eyes and ears.

- Make collages with broken egg shells.
- Make an Easter mural with paintings and collages of blossoms, bunnies, and eggs.
- Decorate with tie-dyed materials.

Music, Drama, Movement

- Records:

"Easter Time Is Here Again" from *Holiday Songs and Rhythms*, by Hap Palmer (Educational Activities).

"Robin in the Rain" from *Singable Songs for the Very Young*, by Raffi (Shoreline Records).

- Sing "The Easter Bunny" from *Singing Bee*, by Jane Hart (New York, NY: Lothrop, 1982).

Math Experiences

- Let the children help to determine how many eggs are needed to have an Easter egg hunt in which they each get one egg.
- Let the children practice counting and weighing hard boiled eggs.
- Use Hap Palmer's record *Math Readiness, Vocabulary and Concepts* (Educational Activities) to practice moving by numerals and clapping sets.

Language Arts

- Stories to read, act out, or adapt to the flannelboard:

Adams, Adrienne. *The Easter Egg Artists*. New York, NY: Macmillan, 1981.

Coskey, Evelyn. *Easter Eggs for Everyone*. New York, NY: Abingdon, 1973.

Holl, Adelaide. *The Remarkable Egg*. New York, NY: Lothrop, 1968.

Milhous, Katherine. *The Egg Tree*. New York, NY: Macmillan, 1950.

Zolotow, Charlotte. *The Bunny Who Found Easter*. Boston, MA: Houghton Mifflin, 1959.

The Physical World

- Buy some fertilized eggs, and place them in an incubator to hatch.
- Learn to care for a rabbit.
- Pick blossoms and flowers for a display in school.
- Plant seeds, and display spring bulbs.
- Have an Easter egg hunt.
- Use the book *Chickens Aren't the Only Ones*, by Ruth Heller (NY: Grosset & Dunlap, 1985), to discuss other animals that lay eggs.

Cooking and Nutrition

- Steam some baby spring vegetables for lunch.
- Make a bunny salad using the ingredients for Raggedy Ann Salad (page 339).

• Make glazed carrots (page 353).
• Make deviled eggs (page 344).

JAPANESE CHERRY BLOSSOM FESTIVAL

Art and Woodworking

• Make cherry blossoms by attaching pink tissue to twigs.
• To make a carp kite, cut two matching fish shapes from lightweight paper. Glue the shapes together along the outside edges. Glue some wire or a pipe cleaner around the mouth, and attach streamers to the tail. Attach kite string to the mouth so that when the kite is pulled, wind will pass through the fish. (See Illustration 9.8.)
• Make a mural for the classroom, depicting cherry trees in blossom. Paint trees, and let the children decorate the limbs with tissue blossoms.
• Do origami (paper folding).

Music, Drama, Movement

• Records:

"Usagi" from *Cloud Journeys,* by Anne Lief Barlin and Marcia Berman (LTM).

"Chotto Matte, Kudasai" (Just a moment, please), from *I Know the Colors in the Rainbow,* by Ella Jenkins (Educational Activities).

"Each of Us Is a Flower" from *10 Carrot Diamond,* by Charlotte Diamond (Hug Bug Records).

• Do creative movement to "Shojoji" the Japanese children's song about badgers who dance in the moonlight, from *Dance-a-Story Sing-a-Song*, by Marcia Berman and Anne Barlin (Educational Activities).
• Invite local Japanese people to visit and perform festival dances for the class.

Math Experiences

• Give children practice in number correspondence by having them place 2 chopsticks (1 pair) at the table for each child.

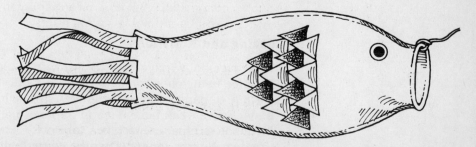

Illustration 9.8 **Carp kite**

- Use Hap Palmer's record *Math Readiness, Vocabulary and Concepts* (Educational Activities) to teach sets and numbers.
- Have the children bring dolls to commemorate *Hina Matsuri,* the Japanese doll festival which begins March 3. Make a chart associating each doll that is displayed with the name of the child who brought it.

Language Arts

- Stories:

Yashima, Mitsu, and Taro Yashima. *Momo's Kitten.* New York, NY: Penguin, 1977.
Yashima, Taro. *Umbrella.* New York, NY: Viking, 1958.

- Show the film *Festival in Japan,* produced by Sakura Motion Picture Company, and distributed by Japan National Tourist Organization, 1420 Commerce St., Dallas, TX 75201. The main office is located at 45 Rockefeller Plaza, New York, NY 10020, if you wish to write for additional information or materials.
- Display posters of Japanese people, and talk about their customs, clothing, and food.
- Invite Japanese families to talk with the class and share some of their artifacts, eating and cooking utensils, materials, kimonos, and kites. (Note: Although the Cherry Blossom Festival is not a major holiday for Japanese in the United States, the celebration offers a good opportunity to introduce the children to the Japanese culture.)

The Physical World

- Find some books at your local library about silk worms; share the pictures and information with the children. You may wish to send away for silk worms to raise in the classroom.
- Take a field trip to a nearby park or area where children can see blossoming trees and shrubs.
- Read *The Very Hungry Caterpillar,* by Eric Carle (New York, NY: Putnam, 1981). Collect caterpillars in jars, feed them, and watch them grow.
- Make and fly kites; talk about the way the air moves things (see page 232).

Cooking and Nutrition

- Make rice balls (page 345). Serve with colorful platters of fresh fruit.
- Practice using chopsticks to pick up food.
- Have a Japanese tea ceremony, using a low table placed on some mats. Serve weak herbal tea in Japanese teapots and cups.
- Invite local Japanese families to provide ideas for foods that the children can help prepare. Display items such as chopsticks, fans, kimonos, and kites.

CINCO DE MAYO

Art and Woodworking

- Make a piñata by covering an inflated balloon with strips of newspaper and taping on crumbled paper to fashion a head, arms, legs, wings, and so on. Cover with papier-mache. Leave a small hole at the bottom to insert toys and candy. Cover with several layers of tissue paper or newspaper strips. Let dry thoroughly, and paint with bright colors. Decorations such as feathers and bows can be added. Stuff some small toys, dried fruits, and other goodies through the opening; pop the balloon and tape the hole shut. Suspend the piñata from a rope or heavy twine so that it can be raised and lowered.
- Make *maracas* by placing rice or beans inside plastic egg-shaped containers. Attach a handle to each container by poking a hole and inserting a wooden dowel. Paint the maracas.
- Fashion clay to make pots; when dry, brush on colorful paint.
- To make *cascarones* (decorated eggshells), poke pencil-tip-size holes in both ends of an egg and blow the raw egg out. Rinse, dry and paint the shell with bright colors. Fill the shell halfway with confetti (see Math Experiences), and glue on colorful paper to cover the ends. (These cascarones will be used later in Physical World activities.)

Music, Drama, Movement

- Records:

"Chiapanacas" from *Rainy Day Record,* by Henry "Buzz" Glass (Educational Activities).

"Cinco de Mayo" from *Holiday Songs and Rhythms,* by Hap Palmer (Educational Activities).

"Los Pollitos" from *Dance-a-Story Sing-a-Song,* by Anne Lief Barlin and Marcia Berman (Educational Activities). This song about baby chicks is sung in Spanish and English.

"La Bamba" from *10 Carrot Diamond,* by Charlotte Diamond (Hug Bug Records).

"Latin American Dances" from *First Folk Dances,* Vol. 2, by Ruth White (Creative Movement).

- Use the maracas made in art to dance to the rhythms of Mexican tunes.
- Invite local Mexican families to bring their records and musical instruments to play for the children.

Math Experiences

- Have the children measure and weigh the confetti to fill each cascarone made in art.
- Practice counting in Spanish.
- Have the children count the number of people in the class and determine the number of trinkets and goodies they will need for the piñata.

• Referring to the bibliography of concept books in Part Four, select some counting, color, and shape books to be translated into Spanish. Display the corresponding English and Spanish words with each picture.

Language Arts

• Stories:

Behrens, June. *Fiesta! Cinco de Mayo.* Chicago, IL: Children's Press, 1978.

Blue, R. *I Am Here: Yo Estoy Aqui.* New York, NY: Franklin Watts, 1971.

Ets, Marie Hall. *Gilberto and the Wind.* New York, NY: Viking, 1963.

Pomerantz, Charlotte. *The Tamarindo Puppy.* New York, NY: Greenwillow, 1980. Spanish and English words are interspersed in poems that have simple themes of interest to young children.

Note: This holiday is celebrated in many areas of the United States where there is a sizable population of Mexican-Americans.

The Physical World

• Talk about some of the common building materials used in Mexico. Make adobe bricks out of clay, water, and bits of straw. Mix the ingredients well to a dough-like consistency. Shape the mixture into flat bricks, and let them dry in the sun.
• Contrast the different sounds made by rice and beans in the maracas.
• Hide the cascarones outdoors, and have the children look for them. In Mexico, the people break the confetti-filled eggs over each other's heads. The children may simply want to break them and scatter the confetti.
• Weigh each egg before and after it is filled with confetti. Compare the weights, and talk about differences in the weights of various materials.

Cooking and Nutrition

• Make tortillas (page 330).
• Make guacamole, using mashed ripe avocadoes, lemon juice, and a dash of hot sauce. Serve it as a dip with vegetables.
• Have a piñata party: display Mexican flags and colors, clothing, gourds, cookware, and other artifacts. Suspend the piñata, and lower and raise it as blindfolded children try to break it with a stick. Have the children take turns until the toys and goodies fall out for everyone to share.
• Make Cinco de Mayo Salad (page 340).

Summer

SUMMER AND THE SUN

Art and Woodworking

- Make sun-dried objects with modeling "goop" (page 23).
- Fingerpaint with bright yellow paint.
- Use easel paints in colors of the rainbow.
- Make mud pies; paint outdoors on washable surfaces with mud.
- To make sun prints, have the children arrange leaves and other objects on black or dark construction paper. Leave the paper in the direct sun for several hours until outlines of the objects are visible.

Music, Drama, Movement

- Records:

Sing a Song of Sunshine: New Songs and Games for Young Children, by Randy Hitz and Diane Brunengo (R&D Records).
"Mr. Sun" from *Singable Songs for the Very Young,* by Raffi (Shoreline).
"Just Like the Sun" from *Everything Grows,* by Raffi; *One Light One Sun* by Raffi (A&M Records).
"It's a Beautiful Day" from *We All Live Together, Vol. IV,* by Steve Millang and Greg Scelsa (Youngheart).

- Let the children dance and move to "Enter Sunlight" from *Movin',* by Hap Palmer (Educational Activities). Another excellent tune from the same record is "Funky Penguin."
- Talk about things the children can do when the sun shines; have them act out or express their feelings through creative movement to songs such as "It's a Beautiful Day" and "Everybody Has Music Inside," by Steve and Greg.
- Use colorful scarves to dance to *My Playful Scarf, Creative Movement and Fantasy with Scarves,* by Stephen Fite (Melody House).

Math Experiences

- Precut circles of easel and fingerpaint paper for painting with bright yellow tempera. Talk about circles and other shapes.
- Keep a record of times on a sundial.
- To provide experiences with conservation of volume, let the children play with water using measuring cups and other containers.
- Use Tana Hoban's book *Round and Round and Round* (New York: Greenwillow, 1983) to talk about objects like the sun that are round.

Language Arts

- Stories:

Cartwright, Sally. *Sunlight.* New York, NY: Coward, McCann 1974.
de Regniers, Beatrice Schenk. *The Shadow Book.* New York, NY: Harcourt, Brace, 1960.

Freeman, Don. *A Rainbow of My Very Own*. New York, NY: Viking, 1966.

Shapp, Martha, and Charles Shapp. *Let's Find Out About the Sun*. New York, NY: Franklin Watts, 1975.

Tresselt, Alvin. *Sun Up*. New York, NY: Lothrop, 1949.

- Using one of the stories about the sun, make flannel pictures so that the children can tell the story in correct sequence on a flannelboard.
- Take children's dictation about the things they do in the sun.
- Talk about people who live in hot climates—their food, clothing, and homes.
- Celebrate the Fourth of July with a picnic, and talk about the reason for the celebration. Introduce and relate the concepts of freedom and equality to children's daily experiences.

The Physical World

- Use chalk to outline children's shadows in the sunlight. Talk about shadows.
- Use Franklyn Branley's book *What Makes Day and Night* (New York, NY: Crowell, 1961) to talk about how the earth rotates around the sun. Follow the simple, detailed explanation to make a flannelboard model of the earth's rotation for children to manipulate.
- Use a globe and flashlight to illustrate how the sun lights only part of the earth at any one time.
- Let the children make rainbows by reflecting light through a prism onto the wall or white paper. Look for all seven colors.
- Use small hand mirrors to reflect light and to make rainbows.
- Make hose rainbows (see page 237).
- Start two avocado plants from seeds; place one plant in the sunlight and the other in a dark place. Notice the effects of sunlight on plant growth over a period of time.
- Display indoor and outdoor thermometers, and record the differences in temperature.

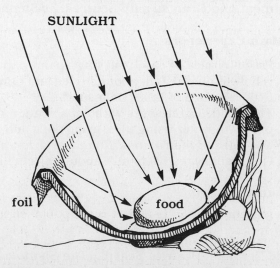

SUNLIGHT

foil   food

Illustration 9.9 **Using sunlight for cooking**

Cooking and Nutrition

- Make melon slush (page 362) and fruit sorbet (page 363).
- Make sun tea by placing 2 herbal tea bags and 1 quart of water in a large covered glass jar and setting the jar in the sun for 2–3 hours. Serve chilled, with lemon.
- Let the children make a solar cooker by positioning a bowl lined with heavy foil so that the sun's rays are focused on the cooking surface. Place bits of cheese on crackers in the solar cooker to make melted cheese snacks. (See Illustration 9.9.)
- Have a Fourth of July picnic. Make ice cream with an old-fashioned hand crank.

THE SEASHORE

Art and Woodworking

- Have the children make a mural of the seashore. Display pictures of starfish for children to use as models for making similar shapes with white glue on construction paper. Shake sand over the glue and let it dry. Paint with water colors. Cut out the starfish and glue them onto the mural.
- Use real sponges to do sponge painting.
- Make collages with seashells, pebbles, and driftwood.
- Let the children add other objects of their choice to the mural.
- Make sanding blocks and musical sand blocks (pages 59–60).
- Make a nature hanging (page 61) with objects collected from the seashore.

Music, Drama, Movement

- Use Hap Palmer's record *Sea Gulls* (Educational Activities) for slow-motion activities and relaxation during quiet time.
- Talk about the different kinds of animal and plant life in the sea, and have the children move the way they think fish move in water.
- Talk about water safety and ways we use water. Dance to tunes such as "Take a Bath" from *Learning Basic Skills Through Music,* by Hap Palmer (Educational Activities).
- Use Ella Jenkins's "The Little Green Frog That Sits by the Stream" from *Hopping Around from Place to Place* (Educational Activities) for listening and singing.

Math Experiences

- Have the children sort and classify a variety of seashells.
- Play a fishing game with numbers. Fashion a small pole with a string and magnet on the end. Let the children take turns fishing for construction-paper fish that have paper clips attached to them. Print numbers or dots on the fish. When all the fish have been caught, add up the numbers on each child's fish. Adapt this game so that children fish for different shapes, counting the number of pairs they can match.

Language Arts

• Stories:

Bellamy, David. *The Rock Pool*. New York, NY: Clarkson Potter, 1988.

_____. *The River*. New York, NY: Clarkson Potter, 1988.

Fitzsimons, Cecelia. *My First Fishes and Other Water Life: A Pop-Up Field Guide*. New York, NY: Harper, 1987.

Jonas, Ann. *Reflections*. New York, NY: Greenwillow, 1987.

Lionni, Leo. *Fish Is Fish*. New York, NY: Pantheon, 1970.

_____. *On My Beach There Are Many Pebbles*. New York, NY: Aston-Honor, 1961.

_____. *Swimmy*. New York, NY: Pantheon, 1963.

Zion, Gene. *Harry by the Sea*. New York, NY: Harper, 1965.

The Physical World

• Take a field trip to some natural body of water, such as a river, lake, or beach. Visit a tropical fish store.
• Collect pebbles and shells (check with local authorities for approval).
• If you live near tidepools, study them and display pictures of life in tidepools (such as described in David Bellamy's book).
• Study the properties of sand and water under magnifying glasses.
• Provide trays of seashells for children to handle and examine.
• Stock an aquarium with fish for the children to take care of.
• Perform a salt water versus fresh water experiment. Have on hand two glasses of water and a raw egg. Add 2 tablespoons of salt to one glass and stir until the salt is dissolved. Try to float the raw egg in first one glass and then the other. The egg will float in the salt water and sink in the fresh water.
• Talk about water safety rules, not only around the seashore, but also at home in the bath and near swimming pools.

Cooking and Nutrition

• Use seafood such as shrimp or tuna in cooking.
• Have the children bring pictures of foods from the sea, such as different varieties of fish and shellfish. Bring samples of kelp and seaweed, and talk about some of the ways people prepare these sea vegetables to eat.
• Use dried seaweed (*nori*, available from Japanese and specialty food stores) in soup or wrapped around rice balls. (See page 345.)

INSECTS AND SUCH

Art and Woodworking

• Make butterfly scarves by tie-dyeing (see page 42).
• Make egg-carton insects by painting sections of empty cardboard egg cartons. Add paper wings, and use pipe cleaners for legs and antennae.
• Collect insects (see page 249), and study their colors carefully. Have the children try to mix water colors to match the colors of the insects.

- Have the children paint collages or make playdough replicas of insects they have seen.
- Make insect homes by taping mesh over the openings of empty juice cans or plastic containers.

Music, Drama, Movement

- Records:

Spin, Spider, Spin, a record by Patty Zeitlin and Marcia Berman (Educational Activities), has several excellent songs suitable for the insect theme: "Just a Snail," "Lots of Worms," "The Way of the Bees," "Night Sounds," and "Frogs and Crickets' Lullaby." Hap Palmer offers such songs as "Flick a Fly" in his recording *Walter, the Waltzing Worm* (Educational Activities).

Math Experiences

- Display a honeycomb, and let the children study the geometric shapes.
- Collect insects and bugs; count the number of legs, eyes, and antennae each has. Keep a record of each child's count.
- Measure out materials needed to stock a terrarium or an ecosystem.
- Have children show the life cycle of a butterfly with sequence cards of flannelboard pieces.

Language Arts

- Stories:

Carle, Eric. *The Very Hungry Caterpillar.* New York, NY: Putnam, 1981.

Ermanno, Christine, and Luigi Puricelli. *In My Garden.* Saxonville, MA: Picture Book Studios, 1985.

Fitzsimons, Cecelia. *My First Insects: Spiders and Crawlers.* New York, NY: Harper, 1987.

Mari, Iela, and Enzo Mari. *The Apple and the Moth.* New York, NY: Dial, 1970.

- Invite a local beekeeper to visit the class and talk about the way bees make honey and how honey is gathered and prepared for consumption. Discuss the fact that bees sting only when angry or frightened. Many people think bees are bad and want to hit or squash them.

The Physical World

- Use the insect boxes that were made in art to collect insects. Place a large sheet under a shrub or bush, and shake the plant. Bring the insects and other bits of plant material on the sheet into the classroom for closer inspection.
- Stock a terrarium with the insects found in the yard. Provide twigs for climbing, water, and other necessities for insects to live.
- After the children have had an opportunity to study the insects more closely, return the insects to their natural habitats.

Cooking and Nutrition

• Make a honey-butter spread for toast or biscuits.
• Talk about the ways honey from bees helps to make our food taste delicious. Use honey in some of the recipes in the cooking section—a dressing for fruit salad, glazed carrots, sweetened yogurt, granola snacks, honey custard—or use honey as a topping for French toast.

TRANSPORTATION/VACATION

Art and Woodworking

• Make boats by hammering and gluing wood scraps. Paint, and add spools or sails if children wish.
• Make wheel pictures by printing with large spools dipped in paint.
• Make a clothespin airplane like the one shown in Illustration 9.10, using a spring-type clothespin and 1½ popsicle sticks. Remove the wire spring from the clothespin, and have the children glue the popsicle sticks on the flat side of one clothespin half to make the wings and tail. The other clothespin half is then glued in place so that the two flat sides are together. Let the airplane dry thoroughly—preferably overnight—before children paint it.
• Cut from magazines pictures of different modes of travel. Display the pictures with a caption such as "This is how we travel."

Music, Drama, Movement

• Records:

"The Wheels on the Bus" from *Raffi Rise and Shine,* by Raffi (Shoreline Records).
"Car, Car Song (Riding in My Car)," by Woody Guthrie from *Fred Penner Special Delivery* (A&M Records).
"Buckle Your Seat Belt" from *Health and Safety,* by Hap Palmer (Educational Activities).

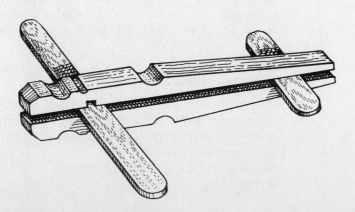

Illustration 9.10 **Clothespin toy airplane**

"This Train" from *You'll Sing a Song and I'll Sing a Song,* by Ella Jenkins (Educational Activities). Also by the same artist is another record with many songs about travel: *Hopping Around from Place to Place.*

"Workin' on the Railroad" and "New River Train" from *More Singable Songs,* by Raffi (A&M Records).

"An Adventure in Space" from *On the Move with Greg and Steve,* Steve Millang and Greg Scelsa (Youngheart).

"Fishing Trip" and "Out to the Country" from *Creative Movement and Rhythmic Exploration,* by Hap Palmer (Educational Activities).

Math Experiences

- Go on a wheel hunt, counting the number of wheels the children can spot in the school.
- Make a list of all the ways children can think of to move or travel from one place to another.
- Build a train of blocks or cardboard boxes. Have the children sell tickets, count money, make change, count out tickets, punch the tickets, count the number of people on board, and so on.
- Build other vehicles such as planes, boats, and buses, and introduce mathematical concepts of shapes, sizes, numbers, and measurement.

Language Arts

- Stories:

Barton, Byron. *Machines at Work.* New York, NY: Crowell, 1987. This same author has created other books with minimal text and bold il-

Illustration 9.11 **Making vehicles from blocks**

lustrations: *Airplanes, Trains, Boats, Trucks, Wheels,* and *I Want to Be an Astronaut.*

Burton, Virginia. *Choo Choo: The Story of a Little Engine Who Ran Away.* Boston, MA: Houghton Mifflin, 1988.

_____. *Mike Mulligan and His Steam Shovel.* Boston, MA: Houghton Mifflin, 1987.

Lenski, Lois. *The Little Airplane.* New York, NY: McKay, 1980.

_____. *The Little Auto.* New York, NY: McKay, 1980.

• Talk about different ways children travel and move from one place to another. Tape their comments and play them back for more discussion.
• Print the modes of transportation on index cards. Give the cards to the children, and let them dictate a sentence or two about each word. Let them paste their cards on corresponding pictures from magazines.
• Talk about vacations, why people take them, and what some people do on vacations. Do animals take vacations?
• Talk about care of pets during vacations.

The Physical World

• Refer to the Physical World, Part Five, for activities using levers, wedges, wheels, pulleys, and pendulums.
• Talk about things that can be moved by air (see page 232). Make and fly paper airplanes.
• Float milk carton boats in water.
• Have the children try to move a heavy object such as a block or box. Then put the object on a wagon. Talk about the use of wheels to make it easier to move things.
• Display posters from travel agencies showing various modes of travel.

Cooking and Nutrition

• Talk about and introduce foods that people eat in other parts of the country and in other parts of the world.
• Talk about the kinds of foods that are easy to eat while riding in a car or bus, such as sandwiches and finger foods. Prepare these foods.
• Talk about foods that might be served on airplanes. Have a make-believe plane trip, and serve foods on plastic plates or trays.
• Have a pretend dining car on a train, and serve from a menu.

ECOLOGY AND THE ENVIRONMENT

Art and Woodworking

• Decorate paper bags and boxes to be used for collecting litter. Have the children help pick up and recycle litter.
• Make a mural showing the interdependence of animals, plants, and weather conditions.

- Have the children help paint and paste on pictures of animals and insects in their natural habitats of shrubs and trees.
- See pages 241–242 for activities about the weather.

Music, Drama, Movement

- Records:

We All Live Together, Vol. 1, by Steve Millang and Greg Scelsa (Youngheart).
"This Land Is Your Land" from *Patriotic and Morning Time Songs*, by Hap Palmer (Educational Activities).
"It's a Small World" from *Mod Marches*, by Hap Palmer (Educational Activities).

- Make up a puppet story about the importance of picking up litter to keep our schools and streets clean.

Math Experiences

- Have the children make miniature ecosystems (see page 265). Let them measure spoonsful of gravel and water and count aquarium plants and snails for each jar.
- Compare the sizes and amounts of materials, using words such as *same, like, different, more than, fewer than, larger, smaller.*
- Reinforce math concepts with music and movement activities such as Hap Palmer's *Math Readiness, Vocabulary and Concepts* (Educational Activities).

Language Arts

- Stories:

Miles, Betty. *Save the Earth! An Ecology Handbook for Kids.* New York, NY: Knopf, 1974.
Peters, Lisa Westberg. *The Sun, the Wind and the Rain.* New York, NY: Holt, 1988.
Tresselt, Alvin. *The Dead Tree.* New York, NY: Parents, 1972
Udry, Janice May. *A Tree Is Nice.* New York, NY: Harper & Row, 1956.
Wosmek, Frances. *The ABC of Ecology.* Los Altos, CA: Davenport Press, 1982.

- June 5 is World Environment Day. Ask the children to dictate some of their thoughts about the environment after reading and discussing the above books. Display their comments along with pictures pertaining to the environment and ecology.

The Physical World

- Refer to Part Five for ecology activities teaching about pollution, erosion, the importance of conserving natural resources, and the interdependence of all life.

Cooking and Nutrition

- Plant vegetables to harvest for cooking.
- Feed leftover food scraps to animals or recycle them for compost.

- Have the children identify fresh versus processed foods.
- Make a trip to the produce market, and select fresh foods to prepare for a snack or lunch.
- Practice conserving water by washing fruits and vegetables in a pan of water and saving the water for plants in the yard. Talk about other ways children can be helpful in conserving natural resources.

Holidays and Celebrations

	January
New Year's Day	1
The Feast of the Three Wise Men (Puerto Rico)	6
Martin Luther King Day	15
Singapore Kite Festival	19 *

	February
Lincoln's Birthday	12
St. Valentine's Day	14
Chinese New Year	*
National Dental Week	*
Battles of the Flowers (France)	20 *
Washington's Birthday	22

	March
National Save Your Vision Week	*
Hina Matsuri, "Girls' Day" (Japan)	3
Purim (Jewish)	16 *
St. Patrick's Day	17
National Wildlife Week	*

	April
April Fool's Day	1
Passover (Jewish)	4 *
Palm Sunday	5 *
World Health Day	7
Good Friday	10 *
Easter	12 *
National Library Week	*
Children's Day (Turkey)	23
Arbor Day	24

	May
May Day	1
Cinco de Mayo (Mexico)	5
Tango-No-Sekku, "Boys' Day" (Japan)	5
Be Kind to Animals Week	*
Mother's Day	14 *
Vesak (Buddhist)	26 *
Memorial Day	30 *

	June
Children's Day	*
World Environment Day	5
Rice Festival (Japan)	7 *
Flag Day	14
Father's Day	21 *
Dragon Boat Festival (China)	*

	July
Independence Day	4
Bastille Day (France)	14

	August
Tisha be-Av (Jewish)	4 *

	September
Labor Day	7 *
Independence Day (Mexico)	16
Rosh ho-Shanah (Jewish)	18 *
Oktoberfest (Germany)	21 *
Yom Kippur (Jewish)	28 *
Native American Day (4th Friday)	*

	October
Sukkot (Jewish)	1
Columbus Day	12
Fire Prevention Week	*
Halloween	31

	November
All Saints' Day	1
Veterans' Day	11
Children's Book Week	*
Thanksgiving (4th Thursday)	27 *

	December
Chanukah (Jewish)	*
Las Posadas (Mexico)	16
Christmas	25

* The date varies.

Additional Themes

Air
America
Animals/Birds
Babies
Body Awareness
Children Around the World
Cities

Colors
Community Helpers
Dinosaurs
Families
Farms
Friendship and Cooperation
Geography
Health and Safety
Machines/Tools
Nursery Rhymes
Nutrition
Outer Space
Self-Concept
Shapes
Sounds
Teddy Bears
Water
Weather

Complete List of Activities and Resources

Student Response Form

We would appreciate hearing a little about your background and having your reactions to this fifth edition of *An Activities Handbook for Teachers of Young Children*. Your comments and suggestions will help us to respond to the needs of users of future editions. Please complete this questionnaire and return it to

College Marketing
Houghton Mifflin Company
One Beacon Street
Boston, MA 02108

1. Do you like the format (large pages, spiral binding) of the *Handbook?*

   Yes _____   No _____

2. Which material or features did you find most useful? _____

   _____

   _____

3. Which material or features were least useful? Why?_____

   _____

   _____

4. Are there too many or too few activities in each of the sections? Should new activities be added in the next edition?

	Too many activities	Too few activities	New activities needed (yes/no)
1 Art and Woodworking	_____	_____	_____
2 Music, Drama, and Movement	_____	_____	_____
3 Math Experiences	_____	_____	_____
4 Language Arts	_____	_____	_____
5 The Physical World	_____	_____	_____
6 Health and Safety	_____	_____	_____
7 Cooking and Nutrition	_____	_____	_____
8 Computers for Preschoolers	_____	_____	_____
9 Themes	_____	_____	_____

5. Did you find the directions for activities clear and easy to understand? _____

6. Did the bibliographies meet your needs? _____

   If not, what is lacking in these lists? _____

   _____

7. How could the book be improved? _____

   _____

   _____

   _____

   _____

8. What was the title of the course in which you used this *Handbook?*

   _____

9. Was this book used as a supplement to another text? _____

   If so, what was the name of that text and by whom was it written

   and published? _____

   _____

10. What other courses have you already taken in early childhood

    education? _____

    _____

11. Are you an undergraduate (if so, what year) or a graduate student

    (if so, have you done any teaching yet)? _____

    _____

12. Do you intend to keep this book to use in your teaching of young

    children? _____

    _____